Dear Carmen,

The Kitchen Garden Cookbook

Have fun!
Love, Sylvia

Also by Sylvia Thompson

Economy Gastronomy

The Budget Gourmet

Feasts and Friends

The Birthday Cake Book

Festive Tarts

The Kitchen Garden Book

THE KITCHEN GARDEN COOKBOOK

Sylvia Thompson

BANTAM BOOKS
NEW YORK TORONTO LONDON SYDNEY AUCKLAND

THE KITCHEN GARDEN COOKBOOK

A Bantam Book / May 1995
Bantam trade edition / May 1997

Book design by Maura Fadden Rosenthal

Library of Congress Cataloging-in-Publication Data

Thompson, Sylvia Vaughn Sheekman.
The kitchen garden cookbook / Sylvia Thompson.
p. cm.
Includes index.
ISBN 0-553-37476-1
1. Cookery (Vegetables) 2. Cookery (Herbs) 3. Vegetable gardening. I. Title.
TX801.T56 1995
641.6'5—dc20 94-35392
CIP

Published simultaneously in the United States and Canada

PRINTED IN THE UNITED STATES OF AMERICA

FFG 10 9 8 7 6 5 4 3 2 1

For Noni and Dote
with love abiding

Contents

Acknowledgments

This book and its companion, *The Kitchen Garden*, have taken seven years. I regret that, for want of space, my gratitude must come down to lists.

Of course recipes are the heart of these pages, and for generously cooking, tasting, sharing their recipes, ideas, and information, I'm in debt to Lorraine Alexander; Julia and Jeremy Azrael; Norah Barr; Margo and Alvin Bart; Gina and Ernie Blanchette; Irving Brecher; Philip and Lois Brown; Peter and Eugenia Caldwell; Victoria and Stan Cutler; Mark and Laury Detrick; M.F.K. Fisher; Nancy and Bert Freed; Marion Gore; Ruth Gottlieb; Carol Hacker; Marie and John Hall; Lynnda and Don Hart; Don Kautter; Diana Kennedy; Betty King & Friends; Susan, Susannah, and Bob Lescher; Jane and Daniel Levy; Hildy Manley & Friends; Olga Matson; Fran and David McCullough; Nancy McKeon; Michelle Mutrux; Russ Parsons; Mima and Arthur Pereira; Jeannine and Dirk Perriseau; Martha and Tom Piwonka; Naomi Price; Ward Ritchie; Suzanne Roll; Lida Schneider; Dolores and John Sizer; Harry and Dianne Stephens; Gloria Stuart; Mary Sutherland & Jeremy Silverman; Caitlin and Bill Szieff; Hoppin' John Taylor; Gene Thompson; Cathy Turney; Maureen Wagstaff & Company; Jim and Amanda Whelan; Paula Wolfert; Nan Wollman; and Dr. George York.

I couldn't be more grateful to those who've made this book possible: The rare Susan Lescher, my editor Frances McCullough—a miracle of grace under pressure, art director Jim Plumeri, copy editor Chris Benton, designer Maura Fadden Rosenthal, assistants Jennifer Webb, Lauren Janis, and Carolyn Larson, photographer Faith Echtermeyer, and gardener par excellence, Ann Cutting.

After trying, I realize I can't find words to thank my friends, mother, children, and husband for their kindness, patience, and indulgence during these exciting but exacting years.

About This Book

Our own kitchen garden is at 5,800 feet in the mountains of southern California. After years of wrestling with the critters—in lieu of caging the whole thing—my husband and I have learned to share our garden gracefully. But you can believe that when I bring a vegetable into the house, it's been hard come by. You can be sure I want to *taste* it.

If you don't have critters to contend with, I'll bet you've got something else that makes gardening a challenge, be it too much shade, a killing schedule, or the neighbor's marauding cat. Your harvest is a triumph, too. You've done it for love and to taste something you can't buy.

So this is a book about love and hard work and gorgeous things from the garden. When you've taken months to bring a cauliflower to the table—given thought to selecting the cultivar, sent away for the seeds, sown them, transplanted seedlings with cutworm collars, watered and fed the little dears, wrapped their leaves to keep the curds from the sun, hosed off aphids and picked off caterpillars, you're going to prepare your cauliflower in a very different way from one wrapped in cellophane you grabbed out of a bin at the supermarket.

Something else about the produce one gets from the supermarket. It was raised and handled with one objective: To get it into those bins without physical damage. Flavor is not the point. Flavor *is* the point when it comes to your kitchen garden. In most books, vegetable recipes have been designed to disguise lackluster store-bought producc—it's smoke and mirrors with razzle-dazzle seasoning. In other books, vegetables are but one element in a complex of ingredients creating a many-leveled taste. In this book, there are no disguises; there's little that's complex. I've gathered notions from all over the world that show off the flavor of your harvest simply.

Now there are a few recipes in these pages, as with chard in lasagne, when a vegetable becomes an ensemble player rather than the star. I do this when a combination of flavors is just so good I want you to know about it, and only with a crop that's so productive you'll have plenty to savor on its own.

I hope you'll like the recipes enough to want to make them when your harvest is over. Then, preparing the dish with market produce—or when you're in the mood for an explosion of tastes—add your favorite aromatics. A handful of herbs, a little lemon or orange juice, plenty of minced garlic, ginger, chilies, fruity nut oils, spices, grating cheeses, and so forth are what you need.

I'm ravenous to taste everything there is to grow and taste—I want to explore all the possibilities of my garden. Often the recipe is for just a few servings because, in my limited space, I grow samplings of dozens of crops. I know how frustrating it can be to come across an ingredient in a recipe I have no hope of finding—my own local markets carry little that's esoteric. That's why, in these entries, I give an alternative for an uncommon vegetable or herb. Often a combination of flavors will give you an idea of its taste.

In addition to obscure crops, all our old favorites are in these pages, too. Be sure to look in the index for ideas—every dish in which you can use one of your beautiful beets, for example, is listed.

In The Cook's Notebook you'll find details on techniques like canning, basic recipes like pizza dough, and dishes that apply to any number of good things, like *crudités,* homemade creamy cheese with herbs, and vinaigrette.

About herbs: Sometimes they can be intrusive—too much sage becomes bitter, too much mint dominates everything else. Added with consideration for balance, herbs can be the single element that gives a dish focus. For example, the recipe for round zucchini and red potatoes (under Summer Squashes) was dull with a handful of flat-leaf parsley. Adding a tablespoon of chopped rosemary made it hum. Both for beauty of form and to pull things together, I often suggest a sprinkling of a particular herb or flower petals just before serving. If what's called for isn't in your garden at the moment, use something that is.

Recipes are organized to mirror the organization of this cookbook's companion, *The Kitchen Garden.* All entries are alphabetical. You should be able to find what you're looking for easily—with this in mind: When presented with the problem of ordering the myriad greens we can grow in the kitchen garden, I decided to gather them in four groups. If you don't know orach exists, how can you look it up? This way, plants in a group are interchangeable in preparation, and you can cruise through the section for inspiration and ideas. You'll quickly get used to the logic of these groups:

Asian Greens are the mild sweet leaves common to Asian cooking.

Mustard Greens are the peppery leaves beloved in Asia and America's Deep South.

Potherbs are the fresh young things that mostly pop up in spring—some are sweet and some are hot, and all are underappreciated. They can go into the pot, or they can go in salads.

Salad Greens include common and not-so-common leaves for salads.

Within an entry, sometimes forms of the plant aren't in alphabetical order, but in order of ripening. Beans are presented first in the snap stage, then the shelly stage, then dried. Cauliflower, eaten in the bud stage, has a recipe for bolting cauliflower at the end of its entry.

To be true to the plants, I've tried to be as botanically correct as possible. But when it came to green onions, I've used scallions, since apparently most of the country thinks of green onions as scallions.

Now, a few idiosyncrasies: In regard to cooking with fat, I generally don't. Nonstick and cast-iron skillets see to that. However, there are times when a little or a lot of sweet butter or cream or extra virgin olive oil finishing a vegetable is the difference between being earthbound and lifted to the stars. At such times, and they are rare in this house, I feel a gilding of fat is warranted.

It's taken a long time to get people to leave the skins on their carrots, cucumbers, even tomatoes (the French peel tomatoes routinely). Here, I take it one step further. You'll find you can eat the delectable stalk of your artichoke. You'll be popping the whole radish into your mouth, from rootlet to leafy tips. You may even join me in not bothering to trim out the seeds of sweet peppers—they add a tad of fiber and flavor, and their speckles are amusing. Seeds of chili peppers, however, are too hot to add routinely.

In the garden, we learn to husband our resources. In these pages, you'll find that none of your harvest—from wrapper leaves to bolted flowers to vines and shoots—none of your effort or your joy—will be wasted.

Sylvia Thompson
The Chimney House
Idyllwild, California 92549-0145
E-mail: chimney-house@compuserve.com

In the Kitchen

Artichokes

The flower buds of enormous plants that love cool weather, artichokes can be harvested from cherry size to buds the size of a small melon. Cut the stalks as close to the plant as you can and leave them long on the artichokes. Plunge into water and refrigerate until ready to cook—*then* rinse.

The peeled stalk's flavor and texture are as delicious as the heart. You can leave a long stalk attached or cut it off at the base and cook it separately. Discard leaves.

The Italians have an elegant way of preparing larger artichokes—if they're not stuffed. A large artichoke is presented like a dinner bell on the plate—cup down, with a 3-inch handle of stalk standing upright.

To prepare artichokes, instead of using scissors, remove the tough thorny top of each leaf by pressing a thumb over its base, then bending back and snapping off the inedible top—this goes faster than trimming with scissors and gives the artichoke a hand-finished look. (This won't work with very large end-of-the-season artichokes from the market, which are fibrous and tough.) Leave enough of the leaf to pluck off and pick up easily for dipping. As you get closer to the center, the leaves will snap farther up the leaf because there's more of the leaf that's tender. Or for family, skip this step entirely, since the thorns become harmlessly soft in the cooking. Rub the cut surfaces with lemon to keep them from darkening. Cut off the stalk at 3 inches. Pare off the stalk's thick skin and rub with lemon. Slice off the top inch of the artichokes with a stainless-steel knife. Pick out all the pink-tipped leaves of the choke—the thistle at the center—then use a sharp-tipped spoon (or a knife with a curved tip) to scrape out the fuzz growing atop the heart—carefully leave the heart intact. Cook the artichokes at once or drop into cold water acidulated with a splash of lemon juice or vinegar if they must wait.

Find a pot in which the artichokes just fit and add cold water to a depth of 3 inches. Set over high heat and add 3 tablespoons cider vinegar, 3 smashed cloves of garlic (no need to peel them), and 1 tablespoon salt. If you and your guests don't mind sticky fingers, 3 tablespoons of fruity olive oil in the water will lightly gloss and flavor the artichokes. Chervil, parsley, thyme, rosemary, and bay are especially good with artichoke, so if there's no herb in the dipping sauce, chop and add one or several of these, too, if you like. Add chervil at the end of cooking.

Fit the artichokes snugly in the pot stalks up—if not snug, they'll probably roll over, which is fine. Add any stalk pieces. Boil uncovered for 25 to 55 minutes, until a thin skewer tests the buds tender through and through. The water will boil down, but you needn't add more—the bottoms may brown a bit, but that's fine, too. The cooking water is tasty and can be used to cook and flavor other vegetables (or use the broth as the base for cooking a second batch of artichokes; just add more water and fresh garlic). Lift the artichokes out with tongs and drain upside down on a folded towel. These are best served neither piping hot nor chilled, but warm, on the day of cooking.

Allow from one large to six tiny artichokes per serving. Artichokes are high in fiber, moderately high in folic acid, and have fair amounts of vitamin C (when eaten raw), magnesium, phosphorus, iron, and protein.

Some people are sensitive to the effects of an acid in artichokes called *cynarin*. Everything tastes sweeter to them for a short while after eating artichoke. You may want to think twice about serving a fine wine with or after the artichokes.

In some parts of the world artichokes are always picked before the choke has developed. In fact some cooks feel that once there are thorns on the leaves the artichoke is past its prime. See what you think.

Cherry-Size Artichokes

You'll find these tiny buds in the very center at the top of an enormous artichoke plant. Their leaves, not having mellowed to nuttiness in the sun, are faintly bitter. Eat them raw with coarse salt as an hors d'oeuvre.

Walnut-Size Artichokes

If you're lucky enough to have lots of plants, harvest the buds this size and brown them in a heavy saucepan in olive oil. Sprinkle with finely chopped garlic, parsley, mint or dill, coarse salt, and freshly ground black pepper. Clap on the lid and cook gently until tender—20 to 25 minutes—shaking the pot from time to time. Sprinkle with lemon zest and taste for seasoning.

Then, holding an artichoke by the stem, bite down, and the center will pop into your mouth.

The Italians thinly slice raw purple artichokes this size and eat them with a lacing of fruity olive oil and salt. They also fry them.

DEEP-FRIED BABY ARTICHOKES: With drinks, Lulu's in San Francisco serves these evocations of Rome. Strip baby artichokes of all but the palest and tenderest leaves—leave only a bit of stem. Slice lengthwise into quarters, keeping the pieces in acidulated water as you work. Pat thoroughly dry, then drop into an inch of mild-flavored olive oil at 375°F and cook, turning occasionally, until brown and crisp through and through, about 3 minutes. Blot with towels, sprinkle lightly with salt, lay a shaved bit of Parmesan cheese on top, and serve piping hot on napkins.

To taste the pure artichoke, omit the cheese. You can also fry the peeled stems.

Large Artichokes

Where artichokes are traditionally picked so small as to be chokeless, artichokes harvested larger than an orange are cooked and stuffed. The centers and pockets between leaves are filled with a savory meat, bread crumb, or rice mixture, then the artichokes are drizzled with oil, baked in a slow oven, and served at room temperature.

But big fat artichokes are a gardening triumph, and we want to savor them with a dipping sauce. Something creamy—homemade mayonnaise on its own or with a little mustard or chopped herbs or garlic or blood orange juice. Served hot, a lighter butter or vinaigrette sauce is ideal—the same seasonings added—or a tangy ravigote sauce, which is an herbal vinaigrette with capers. Garnish with a wedge of lemon or a flower. (Sauces are in The Cook's Notebook.)

CIDER-CARAMELIZED ARTICHOKES: Perhaps you'll have an artichoke or two that seem at the point of being plump but not in imminent danger of bursting into bloom. If the flesh is moist (bite into one raw—you can tell), cut the artichoke into quarters and cook uncovered in a little cider in a nonstick skillet over medium heat, stirring until tender when pierced with a skewer. The pieces will caramelize slightly and be divine. Season and serve hot sprinkled with parsley.

ORANGE-FLAVORED ARTICHOKES: These are marvelous, especially if it's blood orange. In place of cider, simmer quarters in this gorgeous juice. Another time, add garden peas and ribbons of lettuce to the artichoke quarters, cover the skillet, and braise all together. Garnish with wedges of orange and serve hot.

Artichokes with Sorrel Sauce

MAKES 1 1/2 CUPS SAUCE TO SERVE 6

Sorrel shoots are in their glory around the same time as spring artichokes. Their lemony flavor enhances this exquisite sauce that's in a class with hollandaise but is worlds less wicked. If you'd rather, you can compose it with your favorite low-fat mayonnaise, but yogurt doesn't work here.

The sauce also makes a celebration of cold and hot fish and chicken and brightly flavored vegetables such as sliced raw tomatoes, grilled sweet peppers, roasted beets, and asparagus.

This sauce keeps beautifully for several days, tasting better and better. If you're short on sorrel, make up the difference with fresh leaves of watercress, spinach, or Italian parsley—or a combination.

The olive oil must be mild for this sauce. If yours is fruity, temper it with canola or other light oil. Experiment in tiny amounts until you get the right proportions.

2 packed cups chopped sorrel leaves, about 4 dozen medium-size leaves without stems or ribs

¾ cup foolproof mayonnaise (see The Cook's Notebook)

2 teaspoons fresh lemon juice

6 tablespoons cold heavy cream

salt and freshly ground white pepper to taste

6 large artichokes, cooked and cooled

Pour boiling water over the sorrel in a bowl, then immediately drain through a sieve. Press out all liquid.

Add the sorrel to the mayonnaise in the food processor or blender. Process until the leaves are minced and all is thoroughly blended. Blend in the lemon juice, then turn the sauce into a mixing bowl. In a small bowl, beat the cream until stiff, then fold it into the sauce with a rubber spatula. Add salt and pepper, then taste for seasoning. Cover and chill until needed, then stir and serve in small bowls beside the artichokes.

Hearts of Artichokes

ARTICHOKE HEARTS FILLED WITH CAVIAR: My friend Philip S. Brown taught me to pull off all but a few layers of leaves of small cooked artichokes, remove the center chokes as well, then drop in a spoonful of black caviar. Philip surrounds them on a lettuce-lined platter with rosy chunks of cold lobster, crescents of avocado, and rings of out-of-season sweet red peppers, then dresses the salad with a vinaigrette (page 349). Sprinkle with a little chopped fresh tarragon.

Asian Greens: Mild and Sweet

These are plants with leaves of mild sweet flavor that are especially delicious raw and in stir-fries. Asian greens with hot peppery flavor are under Mustard Greens.

Chinese Cabbages

There are three shapes of Chinese cabbage. Two are firm-headed—barrel-shaped napa and celery-shaped michihili—and one is loose-headed. All have thin, crisp sweet leaves. Harvest from seedling to young leaf stages—at which time you can pull the whole plant at the base.

Recipes for heading and loose-headed Chinese cabbages are interchangeable. These cabbages are good sources of calcium, folic acid, and potassium and moderately good sources of fiber.

Any tender raw Chinese cabbage will make the following salad.

CHINESE CABBAGE SALAD: Slice the head crosswise about 1/4 inch thick. Mix in a bowl with a quarter as much thinly sliced celery and a little less of the chopped tender stalks of scallions. Drizzle on a thread of olive oil, then equal parts rice vinegar and low-sodium soy sauce. Add pepper and a pinch of crumbled dried hot red chili (or to taste) and toss with your hands. Taste for seasoning and serve sprinkled with chopped fresh or dried basil.

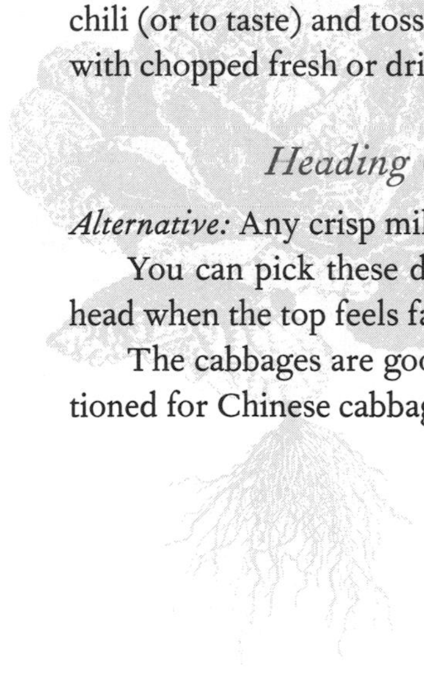

Heading Chinese Cabbage: Napa and Michihili

Alternative: Any crisp mild cabbage or lightly pungent green.

You can pick these delicately flavored cabbages leaf by leaf or cut the whole head when the top feels fairly firm when you squeeze it.

The cabbages are good sources of vitamin A in addition to the nutrients mentioned for Chinese cabbages in general. Best eaten raw or stir-fried.

Hot, Sour, and Sweet Napa Cabbage

MAKES 4 TO 6 SERVINGS

Last-minute, fast, and easy.

- 2 tablespoons rice or cider vinegar
- $\frac{1}{2}$ tablespoon low-sodium soy sauce
- 1 tablespoon cornstarch
- 1 tablespoon sugar
- 1 tablespoon mild oil
- $\frac{1}{2}$ to 1 small dried or fresh hot red chili, seeds removed, crumbled or thinly sliced, or to taste
- a silver-dollar-size slice of fresh ginger, chopped
- 12 cups $\frac{1}{2}$-inch shredded napa cabbage, about $1\frac{3}{4}$ pounds
- $\frac{1}{4}$ cup chicken broth, vegetable stock, or water
- salt and freshly ground white pepper to taste
- chopped cilantro

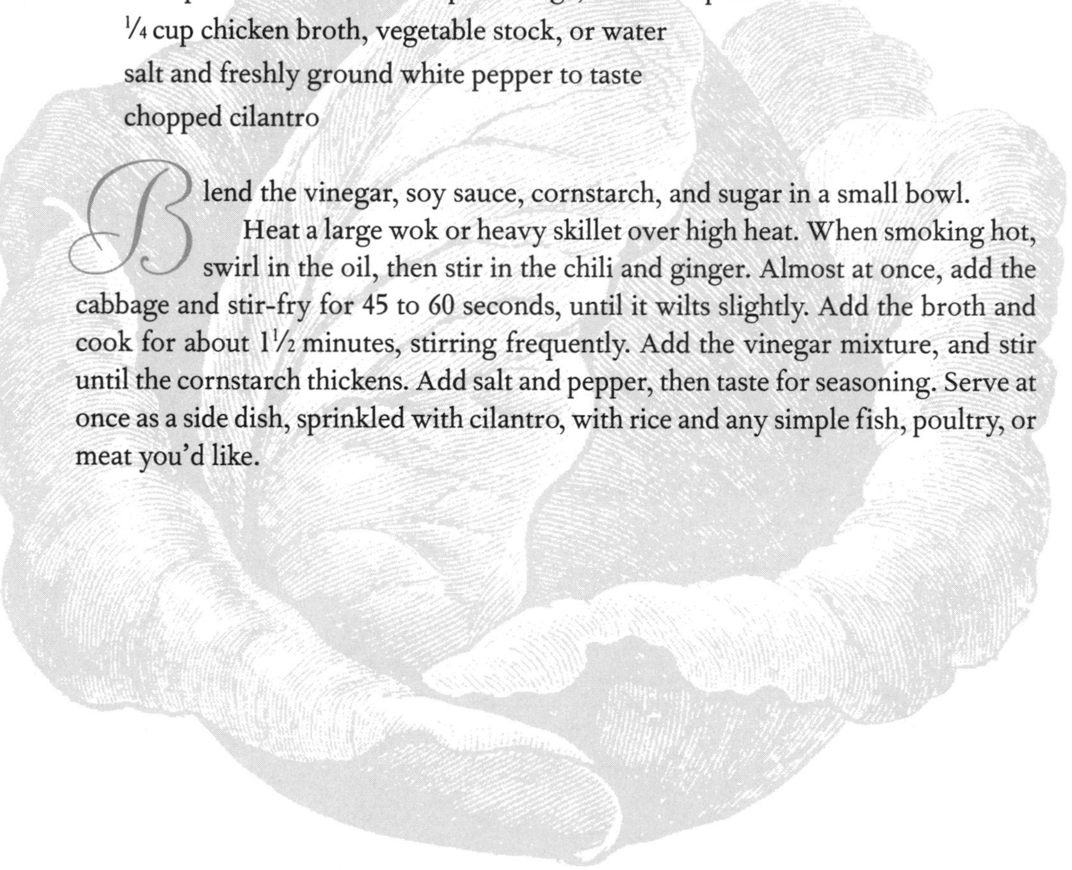

Blend the vinegar, soy sauce, cornstarch, and sugar in a small bowl.

Heat a large wok or heavy skillet over high heat. When smoking hot, swirl in the oil, then stir in the chili and ginger. Almost at once, add the cabbage and stir-fry for 45 to 60 seconds, until it wilts slightly. Add the broth and cook for about $1\frac{1}{2}$ minutes, stirring frequently. Add the vinegar mixture, and stir until the cornstarch thickens. Add salt and pepper, then taste for seasoning. Serve at once as a side dish, sprinkled with cilantro, with rice and any simple fish, poultry, or meat you'd like.

Loose-Headed Chinese Cabbages

Alternative: Any crisp mild cabbage or lightly pungent green.

Pick these leaves singly or wait to take the whole head when nicely developed but when the leaves are still very tender—mature leaves are tough. Some of these open cabbages have pale crisp stalks and dark green leaves, a bit like chard.

You can cook the leafy parts and the stalks separately, treating the leaves like any other greens and the stalks as celery. Cooking sweetens their slightly sharp flavor. Best in stir-fries, these cabbages are remarkably good sources of vitamin A as well as other nutrients mentioned for Chinese cabbages in general.

INDONESIAN SOUP WITH CHINESE CABBAGE: makes 6 servings. This is a rosy soup, thick with vegetables and glorious flavor. It makes your Chinese cabbage shimmer.

Heat 1 tablespoon oil in a large heavy pot. Add 1 minced red onion and 4 minced garlic cloves and cook over medium-high heat until softened, stirring occasionally, about 3 minutes. Add 1 large ripe tomato—half of it chopped finely, half chopped medium-finely. Cook 1 minute, then add 8 cups finely shredded loose-headed Chinese cabbage (about 1 pound) and 1 to 2 small seeded green or red chilies (or to taste) sliced in slivers.

Cook 5 minutes, stirring frequently, then add two 13½-ounce cans of unsweetened coconut milk. Simmer uncovered, stirring occasionally, until the cabbage is tender-crisp, about 10 minutes. Remove from the heat and add 1 tablespoon fresh lime juice. Taste for seasoning and serve, topping bowls with sprigs of cilantro and a thin round of lime.

If there's any left over, when you reheat it, you may wish to add more coconut milk or mild stock.

Garlic Stir-Fried Chinese Cabbage

MAKES 2 TO 3 SERVINGS

This is a delicate accompaniment for everything from grilled fish to roast chicken. The sauce is especially good poured over and mashed into potatoes accompanying grilled fish. The chard adds contrast of color to the pale cabbage leaves. This is a good way to slice a vegetable that has two different textures.

Last-minute but fast.

6 chard leaves, leafy parts separated from the stalks, or use fresh spinach
1 small head (1 pound) loose-headed Chinese cabbage
mild oil
salt to taste
3 scallions, white parts only, thinly sliced
2 large garlic cloves, thinly sliced
$\frac{1}{4}$ cup chicken broth or vegetable stock
freshly ground Szechwan brown pepper or spicy black pepper like Malabar or Tellicherry, to taste
handful of chopped golden lovage or celery leaves

Slice the chard stalks and the thick celerylike base of the cabbage $\frac{1}{4}$ inch thick on the diagonal. Stack and roll the chard leaves and the green leafy ends of the cabbage and slice an inch wide.

Heat a wok or large heavy skillet over high heat until smoking. Swirl in a drizzle of oil, then stir as you add a sprinkling of salt and the scallions and garlic—they'll color instantly. Add the stalk pieces and stir-fry for 45 seconds. Blend in the leaves, sprinkle in the broth, and stir-fry for 1 minute or until the stalks and cabbage are tender-crunchy.

Remove from the heat, add pepper, taste for seasoning, and serve over rice or mashed potatoes.

Chinese Kale

Alternative: The stalks, tender leaves, and florets of a mild mustard or slender broccoli.

The young stalks and loosely bunched flower buds of Chinese kale are reminiscent of broccoli's, but the leaves have a mild cabbage flavor. For the choicest quality, pick stalks while as slender as your little finger, then pick the budding stalks the minute they form. Harvest only the youngest leaves.

To cook simply, follow the method for broccoli, peeling off tough skin when necessary. Any recipe for broccoli or other flowering brassica can be used with Chinese kale.

Like all dark green leaves, these are high in beta-carotene, and the cabbage family is also high in vitamin C, calcium, iron, and folic acid. Best stir-fried, but remember to add tender raw leaves, flowers, and stalks to salad.

Chinese Kale with Chinese Chives

MAKES 5 SERVINGS

This is a generic recipe—substitute any tender leaves and flowering stalks you like. If you don't have Chinese chives, which have a garlicky flavor, use garden chives or scallions and a little garlic.

The slicing can be done an hour or so in advance.

1 head (1 pound) Chinese kale with buds, the stalks no thicker than ½ inch
1 tablespoon mild oil
¼ cup chicken broth or vegetable stock
heaped ½ cup thinly sliced Chinese or garden chives
2 tablespoons fresh lemon juice
1 tablespoon oyster sauce or low-sodium soy sauce
freshly ground black pepper to taste
a handful of buds of Chinese or garden chives, if available

Slice the Chinese kale as directed in the box on page 12.

Heat a large wok or heavy skillet over high heat until smoking hot. Drizzle in the oil, then add the stalk pieces. Stir-fry for a few seconds, until the pieces glisten, then add the broth. Stir-fry for 1½ minutes. Add the leaves and chives and the lemon juice and stir-fry for 15 seconds. Blend in the oyster sauce and stir-fry for another 15 seconds—the stalk pieces should still be crunchy and the leaves bright green. Grind pepper over (the broth and seasoning sauce should provide ample salt) and serve at once garnished with the buds as a vegetable accompaniment.

ANOTHER WAY: Simmer inch-long shoots and ribbons of leaves of Chinese kale in ½ inch of vegetable stock until tender-crisp. Lift out and combine with slivers of lemon zest and small cubes of tofu in a pot of clear broth (wonderful flavored with dried seaweed). Bring to a simmer, grind in a little white pepper, taste for seasoning, then ladle into soup plates—lovely shapes and colors.

Slicing Uneven Stalks to Cook Evenly

Taking a head of Chinese kale or Chinese cabbage as an example, stand the bunch of stalks on end to even their bottoms, then lay them on your cutting board. Starting at the bottom, make slices about 1/8 inch thick. As you move your knife up the narrowing stalks, gradually broaden the slices to 1/4 inch. Continue to broaden the slices until, when there are only leaves at the top, the slices are 1/2 inch thick.

Flowering Brassicas

This is a group of nonheading cabbages grown principally for the flowering shoots, which are beautiful. Their flavors are generally mild and sweet.

Choy Sum

Alternative: Broccoli, cauliflower, or any tender-leaved mild mustard with slender stalks and plump buds on the brink of or just after flowering.

Choy sum is the name not of a plant but of a group of flowering cabbages. Some have green, some purple stalks, and all are delicately flavored if harvested during the first flowering. Pick the flower stalks and leaves while young.

Cook choy sum as you would sprouting broccoli. The buds are as nourishing as the leaves they grace. Stir-fry or add tender leaves and flowers to salad.

Miso is salted soybean paste, delicate, refreshing, and nutritious. A spoonful blended into hot water (boiling miso destroys some of its goodness) makes an instant soup. White miso is sweeter than red. Both are available from Asian groceries in the refrigerated case. They keep for weeks.

FLOWERING SHOOTS IN MISO SOUP: Simmer young choy sum leaves sliced into thin ribbons and their flower stalks cut into ¾-inch lengths in ½ inch of vegetable stock or water in an uncovered skillet until tender-crisp. Timing depends on the plant and its age, but it won't take long. Pour the stock into a heated serving bowl, whisk in white or red miso according to taste, then add the leaves to the stock and ladle into small bowls. Top with more flowers or petals. Pass the white pepper mill on the side.

Do make this soup with the leaves and flowering shoots of young broccoli for a new appreciation of the plant.

Flowering Rape

Alternative: The same as for choy sum, but the nippiest available leaf.

A Chinese name for these golden-blossomed dark greens is "oil vegetable" since the leaves hold so much oil—a relative of this rape is the source of canola oil. This gives cooked leaves—stir-frying is best—an almost buttery taste. With its slightly crunchy, lightly cabbagey green leaves, rape is nothing if not rough-and-ready. It's reviving eaten raw—a crunchy tonic.

Flowers, leaves, and young stalks are all edible and nourishing. Simply remove any hard parts of the stems.

SALAD OF FLOWERING RAPE: Don't try to pair rape with delicate violets and baby lettuces. Instead, make this.

Toss broad ribbons of rape leaves with chopped red onions, crumbled blue cheese, and two or three colors and shapes of cooked dried beans—kidney, chickpea, and black, for example. Snip the flower stalks into small pieces and strew the golden flowers over the bowl. Dress with walnut oil, toasted walnuts, winter savory, and cider vinegar, then mix with your hands. Add salt and pepper to taste. Serve with rustic bread and dark beer. Serve mandarin oranges for dessert.

Garland Chrysanthemum

Alternative: There's no leaf I know whose flavor resembles the slightly musky, slightly lemony, slightly herbal flavor of the chrysanthemum leaves and stems, but you can use any subtly flavored leaf you like in these recipes.

These are leaves of a chrysanthemum whose flowers—unlike the ravishing spoons and spiders and pompoms of autumn—are puny. You're supposed to stop harvesting leaves once the flowers appear, but I keep picking the flowers *and* the leaves. These leaves have a bright, strange, bitter yet flowery flavor that's captivating.

For each serving, snip the leaves from one rinsed 10- to 12-inch stalk, keeping them whole. Trim off and discard the stalk at the point where it becomes thicker than a pencil (it may not). Thinly slice the thin part of the stalk into tiny rounds. These leaves are incomparable in soup, but add them with young buds to salad. To cook, briefly simmer uncovered in ½ inch of vegetable stock or salted water.

GARLAND CHRYSANTHEMUM IN BROTH: This soup is extraordinarily delicate, the sort of thing that lifts your spirits at the end of a dreadful day. Much depends on the broth, which should be no more than chicken trimmings—wings, backs, necks, and skin—simmered in water just enough to color it. Add no seasonings to complicate the simplicity. The barely cooked leaves have the texture of young spinach, and the stems are crunchy, like baby asparagus.

For each serving, in a saucepan, bring 1½ cups delicate chicken broth (homemade or canned broth diluted with equal parts water) to a simmer over medium-high heat. Add 1 lightly packed cup garland chrysanthemum leaves and stalk bits, along with a peanut-size piece of fresh ginger, peeled and minced, and return to a simmer. Remove from the heat, add salt and freshly ground white pepper, taste for seasoning, and serve at once in a beautiful bowl. Garnish with mustard blossoms.

EGG WITH CHRYSANTHEMUM LEAVES: For breakfast, I warm a few finely chopped garland chrysanthemum leaves in a little unsalted butter over medium-high heat, meanwhile beating an egg in a bowl with a fork. I drop in the egg, draw the fork through it until the egg is cooked, then turn it out and spoon a ribbon of sour cream over the top.

Komatsuna

Alternative: Use equal parts leaves of a mild mustard, cabbage, and spinach.

You'll find these thick dark green leaves a delicious discovery, with their sweet mingling of the flavors of mustard, cabbage, and spinach. As with other Asian greens, harvest from seedlings to mature leaves. Pick larger leaves from the outside, leaving an inch or so of stem so leaves will come again. When they bolt, toss tender stems and buds into stir-fries.

Rinse the princely leaves and, if the stalks are at all tough, fold the leaves in half lengthwise and pull the greens away from the stalks. Cook these two parts separately according to the directions for kale. Add tender leaves and crunchy stalks to salad. Although a pile of large komatsuna leaves cooks down considerably, it finishes with more texture and volume than spinach.

Toasted Komatsuna

MAKES 2 TO 3 SERVINGS

The leaves can be prepared for cooking well in advance. Unless you'll be serving this cold or at room temperature, the leaves take minutes and taste freshest just cooked.

6 cups leafy parts of komatsuna leaves (12 large); add chopped stalks if very tender
thread of any flavorful oil you like
squirt of fresh lemon juice
few dashes of ground ginger
salt and freshly ground black pepper to taste
1 tablespoon toasted sesame seeds

Turn the leaves into a big nonstick skillet with the water that clings to them. Cook over medium-high heat, stirring. Keep an eye on them, cooking just until the leaves have wilted and those on the bottom have turned toasty brown and are probably stuck to the pot, about 3 minutes.

Remove from the heat and use a wooden spoon to scrape together all the leaves. Turn onto a board and chop coarsely. Turn into a serving dish, drizzle with oil and lemon juice, shake on a little ground ginger, and add salt and freshly ground white pepper. Taste for seasoning, then serve sprinkled with sesame seeds. The komatsuna needn't be hot—the dark green lustrous leaves are very good at whatever temperature they happen to be. Serve with noodles drizzled with Asian sesame oil.

Mizuna

Alternative: For appearance, use a deeply cut leaf like one of the ornamental kale's. For flavor, combine spinach or a mild mustard with sorrel, or add lemon juice to the dish.

Mizuna's dark green leaves resemble a fernleaf maple's—gorgeous. Harvest them from the seedling stage, then pick tender leaves frequently from the outside of the plant.

Rinse well. When the leaves grow past the all-is-tender stage, fold them in half lengthwise and pull the green parts from the stems. Cook mizuna leaves uncovered in the water that clings to them from rinsing—they'll take about 5 minutes. A dark green leaf means the presence of beta-carotene, calcium, and probably iron, and this exquisite leaf is very dark green. Remember to add tender leaves and stalks to salad.

Use these deeply indented leaves for garnish and keep the small ones whole for stir-fries—I resist chopping up beautiful leaves. The crunch of the stems and the leaves' tangy flavor are something between spinach and sorrel. In the following salad, tartness, spiciness, and sweetness mix with glowing shades of green.

SALAD OF MIZUNA AND KIWI FRUIT WITH GINGER DRESSING (4 servings):

Peel a walnut-size piece of fresh ginger and slice into long slivers. In a mixing bowl, blend 4 teaspoons mild olive oil with 2 teaspoons fresh orange juice and 2 teaspoons rice vinegar. Peel 4 kiwi fruits and thinly slice crosswise. Prepare 6 cups of small mizuna leaves or large pieces of tender parts of bigger leaves. Cover and reserve all these separately.

Just before serving, beat the dressing again to blend then add the leaves and toss with your hands. Add salt and freshly ground white pepper, then taste for seasoning. Arrange the greens on chilled salad plates. Lay the pieces of one kiwi on each plate overlapping in a circle. Strew the ginger over the kiwis, set a nasturtium or other edible flower to one side on the plate and serve.

PUREE OF MIZUNA SOUP: Although I love looking at the raw leaves, mizuna makes a delectable pureed soup. Soften a little chopped onion in a saucepan, add the leafy parts of mizuna, cover with mild vegetable stock, and simmer until tender, 2 to 3 minutes. Puree in the food mill, taste for salt and pepper, then serve sprinkled with finely chopped lovage—the spicy celery and tangy green flavors are wonderful together.

Pak Choi

Alternative: Any cabbage or mild mustard can be used in a recipe for pak choi and vice versa. You can also combine celery and chard and use it in place of pak choi to tasty effect.

The fleshy stalks of pak choi are formed somewhat like an unkempt head of celery, but the broad smooth or ruffled leaves are as kempt as chard's. Harvest from large seedlings to small bundles of "baby pak choi" to individual stalks—or the whole bunch cut at the base, where more shoots will sprout in their place.

In cooking it's usually best to separate the crisp stalks and the leafy greens so neither will end up overcooked. Cooking and other information are the same as for Chinese cabbage.

CUMIN PAK CHOI: An Indian way with cabbage translates deliciously to pak choi. Stir-fry crescents of stalks and shreds of leaves in oil with bay leaves, cumin seeds, and turmeric until tender-crisp. Sliced mushrooms and small black beans added to the wok and bowls of rice and chutney added to the table make it supper.

Gingery Stir-Fry of Pak Choi and Sweet Corn with Beef over Chinese Noodles

MAKES 4 TO 5 SERVINGS

A special pleasure of the garden is discovering that vegetables you hadn't thought would be ripe together are. That sets me thinking about how I can combine them in a dish. When I found I had half a dozen slender pak chois and some fine sweet corn ripe at the same time, I made the following easy stir-fry. It's not elaborate, but it's good enough for company because it's full of flavor, color, and each element holds its own.

Chinese wheat noodles are accommodating and, unlike Italian pasta, can be boiled a day in advance without losing quality. Most come in 1-pound packages, and the noodles are very firm. Use a cleaver or big chopping knife to divide the noodles the long way or simply cook the whole pound, refrigerate, and eat them with other meals.

Since the stir-fry goes like the wind and you haven't a hand free, it's best to have the noodles already cooked, staying warm in the steamer. All other ingredients can be prepared for stir-frying a few hours in advance.

If your butcher isn't amenable to paper-thin slicing, freeze the meat, then, as it thaws, you can slice it yourself with a very sharp knife.

salt to taste

½ pound thin Chinese wheat noodles or any other thin noodles

about ½ tablespoon Asian sesame oil or mild oil

1 medium head (1 generous pound) tender young pak choi, or equal parts celery and chard, or Chinese cabbage

¾ pound tender boneless beef, trimmed of fat and sliced paper-thin

2 teaspoons mild oil

a piece of young fresh ginger the size of a small egg, peeled and cut into slivers

5 garlic cloves, finely chopped

1½ cups corn kernels cut from the cob or thawed frozen niblets

1 small dried hot red chili, seeds removed, crumbled

about 3 tablespoons low-sodium soy sauce

freshly ground black pepper to taste

1 small sweet red pepper, in small dice

Have ready a big pot of boiling salted water. Drop the noodles into the boiling water and stir to separate them—they'll probably be very long. Start testing for doneness in about 3 minutes. When tender but still slightly chewy, lift out with tongs, drain in a colander, then turn into a big bowl. Drizzle on a little sesame oil and toss well to keep the noodles moist. You can refrigerate these for a day and reheat in a steamer for about 15 minutes.

Stack the pak choi on your cutting board and cut stalks from leafy ends at the point where the leafy green begins. Keeping them separate, thinly slice the stalk pieces crosswise, then the leaves crosswise into inch-wide strips. Cut the meat slices lengthwise to make broad ribbons.

To stir-fry, set a large wok or heavy skillet over high heat until smoking hot. Drizzle in 1 teaspoon of the oil, then immediately add half the ginger and garlic and stir to blend. Quickly add the beef a piece at a time so the strips don't stick together as they cook. Stir-fry until there's no more pink in the pan, about 1 minute. Transfer the beef to a bowl.

Heat the wok again, drizzle in another teaspoon of oil, and add the remaining ginger and garlic. Stir-fry briefly, then add the stalk pieces and stir-fry for 30 seconds. Add the leaves and corn and stir-fry for 30 seconds. Return the meat to the wok, add the chili and soy sauce, and stir-fry for 30 seconds more. Add the pepper, taste for seasoning, then ladle the mixture over a bed of the noodles. Garnish with the red pepper. Serve with hot sake or green tea.

Flowering Pak Choi

Alternative: The same as for choy sums.

When the choy sums prove too challenging to grow, the amenable pak chois are allowed to flower.

Prepare them in any way you would the choy sums or other flowering shoots.

FOR A SPRINGTIME PICNIC: Sprinkle slender stalks of golden flowers and mustardy leaves with drops of balsamic vinegar and salt and pepper and munch away.

A WARM SALAD: Simmer the flowering stalks in an uncovered skillet in a little vegetable stock or salted water. When tender-crisp, a couple of minutes, drain well (save the stock), cut into bite-size pieces, and serve as a warm salad tossed with some of the sesame miso dressing in The Cook's Notebook.

Rosette Pak Choi

Alternative: Mizuna leaves, baby squash leaves, or small crisp leaves of mild spinach or Malabar spinach.

These roundish very dark green leaves are at the peak of flavor when picked small. I prefer them raw in salad—their shape is aesthetic, they're pretty, and I dislike turning them into nonentities by cooking them. Remember that the smaller leaves are the choicest. Pick from various parts of a couple of plants—never decimate one plant. Use these leaves anytime you would fresh spinach leaves. For example, basil and spinach are convivial, and so are basil and rosette pak choi.

ROSETTE PAK CHOI, SWEET BASIL, AND NASTURTIUM SALAD: For each serving, into a salad bowl toss a handful of small whole leaves of rosette pak choi with half as much torn-in-half leaves of fresh basil. If you have them, add half a handful each of nasturtium flowers and leaves.

Dress lightly with three parts peanut or other nut oil mixed with two parts rice vinegar—or use red wine vinegar if you'd like it lustier. Add salt and freshly ground white pepper. Taste for seasoning and serve. Tell everyone to eat with their fingers.

ANOTHER HERBAL SALAD: Celery-flavored leaves (lovage, leaf celery, celery) with leaves of rosette pak choi—the light and dark green and the celery/mustardy flavors are lovely. Dress lightly.

Tendergreen

Brassicas cross with cheerful abandon, leaving delicious progeny in their wake. Tendergreen could be related to komatsuna for its blend of mustard and spinach flavors. More and more of these crosses will appear in catalogs. We welcome them into our gardens, as they're richly nutritious and almost trouble free. Harvest and use them interchangeably with komatsuna—which in turn is used interchangeably with other spinachy mustardy leaves.

JAPANESE SALT-PICKLED GREENS: For an amazing taste—something to reach for on a lethargic afternoon when a mouthful will snap you back to the surface, try this Japanese pickle. It's a splendid way to keep any of these greens should there suddenly be too many to eat all at once.

O-shinko is classically done with Chinese cabbage, mustard greens, and spinach. The colors stay uncommonly rich, and surprisingly the pickle isn't too salty. These will keep for at least 3 months in the refrigerator—that's not to say there will be any nutrients left, but the pickle will still taste marvelous.

Rinse and dry leaves—tender stems may be attached. Weigh them. You'll need 1 pound of pure sea or pickling salt for every 5 pounds of leaves.

Note the weight of your crock or other deep flattish-bottomed vessel made of pottery, enamel, or glass. Sprinkle the bottom thickly with salt. Lay leaves an inch or so deep. Sprinkle generously with salt and continue layering this way. If you like, you can strew a little peeled and crushed garlic through the leaves—nontraditional but great. Finish with a thick layer of salt.

Cover with a nonmetal lid and weigh down, ideally with a granite stone (not easy-dissolving sandstone, limestone, or concrete block). Weight accelerates the extraction of water and excludes air, thus permitting the pickler to penetrate the pickle. The heavier the weight, the faster the process and the longer the pickle keeps. However, the faster the process, the tougher the pickle. So a happy-medium weight must be used. With leaf vegetables, that seems to be 70 to 80 percent of the weight of the pickle. So weigh your vessel again, deduct the original weight, then calculate the weight of your stone. If you don't have a river rock handy, use doubled large food storage plastic bags filled with water (do not use garbage bags).

Set in a cool, dark place. You can eat the greens after 12 hours, but if you wait for 2 to 3 days, they'll taste even better. In winter you can keep the crock in a cool place for a couple of months, but when the weather is warm, it's best to refrigerate it.

To serve, rinse the pickled leaves under cool water, gently squeeze out excess moisture, and chop if you wish. Serve in small dishes to accompany anything you like.

Pure salting is the classic way. You may prefer the modification of adding water halfway up the leaves the first day—you can use a chopstick to gauge depth. When liquid completely covers the pickle, it's ready. Less salty, and you don't have to rinse the leaves to eat them.

The Japanese eat lots of pickled vegetables, considering them very nutritious.

To pickle Chinese cabbage, trim off the bottoms, make cuts with a knife at the base to divide the head into eighths, but then pull rather than cut the head apart with your hands. Crosshatch the layers—set pieces at a right angle to the layer before. Proceed as directed.

Asparagus

Harvest asparagus no smaller than 1/4 inch thick, snapping off the spears at soil level—a knife might cut into the crown. Harvest the second spring after planting for just two weeks. By the third year, you can harvest for 4 weeks, and after that, for 6 weeks.

Asparagus shoots, like artichokes, are buds, so if they must wait for cooking, plunge spears into a jug of water. Asparagus loses vitamin C and flavoring sugars rapidly at room temperature, so keep the pitcher refrigerated.

To prepare asparagus, just before cooking rinse the stalks lightly. Unless you've let the stalks go too long, it's unlikely you'll have to peel any part of them as you must with market asparagus. There's an edible center in all but the toughest stalks, and peeling reveals it. Use a carbon-steel vegetable peeler and a light hand just on the very bottom part of the stalk. For company, cut the end on the diagonal to give a finished look.

For the best flavor and color, drop asparagus into an inch of boiling salted water in a wide skillet over high heat, no more than two deep. Cook briskly, uncovered, until tender-crisp—4 to 5 minutes after the water returns to a boil (or 8 minutes or so for those who hate semi-crisp vegetables). Save the stock for soups.

If the stalks are short enough and if you have a pot tall enough, see the method for simmering/steaming budding shoots in the Broccoli entry.

Serve asparagus hot or at room temperature in a heap going one way on a cloth napkin (a European touch that never ceases to give me pleasure) on a plate. If you have English daisies in the garden, their pink sprigs make a charming garnish. Pass melted unsalted butter flavored with a squeeze of fresh orange juice—blood orange if available.

For stir-fries, slice asparagus spears into 1- to 2-inch pieces on the diagonal to expose greater flesh and to allow them to cook fast. Don't forget you can add pieces of tender raw asparagus—cut on the diagonal—to salad.

Asparagus is moderately high in folic acid and vitamin C and a fair source of vitamins E, A, and B.

Asparagus Bundles Tied with Chives in Bloom

ALLOW 1 OR 2 BUNDLES PER SERVING

Cooks since the ancient Egyptians have found asparagus not just good to eat but wonderfully aesthetic as well. One fine spring evening our friend Lynnda Hart gifted us with this handsome composition. The arrangement seems complicated in the describing, but it goes together in minutes.

Cut off 4 to 6 slender asparagus stalks (if thicker than your little finger, halve the stalks lengthwise) at 4 inches, slicing on the diagonal. Drop into a skillet with ½ inch of boiling salted water and boil uncovered until tender-crisp, 2 to 3 minutes. Lift out with tongs and transfer to a deep dish (save the stock for another use).

Moisten with vinaigrette (see Dressings in The Cook's Notebook), and marinate for 1 hour to overnight without turning—handle as little as possible.

Pick chives about 6 inches long—3 for every bundle. Pick as many chive blossoms and buds as you'll have bundles. Arrange chives in heaps of 3 on your work surface. Lift the asparagus from the marinade and set stalks (rounded sides up, if split) on the chives. Tie the bundles once with the chives as ribbons, pulling firmly. Slip a chive blossom and bud into each bundle. Arrange bundles in a herringbone pattern down the center of a serving platter. Overlap slices of unpeeled boiled red potatoes on each side. Drizzle the potatoes with the vinaigrette.

Roasted Asparagus

MAKES 4 SERVINGS

Grilled asparagus is much admired, but roasted asparagus is another thing altogether. The all-embracing heat of the oven cooks the spears more gently and evenly to produce a remarkable and exciting texture. Use a shallow baking dish or several large pie plates in which the spears fit one layer deep. For finest quality, the asparagus should go straight from the garden or refrigerator to the sink to the oven.

Heat the oven to 500°F. Prepare 2 pounds of asparagus spears of roughly the same thickness. Spread a generous tablespoon of fruity olive oil over the bottom of the baking dish or dishes. Add the spears and roll them in the oil until moistened. Arrange them in one layer (if the dish is long, set the butts facing each end and interweave the tips in the center).

Roast uncovered until lightly browned, about 5 minutes, then turn with tongs, sprinkle with salt and freshly ground white pepper, and roast until browned on the other side, another 5 or so minutes. When they test almost tender with a thin skewer, strew the spears with shavings of fresh Parmesan cheese and roast for another couple of minutes. Eat one: it should be tender but still a little crisp. Adjust seasoning. Serve hot from the dish as a first course.

White Asparagus (Blanched)

Alternative: Green asparagus.

These are the stalks you've covered with a pot and blanched—exotic pale beauties. Prepare them just as green asparagus, taking great pains not to overcook.

White Asparagus Pickles

MAKES 3 QUARTS

After you've had your fill of white asparagus with melted butter and lemon juice—butter and orange juice is even finer—turn your blanched asparagus into an unusual pickle. Canning details are in The Cook's Notebook. Use wide-mouth quart jars.

45 to 60 spears (3 pounds) white asparagus, stems peeled, cut to come to ½ inch below rim of jars

3 cups cool water

2⅓ cups distilled white vinegar, 5 percent acidity

⅔ cup bottled lemon juice (acid content of bottled juice is more consistent than that of fresh)

3 tablespoons sugar

3 tablespoons pickling salt

6 whole dried hot red chilies, optional

Heat 3 quart canning jars in hot water, then carefully pack tightly with asparagus, cut sides down. Leave ½ inch of headspace.

In a nonreactive saucepan, combine the water, vinegar, lemon juice, sugar, and salt and bring to a boil over medium-high heat. Taste for seasoning. Meanwhile, add 2 chili pods to each jar, if desired. Pour the boiling solution over the asparagus, leaving ½ inch of headspace. Wipe the rims and threads clean, place hot lids on top, and screw bands on firmly. Process for 15 minutes in a boiling water bath, then cool and store.

Beans and Legumes

When you have a fistful of snap beans warm from the sun in your hand, no matter what their botanical name, you want to know how to cook them deliciously, immediately. And when you've patiently dried your beans on the vines, threshed them, and put them up in jars, the morning you take them down from the shelf you want to simmer them, there and then. These recipes are organized according to the state of the bean—fresh are at the snap and shelly (in-between) stages; dried are winter's stores. Within the group they're interchangeable.

In addition to their delicious flavor, good nutrition, and remarkable versatility, all beans have in common the fact that their leaves are edible—so don't forget to add young ones to your salads.

Fresh Beans—Snaps

"Green" beans are more in the vernacular, but *snap* is the gardener's term that exactly describes the earliest edible stage of the pods—they snap when you break them. In gardener's terms *green* pods are at any stage from snap to shelly—when the seeds inside are little nubbins, just this side of half-mature.

To prepare snap beans, rinse the young things lightly and top and tail only if you're fussy or if the ends are tough. To keep the pods their brightest and crispest, cook them uncovered in abundant water, in advance or just before serving.

To cook, have ready a big pot of boiling salted water and a big bowl of ice water. To keep the water as hot as possible, add the beans to the boiling water by small handfuls. Leave the pot uncovered. According to the thickness of the beans, soon after the water returns to a boil, start picking out beans to taste. You're looking for tenderness with a hint of crisp resistance—less crispness if you'll be serving the beans directly, more if you'll be returning them briefly to the heat. Taste every 30 seconds. Undercook them slightly because they'll keep cooking a little out of the pot.

When they're ready, sweep them out with a sieve and—if they're very thin or if you think you've overcooked them—throw them into the ice water and swish around with your hand to stop the cooking as rapidly as possible. You can pat them dry and set the beans in a cool place for a bit—although it's not the best thing to do to them.

To finish most simply, heat a heavy skillet or wok—use as many vessels as you'll need to have the beans no more than an inch or so deep—over high heat until hot. Drizzle with olive or nut oil or toss in a lump of unsalted butter or use a bit of oil and butter together. Add the beans and toss constantly just until every bean glistens and is heated through—the color should not change. You can also add a sprinkling of chopped herbs—parsley, dill, chervil, mint, and Chinese chives are especially good with snap beans. Sometimes I toss 2 or 3 minced garlic cloves for every 4 or 5 cups of beans in the oil/butter for 10 seconds before adding the beans. And sometimes I squeeze on a little fresh lemon juice just before serving.

An exquisite seasoning with any snap bean is thin ribbons of fresh mint. Add at the last minute with a benediction of extra-virgin olive oil to make it Italian or unsalted sweet butter to make it French.

Add freshly ground white pepper, taste for seasoning, then turn your beans into a hot serving dish, arranging them as best you can to run in the same direction. They're great piping hot or at warmish room temperature as a vegetable or cool room temperature if dressed with oil and offered as a salad.

Snap beans are low in fiber, but they have a decent amount of vitamin C to give us with their sweet taste and a fair amount of folic acid, vitamin A, and iron.

Stir-Fried Scallops and Snap Beans

MAKES 4 SERVINGS

This is a fine dish for early autumn, when summer's passion for just green beans is beginning to pale. All elements can be prepared several hours in advance and refrigerated.

- 1 pound sea or bay scallops, shrimp, or thick fillets of a lean sweet mild white fish cut into inch-size chunks
- 4 whole scallions, cut into 2-inch lengths
- 1 garlic clove, thinly sliced
- 2 tablespoons low-sodium soy sauce
- 1 tablespoon cornstarch
- 1 teaspoon sugar
- 1 teaspoon Asian sesame oil
- 2 tablespoons mild oil
- 4 or 5 cups (1 pound) tender snap beans, trimmed and sliced on the diagonal in 2-inch pieces
- ¼ cup vegetable stock or chicken broth
- salt and freshly ground black pepper to taste
- heaped ½ cup roasted broken cashews, almond slivers, or coarsely chopped peanuts

Cut sea scallops into chunks about an inch in diameter (they'll probably be ½ inch thick); bay scallops are naturally the right size for this dish. If frozen, cover and thaw in the refrigerator.

When you're ready to cook, in a bowl mix the scallops, scallions, and garlic. Sprinkle on the soy sauce, cornstarch, sugar, and sesame oil and stir gently to blend.

Heat a wok or large heavy skillet over high heat until it begins to smoke. Swirl 1 tablespoon oil into the pan, add the beans, and stir-fry until they're on the brink of tenderness, 5 to 7 minutes (more if they're older or thick). Turn into a heated serving dish.

Wipe out the pan, heat it, then swirl in the second tablespoon of oil. Add the fish and stock and stir for 30 seconds, then return the beans to the pan and stir just until the fish is cooked through, the sauce has thickened, and the beans are tender, 1 to 2 minutes. Add salt and pepper and taste for seasoning.

Serve at once over rice, sprinkle with nuts, and offer something bright for the plate—sliced tomatoes or steamed carrots. I like a little more soy sauce for the dish, so I serve a pitcher on the side. I also like to drink beer or gunpowder tea with Chinese food, but some people are happiest with a full-flavored Chardonnay.

Black-Eyed Peas

Alternative: Yardlong beans would come closest in terms of their unusual flavor.

Black-eyed peas harvested at the snap bean stage don't remind me of any other flavor—theirs is unique and captivating. The closest I can come is a fresh verdant nuttiness with hints of cucumber and ginger.

SNAP BLACK-EYED PEAS VEILED WITH CREAM: makes 4 servings. Prepare and blanch 1 pound beans as for snap beans, boiling for about 7 minutes. Just before serving, stack the beans and cut them roughly into 2- to 2½-inch pieces. Turn into a wide heavy skillet with ¼ cup heavy cream. Stir occasionally over medium heat until warmed through, about 5 minutes. Add chopped fresh dill and salt and pepper to taste, and serve.

Fava Beans

Alternative: Snap limas.

These plush pods are the velvet of the bean world. Pick when they're no longer than your longest finger. But save some on the bushes to shell when baby-lima size.

Bear in mind that some people of Mediterranean descent can have a bad reaction to these beans. If you've never eaten them, try only a couple of favas the first time to be sure you won't be affected.

Prepare as for other snap beans.

Snap Fava Beans with Baby Artichokes and Peas in the Sicilian Style

MAKES 2 MAIN-COURSE OR 4 FIRST-COURSE SERVINGS

La frittedda is a classic Sicilian composition that captures the moment in a warm spring garden when peas, baby artichokes, and fava beans are all sweet creamy perfection. Traditionally the favas are shelled along with the peas, but I love the play of pale wedges, bright pods, and green orbs.

This is divinely pure and surprisingly restrained for the Sicilian palate—though perhaps I've seen wild fennel chopped into the mix or dill. Taste the exquisite flavors and textures of this composition all by themselves. Or serve it as a vegetarian main dish: Start with a light soup such as consommé, offer lots of good bread, drink a rosé, and for dessert have lemon sherbet with chopped roasted pistachios and crisp almond biscotti.

You can prepare each vegetable a little in advance, but the final cooking must be last-minute.

4 to 5 cups (1 pound) 3-inch snap fava beans, topped and tailed if necessary
juice of ½ lemon
8 plum-size artichokes or hearts of 4 large artichokes
about ¼ cup extra-virgin olive oil
1 small red onion, finely chopped
about ½ cup hot diluted chicken broth or water
3 cups fresh peas, from 2 to 3 pounds unshelled
a sprinkling of freshly grated nutmeg
salt and freshly ground white pepper to taste
a handful of chopped fresh marjoram or flat-leaf parsley

Have ready a big pot of boiling salted water and a big bowl of cool water. Drop the beans into the boiling water, stir, and set the timer for 8 minutes. Taste to see if the beans are just tender-crisp—depending on the beans, it can take 2 to 4 more minutes. Lift the beans into a flat dish—they'll continue to cook a bit. Cover and reserve.

Meanwhile, mix the lemon juice into the bowl of water. Cut the artichokes with a stainless-steel knife and drop pieces into the bowl as you work to keep them from discoloring. With plum-size artichokes, trim the stems, then cut each bud lengthwise into 6 or 8 pieces about ½ inch at the widest part. With large artichokes, snap off the leaves (they can be steamed for the family), scrape out the chokes, cut the stem flush, and slice the hearts into wedges about ½ inch at the widest part.

In a large heavy skillet (not iron), heat 2 tablespoons oil over medium heat. Add the onion and sauté, stirring frequently, until softened, 3 to 4 minutes.

At this point these vegetables plus the shelled peas can wait in a covered vessel in a cool place for a couple of hours. Before continuing, warm the onion in the pan over medium heat.

Add 3 tablespoons olive oil to the skillet, and when it's hot, add the artichoke pieces. Sprinkle with salt, cover the pan, and cook for 5 minutes. Through the rest of the cooking, frequently shake the skillet, holding the lid in place. Stir in the stock and the peas. When you hear a sizzle, pour on a few tablespoons of broth and repeat as needed. When the artichokes and peas are nearly tender—12 to 15 minutes—mix in the fava beans. Give them 2 to 3 minutes to heat up. Sprinkle with nutmeg, add salt and pepper, taste for seasoning, and turn into a heated bowl. Sprinkle with chopped marjoram and serve.

Filet Beans/French Beans/Haricots Verts

Filet beans are the jewels of beandom. They are fabulously delicate and flavorful—harvest pods when less than ¼ inch across.

To prepare filet beans, line up the beans and trim off just the stem ends—the wisps of tails are a tender reminder they're from a garden. You'll probably want to cook them quickly, then finish them simply.

Filet Beans with Tomato Ribbons

MAKES ¾ CUP PUREE TO SERVE 4

I love the look and flavor of fresh pureed tomatoes—red, yellow, orange, or white—spooned like a ribbon over a heap of filet beans. In fact it would make a charming presentation for guests to alternate colors around the table. Since the sauce is meant to be elegant, here's a rare time we'll remove the tomato seeds.

This sauce is equally delicious and vibrant over cool sliced potatoes, braised celery, summer squash, braised lettuce, roasted onions, cauliflower florets, and so on.

Since the dish is served at room temperature, everything can be prepared in advance.

- salt to taste
- 4 to 5 cups (1 pound) tender filet beans
- 1 large (½ pound) flavorful, meaty tomato of any color, cut in half crosswise
- ½ tablespoon mild olive oil
- a few drops of your favorite mild vinegar
- 4 large supple lettuce leaves, red or pale green
- freshly ground black pepper to taste
- 4 edible yellow flowers, for garnish, optional

Cook the beans in boiling salted water as for basic snap beans, but to your point of perfection since they will not be cooked further. Wrap in a towel and keep in a cool place.

With a fingertip, scoop out the tomato seeds. Whirl the tomato in a food processor or blender until it's a smooth puree. Blend with the oil, vinegar, and salt. Taste for seasoning. The beans and puree can now wait in a cool place for a few hours.

To serve, place a lettuce leaf on each of 4 salad plates. Arrange the beans in the center in a bundle. Spoon the puree in a casual ribbon over the center of each bundle, letting some fall on the leaf. Grind pepper on top and decorate with a fat blossom in the center of the ribbon.

Flageolet Beans

The seeds of these pods are small and kidney-shaped. Whether pale green as shelly beans or white when dried, they're classically used in France for garnishing meats. But at the snap stage they're prepared like other snap beans and are delightful.

MIXED SNAP BEANS WITH HERBS: Here's the sort of dish only you with your uncommon bean patch can bring to the table. Trim equal quantities of two or three different sorts of fresh snap beans such as flageolets, skinny pole beans, filets, and Italian slicing beans. They can all be green, or you can mix colors. Pick them the same size or throw larger beans into the pot first and cook them a little longer. Some cultivars cook quickly, some take longer, so often it's wise to cook each type separately. Boil uncovered in salted water as for basic snap beans until tender-crisp, then lift out, cool quickly, and pat dry.

Turn all the beans into a heated serving bowl and toss with a drizzle of extra-virgin olive oil, a sprinkling of lemon juice, and equal quantities of finely chopped fresh dill, lovage (or cutting celery or celery leaves), and flat-leaf parsley and half as much fresh sage. Add salt and freshly ground white pepper, then taste for seasoning. The beans are prettiest presented on a platter heaped in the same direction. Serve at once.

Another time you can mix the cooked beans in a saucepan, stirring in a splash of hot cream and a sprinkling of minced green onions (scallions) or green garlic, salt, and freshly ground white pepper. Taste for seasoning and serve at once.

Italian Beans

Alternative: Any other large pods.

These luscious broad pods resemble snap fava beans. Prepare and boil as for basic snap beans. Or steam the beans with an inch of water—they will taste drier, and more nutrients will be preserved—then save the stock for another use. And remember to cut young ones up raw into salads, especially with tomatoes.

Italian beans are also marvelous tossed with shavings of Parmesan cheese and with finely chopped rosemary.

The Best Italian Beans

MAKES ABOUT 4 SERVINGS

The incomparably rich flavor and meaty texture of Italian beans fresh from your garden must be preserved. No distractions. There's no finer first course or vegetable accompaniment than these beans my friend Lorraine Alexander was served on a stone terrace overlooking vineyards in Tuscany.

The dressed beans can be kept in a cool place a few hours without harm.

Trim off the stems of 4 to 5 cups (1 pound) of beans. Quickly cook in boiling salted water as for basic snap beans, but begin tasting the beans after about 5 minutes and test every minute thereafter.

Lift out with a slotted spoon, shake off excess water, and if the beans are long, cut them on the diagonal into 6-inch lengths. Spread on a handsome platter. Drizzle with olive oil, then mix with your hands until all the beans glisten. Sprinkle with a little minced garlic, fresh lemon juice (a third as much as oil), a good handful of chopped mint, and freshly ground white pepper. Taste for seasoning. Mix again.

Serve on the platter cooler than room temperature but not cold. Finish with a drift of mixed colors of petals of marigolds and/or calendulas.

Foot-long, inch-wide violet-podded purple pole beans are great cooked this way—and their juices turn the dressing pink.

Purple Pod Beans

Most purple beans turn green when they hit the boiling water. Pity. To relish their color, serve them raw—untopped, untailed—in a crudités arrangement.

Sautéed Purple Pod Beans and Garlic Cloves

MAKES 4 SERVINGS

Here's a company way for cooking these or any other snap beans. The garlic is butter-soft, and with all the chlorophyll in the beans, you needn't worry about becoming antisocial. Everything can be ready ahead of time for the 2-minute finish.

4 to 5 cups (1 pound) young purple pod beans, topped—tailed only if tails are tough or sharp

salt to taste

1 whole head of garlic, 16 or more cloves, separated

2 tablespoons unsalted butter

about 1 tablespoon rice vinegar or fresh lemon juice

a handful of finely chopped parsley

freshly ground white pepper to taste

While you trim the beans, bring a large pot of salted water to a boil. In a small saucepan, bring 1½ to 2 cups of water with a sprinkling of salt to a boil. Drop the whole beans into the big pot and set the timer for 8 minutes. Drop the garlic cloves into the small pot and set the timer for 15 minutes. Keep both pots uncovered. Start tasting the beans at about 7 minutes—they should be tender but still delightfully crisp at the center. Lift them out into a shallow dish lined with a folded towel and cool. (The beans will continue cooking for a bit out of the pot, so if you think you've overcooked them, drop them into a bowl of ice water to stop the cooking. Then lift and lay on a plate. Cover with a towel and reserve in a cool place.)

Peel the garlic cloves, then slice lengthwise about ¼ inch wide. Cover and reserve with the beans.

To serve, melt the butter in a large heavy skillet over high heat. Add the beans and garlic and toss gently until the garlic is lightly colored and the beans are glistening and hot, no more than 2½ minutes. Sprinkle with the vinegar and parsley, add salt and pepper, and taste for seasoning. Then turn into a heated serving dish.

Runner Beans

Runner beans are grown principally for their showy blossoms, which are scarlet, pale pink, or white. If the pods—large and meaty—are picked young enough, they'll be mostly stringless.

Runner snap, shelly, and dried beans are prepared as for the others at those stages. These are certainly worth eating—some runners give uncommonly handsome shelly and dried beans.

Sunny Runner Beans

MAKES 4 SERVINGS

Here is a cheerful way with snap runner beans—a way of remembering the flowers they came from.

Bring a big pot of salted water to a boil. Top 4 to 5 cups (1 pound) of young runner beans; string and tail them if necessary. Snap into inch-long pieces and drop into the water. Return to a boil over high heat and cook at a gentle boil until the beans are tender-crisp, 10 to 12 minutes. Don't overcook—start tasting after 8 minutes.

Meanwhile, coarsely chop 3 ripe tomatoes, chop 1 yellow onion, and mince 1 garlic clove. Turn into a large nonstick skillet and add a drizzle of olive oil and a little salt and freshly ground white pepper. Cook over medium-high heat until the onions have softened, stirring occasionally, about 5 minutes.

Drain the beans and stir them into the skillet. Add a squirt of fresh orange juice, a handful of thyme leaves—lemon thyme, if you have it—and taste for seasoning. When the beans are hot, turn into a serving dish. This is lovely heaped over rice.

If corn is in season, you can add the golden kernels from one cob to the tomatoes at the beginning if you like.

Blossoms of Runner Beans

These are among the handsomest of the edible flowers, looking like plump pea blossoms. Add them at the last minute to any dish of beans. They will be lightly crisp with a sweet bean flavor.

Wax Beans

Their yellow—from straw to gold—is one of summer's special pleasures. All particulars are the same as for green snap beans, except they have less vitamin A since they're paler.

Quick Curried Wax Beans

MAKES 4 TO 6 SERVINGS

This is a dish in shades from cream to gold. Everything can be prepared in advance for a fast finish.

1 tablespoon fresh lime or lemon juice

8 to 10 cups (2 pounds) tender wax beans, cooked as for basic snap beans, hot or cool

1 tablespoon unsalted butter or mild oil

1½ tablespoons curry powder or to taste

3 scallions, both white and green parts, finely chopped

2 garlic cloves, finely chopped

salt to taste

¾ to 1 heaped cup dried shredded unsweetened coconut

¾ to 1 heaped cup chopped roasted peanuts

In a bowl, sprinkle the lime juice over the beans. In a large heavy skillet, melt the butter or heat the oil over low heat. Blend in the curry powder, then the scallions and garlic. Cook, stirring constantly, for 3 to 4 minutes—do not let brown.

Add the beans and a sprinkling of salt (some curry powders are salty—taste yours first). Stir until each glints with the curry and all are hot. Add a knob more butter if the curry is in danger of scorching.

Remove from the heat and taste for seasoning. Serve at once heaped over rice and garnish with coconut and peanuts. Pass your favorite chutney.

You can easily elaborate on this composition by adding coarsely chopped raw yellow tomatoes to the beans at the end and letting them heat through and offering more garnishes such as diced bananas, cucumbers, chopped candied ginger, and so on. Just keep the colors in the same soft hues.

Winged Peas

Alternative: Winged beans or any snap bean.

These resemble winged beans—and long box kites—and I've grown them with pleasure.

For fruits eaten pod-and-seeds-together like snap beans and sugar peas, harvest the early pods when ½ inch thick. They'll be tender with a flavor hinting of artichoke. The leaves and tender shoots can be prepared as for pea shoots. The young tuberous roots are eaten as potatoes.

To prepare winged peas, rinse lightly. Simmer the whole pods in a skillet barely covered in vegetable stock until just tender, about 5 minutes. Some will be edible all the way through, some will have tiny peas in the center, some will have bits of the frame of the kite.

Later in the season even thin winged pea pods will be stringy. Then let them grow until the seeds are big enough to harvest. Cook the immature seeds as for peas, dry and cook them as beans, or roast them like soy nuts. In the 19th century on the island of Mauritius, winged peas were called *pois carrés*—square peas—and were cultivated for their seeds. Are they still? A tasty curiosity.

WINGED PEAS WITH PARSLEY AND BUTTER: For each serving, melt ½ tablespoon unsalted butter in a large heavy skillet and reheat 4 to 5 ounces (a good handful) cooked winged peas over high heat, tossing to coat them with butter—about 2 minutes. Add salt and freshly ground white pepper and sprinkle with a little finely chopped flat-leaf parsley. Taste for seasoning and serve.

Yardlong Beans

Alternative: Snap black-eyed peas or any flavorful snap bean.

Don't let these sweet, rich beans grow longer than 16 inches, or they'll be less than tender. These are among my favorite vegetables. Their sheer exuberance and their meatiness are a joy. But past their length, these are also the snap beans with the most flavor.

Except for the fact these need slicing into manageable size, preparation, nutrition, and serving size are the same as for snap beans.

The entire plant, in early tender stages, is edible. Steam the leaves and serve as you would other greens, with a splash of lemon juice. Slice young stalks on the diagonal and add them to salads with chunks of oranges and red peppers.

You can use yardlong beans in any recipe that calls for snap beans. I find them particularly companionable with sliced mushrooms.

You may see light green, dark green, and even purple yardlong beans at the market—the dark green are considered tastiest by the Chinese, but every Asian culture has a favorite color. Try the purple ones, too. Cook them fast and briefly, and the purple will stay.

Stir-Fried Yardlong Beans with Cashews

MAKES 4 SERVINGS

Rinse, dry, top, and, if necessary, tail 4 to 5 cups (1 pound) of long beans. Slice on the diagonal 3 inches long (or the length you like).

Heat a large wok or heavy skillet over high heat until it smokes. Drizzle 1 tablespoon mild oil around the edges and in 5 seconds add 6 chopped garlic cloves. Stir-fry for 30 seconds, then add the beans, sprinkle with salt, and stir-fry until they're glossy, about 2 minutes—you may need to drizzle in a little more oil. Spread the beans in the pan and cook for 30 seconds, then stir again until the beans are still bright but tender-crisp, 4 to 5 minutes at most.

Remove from the heat, add some freshly ground black pepper, then taste for seasoning. Sprinkle on ½ cup broken roasted unsalted cashew nuts. Good with rice and fish or poultry.

Fresh Beans—Shellies

These are halfway beans. The pods are still considered fresh because they're green, although now they're somewhat leathery. Harvest shellies when the seeds inside—the beans—are well defined. Once you pop out your shelly beans (an affectionate term—it's properly shell beans), you'll find they take longer to cook than pods at the snap stage. Depending on their age and girth, it can be 20 minutes or 45. Shellies take longer to shell than dried beans, too, but they're worth all the time they take.

Shell beans have moderate amounts of fiber, vegetable protein, vitamin C, and iron and fair amounts of magnesium, folic acid, phosphorus, thiamine, and vitamin B_6.

To shell fresh beans, press on the seam of the pod with your thumbs, and the beans should pop right into the bowl beneath. Simmer in salted water, vegetable stock, or other liquid to cover until tender, covering the pot. Shellies have the rare ability to combine with almost any herb you can think of, so mix in chopped herbs before serving.

Black-Eyed Peas

Alternative: Small black-eyes are distinctly flavored, so use the best-tasting shellies you've got—favas in spring and limas in summer.

These shellies take 30 to 40 minutes' simmering to cook to tenderness. They're especially delicious with tomatoes and summer savory. You'll get about 1 rounded cup of beans from 11 ounces of pods, 2 servings.

Butter/Sieva Beans

Alternative: Limas are the closest, but any cowpea will do nicely as well.

Shelly butter beans resemble small limas. Although botanically butter and sieva (pronounced *sivvy*) beans are the same, sievas are the smallest. Carolina Sievas' pods are medium green at the snap stage, and their dried seeds are white. Florida Butter, aka Speckled Butter, beans are speckled buff when dried, but the speckles cook away. Nutrients are the same as shelly beans'.

Lowcountry Shelly Butter or Sieva Beans

MAKES 8 TO 10 SERVINGS

From *Hoppin' John's Lowcountry Cooking,* here is the southern way of cooking butter and sieva beans at the shelly—in-between—stage.

Combine 2 quarts cold water and 1 pound lean bony smoked pork such as neck bones or ham hocks in a big pot. Bring to a boil, add a little salt, turn the heat to low, and simmer uncovered until the water becomes broth, 30 minutes or more. Add a heaped 5 cups of shelled butter or sieva beans (a generous 5 pounds before shelling), return to a boil, again turn the heat to low, and simmer, uncovered, until the beans are tender, about 30 minutes. Stir once or twice. I like a goodly amount of freshly ground black pepper added.

The beans are always fuller-flavored the next day. To serve, lift the beans from the pot, taste for seasoning, and spoon steaming hot over boiled rice.

Add a crisp salad and, for a heartier supper, fried catfish. Juicy melon for dessert.

Leftover ham broth is incomparable for cooking the stronger-flavored greens such as mustards and turnips. Freeze every precious drop.

Cowpeas/Field Peas/Southern Peas

Alternative: Black-eyes and butter beans.

Here are the tiny creams and crowders. Their flavor is very beany and somewhat winey. (Black-eyes, also one of the cowpeas, have their own shelly entry.)

Cook cowpeas at any stage, but they're most delicious as shellies. Simmer the beans until tender as in the previous recipe, 20 minutes or so. Drain, add freshly ground black pepper, and taste for seasoning. Serve with butter or cream.

Cowpeas offer fiber, a moderate amount of protein (complement them with another protein to make it complete), vitamin C, iron, and fair amounts of folic acid, magnesium, phosphorus, thiamine, and vitamin B_6.

Southern Pea Salad

MAKES 6 SERVINGS

The other vegetables should be as close to the size of the beans as possible. The salad can be mixed several hours in advance, but stir it again before serving.

3 cups drained cooked shelly southern peas, about 3 pounds before shelling
1 cup cooked fresh yellow kernels of sweet corn, cooled
1 cup finely chopped red tomato
1 cup finely chopped sweet green pepper
½ cup finely chopped sweet onion
salt to taste
lettuce leaves
about 6 tablespoons chopped toasted peanuts

DRESSING

⅓ cup peanut oil
scant ¼ cup cider vinegar
½ teaspoon sugar
hot pepper sauce to taste

In a salad bowl, mix the southern peas, corn, tomato, green pepper, and onion. In a small bowl, combine the dressing ingredients, then add to the salad. Toss to blend, add salt, then taste for seasoning. Heap each serving on a lettuce leaf and sprinkle with peanuts.

Fava Beans

Alternative: These are among the most flavorful of shellies, so use black-eyes or limas.

Shelly favas are plump and succulent—particularly delicious. You can prepare shelly favas as you would any shelly bean. They have a moderate amount of vitamin C and fair amounts of folic acid, vitamin A, and iron. The leafy tips can be cooked as greens or go raw into salads.

From Rome comes the custom of eating fresh young shelled fava beans with nibbles of pecorino cheese. The sharply flavored ewe's milk cheese makes a stirring contrast to the delicate beans. But unless you're fresh from Rome or a cheese shop that flies in pecorino at its finest, I recommend the round nutted taste of Parmigiano-Reggiano. Any lusty cheese will be wonderful with raw favas. With these sip your favorite Italian white wine, chilled, with the first strawberries of spring floating in it.

Flageolet Beans

Alternative: Baby butter beans or baby limas are closest.

It's at the pale green shelly stage that I find small kidney-shaped flageolets the most beguiling. They're tiny, and a chore to shell, but you who appreciate Mother Nature's treasures will want to give them the time. These are especially good with a steak or chop or roast chicken.

Burgundian Shelly Flageolets

MAKES 4 SERVINGS

Cut 2 small carrots crosswise into 3 even pieces. Slice the pieces on the diagonal 1/4 inch thick, then cut the slices lengthwise in half. Slice an onion 1/4 inch thick, then cut the slices in half.

Heat a heavy dry nonstick skillet and lightly brown the carrots and onions over medium-high heat, stirring frequently, about 5 minutes. Add 2 cups shelled flageolet beans from about 1 2/3 pounds unshelled and 1 cup cold salted water. Turn heat to low, cover loosely, and simmer until the beans are almost tender, stirring occasionally, 30 to 40 minutes. Add 1/4 cup dry red wine and cook, stirring once or twice, until all is thoroughly tender, 5 to 10 more minutes. Add ground black pepper and taste for seasoning. Serve sprinkled with a handful of chopped fresh summer savory leaves.

Horticultural Beans

Alternative: Big plushy limas.

These beans are usually larger than flageolets and often smaller than limas. They come in brilliantly colored pods—the colors of a mountain sunset—and can be beautifully spattered in orange or blue. Horticulturals are meaty beans, with a nutlike aftertaste.

Savory Horticultural Beans

MAKES 4 SERVINGS

This is a classical dish of shelly beans you'll find from Florida's Cross Creek to Rome's Trastevere. They're so good that I'm always tempted to eat the whole batch by myself. It's a small batch because I like to do a great variety of small plantings, so these beans are my entire crop.

Best freshly made, but they can be warmed up.

2 small or 1 large strip of lean bacon, finely diced

1 small onion, preferably red, finely chopped

½ tablespoon finely chopped fresh summer savory leaves or ½ teaspoon crumbled dried

1 teaspoon finely chopped fresh sage leaves or a good pinch of crumbled dried

2 cups shelly horticultural beans, about 1¼ pounds in the pod

1½ cups vegetable stock or cool water

salt and freshly ground white pepper to taste

a little fresh lard, optional

In a medium-size heavy saucepan, cook the bacon over low heat for about 2 minutes. Add the onion and sauté over medium-high heat until the onions have softened, about 2 minutes, stirring frequently. Blend in the savory, sage, and beans and stir for a long minute. Stir in the stock, bring to a simmer, and cover. Turn the heat to low and simmer, stirring occasionally, until the beans are thoroughly tender, 35 to 45 minutes, depending on their stage of dryness.

Use a slotted spoon to lift the beans into a heated bowl and keep them warm. Raise the heat under the pot to high and boil down the stock to a kitchen spoonful. Stir into the beans, add salt and pepper and taste for seasoning. Should you have a spoonful of sweet lard on the premises, drop it in. Serve.

Lima Beans

Snap lima beans can be prepared by any other snap bean recipe. But limas are their richest at the shelly and dried stages. Whether fresh, shelly, or dried, when cooked these pale green kidney-shaped beans are velvety. I like shelly limas seasoned with a lump of sweet butter and a dash of cream.

Fresh limas have a fair amount of protein, a moderate amount of fiber, vitamin C, and iron, and small amounts of folic acid, magnesium, phosphorus, thiamine, and vitamin B_6.

SUCCOTASH: Shelly limas are marvelous as succotash, truly an early American treat: equal parts shelly limas (or any bean for that matter) with fresh kernels of corn. Cook them separately since the corn cooks much faster, then combine with just enough butter and cream for gloss.

Because limas' broad flat pods with lighter borders are a bother to shell, one night, out of patience, I decided to throw the whole beans in to cook with the rice.

The combination is not only lovely—green curls drifting through white rice—but a pleasing change from basic limas and basic rice.

TO SHELL FRESH LIMAS: Using scissors, snip off the band of lighter green on the outside edge of the pods—you can feel where the beans begin, so don't snip there. Run your fingers over the beans, dislodging them into a bowl.

Fresh Shelly Lima or Butter Beans in Jasmine or Basmati Rice

MAKES 6 SERVINGS

All you need is this one dish and a salad to go with whatever else you want for dinner. This is particularly suited to chicken and fish.

The beans can be shelled a day in advance.

1⅓ cups jasmine, basmati, or other long-grain white rice
2 cups shelled fresh lima or butter beans (about 2 pounds before shelling)
scant 2⅔ cups cold water
salt and freshly ground white pepper to taste
a little chopped sage
a walnut-size lump of unsalted butter

Rinse the jasmine or basmati rice in a strainer under cold running water, stirring the rice with your hand, until the water runs clear.

Turn the rice, beans, water, and salt into a large heavy saucepan. Bring to a boil over high heat, stir, cover tightly, turn the heat to low, and simmer without disturbing for 10 minutes. Remove from the heat and let sit undisturbed for 10 minutes more. Taste a bean. If it's not tender, let the rice sit until the beans are ready.

Add the pepper, taste for seasoning, then turn into a hot serving bowl and sprinkle with sage. Take to the table with the butter melting in the center. Eat with a big spoon.

Dried Beans and Legumes

Harvest pods for dried beans as soon as the beans rattle inside and the pods are papery. Keep an eye on them because at some point the pods will twist open and spill the beans.

In their mature dried state, these seeds, aka *pulses,* are the best plant source of protein. Beans are essentially without fat, except for soybeans; half their calories come from fat, but of course it's not unhealthy saturated fat. Dried beans contain almost as much calcium as milk.

Beans are second only to wheat bran as a source of dietary fiber—black, navy, and kidney beans are among the richest in fiber. Beans contain both soluble fiber, which helps lower cholesterol levels in the blood and controls blood sugar, and insoluble fiber. They also provide complex carbohydrates, B vitamins, zinc, potassium, and magnesium. Beans are low in sodium.

To cook dried beans and legumes, rinse them well under cool running water and pick them over carefully in a strainer—particularly those you haven't grown yourself. Little stones and even littler critters lurk. Don't think that just because they're dried they'll cook up tasty 20 years hence. Age tells, even in dried beans.

A slow cooker does a good job of simmering without having to be watched, although if the beans are old and you cook them on low, it can take days. You can of course simmer beans on top of the stove. If you have a pressure cooker, consult the manual about cooking dried beans. Some beans seem to be safe for the cooker, but others can foam and clog the vent, which could be disastrous.

Dried beans are most digestible when cooked thoroughly. Every sort of bean cooks differently. On average, 1 pound dried beans will cook to about 4 cups (limas cook to less), providing six to eight servings. Or allow about ⅓ cup dried beans per serving—depending, of course, on other ingredients in a dish.

From the traditional cooking of bean-loving Mexico (Diana Kennedy is my source) and from contemporary scientific research (Russ Parsons of the *Los Angeles Times*), it has been established beyond a doubt that flavor, texture, and nutrition are superior when you don't soak dried beans before cooking them. The simmering may take slightly longer, but of course it's effortless—all you have to do is stir the pot occasionally and check the water level. All in all, it takes less fussing.

Rinsed dried beans should simply be dropped into a big pot, preferably earthenware. For every pound, add 1 teaspoon salt and at least 3 inches of boiling water. Cover and set in a 250°F oven. Cook, adding boiling water as necessary to keep the beans from burning. Bake until tender, from 1 to 4 hours. If you'd rather, simmer the beans in a covered heavy saucepan on top of the stove—but they really won't taste quite as good as those enveloped in gentle heat. The crucial things in simmering dried beans are that you add salt at the beginning, start with ample boiling water, cover the pot, check every half hour, and if water is needed, add it boiling.

Russ Parsons has further put to rest the notion that discarding bean soaking/quick-boiling/cooking waters has an effect on the flatulence-causing properties of cooked beans. The effect is little or none. What does have an effect on the finished beans is timing of the salt. Added in the beginning, salt is absorbed in simmering—there's no toughening—and flavor is enhanced considerably. Added at the end, more salt is needed to gain the same flavor, but it's not in the heart of the beans as when added initially.

If your beans need a fast pick-me-up, a jot of vinegar will do the trick—especially if it's sweet, tangy balsamic.

Adzuki Beans

Alternative: Any small sweet red bean.

These tiny dried red beans are mild and sweet—and symbolize good fortune in much of the Orient.

Bake them as for basic dried beans. They are high in fiber and have a moderate amount of vegetable protein, a small amount of iron, and a fair amount of calcium.

Certainly you can cook and enjoy these sweet beans tossed into fruit salads or mixed into stir-fries. Or you can blend honey into the pot, make a sweet soup, and ladle it over a toasted rice cake in a small bowl for an elegant warmer on a cold day. You can also coax the beans into sending up sweet sprouts.

But in their native lands, adzuki beans are principally used as an element in other dishes. Sweet adzuki bean paste is venerable—it lies literally at the heart of many Japanese and Chinese treats. The Japanese celebrate the seasons and festivals with adzuki paste, which they call *an,* adding it to soups, jellied squares, cakes, and confections. The Chinese surround a knob of the paste with dumpling dough and steam it into a cloud for dim sum. Then there's red bean ice cream—the color of pureed blackberries in cream, it has a sweet/not sweet flavor that's just right at the end of an elaborate meal.

Red Bean Ice Cream

MAKES 1 GENEROUS QUART: 8 SERVINGS

Bake 1 cup (about ⅔ pound) dried adzuki or other small red beans in salted water as for basic dried beans until tender. Reserve 18 perfect beans. Puree the rest in a food processor or food mill until smooth or mash with a fork (you'll have a rounded 2 cups). Add a pinch of ginger.

In 2 batches in a food processor or with a mixer, blend the beans with 1 quart slightly softened French vanilla ice cream. Taste for sweetness. Turn the ice cream into a 2-quart freezer container and refreeze, whisking until smooth every 45 minutes until firmly frozen. Serve the same day. Before serving—again in 2 batches—whirl the ice cream in a food processor or beat with a mixer just enough to make it soft and smooth. Serve at once, decorating each portion with 3 of the reserved beans.

Black Beans

Black beans come in all sizes and flavors, all of them remarkably delicious. Possibly the color itself has flavor; it seems to give depth. Cooked dried black beans make an inky sauce for themselves and remind us that black is one of the rarest colors in nature.

Prepare and cook dried black beans as for basic dried beans.

Black bean soup is the classic use of these beans. Or make chili with them—splendid as a vegetarian dish or as a dramatic side dish with pale fishes like whitefish and halibut.

Gratin of Garlicky Black Beans

MAKES 6 TO 8 SERVINGS

Like the classic understated little black dress, an understated puree of black beans can be a knockout. The dish can be prepared in advance and refrigerated, but bring it to room temperature before baking.

Bake 2 cups (3/4 pound) dried black beans in salted water as for basic dried beans until tender, about 3 hours. At the same time, roast 2 whole heads of garlic on a baking dish in a 350°F oven until tender, about 1 hour. Pop the garlic cloves out of their skins. Drain the beans, saving the stock. Send the beans and garlic through the coarse blade of a food mill or puree them in a food processor.

Stir in bean stock to make the puree a little more moist than you consider ideal—about 2/3 cup. Add salt and freshly ground black pepper, then taste for seasoning. Smooth into an oiled shallow baking dish (mine is 7 1/2 × 12 inches). Sprinkle with a mixture of 2 cups fresh bread crumbs and 1/4 cup *each* finely chopped celery leaves, the white and some green parts of scallions, and cilantro or flat-leaf parsley. Drizzle with 2 tablespoons olive oil. Bake at 350°F until browned, about 35 to 40 minutes. Serve hot as an accompaniment to ham, pork, or turkey. Orange slices are always right with black beans.

This dish is under a French influence. Were it Mexican, the puree would be plopped into an earthenware cazuela, a branch or two of spicy bitter epazote leaves would be buried in it, and when hot, the puree would be heaped over rice.

Another idea: Cook black beans in an iron pot and they'll get inkier—and more nourishing, absorbing some of the pot's iron.

Sometime, try sieved hard-cooked egg as a garnish for black beans—classic.

Black-Eyed Peas

Prepare as for basic dried beans. Dried black-eyed peas have less protein, iron, and calcium than other dried legumes. Allow 1⁄4 to 1⁄3 cup uncooked dried black-eyes per serving.

Dried Black-Eyed Pea Soup in Turnip Greens Pot Liquor

MAKES 5 TO 6 SERVINGS

When you've made the delicious turnip greens under Turnips, you'll have pot liquor left over. This is what to do with it. Of course you can make the soup without the pot liquor, and you can use any bean you like.

Good the moment it's made or two days later if there's any left over.

2 cups (1 pound) dried black-eyed peas
salt to taste
turnip greens pot liquor plus water to make 10 cups or 10 cups water
1 onion, cut into quarters and thinly sliced
1 fresh mild red chili, seeds removed, finely diced, or to taste
a handful of chopped mixed parsley and cilantro
freshly ground pepper to taste
a little fruity olive oil

Bake the peas with salt, the pot liquor, and the onion as for basic dried beans until tender. Mix in the chili and herbs, add pepper, then taste for seasoning. Ladle into soup plates and tell everyone to drizzle olive oil over the top.

Chick-Peas

Cook dried chick-peas as for basic dried beans. Chick-peas are the trickiest beans to cook—look at them cross-eyed and they won't ever get tender. But because of their round shapes and fundamentally crunchy texture, you can get away with using chick-peas slightly underdone if need be, whereas you can't with other beans. The kala chanas are especially delightful with a bit of crunch left in them.

The skins of chick-peas add fiber to the meal, but if it's a special dish, small translucent wisps of bean skin are distractions. To remove them, when the chick-peas are cooked, lift them into a deep vessel of cool water. Rub the beans gently between your fingers, and their skins will float to the surface.

Chick-peas are very high in folic acid, moderately high in vegetable protein, fiber, and iron, and fair sources of phosphorus, magnesium, and zinc, with a bit of thiamine.

Pilaf of Chick-Peas and Bulgur

MAKES 8 SERVINGS

This combination of chick-peas and bulgur is Turkish. It's light yet earthy, versatile, and keeps well, tasting better and better with time. At any point you can stir in olive oil, lemon juice, and chopped celery (cucumber in summer) for a cool salad. Or add chunks of cooked meat and serve it reheated with chutney.

The terms *bulgur* (also bulghar, bulgar, and burghul) and *cracked wheat* are sometimes used interchangeably. They shouldn't be. Both are wheat berries that have been ground coarse, medium, or fine, but bulgur's berries have been cooked before grinding, and cracked wheat's are raw. Bulgur is available at most health food stores, but whether or not you have a selection of grind depends on the community.

This can be prepared completely a day or two in advance and reheated.

I'm unable to give you precise numbers to get 2 cups steamed bulgur. Amounts of bulgur, liquid, and steaming time vary enormously from package to package. If yours gives no directions, start by stirring 1 cup boiling water or stock with a scant ¾ teaspoon salt into 1 cup bulgur in a heavy saucepan over medium heat, cover, turn the heat to low, and steam until the grains are fluffy and tender—watch carefully and add a little more boiling liquid as needed, and don't overcook. It should take about 20 minutes.

1 cup (¼ pound) dried chick-peas
salt to taste
2 medium-size onions, chopped
3 garlic cloves, chopped
2 cups cooked bulgur, preferably coarse grind
½ cup dried currants
1 tablespoon fruity olive oil
1 tablespoon chopped fresh basil leaves or 1 teaspoon crumbled dried
1 tablespoon chopped fresh mint leaves or 1 teaspoon crumbled dried, optional
freshly ground black pepper to taste
a good handful of chopped parsley, preferably flat-leaf

Bake the chick-peas in salted water as for basic dried beans until tender. Drain, saving the stock for soup. Sauté the onions in a dry large nonstick skillet over medium-high heat for 5 minutes, stirring frequently. Add the garlic and sauté for 2 minutes more. Mix in the chick-peas, bulgur, and currants, then mix in the olive oil and herbs. Add pepper, then taste for seasoning. At this point you can cover and refrigerate the mixture or finish it.

Stirring frequently, cook over medium heat until hot and beginning to brown, about 10 minutes. Mix in the parsley and serve.

Black Chick-Peas

Alternative: Other small chick-peas.

TURKISH ROASTED CHICK-PEAS: One cup (⅓ pound) dried beans makes 1⅓ cups roasted: about 6 servings. These small dark beauties are ideal for turning into a crunchy nibble. You can use any color chick-peas, but the black ones are especially appealing. The scent of chick-peas roasting is sensational.

Bake black or other-colored chick-peas in salted water as for basic dried beans until tender—kala chanas can take 4 hours. Drain, saving the stock for soup. Spread on a heavy rimmed baking sheet, one layer deep. Stirring once or twice, roast in the middle of the oven at 350°F until they smell deeply roasted, about 50 minutes—

they should be dark and crunchy. While hot, drizzle with a thread of fruity oil, and sprinkle with salt to taste.

Kala Chana Beans

Alternative: Small black beans or chick-peas.

Kala chana (aka *channa* and *gram)* beans are earth brown, about half the size of the chick-peas we're used to, with a special crunch and nutted flavor. Cooked, they turn glossy coffee colored, the size of round kernels of corn. Although they're botanically identical to chick-peas, they're not interchangeable in every dish—the way big fat garden peas aren't interchangeable with petits pois. Very small vegetables have an aesthetic quality that must be observed. I wouldn't puree kala chanas—it would be a waste of their diminutive shape.

Tanzanian Coconut Kala Chana Beans Over Rice

MAKES 4 SERVINGS

This marvelous dish was inspired by an elaborate Tanzanian soup—this is simplified but true to the spirit of the original.

There is no reason why everything, including the rice, can't be prepared a day before serving.

1 cup (generous ⅓ pound) dried kala chana beans or other small chick-peas
salt to taste
1⅓ cups rinsed jasmine or basmati or other long-grain white rice
scant 2⅔ cups cold water
1 tablespoon mild oil
1 tablespoon curry powder or to taste
1 tablespoon turmeric
1 large onion, chopped
1 cup canned unsweetened coconut milk
½ to 1 small fresh or dried hot chili, seeds removed, chopped or crumbled
about ¾ cup shredded unsweetened coconut (fresh or dried)
a little chopped sweet or Thai basil

Bake the beans in salted water as for basic dried beans until they're as tender as you can get them. It won't hurt if there's a bit of crunch left, about 4 hours (regular chick-peas will take about 3). Drain, saving the stock for another use.

Prepare the rice in the water as for package directions. Keep hot, or refrigerate, then reheat just before serving.

In a broad, heavy saucepan (preferably nonstick), heat the oil over medium-high heat, blend in the curry powder and turmeric and cook, stirring, for about 20 seconds. Blend in the onion. Sauté, stirring frequently, until lightly browned, about 4 minutes. Blend in the coconut milk, the chili, and then the beans. Scoop up a cupful of the mixture into a food processor. Process until roughly pureed, then stir back into the pot—this gives the bean sauce body. Simmer for about 5 minutes so everything blends. Taste for seasoning, then ladle the beans over snowy rice and sprinkle with coconut and basil.

You can top each portion with chunks of sautéed sea bass browned and cooked without fat in a nonstick skillet. Serve with some of Lida's chutney under Slicing Tomatoes and a salad of grated carrots.

Fava Beans

Alternative: For their flavor, black-eyed peas or black beans.

Do dry some of your fava beans because there's an uncommon stick-to-the-ribs quality about them. They're very like large dried limas, only tastier and meatier.

EGYPTIAN DRIED FAVA BEANS: Bake the beans as for basic dried beans until tender. Meanwhile, prepare your favorite tomato sauce—something light and uncomplicated—adding one or two lightly sautéed chopped garlic cloves for each serving. Drain the beans and stir in enough sauce to moisten. Add salt and pepper then taste for seasoning. Serve hot in soup plates sprinkled with finely chopped parsley as a separate course.

Flageolet Beans

Alternative: Delicate southern peas, butter beans (baby limas), and navy beans come closest.

The seeds of these beans are small and kidney shaped, and whether as pale green shelly beans or white dried, they're classically used in France for garnishing meats.

Dried flageolets are not suited to pressure cooking—they dissolve.

Dried Flageolets Under Toasted Crumbs

MAKES 8 SERVINGS

One of my favorite country dishes is lamb roasted with cream-colored flageolets. The beans lie between meat juices and toasting bread crumbs. When lamb is young and fresh and you have someone special to cook for, spread these delicious beans around the joint while it roasts. Meantime, serve your tiny tasty beans on their own.

It's easiest if the beans are cooked the day before baking. You can prepare the dish for baking in the morning.

2 cups (3/4 pound) dried flageolet beans
salt to taste
1 large unpeeled onion stuck with 8 whole cloves
2 large carrots, quartered
a dozen parsley stalks, a bay leaf, and a few thyme sprigs tied together
2 large onions, preferably white, chopped
2 garlic cloves, chopped
3/4 cup dry red wine
2 tablespoons fresh thyme leaves or 2 teaspoons crumbled dried
salt and freshly ground black pepper to taste
a little olive oil
about 2 cups fine dry bread crumbs
a bunch of parsley—half chopped and the rest left whole for garnish

Bake the beans in salted water with the onion, carrots, and herb bouquet as for basic dried beans until tender. Sauté the onions and garlic in a heavy dry nonstick skillet over medium-high heat, stirring frequently until softened, about 3 minutes.

When the beans are ready, remove the clove-stuck onion, carrots, and herb bouquet and drain the beans, reserving the stock. Mix the beans in a bowl with the sautéed onions, wine, and thyme. Add salt and pepper and taste for seasoning.

Refrigerate beans and their stock if they'll be waiting for more than a few hours to finish.

Heat the oven to 375°F. Smooth the beans into a shallow 2½-quart baking dish. Pour over bean stock to moisten them, drizzle with a thread of olive oil, then sprinkle with bread crumbs. Bake uncovered until piping hot, about 40 minutes. Sprinkle with chopped parsley, tuck parsley sprigs around the dish, and serve.

Kidney Beans—Red

No matter what size they are, rosy pink and brick-red cooked dried kidney beans add wonderful color to a plate.

Cook as for basic dried beans.

A Winter's Bean Salad

MAKES 8 TO 10 SERVINGS

Kidney beans are a super addition to salad because of their warm color and flavor. This salad can be altogether variable. Make it with wurst or nuggets of chicken or forget the meat and make it with greens, bitter or sweet. Or just thread ribbons of sorrel through it. I often make the just-beans part of this salad for lunch. It lasts several days and couldn't be healthier or more satisfying. I make it ad lib—don't worry about measurements. The constants are the herbs. Then use whatever's at hand: celery, shallots or onion, orange or grapefruit, apples, walnuts, for starters.

The number of servings is indefinite because beans swell to volume capriciously according to their cultivar, age, altitude when cooked, and which side of the bed they got up on that morning.

The beans will be more flavorful a day or two after cooking. Just keep them refrigerated in their pot liquor. The bean part of the salad can be prepared several hours in advance.

You can use any richly colored dried bean and any single or mix of wild sorts of greens such as arugula, chicory, endive, escarole, tender kale, sorrel, and mustard.

2½ cups (1 pound) dried kidney beans
salt to taste
⅔ cup dry white wine
⅓ cup cider vinegar
¾ cup plus 2 tablespoons fruity olive oil
2 teaspoons Dijon mustard
freshly ground black pepper to taste
⅓ cup chopped fresh sage leaves or 2 heaped tablespoons crumbled dried
2 to 3 slender celery ribs, thinly sliced
6 walnut-size shallots, thinly sliced, or 1 large white onion, halved and thinly sliced
1 large orange or small grapefruit, peeled and cut into 1-inch chunks
⅓ cup pimiento or marinated sweet red pepper matchsticks
1 pound beef knockwurst
6 to 8 cups lightly packed torn leaves of flavorful greens

Bake the beans in salted water as for basic dried beans until tender. Whisk the wine, vinegar, oil, and mustard together until blended. Add salt and pepper and taste for seasoning. Reserve in a cool place.

Drain the beans (save the stock for another use) and turn them into a large mixing bowl with the sage, celery, shallots, orange, and pimiento. Whisk the dressing to blend and pour a scant cupful over the beans. Mix gently, cover, and keep in a cool place or continue.

In a skillet, cover the knockwurst with water. Bring to a boil, turn the heat to medium, and simmer gently until they swell marvelously, about 10 minutes.

In a large serving bowl, combine the greens with about ⅓ cup dressing and toss with your hands to coat each leaf. Taste for seasoning. Make a lacy bed of the greens on a serving platter. Arrange the bean mixture in the center, making sure all the colors are visible. Slice the hot wurst about ⅜ inch thick and loosely arrange the rounds as a border for the beans. Moisten the meat with dressing and serve.

Kidney Beans—White: Cannellini

These large white kidney-shaped beans are very Italian—the way the little white kidney-shaped flageolets are French and dark dried fava beans are North African. Preparation, serving amounts, and nutritional information are the same as basic dried beans.

Cannellini Soup

MAKES 6 TO 8 SERVINGS

Here is a marvelous harvest soup—when vine-dried beans are pulled up and they're so beautiful you must taste some, when a few leeks can be taken, the sorrel still is perky, and a few potatoes wait to be dug. Of course there's also room in the pot for that small cabbage you've been nursing or a handful of tender mustard greens that poked up in the tomato patch—or a tomato or two that are ripening bravely in October.

You'll notice there are no herbs in this soup, which is based on a Flemish classic. Small white beans are traditional in the soup, but any dried bean will shine here, and I find big buttery meaty cannellini just right.

This soup just improves on standing—the fourth day it's even better.

1½ cups (generous ⅓ pound) dried cannellini
salt to taste
2 tablespoons olive oil
6 medium-size leeks, trimmed, slit, rinsed, and thinly sliced
6 medium-size red potatoes, thickly sliced
2 good handfuls of sorrel, spinach, or chard leaves, sliced into ribbons
fresh lemon juice if you're not using sorrel
2 quarts bean-cooking stock mixed with water or water and chicken broth
2 to 3 tablespoons cream or yogurt
freshly ground black pepper to taste
a little chopped lovage or celery leaves

Bake the beans in salted water as for basic dried beans. When they're tender, drain them, saving the bean stock and turning the beans into a bowl—cover and reserve.

Warm the olive oil in your soup pot over medium heat and stir in the leeks, potatoes, and sorrel (or spinach and lemon juice). When all are glistening, add the bean stock. Bring to a simmer, turn the heat to low, set the lid on askew, and simmer until all is tender, stirring occasionally, a long 20 minutes. At this point, if you wish, you can mash the vegetables so the potatoes become small chunks.

Stir in the beans, then blend in the cream. Add the pepper and taste for seasoning. Cover and refrigerate if you're making the soup ahead. Reheat gently. Ladle into hot soup plates and top with lovage. Good bread and cheese make this a fine supper.

Lima and Butter Beans

Gratin of Dried Lima or Butter Beans

MAKES ABOUT 10 SERVINGS

When some of your elegant beans have dried, treat them to a composition that sings of Provence. Here is a dish at once complex yet simple, impressive yet—if you've sun-dried your own tomatoes—cheap. Coupled with grilled sweet peppers, the gratin can be a main dish or can accompany a festive roast. The dish can be prepared to advantage in the morning or even the day before, then baked and served.

2½ cups (1 pound) dried lima beans, preferably babies
6 cups chicken or beef broth or vegetable stock
6 cups water
salt to taste
½ cup chopped sun-dried tomatoes, about 1 ounce
1 large onion, chopped
about 2 tablespoons olive oil
2 large unpeeled carrots, cut lengthwise into eighths and thinly sliced crosswise
1 celery rib, cut the same way as the carrots
3 large garlic cloves, finely chopped
½ pound mushrooms, sliced
2 tablespoons chopped fresh summer savory leaves or 2 teaspoons crumbled dried
2 tablespoons chopped fresh sage leaves or 2 teaspoons crumbled dried
1 tablespoon fresh thyme leaves or 1 teaspoon crumbled dried
1 large dried or 1 small fresh bay leaf, crumbled
freshly ground white pepper to taste

SAUCE (MAKES ABOUT 2¾ CUPS) AND FINISHES
1½ tablespoons butter
1½ tablespoons olive oil
¼ cup all-purpose flour
salt and freshly ground white pepper to taste
1 cup fine fresh bread crumbs
½ cup finely shredded Parmesan cheese

Bake the beans in the broth and water with salt as for basic dried beans until creamy tender. Drain the stock and reserve it. Cover the beans and keep warm. In a small bowl, cover the dried tomatoes with about 1 cup of the hot bean stock.

In a large heavy skillet over medium-high heat, sauté the onion in a splash of olive oil until tender, stirring frequently, about 5 minutes. Add the carrots, celery, garlic, 1 cup of the reserved bean stock, and a little salt if needed. Simmer uncovered until the carrots are tender but still a little crunchy, about 8 minutes.

Blend the tomatoes with their stock into the beans. Use a slotted spoon to lift the vegetables from the skillet into the beans. Turn their stock into a measuring cup, then add enough of the reserved bean stock to make 2½ cups. Wash and dry the skillet.

In the dry skillet, sauté the mushrooms over medium-high heat until browned, stirring frequently, 3 to 4 minutes. Add to the beans with the herbs. Blend all thoroughly. Add pepper and taste for seasoning. Turn into a wide shallow baking dish with about a 13-cup capacity—mine is oval, 14½ by 10 by 2½ inches.

To make the sauce, heat the butter and olive oil in a small heavy saucepan. Whisk in the flour and cook for 2 minutes over low heat, stirring frequently. Whisk in the 2½ cups bean stock, then whisk over medium-high heat until the sauce simmers. Simmer 2 to 3 minutes, now stirring with a wooden spatula or spoon. Add salt and pepper, taste for seasoning, then gently blend the sauce into the beans. Cover the dish and refrigerate if desired. Bring to room temperature before continuing.

To serve, heat the oven to 375°F. Blend the bread crumbs and Parmesan together and sprinkle evenly over the dish. Drizzle the top with olive oil. Bake until browned and bubbly, 40 to 45 minutes. Let cool for a few minutes before serving.

Soybeans

Alternative: For most recipes, any full-flavored dried bean will do. Where the unique protein and buttery qualities of soybeans are needed, there's no bean comparable.

These are the heavyweights of beans, loaded with nourishment. Their protein is the equivalent of animal protein.

Prepare soybeans as for basic dried beans. Even refrigerated, they can ferment in the blink of an eye, so eat them on the day of cooking. Soybeans have more fat than other beans, but it's unsaturated.

ROASTED SHELLY SOY NUTS: A Thai snack is dried lima beans, soaked, drained, dried, deep-fried in peanut oil until crisp, and salted. In the same vein in Tokyo, with drinks we were served a big bowl of rich roasted soybeans.

Pick the soybeans, whether a green or black variety, when the pods are green (the beans of green varieties are green, and "black" varieties are basically cranberry red). Shell them. Spread on a lightly oiled baking sheet with a lip. Cover lightly with foil (they'll pop) and roast as for chick-peas until crunchy all through.

Tepary Beans

Alternative: Navy beans.

These are small white beans that grow wild in the Southwest—their fine flavor belies their tenacious nature.

Prepare them as for basic dried beans—all other information is the same as well.

You can use tepary beans in any recipe that calls for navy beans, although the flavor will be much different. For a dish true to the bean, make the following ancient mix.

Southwestern Tepary Beans and Dried Corn

MAKES 6 TO 8 SERVINGS

This can be prepared in advance, then heated just before serving. It improves on keeping.

- a scant 1 cup (about ⅓ pound) dried corn chicos (see recipe under Corn)
- salt to taste
- 1½ cups dried tepary beans, about ½ pound
- a good handful of chopped fresh oregano leaves or a heaped tablespoon crumbled dried
- a smaller handful of chopped fresh sage leaves or 1 tablespoon crumbled dried
- 3 tablespoons fruity olive oil
- about 2 tablespoons melted lard, or use all oil
- 1 tablespoon cider vinegar
- freshly ground black pepper to taste
- 2 to 3 cups shredded jack or other mild cheese

Cover the corn with water by 3 inches and soak overnight. In the morning, turn the corn and soaking water into an earthenware casserole, add salt, and bake until tender. At the same time, bake the beans the same way. I usually bake these two at 350°F. At that temperature, the corn takes 3 hours and the beans—depending on their age—somewhat longer.

Drain the corn (about 3 cups) and beans (about 4 cups) and save their stocks for another use. Turn into a mixing bowl. Add the herbs, olive oil, lard, vinegar, and pepper (I add lots). Mix, then taste for seasoning. Either refrigerate, or heat in a covered baking dish at 350°F about 20 minutes or in the microwave until piping hot. Serve topped with cheese.

We like this as a main dish accompanied with a vinaigrette-dressed salad of shredded greens and diced marinated sweet peppers (see Sweet Red Peppers)—they mix deliciously on the plate. If there's any left over (and you haven't added lard), add some diced unpeeled cucumber and dress with your favorite vinegar for a crunchy salad.

Tiny Dried Beans and Legumes

Here is a collection of very small beans with very big flavors, all of which grow and thresh easily.

Prepare and cook as for basic dried beans. You can also sprout these seeds.

Lentils are pulses, and they come in colors from pink to orange to greige. They make one of the world's great soups: Simmer them in salted water or stock with chopped carrot, onion, garlic, and a smoky herb like sage or thyme, and the nubbins are transformed into a texture and taste that's truly meaty.

The rest of this collection is related to cowpeas.

MOTH BEANS: Cook green pods as any snap bean. In pomegranate season in India, moth beans are garnished with the fruit's seeds, a beguiling conceit. Cylindrical dried moth beans are prepared as a snack by soaking, drying, then deep-frying until crispy crunchy.

MUNG BEANS: Stir-fry or steam or blanch the snap beans. The seeds are olive green, the size and shape of grains of barley, only rounder. Mung bean sprouts are stir-fried with spices for breakfast in India.

RICE BEANS: So named because their flavor is reminiscent of sweet nutty rice, these seem to be a secret kept in Chinese, Indian, and Filipino kitchens. At the snap stage tender pods and their leaves are steamed as a vegetable. And of course they can be added raw to salad. The seeds resemble mung beans, only they're more beige.

URD BEANS: The size and shape of large grains of barley but pale black with a pencil line of white down one side, these have a mild and beany taste that combines well with other vegetables.

Indian recipes wreathe their legumes and pulses (called *dals* or *dhalls*) in myriad spices even though the flavor of the bean may be delicate—and amazingly, the beans are enhanced.

Spiced Tiny Dried Beans from Bengal

MAKES 4 TO 5 SERVINGS

By and large, tiny dried beans (actually pulses) don't hold their shape when cooked. This dal, suited to any small bean, is good eaten with a spoon in small bowls—or spoon it as a thick sauce over jasmine or basmati rice.

This may be served at once or reheated after a day (or up to 10 days) in the refrigerator—it just gets better and better. The vinegar stands in for tamarind juice, which you should use instead, should you have some.

1⅓ cups (½ pound) dried small beans or lentils
salt to taste
heaped 1 tablespoon ground coriander
heaped 1 tablespoon turmeric
rounded ½ teaspoon ground cumin
rounded ½ teaspoon ground red chili or chili powder, or to taste
rounded ¼ teaspoon ground fenugreek, optional
3 tablespoons half-strength cider vinegar or fresh lemon juice
1 tablespoon unsalted butter or mild oil
1 large onion, finely chopped
4 large garlic cloves, finely chopped
2 tablespoons nigella seeds *(kalonji)*, optional

Bake the beans or lentils in salted water as for basic dried beans until tender. Drain, reserving the stock.

In a small bowl, blend the coriander, turmeric, cumin, chili, and fenugreek. Slowly stir in the vinegar until you have a thick paste.

In a large heavy skillet, melt the butter or heat the oil over medium-high heat. Add the onion and garlic and sauté for 2 to 3 minutes, stirring frequently. Blend in the spice paste, turn the heat to medium, and stir for 3 to 4 more minutes.

Blend in the beans with a fork, adding enough of the reserved stock to give the consistency of a thick but moist sauce. Add salt then taste for seasoning. Simmer until hot, stirring occasionally, about 10 minutes.

Serve over rice, sprinkled with nigella seeds, should you be lucky enough to have some. Called *kalonji* in Indian groceries (and sometimes mistakenly identified as onion seeds), their flavor is like celery crossed with clove. The coal-black seeds are particularly delicious after a brief toasting in a dry skillet. Poppy or black sesame seeds can be used in their place.

Yankee Beans

Classic Boston Baked Beans

MAKES 8 OR MORE SERVINGS

Whether it's a heritage variety such as Swedish Brown, Mostoller Wild Goose, Vermont Cranberry, or Adventist, or your basic Yellow Eye, White Marrow, or Great Northern, here's the pot to put your beautiful dried beans in. The recipe comes from Ernie Blanchette, whose family came to the New World with Samuel Champlain.

As good, if not better, days after baking.

3 cups (generous 1 pound) dried small white or tan beans
salt to taste
½ pound lean salt pork
1 large onion
¾ cup light molasses
1 tablespoon dry mustard

Bake the beans in salted water as for basic dried beans until tender. Drain well, reserving their stock, and turn the beans into a 2-quart bean pot or deep earthenware casserole. Cut the pork in half, slash each piece deeply in several places, and bury in the pot with the onion. Bring the reserved bean stock to a boil. Blend the molasses and mustard with a little of the stock and pour over the beans, then add more stock just to cover the beans.

Cover the pot and set in the oven, turning the heat to 250°F (Ernie cooks them in his wood stove all night). Bake for 12 hours or until the beans are thick. Add more water a couple of times, stirring it in. The last hour, leave the lid off to get a nice brown top. Serve with steamed brown bread.

Some old bean hands don't bother with the browning at the last, saying only a few beans get browned anyway. The beans taste great either way.

BEETS

Fresh from your garden, these are incomparable. Most beets are best harvested small. The most sensual way to eat a beet is just after pulling it—brush off the earth on your jeans and pop the baby into your mouth there and then. Don't wash or cut off the root before storing.

To prepare beets, rinse them, then scrub with a soft brush only as necessary. Trim stalks at 2 inches, leave the roots intact, don't peel, and don't cut into the beets until after cooking. Steam until tender—25 to 30 minutes for small-plum-size beets or smaller. Leave the skin on for maximum flavor and nutrients.

Rinse all presentable leaves and trim off all but the tenderest stalks. Leaves are cooked as for other greens, but start with the beet green recipe that follows.

Many who adore beets feel that baking them makes their sugar sweetest, their flesh most toothsome—and it also preserves the nutrients. Arrange whole unpeeled beets in a single layer in a shallow baking dish in which they just fit. Moisten with oil (olive, hazelnut, or walnut) and a few drops of lemon juice to heighten their flavor, sprinkle lightly with salt and pepper, and bake at 325°F until tender—1 hour plus. A friend finishes them with a sprinkling of cardamom. Eat hot, room temperature, or cold. Microwaving also preserves flavor and nutrients: Place whole small beets in a microwave-safe vessel with ¼ cup water per pound. Cover and zap until tender, about 10 minutes, turning halfway after 5 minutes.

Beets have the most natural sugar of any vegetable. They are moderately high in fiber and folic acid and have a fair amount of vitamin C and a little manganese.

Grate raw young unpeeled beets into salads at the last minute—particularly goldens, which won't bleed their color.

A French way with cooked diced beets is to blanket them with cream sauce (see the savory recipe in The Cook's Notebook) and a little grated mild cheese in a baking dish, then bake at 375°F for 10 to 15 minutes, until browned. And of course there's borscht, the exhilarating Slavic soup—shredded cooked beets and chopped leaves in their cooking broth finished with a sweet-sour touch of brown sugar and lemon juice, served hot or cold with dill and a plop of sour cream or yogurt.

AN ITALIAN COOKED BEET SALAD: Combine chopped red onions with cooked beet slices, parsley, and mint—oil and wine vinegar dressing.

Cooked beets with potatoes, celery, apples, green onions, and caraway seeds make a fine salad with any dressing you like. Pureed beets and grated horseradish are an essential seasoning for boiled beef. And you can make a lovely instant pickle by just covering skinned and whole, sliced, diced, or matchsticks of beets with a mild rice or other vinegar. A bit of dill, tarragon, celery, or lovage can be added.

Perfection of Baby Beets

MAKES 6 SERVINGS

Here is a simple but incomparable composition. If your beet greens are skimpy, add leafy parts of chard and/or spinach to supplement them.

heaped 4 quarts lightly packed (about 1½ pounds) tender beet leaves and stalks

2 tablespoons olive oil

2 teaspoons fresh lemon juice

3 dozen 1-inch unpeeled beets, steamed until tender

½ cup hot heavy cream

a big handful of chopped dill

salt and freshly ground white pepper to taste

Rinse the beet leaves and stalks, chop them fairly finely, then turn with the water that clings to them into a wide heavy skillet. Moisten with the oil and lemon juice and cook over low heat, stirring once or twice, until tender, 5 to 6 minutes.

Trim off the beets' rootlets, then arrange them on a hot serving dish, stalks all in the same direction. Surround the beets with the greens. Pour the cream over the beets, sprinkle the dill and salt and pepper to taste over all, taste for seasoning, then eat hot in small bowls with large spoons as a separate course. Beets are splendid in a menu with pale fish and poultry.

Beet Greens

Alternative: Chard, spinach beet, or spinach.

Send yellowing and large tough leaves to the compost, then prepare tender leaves as for spinach, rinsing well in tepid water. Cook with the water that clings to them in an uncovered skillet for 4 to 6 minutes or until limp. You can use these leaves in any recipe for spinach—there will be some reddening of the dish from their stalks and leaf veins, but no harm. While beet roots are delectable and nourishing, the greens are far more valuable. The greens contain ample vitamins A and C and a goodly amount of calcium and iron.

In Italy, richly flavored beet leaves are used as often as chard and spinach as one of the greens in filling pasta. You can also use the sweet leaves of collards—or a mix of greens as long as they're non-cabbagey. Remember to add tender leaves to salad.

Beet Greens Soufflé with Beet Sauce

MAKES 4 TO 5 SERVINGS

The flavor of beet greens is less biting than spinach, probably because a few sweet cells from the roots meander up the stalks and settle into the leaves. The pair are a perfect example of the way humble ingredients from the garden can be transformed into something elegant. I can't say which is more appealing in the sauce, its brilliant hue or its undertaste of earth.

For company, all you need do at the last minute is whip the egg whites, fold them in, slip the soufflé into the oven, and warm the sauce.

Chard, spinach, mild mustards, collards, or other mild greens can be mixed with the beet leaves or substituted.

SOUFFLÉ

3 tablespoons unsalted butter, plus a knob for the dish
6 cups lightly packed (½ pound) torn tender beet leaves with tender stalks
½ medium-large onion, thinly sliced
1 garlic clove, sliced in half
1 cup milk (nonfat is fine)
¼ cup all-purpose flour
3 extra-large egg yolks
1 tablespoon fresh lemon juice
½ teaspoon nutmeg, preferably freshly grated
1 tablespoon chopped fresh dill leaves or 1 teaspoon dried
salt to taste and lots of freshly ground white pepper
6 extra-large egg whites

SAUCE (MAKES ABOUT 1½ CUPS)

3 2-inch beets, steamed until tender
1 cup milk (nonfat is fine)
2 tablespoons unsalted butter
2½ tablespoons all-purpose flour
1 teaspoon ground ginger
1 teaspoon finely grated lemon zest
salt and freshly ground white pepper to taste

To prepare the soufflé, butter a 6- to 7-cup soufflé dish or deep baking dish. Set the dish in the freezer (so the soufflé will rise straight up).

In a large, uncovered heavy saucepan over medium-high heat, cook the greens with the moisture that clings to their leaves from rinsing along with the onion and garlic for 5 minutes. Add the milk and cook over medium heat just until the milk begins to simmer. Remove from the heat and cool a bit, then whirl in a food processor or blender until the vegetables are fairly finely chopped.

Melt the butter in a 3-quart saucepan over medium-high heat. Add the flour and stir until smooth. Cook over low heat, stirring frequently, for 2 minutes. Slowly add the greens a little at a time, whisking until blended after each addition. Cook, whisking, until the mixture thickens. Remove from the heat and whisk in the egg yolks (dropping the whites into a large metal or ceramic mixing bowl), lemon juice, nutmeg, dill, salt, and pepper. The mixture can be covered and refrigerated for a few hours at this point, but bring it to room temperature before proceeding.

About 45 minutes before serving, set the bowl of egg whites in a bigger bowl of hot water—stir for a few moments until warmed. Set a baking sheet on the rack in the middle of the oven and heat the oven to 375°F. Beat the whites at low speed until foamy, then add a pinch of salt and beat on medium speed until soft peaks form. Beat on high speed until the whites are firm but still moist, barely 1 more minute.

Immediately blend the whites into the greens mixture: Use the whisk to blend in about a third of the whites quickly but completely. Use a large flexible rubber spatula to fold in the remaining whites in great big strokes, blending until nearly all the puffs have been absorbed. Smooth into the icy dish, then run a finger around the inside of the rim to give the soufflé a bit of a hat.

Set the dish on the baking sheet and bake until puffed and browned, about 30 minutes, or until a thin metal skewer emerges from the center almost clean. Serve at once with the beet sauce.

To prepare the sauce, slice the beets roughly into the milk in a blender or food processor and whirl until pureed. In a medium-size saucepan, melt the butter over medium-high heat. Add the flour and stir until smooth. Turn the heat to low and cook 2 minutes. Add the puree a little at a time, whisking until blended after each addition. Cook, whisking, until the mixture thickens. Blend in the ginger, zest, salt, and pepper, then taste for seasoning. Turn at once into a heated serving bowl. Or cool, refrigerate for a few hours, then reheat gently.

Mangel

This is a field type of beet, coarser and larger but sweet and edible when harvested small. When small, prepare them as garden beets. If they get away from you, feed them to Bossie or chop them up and dig them back into the soil to make humus.

MANGEL TOAST: If you've just had a roast for Sunday supper, steam small mangels until tender, then thinly slice them (no need to peel). Heat the slices in some of the drippings from the roast (poultry or meat, makes no difference), turning once. Season with salt, freshly ground black pepper, and a few drops of lemon juice or mild vinegar. Taste for seasoning, then heap at once onto hot buttered wheat toast, sprinkle with chopped fennel leaves or toasted fennel seeds, and serve for Monday lunch.

Broccoli, Common

Broccoli is a bouquet of hundreds of tiny buds. Harvest while they're firm, cutting the stalk at the base on an angle so water will slide off and the stalk left won't rot. Leave two leaves when you cut side shoots and more sprouts will come.

You should be able to eat almost every bit of your painstakingly raised broccoli. Peel the tough lower parts of the stalks with a vegetable peeler or sharp paring knife to get down to the delicate flesh. It's important to cut thick stalks lengthwise to make them the same diameter as thinner stalks so all pieces cook evenly.

Cook broccoli just until the stalks are tender with a hint of crispness. The easiest way for broccoli is one of the options with asparagus: Stand the stalks upright in an uncovered tall deep pot—there are pots designed for this—in a couple of inches of boiling water. The shoots will steam while the stalks simmer. Start testing with a thin metal skewer after 4 to 5 minutes. Remove from the heat a little before the broccoli is as tender as you like it since the stalks continue to cook off the heat.

To simmer in a skillet, cook uncovered in ½ inch of boiling salted water until emerald green and tender-crisp, as little as 4 minutes with garden broccoli—half as long if the stalk is cut into matchsticks and the florets are cut the same length.

Then a spritz of lemon juice, a drizzle of olive oil, and salt and pepper are all that's needed—but a finish of toasted pine nuts is a delectable touch.

Purple broccoli turns green in the water, so it's cooked according to green broccoli recipes. But of course it's gorgeous in a basket of crudités. And broccoli's young leaves, don't forget, are as edible as cabbage's—prepare in the same manner.

Broccoli has a great amount of vitamin C, moderate amounts of fiber, folic acid, vitamin A, and calcium and a small amount of vitamin B_6 and potassium. Add raw florets and young leaves to salad.

For company, cook broccoli until nearly finished, cool and pat dry, then sauté over high heat with a lively seasoning to finish. It's especially handsome and heats quickly when cut into small florets and matchsticks of stalks all the same length. Toss the pieces in a little olive oil with salty chopped fillets of anchovies and sweet chopped yellow tomatoes, then heighten with balsamic or red wine vinegar. For another bright finish, add matchsticks of red, yellow, and purple sweet peppers to the skillet with slivers of garlic. And tender-crisp broccoli is awfully good cool, decorated with fine shreds of lemon zest and served with an ultra-lemony mayonnaise.

Any recipe for cauliflower can be used for broccoli.

Wrapper Leaves

You won't find them on the heading brassicas at the market. In fact they'll probably come as a surprise with your first harvest. But the wrappers—the large blue-green leaves that protect the flowering stalks of broccoli and cauliflower or heads of cabbages while developing—are eminently edible and supernutritious. See the recipe under Cabbage.

Lemony, Buttery Broccoli Amandine

MAKES 4 SERVINGS

I think most people would agree that the very best way to eat broccoli is with hollandaise sauce. A close second is this delectable finish. Save it for your triumphant first crop. It's equally good with cauliflower, asparagus, brussels sprouts, snap beans, and carrots. This is my mother's luxurious recipe for company; for family, I halve the sauce ingredients and serve the broccoli as a side dish.

Prepare and cook a large head (1 pound) of broccoli. Meanwhile, melt 4 tablespoons unsalted butter in a small heavy saucepan over medium-low heat. Cook until the butter begins to brown—keep an eye on it. Add ½ cup fresh lemon juice and ½ cup fine dry bread crumbs (melba toast crumbs are ideal) and stir until the crumbs are golden. Blend in a good pinch each of minced parsley, chives, sweet basil, oregano and paprika. The moment it's hot, spoon it over the broccoli. Sprinkle with salt, freshly ground white pepper, and about ⅓ cup roasted slivered almonds.

Romanesco Broccoli

Alternative: Purple or green cauliflower or any broccoli.

The fancifully patterned curds of chartreuse Romanesco have a slightly nutty flavor.

Romanesco Broccoli and Seashell Pasta

MAKES 8 MAIN-DISH OR 12 SIDE-DISH SERVINGS

In southern Italy, broccoli, which translates as "hard flower," can be white or green or purple cauliflower or broccoli of any hue. Whatever its name, here is my way with a colorful southern Italian dish, the swirls and flavor of Romanesco coming through. This is equally delicious with any form of broccoli or cauliflower.

The sauce can be cooked and the other ingredients prepared for cooking a few hours in advance.

2 small heads (1½ pounds) Romanesco broccoli, tough parts of stalks peeled
¾ cup extra-virgin olive oil
2 large garlic cloves, thinly sliced
1 cup strips or small pieces of sun-dried tomatoes, not oil-packed
1 cup chopped ripe plum or pear tomatoes
4 dozen Kalamata or oil-cured black olives (don't pit them; just warn everybody)
¼ cup drained capers
1 2- to 3-inch dried hot red chili, seeds removed, crumbled
½ cup dry white wine
salt to taste
1 pound large seashell pasta
½ cup fresh oregano or sweet basil leaves or a scant 3 tablespoons crumbled dried
freshly ground black pepper to taste
freshly grated Parmesan cheese

Cut the broccoli florets leaving 2-inch stems, then slice large florets to make them the same diameter as smaller ones. Cut stalks the same thickness and length as the floret stalks. If you're preparing the broccoli in advance, wrap and refrigerate.

To make the sauce, warm the olive oil in a medium-size skillet over medium-high heat. Sauté the garlic in the oil, stirring occasionally, until pale gold, about 3 minutes. Remove from the heat and add the dried tomatoes, fresh tomatoes, olives, capers, finely crumbled chili pod, and wine. If you're working in advance, cover and keep cool. If you're serving at once, sauté until hot, 2 to 3 minutes, stirring once or twice, then cover and keep warm.

Have ready a big pot of boiling salted water.

Add the broccoli and cook uncovered until tender-crisp—it will be about 5 to 8 minutes after the water returns to a boil. With a strainer, lift the broccoli into a heated serving bowl, cover loosely, and keep warm. Add the pasta to the boiling pot, stir well, cover, and when the water returns to a boil, uncover and cook, stirring frequently, until the pasta is tender but slightly chewy—start testing after 5 minutes.

If the sauce has been prepared in advance, sauté until hot, 2 to 3 minutes, stirring once or twice. Ladle out a generous cup of the pasta water and add it to the sauce. Lift the pasta into the bowl, then add the sauce and oregano. Toss gently but thoroughly. Add pepper, taste for seasoning, then serve with grated Parmesan on the side. A fruity white wine is in order.

Sprouting Broccoli

This is broccoli that doesn't form a central head but sends out lots of smaller shoots. You can harvest sprouting broccoli for a much longer time than heading (common) broccoli. Cut off shoots the same way. These shoots are prepared and cooked the same way as florets of heading broccoli.

BROCCOLI WITH LEEKS AND MUSHROOMS: My husband cuts broccoli florets into even pieces, then slices the tender main stalks crosswise about 1/4 inch thick. While the broccoli simmers, he sautés sliced leeks and quartered mushrooms in a little olive oil until tender. Quantities aren't crucial—whatever's on hand. When the broccoli is ready, he drains and adds it to the leeks and mushrooms. The play of the three flavors is remarkable. This works with sprouting, Romanesco, and regular broccoli.

Roman-Style Sprouting Broccoli

MAKES 4 SERVINGS

The young side shoots—cooked to tender crispness and flavored with the verve of a little minced raw garlic and sunny olive oil and red wine vinegar—make a terrific first course or cold salad, a tradition in Rome.

Of course you can use the tender pieces separated from a young head of broccoli as well.

This can be prepared the night before serving.

Trim and peel any tough parts from a generous pound of 4-inch-long slender broccoli shoots.

Mince 2 garlic cloves and blend them in a small bowl with ⅓ cup richly flavored olive oil and 3 tablespoons red wine vinegar (a splash of this might be balsamic). Add salt and freshly ground black pepper, then taste for seasoning.

Bring a big pot of salted water to a boil. Drop in the trimmed broccoli shoots and return the water to a boil, uncovered, stirring frequently to keep the stalks immersed in water and evenly distributed. Start testing at about 4 minutes—the florets should be tender with a bit of crispness left and still wonderfully green. It can take up to 10 minutes, but no longer.

Scoop out the broccoli and drop it into a storage dish. Beat the dressing to blend it, then pour over the broccoli. Pour the dressing back into its bowl, then drizzle again over the broccoli. Repeat this 2 or 3 times—the florets are too fragile to mix, so this way the dressing will reach every tiny blossom. Cover and chill for at least an hour or overnight before serving.

Taste for seasoning and serve on pretty plates garnished with thin lemon slices and a bright blossom such as marigold or nasturtium.

Broccoli Past Its Prime

Sometimes, between tenderness and bolting, a broccoli plant can get away from you and become tough. When that happens, I turn it into this delicious creamy thick puree. If broccoli stalks aren't as popular in your house as florets, here's the way to get everyone to eat them.

Mashed Broccoli

6 SERVINGS

This may be prepared in advance and reheated.

about 3 quarts loosely packed (1 pound) small pieces of tough broccoli or all broccoli stalks, stalks peeled

salt to taste

2 to 3 tablespoons unflavored oil like canola

⅓ cup flour

2 large garlic cloves, thinly sliced

¼ cup fresh lemon juice

½ to 1 cup milk (nonfat is fine)

2 teaspoons crumbled dried sweet basil

freshly ground white pepper to taste

1 tablespoon unsalted butter, optional

1 small pimento, finely chopped

Simmer the broccoli uncovered in ½ inch salted water in a large skillet until tender, about 10 minutes, stirring occasionally.

Meanwhile, heat the oil in a medium-size heavy nonreactive saucepan over medium heat. Whisk in the flour until smooth, add the garlic, turn the heat to low, and cook for 2 minutes, stirring occasionally.

Lift the broccoli into a food processor. Add this *roux* and the lemon juice and process until smooth while slowly adding ½ cup milk. Return the puree to the saucepan and sprinkle in the basil. Stir over low heat, and add more milk, if necessary, until the mixture is still thick but creamy. Add salt and pepper, then taste for seasoning. Stir in an enrichment of butter and serve in small bowls sprinkled with the pimento. Eat with big spoons.

Flowering Broccoli

Alternative: Any edible flowers, particularly one of the mustards or choy sums.

When my broccoli has begun to flower, I make another version of the Romanesco broccoli dish with the blossoms.

Linguine with Flowering Broccoli

MAKES 3 TO 4 SERVINGS

Last minute, easy.

3 to 4 cups tender broccoli blossoms and flower tips cut in 1-inch lengths, or very slender broccoli florets; include some thin ribbons of tender leaves
salt to taste
½ pound linguine
about 2 tablespoons olive, walnut, or hazelnut oil
3 walnut-size shallots, finely chopped
2 medium-large ripe tomatoes, cut into ½-inch dice
juice of 1 lemon
freshly ground black pepper to taste
½ cup freshly grated Parmesan cheese
a handful of toasted pine nuts

Bring a big pot of salted water to the boil. Drop in the blossoms and ribbons of leaves and boil uncovered until tender-crisp, about 2 minutes. Keep the water boiling while you scoop out the broccoli with a strainer and turn it into a heated serving bowl. Cover loosely and keep warm. Add the linguine to the boiling pot. Stir, cover the pot until the water returns to a boil, then uncover and boil until tender but slightly chewy—start testing after about 7 minutes.

Meanwhile, heat ½ tablespoon of the oil in a large heavy skillet. Sauté the shallots over medium-high heat until softened, stirring frequently—about 3 minutes. Add the tomatoes and lemon juice and stir until the tomatoes are warmed through. Stir in the broccoli and, when it's warm, remove the skillet from the heat—by which time the pasta should be ready. Add pepper, then taste for seasoning.

Drain the linguine through a colander into your serving bowl so the water heats the bowl. Dump out the water, shake the bowl dry, turn in the pasta, then top with the sauce. Drizzle with oil to moisten, sprinkle with cheese, and finish with pine nuts. Drink a golden Italian wine such as an Orvieto Classico and pass Kalamata olives.

Brussels Sprouts

You won't know these are the same vegetable as the hard old things you buy at the market for Thanksgiving dinner. These are light, sweet, tender morsels that will make you wonder why you've wasted so much time not eating brussels sprouts. Pick the sprouts when they're no bigger than your thumb.

To prepare brussels sprouts, just before cooking, flush out any critters in the folds of the outer leaves by soaking sprouts in warm water—weigh them down so they're submerged—for about 30 minutes. Rinse in fresh water. Trim the stems to ¼ inch. Remove any yellowing or imperfect leaves.

To cook the diminutive heads whole, cut a cross into the stem with a knife—so heat will travel into the base of the head and cook it more evenly and quickly. Over high heat, drop the sprouts into a skillet with an inch of boiling lightly salted water. Return the water to a boil, give the sprouts a stir, then boil uncovered until they test tender with a thin skewer—start testing after 4 minutes. Eat one to see; they're best when tender but still a bit crisp in the center. Drain (save the nourishing stock for another use) and turn into a hot bowl. Add butter, salt, and pepper and serve. Dill is a tasty herb with sprouts.

Slicing the sprouts in half cooks them even faster and gives a larger surface to absorb seasonings. Boiling time is 2 to 3 minutes for young things, longer if the sprouts are older. Paul Bertolli, poet and inspired cook (*Chez Panisse Cooking*), suggests pulling the globes apart altogether to make heaps of diminutive cabbage leaves—the remaining heart is thinly sliced. Paul simmers the leaves until tender with diced carrot, celery, onion, and pancetta (Italian bacon) softened in olive oil. The composition is sharpened with a dash of white wine vinegar. Brilliant!

Don't neglect the tender leaves from the brussels sprout plant—cook them as if they were cabbage. Sprouts are wildly rich in vitamin C, moderately rich in fiber and folic acid, and offer fair amounts of vitamin A, vitamin B_6, and iron. Add tender raw leaves of the stalk to salad.

Assertively flavored sprouts are best with other flavors that can hold up their end, such as beef, turkey, and duck. The Belgians sprinkle nutmeg on their sprouts, and since they invented the vegetable, I like to do as they do. The ultimate sprout combination, I think, is with cooked chestnuts, tossed together in brown butter and parsley.

Sesame-Seeded Brussels Sprouts

MAKES 4 SERVINGS

The Japanese do simple and lovely things with their brassicas. The sauce can be prepared in advance, but put it together just before serving.

- 3 tablespoons sesame seeds
- 1 tablespoon peanut or other mild oil
- 1 tablespoon sugar
- $\frac{1}{4}$ cup low-sodium soy sauce
- 4 cups (about 1 pound) brussels sprouts, trimmed, sliced in half lengthwise, and cooked
- freshly ground white pepper to taste

In a large heavy skillet over medium-high heat, toast the seeds by shaking the skillet until they're golden, about 2 minutes. Add the oil and sugar and stir until the sugar dissolves. Blend in the soy sauce. You can cover the sauce and set it aside for now. Reheat before continuing.

Add the sprouts to the skillet. Toss over high heat until the sprouts are hot and each morsel is touched with the sauce. Add pepper, taste for seasoning, then serve at once.

Burdock, Great

Alternatives: Parsnip, scorzonera, salsify.

The very long, very thin white-fleshed roots of burdock have the hint of the taste of the earth. Harvest these remarkable roots with a post hole digger, if one's available—the root is liable to be 2 feet long. For sweetness, dig it while it's no more than $\frac{1}{2}$ inch thick.

To prepare burdock, trim and gently scrub the roots just before cooking, then cook any way you would carrots. They'll be delicious.

Burdock is very high in fiber and offers a good amount of potassium and a small amount of calcium and iron. The young leafy shoots are also edible—use them in salads.

Since it takes months to come to the table, I give this prized vegetable the royal treatment. Once a year, when burdock is ready, I make tempura. One of the translations of the Japanese characters for tempura is "veiled in batter as a woman in silken gauze, desire rises in the beholder at the glimpse of heaven beneath." I'll say.

Tempura

MAKES 4 SERVINGS

Garden-fresh vegetables cooked lightly in a veil of crispy batter are incomparable. But don't try to make tempura for more than four. The cooking must go like the wind, and the pieces are ideally served at once, although they will hold in a 250°F oven on brown paper for 10 to 15 minutes.

The Japanese also make tempura with thin sweet pepper rings, whole okra pods, broccoli and cauliflower florets, and 1/4-inch-thick slices of mushroom, carrot, turnip, and kohlrabi. We like a bit of fish mixed with the vegetables—succulent fillets or medium-large raw shrimp with tails on or rings of squid. If you want an all-vegetable tempura, in place of the fish add 1/4 pound each of two more vegetables. If burdock isn't available, you can use any sweet slender root.

There are some untraditional elements here. Baking powder makes the batter especially puffed and lacy, and sugar and salt heighten flavor and aid in browning. The dipping sauce should be based on dashi (broth of dried kelp and dried bonito), but I find such assertive flavors can overwhelm delicate vegetables.

I also peel most vegetables for this luxury treatment, but you can leave skins on if they're delicate.

Since tempura cooks in 1 to 4 minutes, everything must be prepared in advance—the fish and vegetables can wait for a long hour.

Secrets of frying without absorbing fat: the oil must be very fresh, the temperature must be maintained, and the finished pieces drained and patted dry with paper towels.

VEGETABLES AND FISH

a splash of lemon juice or vinegar

2 to 2½ feet of ½-inch-thick burdock, scrubbed

1 to 2 slender sweet potatoes, peeled

4 slender Asian eggplants, 4 to 5 inches long, peeled

4 slender zucchini or other summer squash, 4 to 5 inches long

½ pound fresh fillets of fish or shelled shrimp with tails or rings of squid

12 to 16 slender green beans, about 4 inches long, topped and tailed if necessary

4 green or purple perilla leaves, optional

BATTER

1 cup all-purpose flour

2½ tablespoons cornstarch

2½ teaspoons baking powder

⅔ teaspoon sugar

⅔ teaspoon salt

1⅓ cups ice water

DIPPING SAUCE (MAKES ABOUT 2 CUPS)

1 cup mild chicken broth, vegetable stock, or dashi

⅓ cup mirin, sake, or dry sherry

⅓ cup low-sodium soy sauce or to taste

½ tablespoon sugar

½ cup finely shredded daikon or other white radish

a piece of fresh ginger the size of a walnut, peeled and finely shredded

COOKING

about 6 cups corn or other light oil, enough to give at least 2 inches' depth

flour for coating the vegetables

cornstarch for coating the fish

Have ready a big bowl of cold water with the lemon juice in it. As you prepare the first four vegetables, drop the pieces into it.

Cut the burdock into 2½-inch lengths (cut thicker roots like the sweet potatoes). Cut the sweets into ¼-inch-thick rounds. Slice the eggplant and zucchini lengthwise ¼ inch thick. Cut the fish into 2-inch squares. Wrap and refrigerate the fish, beans, and perilla until needed.

To make the batter, in a bowl in which all the pieces can easily be dipped, mix the flour, cornstarch, baking powder, sugar, and salt with a fork. About 15 minutes before cooking, add the water and blend lightly with chopsticks or a fork. The batter must be no thicker than heavy cream and beaten no more than to blend—tiny lumps become delicate beads on the fritters.

To make the dipping sauce, in a small saucepan or microwave-safe dish, blend the broth, mirin, soy sauce, sugar, daikon, and ginger. When the tempura is about to be cooked, heat the sauce until hot, then stir, taste for seasoning, and divide among 4 small bowls.

To make the tempura, drain the vegetables that are in the water. Have all other vegetables ready. Pat the vegetables and fish thoroughly dry.

To deep-fry the tempura, slowly heat the oil in a wok or wide heavy pot to 340°F—the temperature at which a drop of batter will drop below the surface, then quickly bobble up.

While the oil heats, arrange everything you'll need within reach of the stove. Ask your guests to be seated at the table.

Adjust the heat under the wok to maintain the temperature.

With your fingers or chopsticks, dip each vegetable piece in flour, shake well, dip in batter, then slip into the oil. Fry until golden, turning once or twice—allow 1 to 4 minutes, depending on density. Test dense pieces for tenderness with a thin skewer until you get a feel for timing. Don't crowd the pieces. Cook for each person, dipping the fish in cornstarch and frying it last. Lift out and drain finished pieces on several thichnesses of paper towels, blotting with towels as well. Frequently skim off bits of cooked batter—if they burn, the oil turns bitter.

Serve at once with dipping sauce on the side as well as rice and little bowls of pickled vegetables. Serve warm sake, cold beer, or hot green tea.

Small bowls of light soup classically precede the tempura—the miso soup under Choy Sum perhaps. And for dessert, a palate-cleansing ice made of fruit.

At high altitude, have the oil at about 365°F—a drop of batter will fall to the bottom for an instant, then bobble to the surface, sizzling.

The Greener, the Better

The longer time leaves of greens have been exposed to light, the more nutrients they'll contain. The leaves will contain more chlorophyll—the green pigment produced by photosynthesis, the biological synthesis of chemical compounds in the presence of light. Chlorophyll seems connected to the presence of beta-carotene, vitamin C, and calcium—for starters. So the darker outer leaves of a head of greens may have twice as much beta-carotene and many times more calcium and vitamin C than the pale inner leaves. That's why brassicas' wrapper leaves should be saved. If they're tougher, cook them separately a little longer, then mix them with the rest of the leaves.

CABBAGES

In early spring, the thinnings of autumn-sown cabbages that have finally begun to grow provide early greens—pull and toss them into salads. Heads form later, and then comes the harvest of cabbages sown in spring. You can cut a cabbage at any stage—I've seen whoppers—but a big reason to grow your own is to harvest a cabbage when it's glossy, sweet, and small—the size of a large orange. Make a clean cut at the base of the plant just above the ground. With autumn- and spring-sown cabbages, cut a cross ½ inch deep in the stump, and wee cabbages will sprout.

Cabbages have developed from a mustardlike weed that loved the sea. No other vegetable except peppers has as high a concentration of vitamin C. Cabbages have more moderate amounts of fiber and folic acid.

The first thing to know about homegrown organic cabbage is that you'll have aphids unless you keep the plants covered with floating row covers from start to finish. I've done that, but it deprived me of their beauty—I'd rather rinse off the aphids and see the gorgeous cabbages coming along. So after you cut off the root outdoors, bring the head into the kitchen and submerge it in a sinkful of cool water (weight it down with a can or a large plate). After 10 or 15 minutes you'll have to start at the bottom and use a stream of running water to wash away aphids hiding in crevices. Leave what water clings to the leaves, because this will help cook the cabbage and help conserve nutrients. Slice it into quarters lengthwise. If the core is tender, leave it; otherwise trim it out. Trim thickened stems of large outer leaves flat.

Steaming is one of the best ways to cook cabbage for every reason. Cut up the head and set the chunks in or over 1 inch of boiling water. Loosely cover with one of the wrapper leaves (or a piece of brown shopping bag paper, not foil) to help retain vitamins. Steam until tender-crisp, 7 to 10 minutes. Slice the pieces into thin ribbons. Trim out any hard ribs and toss them into a soup. For a delicious finish, melt ½ tablespoon unsalted butter per serving in a skillet. Add the ribbons and stir over low heat until the texture desired. Do not overcook. Remove from the heat and season with salt, freshly ground black pepper, and perhaps a pinch of caraway or dill seeds. Turn into a hot bowl and serve at once.

Pulling up my first cabbage on a drizzly September day was a thrill. It was a Perfect Ball, seeded at the end of April, and perfect it was. All the recipes said to throw the tough leaves from the stalk and around the head into the compost. But the leaves were blue-green and flawless, and I wasn't going to waste one bit of this beauty. So I tried the following recipe for the wrapper leaves. After washing them well, drop the leaves into a kettle of boiling salted water. In 7 minutes the leaves will be a match for those of the head.

Cabbage Wrapper Leaves from Ceylon

MAKES 3 TO 4 SERVINGS

This recipe applies to the quasi-tender outer leaves of cabbages, cauliflower, broccoli, and the leaves of brussels sprouts.

Combine in a nonstick skillet the thinly sliced outer leaves of a cabbage (which you've rinsed well), 1 thinly sliced onion, 2 or 3 sliced fresh green chilies (or to taste), 2 or 3 minced garlic cloves, and a finely chopped slice of fresh ginger. Cook uncovered over high heat, stirring frequently, until tender-crisp (add boiling water if the leaves are in danger of scorching). Stir in a handful of shredded unsweetened coconut dredged in 1/4 teaspoon curry powder. Add salt and freshly ground white pepper, then taste for seasoning. Serve the moment you can smell the curry.

Green Cabbage

Cabbage Stew

MAKES 4 TO 6 SERVINGS

Even my mother, who hates vegetables, likes this dish. The flavor of the sausages has everything to do with success of the composition. Use something highly seasoned such as kielbasa, chorizo, or pepperoni.

This can be cooked several hours in advance and warmed up.

1 small (1 1/4 pounds) tender green cabbage, wrapper leaves included
salt to taste
2 tablespoons olive oil
1 large red onion, coarsely chopped
6 fine carrots, cut into small dice
3 garlic cloves, finely chopped
2 tomatoes, cut into small dice
1 tablespoon fresh thyme leaves or 1 teaspoon crumbled dried
1 pound tasty smoked sausages, cut into 1 1/2-inch pieces
2 cups dry white wine
1 cup good chicken broth
freshly ground black pepper to taste

Soak, quarter, and trim the cabbage. Drop the wrapper leaves into boiling salted water and boil 7 minutes. Skim with a fine sieve to catch any last critters. Drain well. Chop these leaves with the rest of the cabbage into 2-inch squares.

In a large heavy nonreactive saucepan, warm the olive oil. Add the onion and carrots and stir over medium-high heat until glistening, about 2 minutes, then blend in the garlic, tomatoes, and thyme. Stir for a minute or two, then turn the heat to low and arrange the cabbage over this bed. Strew the sausage pieces over the cabbage. Pour in the wine and broth, cover tightly, and cook until the cabbage is redolent and tender, about 40 minutes. Stir with a wooden spoon after 20 minutes, distributing the cabbage and sausages through the vegetables. Add pepper, taste for seasoning, then serve in soup plates with boiled potatoes.

A Czech or Pole would also season the stew with a good pinch of caraway seeds and top it off with sour cream or yogurt.

Doukhobor Borscht

MAKES 4 TO 6 SERVINGS

Years ago a friend made us soup from her childhood that had cabbage at its heart. Olga Matson grew up in Canada near a settlement of Doukhobors, a religious sect who fled persecution in Russia at the end of the 19th century. The Doukhobors are singular cooks. Olga learned this soup from them, she handed it on to me, and I hand it on to you. The steps may seem fussy, but that I've remembered the soup for 30 years speaks to their success.

Olga says, "This is especially good with new vegetables. New little beets can be added and the beet greens chopped up if very young." The chopped raw leaves can go in with the first cup of cabbage. Add the hot cooked beets just before serving.

Serve this when made—if you reheat it, the cabbage will no longer be crunchy.

6 small unpeeled red or white new potatoes (1 pound) cut into 1-inch pieces
1 quart water
salt to taste
1 medium-size onion, chopped
4 tablespoons unsalted butter or 3 to 4 tablespoons mild oil
4 fresh or canned plum tomatoes, chopped
2 cups chopped red or green cabbage, about 1 pound
½ cup sour cream
1 tablespoon chopped fresh dill or 1 heaped teaspoon crumbled dried
freshly ground black pepper to taste

In a soup pot, combine the potatoes, water, and salt. Bring to a boil, turn the heat to low, set the lid on askew, and simmer until tender, about 15 minutes.

Meanwhile, sauté the onion in the butter in a saucepan over medium-high heat until golden, about 5 to 6 minutes. Add the tomatoes and simmer for a few minutes, stirring occasionally. Add 1 cup of the cabbage and simmer for 2 to 3 minutes.

Lift about half the potatoes from the soup pot into a bowl and reserve. Add the remaining cabbage to the soup pot and simmer just until the cabbage is tender but still crunchy, 2 to 3 minutes. Add the tomato mixture to the soup and turn off the heat. Mash the reserved potatoes with a fork and blend in the sour cream. Stir into the soup. Add the dill and pepper, then taste for seasoning. Serve with rye bread and cream cheese, then apple pie for dessert.

Coleslaw Greek Style

MAKES 4 TO 5 SERVINGS

Coleslaw is surely the most popular way green cabbage is enjoyed in this part of the world. My mother adds about one third as much chopped flat-leaf parsley as shredded cabbage to her coleslaw—everyone adores its clean sweet flavor. I add celery seeds to my coleslaw, and I like the dressing to be half mayonnaise, half yogurt, loosened with buttermilk, and spiked with lemon juice. My husband, with an affection for all things Greek, created this coleslaw, which is unbelievably delicious. It's best when the cabbage is still freshly crisp, but it's still plenty tasty the next day.

1½ quarts shredded tender cabbage, green or red or a mixture (½ large cabbage)
1 cup plain yogurt (nonfat is fine)
¼ cup feta cheese, 1½ ounces
½ teaspoon ground coriander or a heaped tablespoon finely chopped chives
freshly ground black pepper to taste

Combine the cabbage and yogurt in a big bowl and toss with your hands until every piece is coated. Add the remaining ingredients and blend with a spoon. Taste for seasoning and serve cold.

Red Cabbage

I love what the reds do to a composition of food. Very thin shreds of red cabbage make a dull salad shimmer in its bowl. For its rich tint alone I'd keep red cabbage around. But it has crunch to offer—even when cooked, if you're careful. And its flavor is sweet yet snappy—a fine vegetable indeed.

When you cook red cabbage, add a little cider vinegar to the water to help hold the color. The vinegar also adds just the point the cabbage needs for great flavor. Red cabbages offer lots more vitamin C than green ones, as well as all the other good things green cabbages offer. Use stainless-steel implements with red cabbages—carbon steel discolors the leaves.

MARINATED SHREDS OF RED CABBAGE: Marinated red cabbage is a crispy, colorful, and flavorful accompaniment to summer grills and roasts. My father kept a crock of it in the refrigerator, next to his jar of marinated red onions. This keeps for at least a couple of weeks.

Remove the wrapper leaves of a fine large red cabbage (save them for another dish). Soak, trim, quarter, core, and very thinly slice the cabbage. Cut in 2-inch pieces. You'll have about 11 cups. Turn it into a crock or deep bowl and sprinkle with salt (preferably pure sea or pickling salt)—for a small cabbage, use about 2½ tablespoons. Mix with your hands, then cover and refrigerate for two days, stirring occasionally.

Drain the cabbage, squeezing it dry. Rinse well in several changes of cool water. Return to the crock with slivers of garlic cloves to taste (I use three), 1 heaped teaspoon celery seeds, a bay leaf, and lots of freshly ground white pepper. Cover the cabbage with about 3½ cups cider vinegar and 3½ cups red wine. Cover (not with foil) and refrigerate for another day or two, stirring occasionally. This recipe makes 2 quarts. To serve, lift out and pat dry, then heap over poultry or meat as garnish or beside it as a crunchy condiment.

FLEMISH RED CABBAGE: Here's a splendid dish the color of lavender. It keeps for days and makes a satisfying lunch. This recipe makes 9 servings.

Soak, trim, and quarter a firm medium-size red cabbage (about 1½ pounds). Slice the quarters ¼ inch thick, then turn the slices and cut them crosswise the same way.

Preheat the oven to 325°F. In a hot dry nonstick skillet, sauté a chopped onion over medium-high heat until golden, stirring frequently, about 5 minutes. In a bowl, use your hands to mix the cabbage, onion, 3 coarsely grated unpeeled spicy red cooking apples, ⅓ cup fresh thyme leaves (or a scant 2 tablespoons crumbled dried), and ⅓ cup light brown sugar. Add salt and freshly ground black pepper then taste for seasoning.

Turn into a 3½ quart baking dish and pour over ½ cup cider vinegar, then 2 cups dry red wine. Stir, cover, and bake 2 hours, stirring 2 or 3 times. Blend in 2 tablespoons unsalted butter for gloss. Serve in bowls as a side dish for poultry and meat, to be eaten with a big spoon.

Savoy Cabbage

Ruffled and puckered savoys can be small and charming or large and magnificent. They can even be used as table decorations. Beyond beauty, savoys are considered the finest flavored of cabbages. By and large the thinner the cabbage leaves, the richer the flavor. Savoy leaves are the thinnest—and when you cook them, they release very little odor. Savoys are not good keepers, so use the cabbage at once.

Nutrients and preparation are the same as for other green cabbage.

SWEDISH CABBAGE SALAD: Because of their flavor and delicacy, savoy cabbages lend themselves especially to salads. A Swedish friend mixes shredded raw cabbage, grated unpeeled red apples, and curly parsley (an apple for every 2 cups cabbage, plus a handful of chopped parsley). Her dressing is inspired: one part fresh orange juice to two parts heavy cream. The citrus keeps the apple from turning dark, and the salad is served very cold.

Savoy Cabbage with Noodles

MAKES 6 SERVINGS

For my father, my mother often made *krautfleckerel,* a spicy and satisfying Austro-Hungarian dish from another era. When she gave me the recipe, I said, "I can't use that much butter!" My mother pointed out that the butter is for both the cabbage and the noodles and changed the subject. I notice that Mimi Sheraton's mother (*From My Mother's Kitchen*) used as much butter in her dish, too. This recipe from the forties also called for a common cabbage and cooked it for an hour till it was *brown.* I told my mother I couldn't do that either. So she graciously adapted the recipe to a light savoy, making it even more delicious.

If you undercook the noodles slightly, the dish can be prepared, refrigerated, then warmed up in a covered dish in a 350°F oven.

¼ pound butter, preferably unsalted

2 large onions, coarsely chopped

1 teaspoon paprika

2 tablespoons tomato puree

1 tablespoon Worcestershire sauce

1 tablespoon sugar

1 teaspoon freshly ground black pepper or to taste

1 cup boiling vegetable stock or water

1 medium-large (2 pounds) savoy cabbage, wrapper leaves removed, cored, and sliced ¼ inch thick

1 pound broad egg noodles

salt to taste

1½ to 2 pounds cooked fresh or smoked European-style sausages, thickly sliced, optional

Melt the butter in a large heavy skillet and sauté the onions over medium heat, stirring frequently, until softened, about 5 minutes. Blend in the paprika. Cover and turn the heat to low while you blend the tomato puree, Worcestershire, sugar, and pepper with the boiling stock. Add the cabbage and sauce to the onions and stir to blend. Cover and simmer until the cabbage is tender-crisp, 5 to 10 minutes—stir once or twice. Turn off the heat.

Cook the noodles in a big pot of boiling salted water until tender, or just this side of tender if you're going to reheat the dish. Heat the sausages in a covered skillet until piping hot. Drain the noodles and mix them into the cabbage. Add salt, taste for seasoning, and serve topped with the sausages. Accompany with sliced sweet red peppers or marinated peppers (see recipe under Peppers). You'll want great beer with this and chocolate ice cream for dessert.

Sauerkraut Cabbage

For tangy old-fashioned sauerkraut, the secret is to use a cabbage that has been growing long enough to accumulate lots of sugar in its leaves. In fermentation the sugar turns to lactic acid, which gives the kraut its sauer. Cool weather, even a nip of frost, helps. Though sauerkraut is traditionally made from cabbages sown in late summer, tender juicy early spring-sown cabbages make fine fresh sauerkraut. Just don't use savoy cabbages—their delicate leaves will disintegrate.

Since my idea of fun in the garden is to grow just a small patch of a great number of things, I never expect to have 30 or 40 pounds of sauerkraut bubbling away in the kitchen. But I have made it with two large heads of Perfect Ball, and I urge you to do the same with your favorite cabbage, early or late. What might seem a mysterious process couldn't be simpler.

Sauerkraut

MAKES 1 SCANT QUART

Never in your life will you have tasted sauerkraut—or any form of cabbage for that matter—to compare to this deliciousness. It has nothing at all to do with the stuff in the jar from the market or even from the deli. Detailed notes on canning are in The Cook's Notebook.

Working with about 2 large heads (5 pounds) of cabbage, trim off the wrapper leaves (use them in soup), then wash and drain the heads. Cut into quarters, leaving the cores if they're tender; otherwise add them to soup. Slice the quarters the thickness of a dime, using a shredder, mandoline, or stainless-steel knife—the blades give long fine curls, the knife shorter pieces. In a large stainless-steel, ceramic, or plastic bowl, combine the cabbage and 3 tablespoons pickling salt and, if the cabbage isn't sweet, 1 teaspoon sugar. Toss with your hands until thoroughly blended. Let stand for about 5 minutes, then turn into a clean uncracked stoneware crock or glass jar (a gallon jar holds about 8 pounds of cabbage). Press down gently until juice covers the shreds.

Cover the cabbage (not the jar) with plastic wrap, smoothing it to the edges so no shred is exposed to air. To weight the cabbage down in the vessel, put a 1-gallon freezer-weight plastic food storage bag inside another, set it on top, and fill with cool water until the shreds rest well beneath the juice. (If you're fermenting cabbage in a broader crock, don't think of using garbage bags—that plastic is not food-safe. Instead, lay a clean plate that just fits inside the crock on the plastic film, then weight down evenly with capped canning jars filled with water. Juice must cover the plate.) Cover the weights with a damp clean white cloth, tucking corners inside the vessel. The cloth will absorb some of the fermenting liquid.

Old-time kraut makers say that for best quality the cabbage must ferment at 70°F. It will ferment as low as 55°F but take about 2 weeks longer. Warmer than 75°F and the cabbage may spoil. Once, in a cool October, I had to set the crock in a heavy cardboard box and wrap the box in a blanket. It still came just to about 62°F, but it worked. Don't put the crock somewhere inconvenient, because you've got to spoon off the scum and rinse the covering film and cloth occasionally (daily if it's fermenting briskly). Fermentation will begin the day after packing and end 2 to 6 weeks later, depending on the temperature. When the bubbling stops, it is ready.

A week or so after starting the crock, when the cabbage is still crisp but souring has commenced, to me that just may be the peak of sauerkraut delight.

You can refrigerate the sauerkraut at any stage, and it will keep for up to a few weeks. But for long keeping, turn the finished sauerkraut into a large nonreactive saucepan. Stir frequently over medium-low heat until the juice comes to a boil. At once pack into clean hot pint or quart canning jars, distributing the juice evenly and leaving ½ inch of headspace. Run the handle of a wooden spoon up and down inside the jar a few times to release any air bubbles. Seal as usual. Process quarts for 15 minutes and pints for 10 minutes in a boiling water bath.

Serve the sauerkraut cold with a sprinkle of caraway or celery seeds next to potato salad. To serve hot, you'll have the most tang if you just heat and serve it—longer cooking blunts the flavor and texture. Some Pennsylvania Dutch sauerkraut makers serve it with roast turkey. Serve pork chops on a bed of sauerkraut with applesauce on the side. A midwestern treat is to heat sauerkraut in the oven topped with slices of cheddar cheese. And look up a recipe for Alsatian *choucroute garni* (aka *à l'alsacienne*) for—to me—the ultimate in sauerkrautery.

Cardoons

Alternative: The only vegetable comparable in flavor is slender stalks of artichokes.

If you didn't know this tall, stately fountain was a cardoon, you'd think it was an artichoke plant. The two are closely related, except the part of the cardoon we eat is not the bud but the stalk. Cardoons take fussing to grow, since stalks must be wrapped against the sun. Cardoon's flavor is bittersweet artichoke—fascinating eating.

Harvest by cutting stalks off at ground level about five weeks after you've wrapped the plant to blanch it. There may be lots of uninvited guests nestling among the leaves. Discard the outside stalks of the plant if they're hard or dry. To prepare cardoons, trim off the leaves and cut off stalks where they narrow to about ½ inch. Rinse well again. If necessary (it usually isn't from garden cardoons), pull off the strings as you would from superlarge ribs of celery. Cut the stalks into pieces about 2½ inches long, stopping when the stalk starts becoming resistant to the knife. Soak in cold water with lemon or lime juice for 30 minutes.

Bring a big pot of water to a boil. Whisk in 1 tablespoon all-purpose flour (the acidulated water bath and flour in the cooking water are meant to keep the cardoons white, which helps keep them sweet). When the water boils, add the cardoon pieces, return to a boil uncovered, turn the heat to medium, and boil gently until the pieces are tender-crisp, 15 to 30 minutes. Drain and pat dry. The pieces can now be covered loosely and kept in a cool place for a few hours. Cardoons are moderately high in sodium (you won't need to add salt) and contain fair amounts of folic acid and magnesium.

Cardoons with Gorgonzola Cheese

ALLOW ABOUT 5 STALKS FOR 2 PEOPLE

Heat a splash of olive oil and a nut of unsalted butter in a large heavy skillet over medium-high heat. Dip cooked cardoon pieces in flour, shake off excess, then sauté them without crowding, turning frequently, until browned, 5 to 6 minutes. Arrange on a hot platter and sprinkle each serving with the juice of ½ lemon, 1 ounce of crumbled Gorgonzola cheese, and a little finely chopped fresh sage. Grind white pepper over all and serve with glasses of Frascati.

It's traditional in the Piedmont region of northern Italy—where cardoons grow gloriously—to serve the tender center stalks with bagna cauda. In a pot over hot water, cook ¼ cup butter, 1 cup olive oil, and 5 minced garlic cloves until hot. Turn off heat and blend in 5 minced anchovy filets. Cover and wait 20 minutes, then stir and serve. Run a cardoon stalk or tiny raw artichoke or chunk of chicory, celery, Jerusalem artichoke, fennel, scallion, or sweet red pepper through this sauce, and your mind will race, thinking what else you can bathe in its glow. The answer is any raw vegetable you please.

Carrots

For best flavor and texture, harvest carrots while small. For a sweeter more nutritious carrot, let it grow to the size described on the seed packet. You won't want to peel your homegrown carrots—and you shouldn't. So much flavor and many of the vitamins are lost in the peelings. Just scrub them with a vegetable brush in a bowl of cold water to get the soil out of the creases.

I think the way to cook carrots for maximum flavor and nutrition is to skillet-steam them—the carrots, in whatever form you like, spread shallowly in a heavy skillet, ½ inch of cold salted water added, and the carrots cooked uncovered over medium-high heat until tender-crisp. Save the valuable stock. Slices and matchsticks take 3 to 4 minutes, whole slender carrots 8 to 10 minutes. Butter is nice with simple carrots but not necessary. In fact, well-grown carrots taste buttery on their own and are the quintessential diet food.

Carrots, as every schoolchild knows, are abundant in vitamin A and beta-carotene. Carrots also have a moderate amount of fiber, a fair amount of vitamin C, and a jot of potassium.

Surprisingly, carrots cooked tender-crisp are more nourishing than raw. That's because their cell walls are so strong that digestive juices can't completely break them down. A fast pass through the heat does the job, and the nutrients are released. But too much cooking destroys these nutrients, so be watchful.

Herbs especially good with carrots are parsley, dill, chervil, tarragon, marjoram, mint, and thyme—spices are nutmeg, mace, celery seeds. Also sesame, fennel, nigella, celery, anise, and caraway seeds.

Since I adapted the recipe under Turnips from a carrot recipe, retrieve it and make it with carrots.

If you think peas and carrots are horrible, you haven't tasted your own baby carrots simmered with your own freshly picked peas.

ROASTED CARROTS: As with beets, whole carrots roasted to tenderness in their skins then moistened with olive oil and melted butter are heaven. Although sugar-sweet, they won't look like much, so sprinkle with chopped chervil and close your eyes.

Grated Carrot Salad in the French Style

ALLOW 2 CARROTS PER PERSON

Even though slightly cooked carrots have more available nutrients than raw, I dearly love a grated carrot salad. Here's a fast pure French way with carrots that's frequently on our table.

Grate scrubbed unpeeled sweet carrots 1/8 inch or so thick into shreds that are longer rather than shorter—a grating blade on the food processor or Moulin Julienne is ideal. Turn into a big bowl, drizzle with mild olive oil, and add fresh lemon juice, salt, and freshly ground white or black pepper. Toss with your hands then taste for seasoning.

Candied Brandied Carrots

MAKES 4 SERVINGS

When I was in high school, I watched my mother make candied brandied carrots. I thought they were the most sophisticated things imaginable and among the most delicious. When I harvest my prized Nantes carrots, this is how I serve them.

The carrots can be almost cooked, then candied just before serving.

8 skinny or 4 to 5 medium-size (about 1 pound) tender carrots sliced into matchsticks

salt to taste

2 tablespoons brandy

2 tablespoons unsalted butter

3 tablespoons sugar

heaped 1 tablespoon very fine shreds of lemon zest or chopped chervil

Turn the carrots into a heavy skillet in which they fit in a single layer if possible. Add ½ inch of boiling salted water and simmer uncovered until tender-crisp, 3 to 4 minutes. The carrots can be removed from the stock (save it for another use), quickly cooled in ice water, dried, and refrigerated for a few hours at this point. Bring them to room temperature before continuing, or they'll be cold in the center.

To serve, combine the carrots and brandy in a nonstick skillet. Cook uncovered over low heat, shaking the skillet, until all the brandy has been absorbed by the carrots. Turn them into a bowl and cover. Without washing the pan, quickly add the butter and sugar. Stir over medium heat until the butter has melted, then add the carrots. Stir and shake until the sugar has caramelized and each piece of carrot is coated with caramel. Turn into a heated serving dish and sprinkle with the lemon zest or chervil. Serve at once.

Carrots with Black Sesame Seeds

MAKES 5 SERVINGS

For its flavor and colors, we're fond of this recipe inspired by a note in a Chinese cookbook. Shimmering orange matchsticks speckled with coal-black sesame seeds are luminous beside pearly fish, and their flavors make a sweet and nutty contrast to mild flesh. Black sesame seeds taste like white sesame seeds to the second power. Another time use nigella seeds for a perfumed flavor.

The carrots can be prepared for cooking several hours in advance, covered tightly, and refrigerated. Don't worry that the skin darkens and looks disagreeable; it will brighten with heat. This dish is also good cold.

2 tablespoons black sesame seeds (*kuro goma,* inexpensive in Asian markets) or use white seeds

8 skinny or 4 to 5 medium-size tender carrots, about 1 pound, sliced into matchsticks

1 cup vegetable stock or water

salt to taste

2 tablespoons any nut oil, mild olive oil, or Asian sesame oil

1 tablespoon fresh lemon juice

freshly ground white pepper to taste, optional

Toast the seeds in a dry large heavy skillet over low heat, shaking the skillet, just until they start to pop—about 2 minutes. This is called *parching.* Turn them into a bowl and spread the carrots in the skillet. Add the stock and salt if the stock is unsalted or you're using water. Cover and set over high heat. Don't leave the kitchen, because in a few minutes the water will be gone and the carrots will be tender with just a hint of crispness left.

Remove from the heat and stir in 1 tablespoon of the oil, then the seeds, mixing thoroughly. Sauté again just enough to heat the seeds, stirring constantly, about 2 minutes. Remove from the heat and stir in the remaining tablespoon of oil, if desired, the lemon juice, and taste for seasoning—I don't think it wants pepper, but you may disagree.

Carrot Greens

In the reign of James I, Scottish ladies of fashion decorated their headdresses with carrot fronds.

Unlike beets, whose greens are traditionally well regarded, carrot greens are usually dumped, except in the eastern Mediterranean. It has always bothered me that I've had to send great ferny bunches of greens to the compost. As delicate as they appear, the greens are a tad sharp and quite chewy.

To prepare carrot greens, plunge them deep into cool water, inspecting the leaves and stalks for browned bits while you ruffle and shake them. Change the water several times until the water is clear. Fold up the stalks and chop the greens coarsely. Don't forget to throw a handful into salad.

Puree of Carrot Greens Soup

MAKES 6 SERVINGS

In the spirit of not wasting a smidge from the garden (and having more than I could really wear), I invented this soup. The flavor is tangy, and the texture is velvety (thanks to the blender). As good (if not better) the next day cold, creamed with a little yogurt.

1 tablespoon mild oil
1 large white or yellow onion, cut up
carrot greens, from about a dozen carrots, coarsely chopped
3 cups cool water or use water and mild vegetable stock
1½ tablespoons rice vinegar
salt to taste
2½ cups mixed vegetable juices, including tomato
1½ teaspoons chopped fresh dill or ½ teaspoon dried
2 cups cooked white or brown rice
freshly ground white pepper to taste

In a large saucepan, heat the oil and sauté the onion over medium-high heat until softened, about 3 minutes, stirring frequently. Add the greens and stir until wilted and mixed with the onion, about 1 minute. Add the water, vinegar, and salt. Stir to blend, then bring to a simmer. Turn the heat to low, then simmer, stirring occasionally, for about 15 minutes. The greens will be cooked and the stems still slightly crunchy.

In small increments, whirl the contents of the pot in a blender until absolutely smooth. Either return the puree to the pot or turn it into a bowl, then blend in the vegetable juices, dill, and rice. Add pepper and taste for seasoning. Heat and serve or cover and refrigerate until you're ready to present it hot or cold. Add crisp crackers and mild cheese, and this can be supper.

Cauliflower

Harvesting your own cauliflower is a thrill—and it will have been worth your while. Cut when a head is 6 to 9 inches in diameter (according to the cultivar), while the curds are still tight. Pull the plant, because a new head won't form.

I thought I had invented cooking cauliflower in a wet brown paper bag in the microwave, but of course I didn't. I always get a kick out of how well the flower head comes out. I just trim a medium-size cauliflower (to 1 pound), tuck it inside, wet the bag under cold running water, prick it in several places with the tip of a sharp knife, roll down the top, and cook it on full power, turning it a few times until tender, about 10 minutes. Another handsome way to cook cauliflower is to steam the whole head with some of its leaves attached in a deep steamer. Add a squeeze of lemon juice to an inch of water to help keep the cauliflower white (and save afterward for stock). A medium head takes 10 to 12 minutes. Present the whole head on a platter as a bouquet. I drizzle it with a little melted butter and a little fruity olive oil—the green and gold running together—dust with paprika, then serve cut into wedges (including the main stalk if it's tender) with crescents of lemon.

Just don't boil cauliflower in lots of water—you'll waste its valuable nutrients. And please cook the cabbagey wrapper leaves.

Your painstakingly raised cauliflower is a very good source of vitamin C, a moderate source of fiber and folic acid, and a smallish source of B_6. While brisk cooking helps retain nutrients, the folic acid is volatile, and most of it will be leached into the cooking water. So it's very important to use little water when steaming cauliflower and to use that water in a soup so the folic acid won't be wasted.

Purple cauliflower and broccoli-cauliflower are treated like cauliflower in cooking. Any of them can be cooked according to any recipe for broccoli.

Do not cook cauliflower in aluminum or iron—chemicals in the vegetable react with chemicals in the metals to discolor the florets.

Remember to add tender cauliflower leaves and raw florets to salad.

A FEW DISHES FROM THE FRENCH: Comtesse du Barry, mistress of Louis XV, so relished *chou-fleur*—French for "cabbage flower"—that her name after a dish on the menu signals cauliflower. *Potage à la du Barry* is a puree of cauliflower and potato (by weight, four parts cauliflower to one of potato) thinned with rich broth or milk, splashed with cream, and sprinkled with chervil or parsley. Delightful *salade du Barry* is florets of cool steamed cauliflower tossed with sprigs of watercress, dressed with a lemony vinaigrette, sprinkled with chervil, chives, and flat-leaf parsley, and garnished with whole baby radishes. And cauliflowers du Barry are cooked florets sprinkled with grated cheese, browned under the broiler, then slipped onto small hot saucers of artichoke bottoms.

CAULIFLOWER WITH A DRIZZLE OF BROWNED BUTTER: One of the best of all adornments for cauliflower. Fine bread crumbs stirred in a skillet in a bit of butter until both brown is even more exciting, since the crumbs are crunchy and richly colored against the white softness. My husband adds sautéed quartered mushrooms to buttered toasted crumbs with a squeeze of lemon—sublime.

WARM CAULIFLOWER SALAD: Steam a whole head until tender-crisp, separate into florets, and slice the stalk crosswise. Toss with dark raisins and chopped raw red onion, then dress with walnut oil and red wine vinegar.

Scalloped Cauliflower

MAKES 4 SERVINGS

This dish turns back to an innocent period in our cooking history, and there's great affection for it. The dish is an updated version of a recipe from my grandmother's 1928 edition of the *Rumford Complete Cook Book*. Prepare it for the final baking a few hours in advance if you like.

1 cup milk
salt to taste
1 whole (1¼- to 1½-pound) cauliflower
1 tablespoon butter, preferably unsalted, plus more for the dish
½ cup dry bread crumbs
½ cup cream or half-and-half
freshly ground white pepper to taste
½ cup sliced or slivered almonds or cashews, toasted
a handful of chopped curly parsley

In a deep saucepan, bring the salted milk to a boil (milk is thought to keep the curds white). Add the cauliflower and boiling water to make the liquid ½ inch deep. Cover and simmer over medium heat until tender, 10 to 12 minutes.

Butter a 6-cup baking dish and sprinkle it with some of the crumbs. Drain the cauliflower (freeze the milky stock for a cream soup) and break it into small pieces. Heat the butter and cream together in the microwave or a saucepan until the butter melts. Add salt and pepper then taste for seasoning. In the baking dish, layer cauliflower and cream, sprinkling each layer of cauliflower with nuts. Cover and refrigerate until needed, then bring to room temperature.

To bake, heat the oven to 400°F. Sprinkle the remainder of the crumbs on top, and bake until bubbling, 15 to 20 minutes. Serve sprinkled with parsley.

Golden Cauliflower and Rice

MAKES 4 SERVINGS

One night I realized that my garden's cauliflower and long-grain rice cook in about the same length of time. So I combined them felicitously. This is the same easy-cooking notion as for the dish of rice and shelly lima beans.

1 medium (1¼- to 1½-pound) cauliflower, including tender leaves
1 teaspoon turmeric
⅔ cup rinsed jasmine, basmati, or other long-grain rice
1⅓ cups mild chicken broth, cold water, or vegetable stock
salt to taste
1 large garlic clove, thinly sliced
1 tablespoon olive oil
1 small tomato or 1 steeped sun-dried tomato (see The Cook's Notebook), chopped
freshly ground white pepper to taste

Slice the florets crosswise into quarter-size pieces (reserve the stems). Sauté in a dry nonstick skillet over high heat for about 2 minutes, stirring frequently. Add the turmeric and stir for another minute to coat the pieces.

Bring the rice and the salted broth or other liquid to a simmer uncovered. Cover and simmer for 10 minutes. At the same time, cover the turmericked florets in the skillet and cook gently in dry heat for 10 minutes. Stir them into the rice after its 10-minute simmering, then let both set undisturbed for 10 minutes.

Meanwhile, cut up tender leaves and stalks from the cauliflower into ½-inch pieces and thinly slice the tender part of the main stalk. Turn into the skillet with the garlic, drizzle with the oil, and sauté over medium-high heat until tender.

Just before spooning up, stir the tomato into the rice, then taste for seasoning. Serve immediately, with the cauliflower rice surrounded by the leaves.

Flowering Cauliflower

Because it's so hot and dry where I garden, I have difficulty keeping curds of cauliflower from flowering. Finally I've stopped fighting the inevitable, and I turn disadvantage to advantage. The bolting sprays look like pins of emerald enamel designed for Tiffany, with clusters of seed pearls—the tiny curds—at the ends.

BOLTING CAULIFLOWER: To cook, cut off and discard the stems at the point where the knife tells you they're no longer tender—where they snap naturally, like asparagus. Steam over an inch of water just until tender-crisp, then arrange on a heated platter. Dress with browned butter, a dash of lemon juice, salt, and white pepper and color with a drift of finely chopped green garlic or Chinese chives or chives.

Mini-Cauliflowers

Alternative: Larger cauliflowers trimmed down to 3 inches or cut into small florets.

These are a kitchen garden version of Japanese bonsai—standard-size plants so crowded that they produce miniature heads. They are delightful one-serving cauliflowers, ideal to grow when your space is limited. Harvest them by slicing off at ground level.

Italians have been growing and cooking cauliflower for generations. In southern Italy florets are sautéed in fruity olive oil with chopped tomatoes, diced ripe sweet peppers, salty black olives, slivered garlic, capers, oregano, and white wine to moisten—*maraviglioso.*

Cook the outer leaves on their own as you would cabbage.

MINI-CAULIFLOWERS FROM PIEDMONT: (makes 4 servings). Should you be growing the small heads in a small space, here is a northern Italian way called *cavolfioriti alla Piemontese* that sets off small bouquets beautifully. It can be served hot or at room temperature.

Steam 4 mini-cauliflower heads—stems trimmed flush—until tender-crisp. Cover and keep the curds hot if you plan to serve them hot. Otherwise, cover loosely and cool.

Meanwhile, film a small heavy nonstick skillet with a mild oil. Sauté 1 coarsely grated red onion over medium heat until softened, stirring frequently, about 5 minutes. Add 2 tablespoons mild olive oil, 2 tablespoons dry white wine, 1 tablespoon tomato paste, 1/2 tablespoon balsamic vinegar, and 6 finely chopped flat fillets of anchovies. Heat until hot, shaking the skillet occasionally. Add freshly ground white pepper, then taste for seasoning.

Arrange each cauliflower on a salad plate, spoon sauce around it, grind white pepper over, and sprinkle the top with a little finely chopped fresh sweet basil. Serve hot or at room temperature as a first course garnished with a sprig of basil leaves or basil in flower.

Celeriac

Alternative: Jerusalem artichoke, salsify.

This underappreciated root with creamy white flesh, velvety texture, and warm celery flavor is an autumn and winter vegetable. Pull it up when the bulbous part is 2 to 3 inches in diameter. Celeriac's stalks and leaves are used as leaf celery. When an Asian recipe calls for celery, if you haven't any Chinese or leaf celery, the diminutive stalks and leaves of celeriac are a better substitute than mild-flavored trenching celery.

To prepare celeriac, first slice off what's left of the celery stalks. Then rinse and scrub the root well to rid it of the earth that will have worked its way into crevices. Celeriac is marvelous baked in its skin—350°F for an hour or so—then peeled or the skin eaten if tender. Otherwise peel the skin before cooking. So the flesh won't darken from exposure to the air, keep pieces you're not working with in water with lemon juice—and always use a stainless-steel knife. Simmer slices in ½ inch of salted water, uncovered, for 3 to 5 minutes. Do not overcook. Add tender leaves to salad.

Treat yourself to celeriac soup—pare, slice, and steam the root until tender, whirl in a food processor, then thin to the desired consistency with milk. Pureed cooked celeriac whipped into mashed potatoes is great. And serve celeriac au gratin—cooked matchsticks sprinkled with cheese and butter and baked until brown.

Celeriac provides vitamin C, phosphorus, and potassium.

Mustard-Flavored Celeriac and Sweet Red Peppers

MAKES ABOUT 6 SERVINGS

Most of us know celeriac best as the classic French hors d'oeuvre, *céleri-rave en rémoulade,* raw strips dressed with mustard-flavored French dressing. Here is a lean variation, tasty and colorful—sweet red pepper strips are added—based on a recipe from J.-B. Reboul's 19th century *La cuisinière Provençale.* You can serve this the next day or in 10 days.

salt to taste

1 medium-large (1 pound) trimmed and peeled celeriac, cut into ⅜-inch-thick matchsticks

2 medium-size sweet red peppers, sliced into ⅜-inch-thick strips

DRESSING

1 cup water

½ cup cider vinegar

¼ cup distilled white vinegar

2½ tablespoons dry mustard

2½ tablespoons olive oil

salt and freshly ground white pepper to taste

Bring a big pot of salted water to a boil. Drop in the celery root and return to a boil uncovered. After about 3 minutes, taste—the pieces should be tender on the outside and distinctly crisp inside. When ready immediately lift out with a strainer and turn into a mixing bowl. Drop the peppers into the boiling water and cook just until slightly softened, 3 to 4 minutes altogether, then lift out and add to the celery root. Drain off water in the bowl.

To make the dressing, in a nonreactive saucepan combine the water, cider vinegar, white vinegar, dry mustard, and oil. Bring to a boil over medium-high heat, stirring. Pour over the celeriac and peppers and stir to blend. Add salt and pepper and taste for seasoning, then cover the bowl and keep it in a cool place until the next day. Either serve it or turn the mixture into a jar, cover, and refrigerate.

Include in a mixed hors d'oeuvre plate, to be eaten with a fork—black olives, red radishes, rolled-up paper-thin slices of salami, pickled chilies, curled fillets of anchovies, blocks of salty cheese—with crusts of French bread for sopping up the mustardy dressing.

Once the celeriac and peppers are gone, use the dressing for salad.

Celeriac combines superbly with potatoes, especially mashed potatoes—their flavors embrace one another. Use equal amounts and serve garnished with chopped celeriac leaves. Good with beef and game.

CELERY

I can't remember when anyone has served us celery as a vegetable dish at a dinner party. These recipes deserve to come to the party.

Harvest celery in a cut-and-come-again way, cutting each stalk at the base with a sharp knife, always leaving ⅔ of the bunch intact. However, if you cut all the stalks flush with the ground, more will sprout up.

To prepare your carefully cultivated celery, soak it in a sinkful of cold water for an hour or so to plump it. Drain and pat it dry before continuing. It's unlikely you'll want to harvest a whole head at once, as you would bring it home from the market, but if you do, trim off the roots and any tough outer ribs and flush the interior with cool water. If any ribs are stringy, pare with a vegetable peeler. To preserve vitamin C and folic acid, simmer celery pieces in ½ inch of chicken broth or water with a drizzle of olive oil just until tender-crisp, about 10 minutes. Drain and pat dry, then finish as desired.

Add tender stalks and leaves to salad.

Most recipes that suit celeriac suit celery and vice versa.

We love celery cut into crescents and simmered until tender in lightly salted milk, then drained and served with a pinch of nutmeg and a drift of grated cheese.

BRAISED CELERY: (makes 4 servings). Here's the celery dish for company, a classic French dish that tastes complex but is not hard to put together. Braised celery is particularly good with chicken, fish, and beef. This is ideal for homegrown celery that's more flavorful but less presentable than market stuff.

Serve as soon as the celery is ready, but the slow baking makes that easy. As a friend says, it smells like Thanksgiving.

Trim 4 whole small heads or cut 2 large heads lengthwise in half. Tie each bundle of celery together with cotton string to preserve its shape. Butter a deep earthenware or glass baking dish—ideally one in which the celery just fits. Heat the oven to 250°F.

Thinly slice 4 tender unpeeled carrots on the diagonal, chop 1 onion, and mince 2 garlic cloves. Strew over the bottom of the dish and sprinkle with leaves from 4 thyme sprigs or 1 teaspoon dried thyme leaves. Lay the celery on the vegetable bed—cut side up if cut.

Bring about 3 cups mild broth—half chicken and half beef or a vegetable stock—to a boil. Pour it over—just to cover the seasoning vegetables, not the celery. Add salt and freshly ground white pepper to taste. Lay a buttered sheet of wax paper over the celery, buttered side down, then cover loosely with foil, shiny side down. Bake in the middle of the oven, shaking the dish a few times, for about 1½ hours. Remove it from the oven. Serve sprinkled with chopped flat-leaf parsley and more fresh leaves of thyme.

Puree of Celery Soup

MAKES ABOUT 6 SERVINGS

Italians are also fond of celery. In Tuscany, cuts of cooked garlic-seasoned celery the same size as a ridged tubular pasta called *sedanini,* "little celery," are tossed with the pasta and finished with parsley. The third Sunday in October, the town of Trevi in Umbria has a celery festival in which the townspeople dip branches of celery in a dressing of extra-virgin olive oil, salt, and pepper—*pinzimonio* under Dressings in The Cook's Notebook. Farther north in Friuli, in Venezia Giulia, a celery soup, *sopa friulana,* is traditionally served on Christmas Eve. Inspired by the idea, when I grow celery I often make this. Like so many other soups, this one is equally good cold.

¼ cup olive oil
8 cups chopped celery stalks, leaves, and flowers; any or all can be tough—this is a good place for Chinese celery
2 cups chopped onion, about 1 very large
1½ cups chopped tomatoes, about 3 medium-size
3½ cups unpeeled floury potatoes in 1-inch dice, 2 medium-size
3 large garlic cloves, chopped
1 quart mild vegetable stock or chicken broth
1 quart cool water
salt to taste and lots of freshly ground black pepper
about ½ cup heavy cream, sour cream, or yogurt, optional
nasturtium blossoms or any fresh herb sprigs available for garnish

In a large heavy skillet, warm the olive oil over medium-high heat, then add the celery and onion. Stir with a wooden spoon to coat the vegetables with oil, then cover and sauté for about 12 minutes, stirring frequently toward the end so nothing browns. Turn into your soup pot and stir in the tomatoes, potatoes, and garlic, then the stock, water, and salt. Cover, bring to a simmer, turn the heat to very low, and simmer for 1 hour, stirring occasionally.

Puree roughly in a food processor, then pass through the medium blade of a food mill or a coarse sieve to catch the strings. Add pepper and taste for seasoning. Heat if necessary—or chill—then ladle into soup plates. Add a swirl of something creamy if you like and garnish as you please.

Celery Seeds

Like the vegetable they create, these seeds are too little used. Their flavor is like toasted celery—remarkable. Should your celery get to the point of making seeds, gather them carefully and keep in a tightly closed jar in a dark place. Then when you might have reached for caraway seeds, you can take down your celery seeds instead. Add them to salad dressing or potato or bean or pasta salad. Add them in place of celery for flavor, such as in soup or stew or savory pie.

CELERY-SEEDED FILLETS OF SOLE: (makes 2 servings). Gray, Dover, and petrale sole will hold their shape in this simple, fast dish.

In a large heavy skillet over medium-high heat, melt 3 tablespoons unsalted butter. Sprinkle in 1 tablespoon celery seeds and stir them, sautéing, until the butter and seeds are hot, about 30 seconds. Lay in 4 thin fillets of sole and cook for 1 minute. Turn with a pancake turner and cook for another minute. The flesh should be pearly and opaque.

Lift the fish onto heated plates. Set the skillet over high heat and reduce the pan juices to a lightly browned spoonful or two. Stir in 2 tablespoons fresh lemon juice, pour the sauce over the fish, grind white pepper over it, then tuck a sprig of celery beside the fish. Serve at once. New potatoes steamed with carrots and sprinkled with flat-leaf parsley are fine companions.

Chinese Celery

Alternatives: Celeriac stalks, celery, or lovage.

With its slim hollow stalk, abundance of leaves, and complex flavor, Chinese celery seems a happy combination of trenching and leaf celeries. Pick before they flower. These stalks aren't their best raw; they need a bit of heat to shine. Chinese celery is especially good in stir-fries combined with nuggets of chicken, ginger, and chilies. Preparation and nutrition information are the same as for celery.

Leaf Celery or Par-Cel

Alternative: Young celery leaves.

When you grow this, you'll see how fresh and springlike the leaves are, how rich the flavor. Harvest the same as celery. You can, of course, use these leaves in any way you'd use basic celery leaves, but expand your horizons. Try them in place of flat-leaf parsley—whose shape the leaves of par-cel resemble.

Salad of Oranges, Lemons, and Leaf Celery

MAKES 6 SERVINGS

This salad is especially delicious with bland roast poultry and meats. The skins of the oranges and lemons must be thin and smooth. The salad can be prepared 8 or so hours in advance.

- a good handful of young leaf celery leaves, roughly chopped
- 1/4 cup extra-virgin olive oil
- a sprinkling of sugar
- salt and freshly ground white pepper to taste
- 3 unpeeled sweet oranges, sliced into the thinnest possible rounds, seeds removed if any
- 3 lemons, preferably Meyer, prepared the same as the oranges
- 6 leaf celery sprigs for garnish

Combine the celery leaves, oil, and sugar in a mixing bowl. Add salt and pepper and taste for seasoning.

On individual salad plates, overlap alternating slices of oranges and lemons in a ring (or any shape you like). Spoon over the leafy dressing. Each salad can then be covered with plastic wrap (it will eat holes in foil) and refrigerated until serving time. Serve garnished with a leafy sprig.

Celtuce

Alternative: Celery makes a fine substitute.

In northern China, *woh sun* has been grown for centuries. Harvest when the stalk is about 1½ feet tall and 1½ inches thick—or whatever height yours reaches at that girth. Any thicker, and it will be tough. The plants with the thickest stalks and whitest flesh are chosen because the heart of the stalk is the prize.

Remove the leaves from this odd stalk. Pare the skin down to the tender flesh—it will look like translucent pared broccoli. One stalk makes about four servings. Cut it into matchsticks either for pickling or for stir-fries. Slice the leaves crosswise about an inch wide and use them in a stir-fry. Quite nice on their own or added to a mix and finished with soy sauce. Celtuce is very high in vitamin C.

But the considerable amount of vitamin C in the stalk is lost when cooked, so the best thing is to eat the vegetable raw. Even if you end up with—or buy at the Asian market—a celtuce stem as big as your arm, you must pare down the tough stringy exterior, and you'll finish with the same amount that's edible as if you'd harvested it young.

California/Chinese Celtuce Salad

MAKES 4 SERVINGS

This is my sort of salad made with Chinese ingredients. Since there's little taste in the celtuce itself, the excitement is in its crunchy texture, in any accompanying vegetables, and in the dressing—a delicious change from the ubiquitous olive oil and lemon juice.

The salad can be prepared hours in advance. Refrigerated in a tightly covered jar, the dressing will last until eaten.

1 tender celtuce stalk, pared and sliced into matchsticks
1 carrot, scrubbed and trimmed
3 whole scallions or green garlic stalks, thinly sliced

DRESSING (MAKES 2 CUPS TO SERVE ABOUT 16)
1 cup peanut oil
½ cup low-sodium soy sauce
⅓ cup fresh orange juice
¼ cup rice vinegar
1 tablespoon toasted sesame seeds, optional

Turn the celtuce into a salad bowl. For contrast of color and shape, pull a zester along the carrot, making long orange wisps, or shred the carrot finely. Add the carrot and green rings to the celtuce.

In a mixing bowl, combine the dressing ingredients. Whisk or beat with a fork until thoroughly blended.

Pour on just enough dressing to moisten the ingredients and toss with your hands to blend. If you're making this in advance, toss the salad again before serving. Turn extra dressing into a jar, cover, and refrigerate.

CHARD

"So what does chard taste like anyway?" asked my friend as I was harvesting some leaves. I suppose the largeness of the leaves makes them look like monster spinach, but close your eyes and taste a young leaf from the center of the plant, and you'll think it's lettuce. In older leaves the flavor of lettuce moves toward spinach—with a hint of earth—but with none of spinach's metallic bite. Harvest chard stalks at the base, taking outside leaves first, and cutting with a knife.

Chard may not be as richly nutritious as some greens, but it grows readily, and I find its mild flavor goes down more gracefully than some other greens. So it's chard more often rather than bitier greens less often, and it all works out in the end.

In the West, chard is cooked in nearly all the same ways as spinach. Pull the greens from the stalks—fold the leaf lengthwise and pull down from the top; the two leafy sides will come away. (To preserve their flavor, steam the stalks whole and then cut them up if you wish.) Wash the greens in a couple of sinkfuls of lukewarm water until clean. Shake off water from the leaves and turn them into a big pot with the water that clings to them. Cover and cook over medium heat until tender, 12 to 15 minutes, stirring a couple of times. Drain in a colander and, when cool, squeeze out juices until the leaves have the texture of a moist sponge.

For maximum color, simmer the leaves uncovered in an inch of salted water. Chard is lower in beta-carotene than most dark leaves, with as much vitamin C as beet greens (in fact the plant is a form of beet), two thirds of the iron of spinach, but only half the calcium of most other leaves. Add tender pieces of leaves or stalks to salad.

The Italians and French regard chard highly. Italians cook the green leaves as they do spinach and dress them with oil and lemon juice (the way we've come to enjoy turnip and other mustard greens). The French add chopped greens to pâtés. I stumbled on this pleasure when I snipped the greens of a chard going to seed into ribbons and mixed them into my meat loaf—now I always add them. In Genoa shredded greens are combined with sautéed onions, parsley, garlic, mushrooms, beaten eggs, and Parmesan, topped with bread crumbs, and baked until set—wonderful cold on a picnic. Chard- and ricotta-stuffed tortelli have been part of the midsummer Feast of San Giovannia in Parma since the year 1210.

Creamy Chard, Tomatoes, and Mushrooms in Fresh Paprika-Pasta Lasagne with Basil and Three Cheeses

MAKES 12 SERVINGS

Picking stalks for supper one afternoon, I was thinking about our summer in Rapallo and our cook Tina and her freshly made pasta and chard: the little hats and half-moons and ravioli and lasagne stuffed with creamy greens. A few hours later I pulled my own lasagne from the oven. It takes only a little longer to prepare than standard lasagne, but it's lyrical—layers of creamy pink pasta, rosy tomatoes, and soft green chard. As I put the dish together, I thought again that much of what I treasure about my garden is that when I feel like being creative in the kitchen, the materials are just outside my door.

Fresh pasta, the way I make it, takes about 35 minutes to prepare and it makes an extraordinary difference in this dish. If this is impractical for you, 9 ounces of fresh thin wonton wrappers are a good substitute. Separate the pieces and boil them just until al dente, usually about 3 minutes. Keep covered with a towel.

1 RECIPE PAPRIKA PASTA, UNDER PASTA IN THE COOK'S NOTEBOOK

CREAM SAUCE (MAKES ABOUT 4 CUPS)

6 tablespoons unsalted butter
6 tablespoons all-purpose flour
½ cup whole tender scallions, chopped, about 3
3 cups milk (nonfat is fine)
¾ cup freshly grated Parmesan cheese, about 3 ounces
¼ cup thin ribbons of fresh basil or 1 rounded tablespoon crumbled dried
tiny pinch of nutmeg, preferably freshly grated
freshly ground white pepper to taste

FILLINGS AND FINISHES

about 10 cups (1½ pounds) green part of chard leaves, chopped into ½-inch pieces

1 cup ricotta cheese (low-fat is fine)

2 tablespoons unsalted butter, melted

1 tablespoon fresh lemon juice

salt and freshly ground white pepper to taste

1 pound mushrooms, thinly sliced

8 to 9 (1 pound) plum or pear tomatoes, cut into ¼-inch dice

a little unsalted butter and olive oil

½ pound mozzarella cheese, shredded

Prepare the pasta dough. To make the lasagne, roll it out into the thinnest, largest sheets you can handle. Cut into 12 4-inch squares and 8 3- by 4-inch rectangles. Cook, cool, and keep on towels as directed.

To make the cream sauce, in a large heavy saucepan over medium heat, melt the butter, then whisk in the flour. Cook over low heat, stirring occasionally, for 2 minutes, then blend in the scallions. Slowly whisk in the milk, then whisk occasionally until the sauce thickens. Turn the heat to low and cook for 5 minutes, whisking frequently. Whisk in the Parmesan, basil, and nutmeg and, when the cheese has melted, add the pepper. Remove from the heat and lay plastic wrap directly on the surface to prevent a skin from forming.

To make the fillings, in a mixing bowl combine the chard, ricotta, butter, and lemon juice, then blend in 1 cup of the cream sauce. Add salt and pepper and taste for seasoning. Cover.

Heat a dry large heavy skillet over medium-high heat and sauté the mushrooms, stirring occasionally, until all moisture has evaporated and the mushrooms brown slightly—stir almost constantly at the end. Combine in a mixing bowl with ½ cup of the cream sauce. Add salt and pepper, taste for seasoning, and cover.

Combine the tomatoes in a mixing bowl with ½ cup of the cream sauce, season, taste, and cover.

To assemble, film the bottom of a 9- by 13- by 2-inch baking dish (the sort that slants to 8 by 12 inches on the bottom) with butter and oil. Cover the bottom with four 3- by 4-inch pieces of pasta. Spread half the chard filling evenly on top, then sprinkle with a handful of mozzarella.

Next layer, fit two 3- by 4-inch pieces and two 4- by 4-inch squares of pasta on the chard. Spread three quarters of the tomato filling on top and sprinkle with another handful of cheese.

The next layer of pasta is the same as the last. Cover it with the rest of the chard and another handful of cheese.

The next layer of pasta is 4 squares, then cover with all the mushroom filling and more cheese.

The final layer of pasta is the same as the last. Blend the remaining cream sauce and tomato mixture and smooth over the top, then sprinkle with the rest of the cheese.

Shake the pan to even things out. Either bake at once in a preheated 375°F oven until the top has browned richly and the sauce is bubbling, about 30 minutes, or cover and refrigerate for a few hours, then add about 10 minutes to the baking time if the lasagne is cold.

Serve hot or at room temperature with a sunny dry Italian white wine—Orvieto Secco or Soave, or California Chardonnay.

Stalks of Chard

Europe and Asia have taught us to prepare the leaves and stalks as separate vegetables. Chard stalks taste faintly of asparagus.

SPRIGHTLY CHARD STALKS: About 12 minutes before serving, barely cover the whole pieces with salted water in a large heavy skillet, cover, bring to a boil over high heat, turn heat to medium-low, and cook briskly until tender, 8 to 10 minutes. Drain (save the stock for another use) and slice on the diagonal about 3/8 inch thick. Sprinkle lightly with fruity olive oil, balsamic vinegar, salt, and cayenne pepper. Taste for seasoning, turn into small bowls, and serve with big spoons. Pass freshly grated Parmesan or Romano cheese on the side.

CHINESE ARTICHOKES

Alternative: Jerusalem artichokes cut into long small chunks.

These are fascinating little tubers that look like small whorled seashells. They are crunchy and taste like a sweet blend of artichoke, Jerusalem artichoke, and salsify. Their nutritional value is unknown. Harvest after the leaves die down and use at once since they dry out rapidly.

You can fuss with peeling the swirls, but the skin is thin and tasty—don't peel.

If you're serving them to company and you want their pearliness to glow, however, lay them in a tea towel, sprinkle coarse salt over them, and rub and rub—somewhat the way you rub the skins off blanched nuts. Rinse and rub off any remaining skin. Classically these little nubbins are blanched in a small amount of boiling salted water for about 5 minutes—save the delicious stock—then finished in butter or broth.

Few vegetables you'd serve could be more impressive than Chinese artichokes. Any recipe you find for Jerusalem artichokes can be adapted, but the simpler the better—don't smother their beauty in a cream sauce, for example. Braised Chinese artichokes—the tubers cooked until tender in rich meat or poultry juices—are a delectable accompaniment to a roast.

Think of them as decoration rather than as a dish unto themselves. Set off their whorled shapes against smooth shapes. Spoon braised Chinese artichokes in a ribbon over braised heads of romaine lettuce or whole bunches of celery or bunches of spinach. Also think of their crunch as an element in garnishes and sprinkle them over purees of a contrasting color such as carrots, sweet potatoes, and winter squashes. Wherever you'd use croutons, you can use Chinese artichokes.

CHINESE ARTICHOKE SALAD: As with Jerusalem artichokes, you can add the tubers raw to a delicate salad—fruit salads in particular. Here is a traditional French way with Chinese artichokes.

Simmer the cleaned tubers, adding a squeeze of fresh lemon juice and a drizzle of olive oil. When tender-crisp, drain and turn into a vinaigrette dressing (see recipe in The Cook's Notebook under Dressings) seasoned with a soupçon of dry mustard. Cool the tubers in the dressing, turning them occasionally to moisten all sides. This can be done several hours in advance.

Taking half as many small cherry tomatoes as you have Chinese artichokes, slice them into quarters or halves according to their size. Combine the tomatoes and tubers in their dressing in a colorful bowl. Sprinkle on a finely diced anchovy fillet for each serving, breaking apart any pieces that stick together. Toss with your hands to blend, taste for seasoning, and serve on red lettuce leaves sprinkled with chopped marjoram.

COLLARDS

The flavor of collards' large smooth dark green leaves is more mustardy than cabbage and less mustardy than turnip greens. It's very pleasant, and can even be sweet. Harvest by the leaf or take the whole head.

To prepare collards, bring a big pot of salted water with a glug of vinegar in it to a boil. Meanwhile, stack the collards and cut off their stems. Cook the stems separately: Chop the stems and turn them into a saucepan with a splash of vinegar. Cover with cold water, sprinkle with salt, and simmer, loosely covered, until tender—about a quarter more time than it will take to cook the greens. Add water if needed.

Cut the leaves crosswise into ribbons from 1/4 to 1 inch wide or tear the leaves into large bite-size pieces, according to the recipe. Drop into the boiling water and simmer uncovered until tender, from 1 to 40 minutes, depending on the size of the leaves, their age, and their venue. With a sieve, lift the leaves out, shaking off excess moisture. Save the pot liquor for cooking black-eyed peas. Collards need only the seasoning of a sprightly vinegar and hot pepper sauce if it's to your liking.

Collards are major players on the nutritional field, high on the list of vegetables thought to be cancer fighters. Add ribbons of tender leaves to salad.

Sara Belk, in her superb *Around the Southern Table,* calls for a dressing of warmed walnut oil, red wine vinegar, and chopped toasted walnuts—marvelous. I also love Hoppin' John Taylor's suggestion to heat leftover collards in a skillet with roasted peanuts and crushed red peppers. Brown diced ham in the skillet first, then add the greens, peanuts, and peppers, serve it over rice, and have cold sliced tomatoes on the side—a terrific supper.

For a satisfying main-dish salad, mix drained cooked beans—white, red, and black together—with cooked collards and dress with oil and vinegar.

SIMPLE COLLARDS: (makes 2 servings). The color of cooked collards—when your eye has been accustomed to brilliant greens—is army drab. But seasoned this way, who cares?

Cook 3 cups (about 1/2 pound) collard leaves. Strew the tender stems over the leaves. Dress with 2 tablespoons extra-virgin olive oil, 2 teaspoons rice vinegar, and 2 minced garlic cloves. Season with salt and cayenne or freshly ground black pepper.

Serve with rice and corn bread and some sort of fish or fowl or meat if you wish.

Corn

We harvest corn at two stages. The milk or green stage is when the kernels are so soft they spurt a milky substance when you pierce them with a thumbnail—it's the equivalent of the snap stage in beans. There's no shelly stage with corn, so the second stage is when the kernels are so hard a thumbnail can't make a dent—this is the dried stage, the same as with dried beans.

The best way to cook corn at the milk stage, in my opinion, is to microwave it just as it comes from the stalk. Set unhusked ears around the perimeter of the microwave oven but not touching the walls or each other. Cook at full power for 2 to 7 minutes per ear, depending on the size of the ears and your oven. The time increases geometrically as you add ears, so it's unpredictable. Just have everything else in the meal about ready before you start the corn. Give each ear a quarter turn every couple of minutes and rotate all the ears every 4 minutes. The corn is done when you can smell it. Serve with butter and perhaps some shredded grating cheese.

Before I had a microwave, I lined the bottom of a large skillet with corn husks and added an inch of water and a splash of milk (no salt). When the liquid boiled, I laid in the ears (no husks or silks this time), clapped on the lid, and steamed them for 4 to 5 minutes. Milk brings out the sweet corn flavor. Except for heritage open-pollinated sorts, today's hybrid sweet corn fresh from the garden wants no more than a minute of boiling.

To cut fresh kernels from the cob, stand the ear in a shallow bowl. Use a sharp chef's knife to cut the kernels into the bowl, then use a flat-edged spoon to scrape down the remaining pulp and cornmilk.

Corn needs companions at table to give you its full nourishment. It's high in protein but lacks certain elements that make the protein useful—so eat beans with your corn and you've got it. Similarly, corn contains niacin, but it's locked up and useless on its own. Mixed with the alkalinity of lime to make tortillas, the niacin is freed. The question is, how did the people in whose backyard corn was a native learn to eat their corn this way? Corn also offers a moderate amount of fiber and folic acid and small amounts of vitamin C, magnesium, phosphorus, and thiamine.

When corn kernels are mixed with other ingredients—blending their sweetness with other voices—I enjoy any seasoning that doesn't drown out those voices. But when kernels are pure on the cob? Shreds of mild cheddar cheese sprinkled over the rows as I chomp and slurp up and down are all I want. Past cheese, I can think of nothing that ought to mantle their golden or creamy little shoulders except butter.

Sweet corn is one of the tastes I never tire of and can't imagine sullying. Raspberries, garden peas, and peaches are others.

In Thailand, *kao pot ping* is husked ears of corn dipped several times in coconut milk while roasting over charcoal. A quick coconut milk is made with the blender: On medium speed, whirl 2 parts dried shredded unsweetened coconut with 1 part boiling water for 20 seconds. Strain the liquid through a cloth, squeezing hard, and lightly salt the milk (discard the coconut).

Don't forget that corn eaten raw off the cob fresh off the stalk is superb. That's how Mayans ate their maize as they tramped along the road. Remember to cut tender raw kernels of corn into salad.

Sweet Corn

Harvested at the milk stage, standard open-pollinated or hybrid corn should be cooked as little as possible. Taste a few kernels at the tip. If they're not starchy, just pass them through the heat—like the bottle of vermouth over the martini glass. Heat presses the conversion of corn sugar to starch, so the more cooking, the tougher the kernels become.

If you grow and dry kernels of Black Aztec—surprisingly a sweet corn—grind them into meal and make the corn sticks under Dent Corn.

The following two recipes are pure and delicious. I like to cook delicate white corn on top of the stove and to pull somewhat richer yellow corn from the oven. But of course you can cook any color of kernels either way.

SWEET WHITE CORN ON TOP OF THE STOVE: For each person, stand a freshly picked ear or two in a deep bowl and slice off the kernels. Turn the kernels into a small heavy skillet and for each ear slice off 1 to 2 tablespoons from a stick of unsalted butter into the pan (or add butter to taste). Cook over medium heat, stirring occasionally, until tender—3 to 5 minutes. Salt and pepper to taste, turn into a bowl, and eat with a big spoon with your eyes closed. Don't let anybody talk to you while you're doing it.

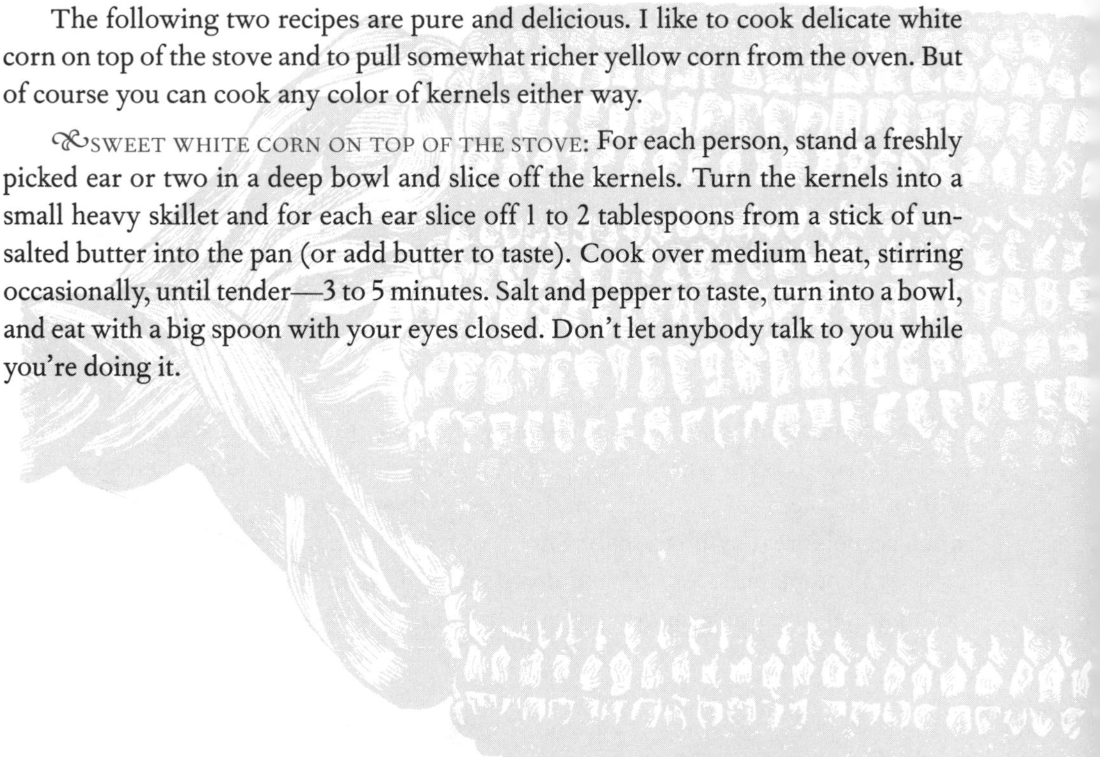

Sweet Yellow Corn in the Oven

MAKES 4 SERVINGS

4 large ears of yellow sweet corn
1 cup milk (low-fat is fine, as is half-and-half)
pinch of salt
freshly ground white pepper to taste
pinch or 2 of sugar if needed
generous 2 tablespoons unsalted butter
a little minced parsley

Heat the oven to 350°F. Scrape kernels from the cobs, making the first cut about two thirds of the way down the kernels, then using a spoon to scrape the rest into the bowl—you'll need about 3½ cups. Turn into a shallow baking dish, roughly 9 by 1½ inches, breaking up connected kernels.

Add the milk, salt, and pepper. Taste a few kernels. If they're not marvelously sweet, sprinkle sugar over them. Stir to blend, then shake the dish to even the corn. Top with flakes of butter. Bake until the kernels are tender and the top is lightly browned, 45 to 50 minutes. Sprinkle with parsley. Serve hot in small bowls with big spoons.

MAINE CORN CHOWDER: The best I ever had. Soften sliced onions in Canadian bacon drippings, then simmer with chunks of potatoes in water. When tender, stir in freshly cut corn (the same amount as the potatoes) and milk (the same amount as the water) and heat. Top the bowls with slivers of the hot Canadian bacon and shredded white cheddar cheese.

The best corn pancakes I ever had were sweet milk pancakes with so much fresh corn folded in that the batter barely held the cakes together (for every cup of flour in the batter, add 1 cup corn kernels). They were served with blueberry syrup.

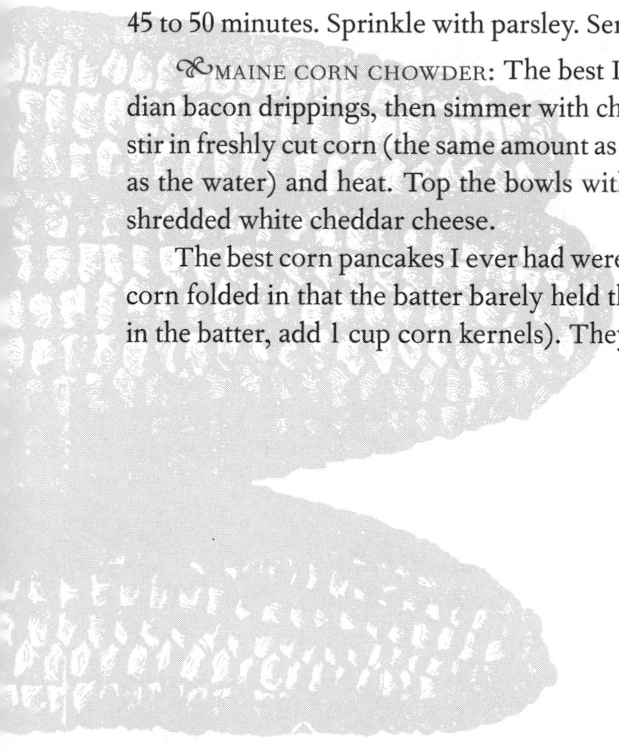

Good and Easy Fresh Corn Relish

MAKES ABOUT 4 CUPS TO SERVE 12 TO 16

One of the best corn relishes I ever tasted is this one. Don't bother putting it up because it will all be gone in a trice. A heap brightens up the palest food. Make this at least a few hours in advance so the flavors can mingle. It will keep refrigerated 7 to 10 days.

2 ears corn, kernels removed
1/4 cup cider vinegar
1/4 cup canola oil
2 ribs celery, finely chopped
1/2 red sweet pepper, cut into small dice, including some seeds
1/3 cup drained piccalilli or sweet pickle relish
3 whole scallions, thinly sliced
2 small fresh hot chilies, seeds removed, minced, or to taste
1 teaspoon dry mustard
1 teaspoon paprika
salt and freshly ground white pepper to taste

While you're preparing the remaining ingredients, simmer the corn in the vinegar and oil in a covered nonreactive skillet over medium-high heat until the kernels are tender-crisp, 3 minutes—shake the skillet frequently. Turn into a mixing bowl and cool. Combine with the remaining ingredients, then taste for seasoning. Chill before serving in a glass bowl.

Baby Corn

Baby corn, the wee ones you see packed expensively in jars, is nothing more exotic than standard corn (usually white because it's sweeter) grown so close together that the ears mature but are dwarfed—like mini-cauliflowers. Pick not long after the silks emerge, when you can feel the ear is no more than 3 inches long. The ears mature somewhat erratically, so if you want a great many of uniform length for putting up, grow a lot of plants.

Shuck these teenies, remove all silk, trim as needed, and rinse lightly.

Baby corn can be tossed briefly in butter until fragrant and hot and offered as a garnish for delicate poultry or meat. It's delightful raw on the hors d'oeuvre tray.

The classic way is to pickle them, but my crop of baby ears is always small. If yours is larger, multiply the recipe.

BABY CORN PICKLES: (makes 4 1-cup jars). Any baby vegetable can be pickled this easy way—try cucumbers, onions, carrots, green tomatoes, and eggplants. The pickling spice could be just mustard seeds or celery seeds.

Please read the canning notes in The Cook's Notebook.

In a bowl, combine 4 cups baby corn ears—as much the same size as possible—and 1 tablespoon plus ½ teaspoon pickling salt. Stir to mix and set in a cool place for 3 hours. Drain well, but do not rinse.

In a large nonreactive saucepan, blend 1 cup white vinegar (5 percent acidity), 1 cup sugar, and a rounded tablespoon of mixed pickling spice. Bring to a boil, stirring until the sugar dissolves. Add the corn and stir over medium-high heat until the ears are hot—remove from the heat before the syrup starts to boil.

At once use tongs to pack hot canning jars with the ears, then pour the syrup into the jars, leaving ½ inch of headspace with both corn and syrup. Slip a chopstick or thin plastic spatula up and down a few places inside the jars to force out any trapped air, wipe the tops of the jars clean, put on hot lids, and screw bands on firmly.

Process in a boiling water bath for 10 minutes, then cool and store.

Field Corn

Field corns are the rugged plants that give us cornmeal, corn flour, cornstarch, and all the glorious good things that come from them. These are the ancient corns, many with colorful kernels and cobs, all with robust flavor. Usually the corn we love fresh on and off the cob is sweet corn.

There are four sorts of field corn: dent, flint, flour, and pop. What distinguishes them is the amount and type of starch in the kernels. Each has its special use. Dent corn kernels have centers of soft starch with flint-hard exteriors, so they pucker when they dry—producing a dent. Flint corn is superhard and smooth through and through, with little if any soft starch in the kernel. Flour corn is just the opposite of flint—almost completely soft starch. A combination flour-dent-flint corn has been bred by Native Americans to have some of each sort of kernel on each ear. Popcorn is the smallest of the kernels, as hard as flint, and it retains a dot of moisture in the center so when it's heated the moisture turns to steam, and you know what happens.

Mostly field corn is raised to be eaten from the dried stage. But some—particularly dents—roast deliciously at the milk stage. That's why field corn that's tasty when young is called *roastin' ears*. So harvest whenever you please.

ROASTIN' EARS: For hundreds upon hundreds of years, ears of corn have been roasted in the ground. In the old Southwest, corn is still roasted in a pit or adobe oven in embers overnight. Here's a less romantic but easier way to get delicious lightly charred roasted corn.

Using any type of corn at the milk stage, pull back the husks, leaving them attached, and remove the silks. Smooth the husks back in place and tie around the ear with a ribbon of husk or string.

When your fire's about 30 minutes from being ready (when gray ash covers the coals—which I hope are mesquite or other tasty wood), cover the unhusked ears in a vessel with tepid water. After about 30 minutes, roast the soaked ears 6 inches above the coals, turning with tongs every 5 minutes so they're evenly cooked. They're ready when you can smell them, 10 to 30 minutes, depending on the fire, the corn, the wind, and how impatient you are. Don't rush it.

Or you can roast ears on the rack in the center of a preheated 300°F oven for about 45 minutes.

Remove the husks and serve at once with sweet butter, salt, and freshly ground white pepper.

TO SHUCK, WINNOW, AND STORE FIELD-DRIED KERNELS: First be sure both cob and kernels are bone-dry. Then get a big grocery bag. Put on gloves if your skin is tender. Holding them deep inside it, rub two ears together. If the kernels are as dry as they should be, soon some will skip off the cob, and you can turn the cobs as the kernels are chipped off.

Lay the kernels about ¼ inch deep on a tray with a 1- or 2-inch lip. Use a hair dryer or fan to blow off the debris. Best to use pure air, no heat. If you must use heat, apply it in 10-second bits, then cool the kernels.

Store dried kernels in an airtight moisture-proof container in a cupboard or the freezer until ready to grind them or turn them into hominy or use them for seeds.

GRINDING DRIED CORN: For the freshest, deepest-tasting corn sticks, corn bread, Italian sponge cake, and other rare treats, grind your dried corn yourself. First of all, try to grind only as much as you'll use that day: ¼ cup kernels yields about ⅓ cup fine meal. Once the integrity of the kernel is broken, oxidation begins, and flavor and nutrients suffer.

If you're going to be doing this regularly, invest in a Corona burr mill (available from Johnny's Select Seeds and a number of other seedsmen). Your corn won't be stone-ground, and you won't be able to grind it finely, but it will have a texture as close as you can get to the traditional—next to bending over a metate. A coffee mill will grind kernels beautifully, but it's not a great idea to start with the whole kernel. A blender set on grind is better. Best to send kernels through the Corona hand-turned grain mill first, then refine it in the blender or coffee mill. Grind small amounts, no more than ½ cup at a time unless your machine has a powerful motor.

Dent Corn

Dried dent corn kernels are good for hominy, grits, meal, tamales, tortillas, and flour. Dent kernels are easier to grind than flint.

Dent Corn and Ancho Chili Pudding

MAKES 5 TO 6 SERVINGS

At the milky or tender kernel stage, these are roastin' ears, called *elote* in the Southwest and Mexico. A classic way of cooking kernels of roastin' ears is to turn them into pudding—dent corn's starch thickens the pudding nicely. In Mexico it's called *budín de elote* and served with hot salsa or crème fraîche; in the Midwest and South it's called corn pudding and finished with a drizzle of butter.

Proportions of corn to eggs are much the same everywhere, but what differs is the amount of milk. Add less, and you can unmold this fragile beauty. Add more, and the pudding quivers on the spoon. You can coarsely puree the kernels to release their starch and have a smoother custard, or you can drop the kernels in as they come from the cob for a pleasing bumpy texture. You can add more butter or less. The sweet part is that every choice you make will give you heavenly pudding. Mine was inspired by Diana Kennedy's *budín*.

I untraditionally flavor my corn pudding with ancho chili, a large reddish brown dried chili that's mild, sweet, toasty, and fruity—perfect with corn. I finish the dish with shredded cheese. My husband and I divide one pudding between the two of us, it's that good. Of course you can make this with any fresh corn and any chili. The amount of chili I use adds a smoky dimension without dominating the corn. You can certainly make the pudding without chili, in which case if the field corn isn't sweet, add a pinch of sugar to make up for the missing chili's sweetness.

Serve with grilled fish or chicken, a colorful crisp salad, beer, and watermelon for dessert.

The pudding can be prepared several hours in advance of baking, but serve as soon as it comes from the oven.

To unmold this pudding onto a platter, butter the bottom of the dish, line it with wax paper, and butter the paper—*then* dredge with the crumbs.

Wear rubber gloves when you work with chilies. To keep the remaining reconstituted chili almost indefinitely, cover it in a jar with half vinegar, half water, then float 1/4 inch oil on top. Cover tightly and refrigerate.

1 ancho chili or to taste

2 cups freshly cut dent or other corn kernels, about 3 ears

1/2 cup milk (nonfat is fine)

2 tablespoons melted unsalted butter plus more for the dish

3 large eggs

1/2 teaspoon salt or to taste

3 tablespoons dry bread crumbs or unsalted cracker crumbs

about 1 1/2 cups thinly shredded Swiss or spicy grating cheese

To prepare the chili, slit the dried pod down the sides and discard the seeds. Drop into an inch of simmering water in a small saucepan and simmer, covered, for 5 minutes. Turn off the heat and let steep for 5 minutes. Lift out, pat dry with paper towels, chop finely, and reserve. This can be done several hours in advance.

Turn 1 cup of the corn, the milk, and the butter into a food processor. Pulse until you have a rough puree, about 10 strokes. In a mixing bowl, beat the eggs with a fork until the yolks and whites are blended. Add the corn puree, the whole kernels, 2 tablespoons of the chili, and the salt. Blend with the fork, trying not to incorporate air (it makes tiny bubbles in the custard). You can cover the bowl and chill at this point or proceed to bake.

To bake, have everything at room temperature. Heat the oven to 300°F, setting a heavy baking sheet (or 2 thin sheets stacked) on the lowest rack of the oven. Butter a 1-quart baking dish, then dredge it with some of the crumbs. Pour the pudding carefully into the baking dish, then shake to even out the ingredients. Sprinkle the top with the remaining crumbs.

Bake on the baking sheet until the pudding is puffed and gilded and the center is firm but has a moist air about it, 30 to 35 minutes—better to underbake than overbake.

Serve from the dish, passing the cheese on the side for garnishing the top.

At high altitude, bake at 320°F.

Buttermilk Blue Corn Sticks or Corn Bread

MAKES 21 CORN STICKS TO SERVE 10 TO 12

Make as many corn sticks as you have pans, because the breads freeze beautifully. These are crispy, light, and fill your mouth with an astonishingly deep and warm corn flavor—and the acid in the buttermilk intensifies the color. If corn stick pans are on your wish list, make corn bread. Of course you can make this corn bread with any color cornmeal.

2 large eggs, at room temperature
¼ cup mild oil such as canola
1 cup buttermilk, at room temperature
1 cup finely ground cornmeal, preferably from black or blue corn
1 cup all-purpose flour, lightly spooned into the cup
3 tablespoons sugar
2 teaspoons baking powder
½ teaspoon baking soda
1 teaspoon salt

Set the oven at 425°F. Brush 3 iron corn stick pans (7 sticks each) or a 9-inch iron skillet with oil and set in the oven. Add the eggs and 1/4 cup oil to the buttermilk in a bowl and whisk until blended. In another bowl, blend the remaining ingredients. Turn the dry ingredients into the liquids and whisk just until smooth.

Remove the pan or pans from the oven and spoon the batter into the corn stick molds, almost filling them—use all the batter. Or smooth the batter into the skillet. Bake in the middle of the oven until the corn sticks are golden—12 to 15 minutes—or until a toothpick emerges clean from the center of the corn bread, 20 to 25 minutes. Serve hot with butter.

At high altitude, bake just below 450°F and use ¾ teaspoon baking powder and ¼ teaspoon baking soda.

LAZY CORN MUSH: Just before she goes to bed, a friend mixes ½ cup freshly ground cornmeal with 2 cups boiling water in a wide-mouth thermos (preheated with boiling water for 15 minutes). She caps it, shakes it for a full minute, then sets it by. In the morning her breakfast mush is thick and hot and ready for honey, butter, a dash of cinnamon, and milk.

One large ear or two small ones provide enough kernels for 2¼ cups, 2 servings. Of course, you can use store-bought cornmeal, preferably from the health food store, since it will have the whole of the kernel.

Flint Corn

Alternatives: Dent and flour corn.

Just like dent corn, flint ears are roasted at the milk stage—or turned into chicos, under More Dried Corn. Dried flint kernels make fine hominy, kernels of white cultivars being favored.

Native Americans call it *pozole,* we call it hominy, and Mexicans call it *nixtamal*—dried kernels of corn that are treated with lime to soften them and remove their skins.

In Mexico, nixtamal corn is dried and then ground into masa—the makings of tortillas (the finest grind) and tamales (less finely ground).

Don't be alarmed by the lime. Remember, it acts as a nutritious catalyst. If you have sensitive skin, wear rubber gloves when working with the rinse waters. And don't let the fumes from the lime get into your eyes—they will irritate them. Other means of pulling off the skins are with lye—it's terribly caustic and I don't like it—and culinary ash, which is the traditional way. I once spent a week in Santa Fe and couldn't find culinary ash. No one had ever heard of it. They made their pozole the following way.

HOMINY/NIXTAMAL: Turn 4 cups dry white flint corn kernels into an enameled or stainless-steel pot (the right material is crucial). Cover with cold water by 1 inch. Dissolve 1 tablespoon powdered lime (calcium oxide, from a builders' supply store) in a little cold water. Pour through a strainer into the corn. Cover and cook over medium heat until bubbles float to the surface—do not let the water boil. Turn the heat to low, stir well, then simmer until the hulls soften and loosen from the kernels, 15 to 30 minutes—test by rubbing a few kernels in your hands. Let soak in this water overnight or up to 2 days.

Drain, then cover again with cool water. Use your hands to push off the skins gently. Continue draining and rinsing and worrying off the skins until the water is clear and no more (or few) skins remain.

For grinding, spread the kernels on towels to dry. To use as hominy, store moist kernels in a jar in the refrigerator, where they will keep for 2 weeks.

After this, the kernels still need cooking. Cover amply with cool water in a heavy pot, cover, and cook over low heat for 4 to 5 hours, or until puffed and tender. Then make pozole.

Pozole

MAKES 10 TO 12 SERVINGS

In the Southwest, pozole means not only hominy but also one of this country's most glorious dishes, a rich hominy-based stew. As with Yankee beef stew, every cook has his or her own recipe. The stew is cooked slowly until the pork falls apart and you can hardly bear to stay in the same house with the scent without running away with the pot. Here are the basics. Play with them and make the recipe your own. In the Southwest pozole is traditional for the Christmas holidays. Some quarters garnish their pozole with chopped raw cabbage and fresh limes; others wouldn't think of it.

This pozole recipe is essentially my recipe for carnitas with hominy added—with invaluable asides from pozole master Maureen Wagstaff.

Let this rest for a day or two before serving if you can. When it's hot it can wait in a low oven for an hour or more.

4 cups (1½ pounds) dried hominy
salt to taste
1 large onion, coarsely chopped
3 large garlic cloves, chopped
3 tablespoons fresh oregano leaves or 1 tablespoon crumbled dried
1 teaspoon ground cumin
1 teaspoon ground coriander
6 fresh thyme sprigs or 1 teaspoon crumbled dried
1 dried bay leaf
4 dried hot red chilies, seeds removed
4 pounds bone-in pork shoulder at room temperature, trimmed of fat
5 to 6 limes, quartered
cilantro sprigs for garnish

If you want tender rather than crunchy or chewy kernels, prebake the hominy in salted water for 2 hours following the recipe for dried beans, then proceed.

Heat the oven to 350°F. In a deep 4-quart casserole—preferably earthenware (a cazuela)—mix the hominy, salt (if not prebaked), onion, garlic, oregano, cumin, ground coriander, thyme, and bay. In a blender or with a mortar and pestle, grind the chilies and slowly add a little water to make a thin paste. Stir into the hominy. Set the meat in the center of the pot and add cold water to cover the meat. Cover and bake in the middle of the oven for 2½ hours.

Remove the lid, turn the heat to 275°F, and roast 3 more hours or until the meat is as soft as butter. Turn the meat over after 1½ hours, and add cool water as needed to keep the hominy covered.

Remove the bone, then use two forks to pull the meat into large shreds. Mix with the hominy. For more sauce, stir in cool water. Taste for seasoning. Cover and keep warm in a low oven until serving, or refrigerate and reheat.

Serve with limes for squeezing over the dish and sprigs of cilantro. Offer hot buttered tortillas, your favorite salsa, pickled chilies, and beer.

Flour Corn

Alternatives: Dent and flint corn.

These dried kernels grind to airy light flour, and the flour makes superb corn griddle cakes and others of their ilk.

Italian Cornmeal Sponge Cake

MAKES 10 TO 12 SERVINGS

If you're not off to Venice or you don't live near a baker with a nostalgia for the Veneto, you won't be able to taste this heavenly airy and lightly sweet cake made with freshly ground corn flour unless you bake it yourself. The corn, especially if it's richly flavored blue, contributes a haunting depth. This is an interesting cake to make, and it's easy, despite the directions. They're long so you'll be assured of baking a perfect cake for your friends. Don't expect a tall cake. In European tradition, it's about 2½ inches tall. Alas, it won't work at high altitude.

Wrapped airtight and kept in a cool place (not the refrigerator), the cake keeps for at least 3 days.

For the cake to be its lightest, you must use cake flour or southern White Lily flour. If it's hard to find, use ½ cup plus 2 teaspoons sifted all-purpose flour.

unsalted butter for the pan
½ tablespoon finely grated lemon zest
¾ cup plus 2 tablespoons sugar
½ cup plus 2 tablespoons sifted cake flour
½ cup sifted finely ground cornmeal, preferably blue
½ teaspoon plus ⅛ teaspoon baking powder
pinch of salt
7 extra-large eggs, warmed in their shells in a bowl of hot water
⅓ cup lukewarm water
2 tablespoons fresh lemon juice
½ teaspoon cream of tartar
confectioners' sugar
dried corn leaves and tassels from your corn patch for decoration, optional

Mixing speeds are for a portable mixer. With a standard mixer, lower the speed by one notch. Use the wire whip attachment, if available.

Heat the oven to 350°F. Butter the bottom of a 10-inch tube pan. To line the bottom, use the pan as a template and cut out a ring of wax paper. Smooth it into the bottom of the pan, then butter the paper. In a small bowl or a food processor, blend the lemon zest into ¾ cup of the sugar. Sift the flour, cornmeal, baking powder, and salt together onto a sheet of wax paper. Separate the eggs into 2 measuring cups. Save 1 yolk for another purpose—you'll need 1 cup whites but only ½ cup yolks. Turn the yolks into a large mixing bowl.

Beat the yolks at high speed until creamy. Continue beating while you trickle in the water and lemon juice. Beat until frothy and increased in volume, then continue beating while sprinkling in ¾ cup of the sugar a tablespoon at a time. Beat until, when you lift the beaters, the batter mounds up on the surface for a second or two and then sinks. Reserve.

Immediately beat the whites with clean beaters at low speed until frothy. Sprinkle in the cream of tartar and beat on medium speed until soft peaks form when you lift the beaters. Beat on high speed while sprinkling in the remaining 2 tablespoons sugar a tablespoon at a time. Beat until, when you lift the beaters, the peak holds, then drops.

Add a third of the whites to the yolks and blend in with a large rubber spatula. Sprinkle in the flour mixture and fold until almost but not quite completely blended in. Add the rest of the whites and fold the batter with the spatula to blend thoroughly. Smooth into the pan, slightly pushing the batter up against the center tube and the sides.

Bake in the center of the oven until a wooden toothpick emerges clean from the center of the cake, 35 to 45 minutes. Immediately turn the pan upside down over a cake rack.

The cake will probably drop from the pan by itself. If not, when cool, free the cake by running a long knife around the sides of the pan and the tube. Invert onto plastic wrap for storing or onto a platter (with a paper doily in place) for serving. Just before serving, shake confectioners' sugar through a sieve over the cake—ask someone to tilt the dish for you so you can drift the snow over the sides. Wreathe the platter with corn leaves and tassels if you have them and take the cake on a picnic.

Flour-Flint Corn

These remarkable all-in-one ears have become adapted to growing conditions as needed. Cooking them is a matter of experimenting with the ears of each plant since strains are so individual. Certainly you can roast milky ears, and you can make hominy and grind dried kernels to the texture best suited to their makeup.

Corn Fungus

Because I've never had the silvery fungus on my corn, I've never had the opportunity to prepare it. For those of you who have this windfall gift from the corn patch, here's Diana Kennedy's recipe from *The Art of Mexican Cooking*. Epazote is a wild strong-flavored herb.

TO PREPARE CUITLACOCHE: Unfurl the green husks around the ear of corn and discard. Pull off the fine strands of corn silk and discard. Cut the fungus and corn kernels that remain off the center core as closely as you can—do not shave them off by degrees, because this will spoil the texture. Remove any more stray bits of corn silk that were tucked inside and roughly chop the fungus. Weigh at this point.

To Cook Cuitlacoche

MAKES ABOUT 5 CUPS

Cooked by the following method, cuitlacoche can be used for *crepas, quesadillas, budín,* or in plain tacos.

3 tablespoons safflower oil

2 tablespoons finely chopped white onion

2 small garlic cloves, finely chopped

rajas (strips) of 4 poblano chilies

1½ pounds (about 6 cups) cuitlacoche

sea salt to taste

2 tablespoons roughly chopped epazote leaves

Heat the oil in a frying pan, add the onion and garlic, and fry gently until translucent—about 3 minutes. Add the chili strips and fry for 1 minute more. Add the cuitlacoche and salt, cover the pan, and cook over medium heat, shaking the pan from time to time, for about 15 minutes—the fungus should be tender, retaining some moisture, but not soft and mushy. Stir in the epazote and cook, uncovered, for another 2 minutes.

Note: If the cuitlacoche is rather dry, sprinkle on ¼ cup water before covering; if, on the other hand, it is too juicy, remove the lid before the end of the cooking time and reduce over higher heat.

Popcorn

Popcorn has been used traditionally by Native Americans both for popping and for pinole—toasted kernels that are ground. Harvest at the dried stage.

People in Central America popped corn for centuries in clay pots over an open fire. In the Rodale test kitchens, comparisons were made with various methods of popping. Popcorn popped in a hot-air popping machine gave the best results, yielding the most kernels popped with the best flavor. Corn popped in a heavy pot on top of the stove yielded almost as much, but the kernels had an oily flavor. Kernels popped in a popper designed for the microwave were the driest, but the yield was less. They even popped in a wok, but it wasn't satisfactory.

Caramel Corn

MAKES A GENEROUS 4 QUARTS TO SERVE 8 TO 10

Here it is, folks, the best caramel corn you ever ate. If you can find a place to hide it, this keeps for at least a couple of weeks in a tin in a dry place.

- 4 quarts popped corn
- 1 cup granulated sugar
- ⅔ cup firmly packed light brown sugar
- ½ cup dark corn syrup
- ½ cup water
- ½ teaspoon salt
- 4 tablespoons unsalted butter
- ½ teaspoon baking soda
- 1 teaspoon vanilla extract

Heat the oven to 250°F. Spread the popcorn on a large shallow baking sheet and set it in the oven. In a large heavy saucepan over medium heat, stir the granulated sugar, brown sugar, corn syrup, and water until the sugar dissolves. Cover and boil for 1 minute, then uncover and continue cooking without stirring at a steady low boil until a little syrup dropped into cold water forms a firm ball (290°F on a candy thermometer), about 5 minutes. Stir in the salt and cook until a little dropped into cold water now cracks (300°F), another minute or so. Remove from the heat and blend in the butter, baking soda, and vanilla—it will foam up.

Pull out the popcorn and drizzle the syrup over it, stirring constantly with a wooden spoon (don't let the syrup touch your skin; it will burn). Stir until all the popcorn has been coated, then return to the oven and bake for 45 minutes, stirring 2 or 3 times. When cool, store airtight in a cool place.

Once, for a Valentine's Day present, I added ½ cup cinnamon hots to the syrup—delicious.

More Dried Corn

Of course the easiest way to dry corn is on the stalk in the field—let Mother Nature do it for you. But hand-dried kernels have a deeper flavor. You can dry all sorts of corn—some for grinding into flour, some for meal, and some to soak overnight and use in the manner of fresh corn. Store the kernels in tight jars in a cool dry place.

To use dried corn, soak 1 cup in 2 cups boiling water for at least 1 hour, then add salt and simmer, uncovered, over low heat for about 30 minutes—stir occasionally and watch for scorching. Flavor with a little butter, sugar, and salt, then finish with a bit of cream. Or reconstitute in milk, cooking very slowly until tender.

Just think how long corn-drying rituals have been performed in this country. Native Americans toasted corn kernels that had already dried in the field until the kernels were crunchy and the color of walnuts. The early settlers boiled husked ears of corn in the milk stage, cut the kernels from the cob, and roasted them slowly until they were dry and the color of walnuts.

CHICOS: Choose flavorful cultivars—those that are blue or blue-black certainly should be included. Use unhusked sweet or field corn at the milk stage straight from the garden. Roast on a rimmed baking sheet in a 350°F oven until the kernels are bone-dry when you try to pierce them with a thumbnail, about an hour. Turn the ears once or twice. Remove from the oven.

When cool, discard the silk, pull back the husks, and hang the ears by their husks in a cool dry place. Wait until you need kernels before you take them from the cob.

Cucumbers

Harvest cucumbers with scissors so as not to tear the vines. Pick gherkins at 1 to 3 inches, lemon cucumbers at plum size, picklers shiny green and 3 to 4 inches, American slicers at 7 to 8 inches, Beit Alpha slicers at 5 inches, and West Indian gherkins no longer than the first joint on your thumb. Just pick 'em, rub the dust off on your jeans, and proceed from there. To cook cucumbers—delicate and delicious—see the recipe further on in this entry. Cucumbers are the bonbons of the kitchen garden: scant redeeming nutritional value but wonderfully refreshing. They're mostly water.

Gherkin/Cornichon Cucumbers

RUSSIAN SLIGHTLY SALTED GHERKINS: This recipe is for the little-finger-size cucumbers called *gherkins*. It will work as well with pickling cucumbers, but don't let them get too large, or their skins will be tough. The Russians call these *ogurtzi*.

After 24 hours the pickles have a crisp innocence. At the end of a week, they're roundly salty. I say catch them early.

For each 16 (1 pound) gherkins you'll need 1 pint of brine made by dissolving 1 tablespoon pickling salt and ½ teaspoon sugar in 2 cups cool water. Thoroughly rinse 2- to 3-inch gherkins. Line the bottom of a scrupulously clean crock or jar with rinsed grape, black currant, or deciduous oak leaves (the leaves add crispness). Arrange a single layer of gherkins, dill or fennel sprigs to cover, and more leaves. Continue in this manner, finishing with leaves. Pour the brine over the stack. Fit a 1-gallon freezer-weight plastic food storage bag in another and fill with water. Set on top as a weight to keep everything submerged—the brine must come at least 2 inches above the leaves. Keep in a cool place from 24 hours to 1 week. One pound makes a scant 3 cups.

Fish out the pickles and serve with small glasses of iced vodka. Refrigerate pickles in the brine, but eat them up, because eventually they'll be too salty to enjoy.

Lemon Cucumbers

Alternative: Small slicing cucumbers.

The size and shape of a lemon and pale yellow, these are meant for eating simply.

I love the roundness of a lemon cucumber in my hand. Of a summer morning I may go out to the vine in my nightgown and bare feet to pluck a fruit, sit down on a log, and take a long, deep, cool crunchy bite. As the small round fruit settles into my hand, sometimes I think about the cucumbers farmers grew 3,000 years ago on land that would be India, and I wonder whether any of them were golden.

SZECHWAN LEMON CUCUMBERS: If you want to make them fancy, slice unpeeled lemon cucumbers into a glass or pottery bowl and grind on Szechwan peppercorns (from an Asian market) that you have first lightly roasted in a dry heavy skillet over low heat until you can smell their fragrance. (Spicy Malabar pepper makes a good alternate.) Serve with chopsticks.

SIMPLE SALADS: Wedges of lemon cukes and wedges of cooked beets make a spiffy salad with fresh dill and vinaigrette. Or pair them with halved cherry tomatoes the same way.

Pickling Cucumbers

Picklers are squat and warty and hold their crispness. Pick 3 to 4 inches long and shiny green. Rinse these well before proceeding with a recipe.

Kosher Dill Pickles

MAKES 4 TO 5 QUARTS

The families of many American Jews emigrated from Russia and Poland, bringing an affection for dill pickles with them. Irving Brecher wrote *Go West* for the Marx Brothers and other comedy classics. If Brecher weren't famous for his writing, he'd be famous for his pickles.

To connoisseurs, "new dill" is the pickle of choice. That's a cucumber that has been in brine for about a week. The longer it's processed, the less crisp.

Brecher writes, "Select only the very firm cukes, dark green . . . if the raised warts are brownish, reject them." Brecher uses a 5-gallon crock. When I made half the recipe with 3 pounds of cucumbers, I found that a 5-quart crock was just right, so 3 gallons really should be big enough. However, air is the great spoiler in brining, so there must be 2 cups of solution above the cucumbers at all times.

Brecher has always used packaged pickling spice. I like the pickling herbs and spices called for in old Jewish cookbooks. For this recipe I blend 6 tablespoons mustard seeds, 12 dried bay leaves (crumbled), 4 3-inch dried red chili peppers (crumbled, seeds included), 48 allspice berries, 48 whole black peppercorns, 4 teaspoons ground coriander (when I have the whole seeds, I use 1/4 cup instead), and an egg-size piece of unpeeled fresh ginger, grated.

Once they have cured, the pickles will keep under refrigeration and remain crisp for at least 5 weeks. In fact, a pickle from my first batch got lost in the refrigerator and was marvelous a year later. Be sure to remove a thin slice from the blossom end of cucumbers, because they contain an enzyme that can cause spoiling.

30 to 40 (6 to 7 pounds) very fresh pickling cucumbers of uniform size, 3 to 4 inches long

6 or more (I use 10) fresh dill stalks, cut into short pieces

1 1/3 cups mixed pickling spice, 1/4 pound

10 large garlic cloves, peeled and thinly sliced

6 1/2 quarts water

1 1/2 cups kosher salt or 1 cup pickling salt

Soak the cucumbers in cold water for a few minutes to clean them. Line the bottom of the crock with dill. Sprinkle pickling spices and garlic on it. Place a double layer of cukes on top—do not pack too tightly. Repeat until all cukes are in the crock, topping off with dill, spices, and garlic.

Stir 6 quarts of the water and salt together until the salt has dissolved, making the water clear. Pour this brine into the crock, covering the cucumbers by at least 2 inches. Place a dish on top and on the dish a 12-ounce weight—just enough to hold the cukes beneath the brine (for the weight, see the recipe for gherkins or sauerkraut). Cover with a cloth and set in an airy place at around 75°F.

In 3 days, add 2 cups water to the brine. In 6 or 7 days, the cukes should have changed color. Try one. How much longer to cure them depends on your taste. When they're right, pack closely in jars, including lots of the dill and spices if desired, and cover with brine.

Refrigerate, covered. They'll keep for months—a year!

Slicing Cucumbers

Slicing cucumbers come in all lengths, including the superlong from Asia. A good rule for maximum quality is to pick them shorter than the length given in the seed packet. The only way to know if a cuke is ready is to slice into it and taste.

Cold Russian Cucumber Soup

MAKES 8 OR MORE SERVINGS

The Slavs have many wonderful ways with cucumbers. There are as many versions of okrochka—cold Russian summer soup—as there are of beet borscht, but cucumbers and kvass are constant ingredients. Kvass is a lusty brew fermented from black bread, and friends who've dined on okrochka many times in Moscow suggest malt liquor and apple juice to approximate kvass's flavor.

This keeps for a week if not gobbled up first.

2 large slicing cucumbers, peeled only if the skin is bitter
a dozen large sorrel or spinach leaves, pulled from their ribs
1 quart plain yogurt
2 cups malt liquor
1 cup unsweetened unfiltered apple juice
4 medium-size new potatoes, cooked, peeled, and cut into thick matchsticks
2 hard-cooked eggs, chopped
6 whole scallions, thinly sliced
2 rounded tablespoons chopped fresh dill or 2 teaspoons crumbled dried
salt and freshly ground black pepper to taste
4 or 5 small whole beets, cooked, peeled, cut into thin matchsticks, and chilled

Liquefy half a cucumber in a food processor or blender. Add the leaves and process until they are specks. In a 4-quart serving bowl, whisk this mixture with the yogurt, malt liquor, and apple juice until smooth. Thinly slice the remaining cucumbers, then cut the slices into quarters. Stir them into the soup with the potatoes, eggs, scallions, and dill. Season to taste, then cover and refrigerate until cold, at least 5 hours. Garnish the center of each bowl with a heap of beets. Serve with black bread and more malt liquor.

Turkish Cucumber Salad

MAKES 4 SERVINGS

Perhaps because of their translucent sweetness, cucumbers are paired all over the world with something thick, pale, and creamy—sour cream, crème fraîche, yogurt. To my taste, this simple salad is cucumber salad nonpareil. With dark peasant bread, olive oil for moistening the bread, bowls of black olives, cherry tomatoes, and toasted walnuts, you'll have quite a meal.

This can become a refreshing cold soup if you use half as many cucumbers and four times as much yogurt.

You can prepare this several hours in advance and chill it. It's delicious for 3 to 4 days.

2 medium-large slicing cucumbers, peeled only if the skin is bitter, cut into small dice

a thread of olive oil

a large handful of dark raisins

a small handful of chopped fresh mint

½ cup plain yogurt (nonfat is fine), chilled

salt and freshly ground white pepper to taste

bright flowers such as nasturtiums for garnish

Combine the cucumbers, olive oil, raisins, and mint in a salad bowl, preferably glass. Add yogurt and mix with a wooden spoon. Add salt and pepper, taste for seasoning, cover, and refrigerate until cold. Serve in soup plates with flowers on top.

Salad of Cooked Cucumbers in the Greek Style as Made by the French

MAKES 4 TO 6 SERVINGS

This composition is another Mediterranean way with cucumber salad—an example of how delicious cooked slicing cukes can be. They are delicately flavored—don't make them for people who must have lusty tastes. A Belgian friend who loves them suggests they'd be a great change for salad on a hot summer night. If you want to make this for a crowd with mixed tastes, pass a bottle of balsamic vinegar on the side.

Prepare this 24 hours in advance—but the salad will keep tasty at least a week.

2 large unpeeled crisp salad cucumbers, quartered lengthwise and trimmed to be even

2 celery ribs

2 fennel ribs or slender carrots

3 fresh thyme sprigs

3 fresh bay leaves or 1 dried

1½ cups chicken broth or vegetable stock
1½ cups water
½ cup olive oil
½ cup fresh lemon juice
good pinch of ground coriander
salt and freshly ground white pepper to taste
marigold petals for garnish

Turn the cucumbers into a nonreactive skillet in which the pieces just fit. Slice the celery and fennel (or carrots) in half lengthwise. Lay the celery, fennel, thyme, and bay on top of the cucumbers. Add the chicken broth, water, olive oil, lemon juice, and coriander. Simmer uncovered until the cucumbers are tender-crisp, 5 to 8 minutes. Lift the vegetables into a serving dish, reduce the cooking liquor to half by boiling hard, then pour it over the salad. Add salt and pepper, then taste for seasoning. Marinate in a cool place for 4 to 24 hours, then serve sprinkled with the petals of marigolds.

West Indian Gherkins

These are fuzzy-prickly little barrel-shaped devils with soft insides that absorb pickling solutions wonderfully. It's possible your great-grandmother grew these to make her sweet pickles.

These can be eaten out of hand, of course, but they've been valued for their pickling quality for generations.

Golden Sweet West Indian Gherkin Pickles

MAKES ABOUT 7 PINTS

Please read details on canning in The Cook's Notebook.

5 quarts West Indian gherkins, rinsed
10 cups sugar
3 cups cider vinegar, 5 percent acidity
2 cups white vinegar, 5 percent acidity
2 heaping tablespoons pickling salt
1 heaped teaspoon turmeric
2 tablespoons plus 1 teaspoon mustard seeds

Days 1–4: Cover the gherkins in a vessel with boiling water, then pour it off. Wrap and refrigerate.

Day 5: In a nonreactive saucepan, blend the sugar, vinegars, salt, and turmeric over medium-high heat, stirring until the sugar dissolves. Bring the syrup to a boil and pour it over the gherkins in a heatproof nonreactive 8-quart vessel. Cover and refrigerate.

Day 6: Drain the syrup into its saucepan, bring to a boil, and pour over the gherkins. Cover and refrigerate.

Day 7: Heat seven 1-pint wide-mouth canning jars in boiling water. Pour the syrup into a saucepan and bring to a boil while you pack the gherkins into the jars—leave ½ inch of headspace. Sprinkle 1 teaspoon mustard seeds into each jar, then pour in the boiling syrup, observing the headspace. Run a chopstick or other non-metal implement up and down in the jar in a few places to force up any air bubbles. Wipe the rims and threads clean, place hot lids on, and screw the bands on firmly. Process for 5 minutes in a boiling water bath. Cool and store.

EGGPLANT

Harvest eggplants while the skin is glossy and the fruits are about half the size of the seed packet's description. Small eggplants, no matter what type, are of the finest quality. Always cut the fruit from the plant.

The flesh of eggplants is enormously versatile, tasting like rich meat one minute, creamy sauce the next. They are low in fat and also skimpy in the nutrition department—a little folic acid. Rinse them lightly.

Eggplant soaks up fat like a sponge, so the trick is to avoid cooking it in fat whenever possible. Often in Mediterranean recipes it's customary to sprinkle cuts of eggplant with salt and let them steep awhile before cooking. This coaxes out bitter juices or excess moisture, and the flesh absorbs less oil. I don't do this because I don't find our eggplants bitter or wet. I also don't brown eggplant in inches of oil. Instead, I film a cast-iron or heavy nonstick skillet with oil, heat it over moderately high heat, then add the eggplant pieces and move them around and turn them like crazy until they're a pleasing color.

Do not prepare eggplants with carbon-steel implements or cook them in aluminum—the flesh will discolor.

Roasted eggplant is delicious, rendering the flesh soft and sweet. Should you ever roast the fruits in a convection oven, prick them first, or they'll explode. Ask how I know.

Asian Eggplants

Alternative: Small European eggplants.

These are the long, slender and small round shapes.

The beguiling little round green-striped eggplants may be seedy, but that just makes them crunchy beneath the softness of their cooked flesh. They should be harvested no bigger than a large walnut, then the stem and cap sliced off. I like to quarter them from top to bottom and add them to any mixed-vegetable stir-fry or sauté. They're ready in about 15 minutes. Sweet and nutty.

Small round Thai and Hmong red and orange eggplants are also seedy and crunchy and sometimes bitter. They're considered a great delicacy in Asian cuisines. All of these add considerable interest to a stir-fry.

Cold Pickled Small Asian Eggplants

MAKES 4 TO 5 SERVINGS

Pickled eggplant is popular in Asia. Instead of always stir-frying the small ones, pickle them.

This must be prepared several hours before serving. It may be to your taste a day later—save a piece or two to see.

16 plum-size (1 pound) round green or 5 (1 pound) long dark Asian eggplants
1 teaspoon salt
3 tablespoons mild oil
3 tablespoons rice vinegar
2 tablespoons sugar
1 tablespoon low-sodium soy sauce
a little finely chopped Thai or sweet basil

Use a vegetable peeler to peel the eggplants. Cut the small round ones into quarters or cut the larger long eggplants into small chunks. As you go, turn the eggplant into a bowl and sprinkle with salt. Let steep for about 10 minutes. Turn the eggplant into a towel and squeeze out the liquid. Rinse and dry the bowl and return the pieces to it.

In a small saucepan, bring everything but the basil to a boil and pour the mixture over the eggplant. Taste for seasoning. Cover and refrigerate until chilled, at least 4 hours. Serve sprinkled with basil as an accompaniment to hot rice.

European Eggplants

These are the large teardrop and round eggplants, which are meaty.

Sicilians, too, are fond of a tart-sweet blend. It's marvelous as the finish of caponata, sautéed diced unpeeled eggplant, celery, red onions, and tomatoes piqued with capers, green olives, wine vinegar, and a sprinkling of sugar.

Farther north up the coast there's the luminous Provençal ratatouille—from *touiller,* to mix or stir—cubes of eggplant, tomatoes, onions, sweet peppers, zucchini, and garlic simmered in olive oil and herbs. Farther south in Morocco, sautéed eggplant and tomato are blended with garlic, paprika, and cumin. In all these mixtures each vegetable is cooked separately, then all are combined and cooked until nearly the texture of preserves.

And from lands between the Adriatic and the Sea of Okhotsk comes a spread my father adored that his Russian-born mother taught my mother, who taught me. Peasant Caviar is eggplant roasted slowly overnight, peeled, and the flesh whipped to a coarse puree with a little olive oil, lemon juice, and chopped onion. In the Middle East, garlic replaces the onion, and parsley is often added. Bulgarian friends tell me that in Sofia they add chopped roasted almonds. There's something eerily ancient about this.

Now that you have a sense of eggplant caviar, see the Golden Zucchini Caviar recipe under Squash.

Turkish Eggplant Cream

MAKES 6 SERVINGS

The most unusual and perhaps the most sensuous way I've tasted eggplant was at a seaside café in Turkey, where a startlingly white puree of eggplant was served beneath a sweet-spiced lamb stew. In individual bowls, the creamy puree makes an intriguing side dish with grilled meat and poultry. It's called Hünkâr Beğenodi, Sultan's Delight. It can be prepared in advance, refrigerated, then reheated gently over boiling water.

- 3 small (2½ pounds) European or 10 (2½ pounds) Asian eggplants
- 1½ tablespoons fresh lemon juice
- 2 tablespoons butter, preferably unsalted
- 2 tablespoons fruity olive oil
- ¼ cup all-purpose flour
- ½ cup whole or low-fat milk
- 1 large egg
- ½ cup finely shredded Gruyère or Swiss cheese or ¼ cup freshly grated Parmesan
- pinch of ground cinnamon
- salt and freshly ground white pepper to taste

To preserve their whiteness, steam the eggplants whole—pricking them first—until they have collapsed and the flesh tests meltingly tender with a thin skewer, 15 to 30 minutes. For a deeper color and the sexy undertaste of smoke (and speckles of char), roast the eggplants directly on gas burners or under the broiler at its hottest setting, turning frequently with tongs, until the flesh tests tender. Either way, lift the eggplant onto a plate, slit open, and cover with a towel until cool enough to scoop the flesh into a bowl. (Some say the juice that pools on the plate is bitter, but I always add it, not to waste a drop of flavor.)

Beat the lemon juice into the flesh in the bowl, then puree it in a food processor or through the coarse blade of a food mill until smooth. Cover and reserve.

In a large saucepan over medium heat, melt the butter with the olive oil, then whisk in the flour. Cook over very low heat for 2 minutes, stirring occasionally. Whisk in the puree, then the milk. Cook over very low heat for 10 minutes, stirring occasionally. Beat in the egg, then the cheese and cinnamon. When the cheese has melted, remove from the heat and add salt and pepper. Taste for seasoning and serve at once or cool, refrigerate, and then warm up.

Sicilian Caponata

MAKES A GENEROUS 8 CUPS TO SERVE ABOUT 32

Caponata, a Sicilian classic, is to me one of the great mixes of flavors in this world. It takes some doing, but it's worth every second—a friend's help makes it go faster. If you have a pressure canner, you can put caponata up for keeping—double the recipe in that case. This is the perfect summer appetizer and a great gift.

A jar of caponata with oil floating on top will keep for 10 days in the refrigerator. You can also freeze it for up to 4 months, although the texture is altered somewhat.

The trick of this extraordinary mix is that each element is prepared individually for the final roasting.

a few tablespoons olive oil

8 cups (about 2 large) unpeeled eggplant cut into 1-inch dice

1½ cups (2 medium) onions cut into ½-inch dice

2 cups (4 ribs) celery sliced crosswise ½ inch thick

1 dozen small (1 pound) plum tomatoes, dropped into boiling water, lifted out, and peeled

2 cups thick plain tomato sauce

1½ cups (½ pound) pimento-stuffed green olives, drained

½ cup (¼ pound) drained capers

½ cup firmly packed chopped fresh basil leaves

1 teaspoon pressed garlic
½ cup dry red wine
½ cup cider vinegar
1 tablespoon sugar
salt and freshly ground black pepper to taste

Film a couple of heavy vessels—a wok and a cast-iron skillet, for example—with olive oil. Lightly brown the eggplant in them over medium-high heat, stirring frequently—5 to 6 minutes. Turn the eggplant into a bowl and brown the onions in one of the vessels the same way, about 5 minutes. Cook the celery in the other pan over medium heat until tender-crisp—also about 5 minutes—toss frequently; if necessary, add a little water.

Heat the oven to 325°F. In a 3-quart baking dish, mix all the ingredients except the salt and pepper. Bake uncovered until the celery is nearly tender if you're going to can it, tender if you're going to refrigerate or freeze it—plus or minus 1 hour. Stir frequently. Add salt and pepper and taste for seasoning.

Either pack into jars, float ¼ inch olive oil on top, and refrigerate or freeze or pressure-can: Pack into hot pint jars leaving 1 inch of headspace and filming the tops with olive oil. Process for 30 minutes, following the directions that come with the canner.

Serve at room temperature on thin unsalted crackers.

Florence Fennel/Common Fennel

Alternative: Celery with fennel seeds.

Florence fennel has a fat celerylike head with great feathery fronds. Harvest the whole plant when the bulb is no more than 3 inches across. Cut off the leaves where the ribs start getting tough—deeper green is an indication. Set the ribs in a jug of cold water and use the leaves as seasoning. Rinse the bulb. You can use it whole or pull off ribs individually as you would celery. When you cut the bulb lengthwise for serving portions, be sure to leave the heart intact so it will hold the ribs together. Cook any way you like, but few things are more delicious roasted with poultry or meat than whole bulbs of baby fennel. Just trim off the leaves and lay the bulbs in the pan and baste with pan juices. Doesn't matter that they cook to softness (about 1 hour) rather than tender crispness. Fennel is an excellent source of vitamin C, a moderate source of iron and vitamin A, and a fair source of calcium and magnesium.

Fennel can be cut into slices clean through until the time it prepares to send up a flower. Then—as with leeks—it forms a hard core. If this should be happening to your bulb, just pull off the translucent leaves from the woody rib and discard it.

But then, should it flower, fennel flowers are edible and fennel-flavored.

Fennel is one of the rare plants that likes being sown in the heat of the summer and is ready for the table in chilly winter—no surprise it grows wild all over Greece and southern Italy and that both cuisines celebrate their fennel.

FOR AN ITALIAN FENNEL SALAD FOR TWO PEOPLE: Thinly slice 1 medium-size Florence fennel bulb and 1 unpeeled sweet orange. Arrange—alternating and overlapping or however you like—on two salad plates. Strew with half a dozen salt-cured or Kalamata olives, and sprinkle each plate with ½ tablespoon extra-virgin olive oil, a few drops of fresh lemon juice, a teaspoon of finely chopped young fennel leaves, salt and freshly ground white pepper. Serve at once or let the ingredients mingle an hour or two. Warn about the pits in the olives.

Fennel, Mushroom, and Parmesan Cheese Salad

MAKES 4 FIRST-COURSE SERVINGS

Florence fennel lends itself to invention—for example, this uncommonly decorative and delightful salad of raw fennel inspired by Paul Bertolli in *Chez Panisse Cooking*.

You can prepare the dressing an hour or two in advance, but the salad ingredients won't keep pristine for more than half an hour.

DRESSING (MAKES ½ CUP)
½ cup less 1 tablespoon mild olive oil
2 tablespoons fresh lemon juice
salt and freshly ground white pepper to taste
a tiny pinch of nutmeg, preferably freshly grated
1 firmly packed tablespoon finely snipped feathery fennel leaves

4 small bulbs (½ pound) of translucent Florence fennel, sliced paper-thin

1 ounce Parmesan cheese, shaved paper-thin with a cheese slicer or vegetable peeler

4 plump mushrooms, about 1 ounce each, sliced paper-thin—keep each mushroom separate

freshly ground white pepper to taste

Use a fork to blend the dressing ingredients in a small bowl. Taste for seasoning. Cover and keep in a cool place.

Combine the fennel and cheese in a mixing bowl. Beat the dressing to blend it and add ¼ cup to the bowl. Blend carefully with your hands—the cheese tends to sink to the bottom, and you don't want to end with just crumbles.

Spread a handful of this mixture on 4 colorful salad plates, filling the plates. Heap the mushroom slices lightly over the fennel, leaving a curly border of the fennel. Beat the dressing again and spoon 1 tablespoon over the mushrooms on each plate. Grind pepper over the salads and serve at once as a separate course with bread sticks.

Flowers of Common Fennel

The pale yellow flowers of common fennel—resembling the sprays of dill and caraway and others in the family—have the same anise flavor as their ribs. Of course they are edible and make a delicate garnish. A friend makes apple pie with a handful of fennel flowers—interesting.

Leaves of Common Fennel

These ferny anise-flavored leaves can be used any way that strikes your fancy. They have a marvelous affinity for fish. Chop them into fish soup or sprinkle over a seafood salad. Fennel is one of the great grilling seasonings for fish—lay a few leafy branches on the rack, then rest your fish on them. Think of fennel leaves when the recipe calls for dill.

Seeds of Common Fennel

Common fennel grows wild, and its seeds are much used as a flavoring in a few corners of the world—Italy and Southeast Asia are two of them, curiously. Florentine culinary maestro Giuliano Bugialli describes the flavor of fennel seeds as "a sweet-and-sour effect," referring to their hint of licorice. The Malay name translates as "sweet cumin"—if you see that term in an Indonesian cookbook, it means fennel seeds. I love them in rye bread instead of caraway, and I'm crazy about fennel seeds in sausage. And in tomato sauce over pasta. And especially in what has become our house bruschetta, rustic garlicky toast.

BRUSCHETTA WITH FENNEL: For each serving, chop a medium-size ripe sweet tomato medium-fine. Smash and peel a garlic clove, then slice it lengthwise in half. Cut a ½-inch-thick slice from a large loaf of country-style bread. Get out your freshly dried fennel seeds and extra-virgin olive oil.

Warm a dry heavy skillet over medium-high heat and spread the tomato in it. Cook for 5 minutes, stirring occasionally as the juices evaporate. Add 1 teaspoon fennel seeds and stir until the tomato has thickened a bit, another minute. Blend in ½ tablespoon extra-virgin olive oil and remove from the heat.

Meanwhile, toast the bread. While hot, rub all over on both sides with the garlic.

Set the toast on a plate, smooth on the tomato, sprinkle with coarse salt, and grind on black pepper. Serve at once.

Garlic

Harvest garlic for curing (what we're accustomed to using) when about a third of the leaves are brown and dry. Lift carefully, snip off the roots, and dry out of the sun on a rack until the wrapping is papery but the stalks are still flexible, about 1 week. Store in a cool dark dry place. Keep heads of cured garlic intact, pulling off cloves as you need them—this helps keep cloves from drying out.

If you've got the garlic press habit, consider burying the press at the back of a drawer. It's a pity to leave so much of the clove behind in the press. Besides, once cooked, garlic is mild, so you don't have to mince garlic when it's going to be cooked. If you love garlic, finding a lusty bit in your mouth is pleasurable anyway.

Instead of using a press, lay the clove on your counter and, with the flat of a large-bladed knife, simply push down gently on the clove to smash it slightly, giving it a push to split the skin. Pull the skin off and use the garlic clove whole if it will be cooked in a stew or the like. Or you can chop the clove coarsely or finely with the knife, tap, tap, tap—the whole operation takes less time than niggling out the bits in the garlic press. The only time I use a press is when it's mandatory that no speck of garlic be seen. A bit of salt rubbed into wet fingers—or the chopping board—rinsed with cool water and soap, removes garlic scent.

Garlic and Herbs in Olive Oil

This is such a picturesque idea, but in fact it's potentially lethal.

Spores of *Clostridium botulinum* are in all soil and in dust and thus can be clinging to any produce brought in from the garden—plants well above ground can have spores splashed on them by rain or water from the hose. At this point the spores are harmless, because they're in the presence of oxygen, which prevents them from reproducing rapidly. The spores cannot reproduce in an acid environment, so food with a pH of 4.6 or lower is 100 percent safe stored at room temperature—that's almost every fruit preparation and everything pickled in vinegar. The FDA's breakpoint for tomatoes is 4.7. Then temperature plays a role. At room temperature food with a low level of acid, such as garlic, in an airless environment such as olive oil gives botulism spores the opportunity to multiply, producing poisonous toxins. That doesn't mean they will—spores are capricious. But they have no off flavor to warn you, so there's no telling. Refrigerating such a combination will stave off trouble for 10 days for sure—longer, and there's no guarantee.

To be safe, when you're making a salad dressing or marinade with garlic or herbs or anything nonacid from the garden, even though there's vinegar or lemon juice in it, refrigerate the mixture and throw it out after 10 days—by then other harmful properties may start developing. This is also true with garlic butter—refrigerate as soon as possible after preparation and throw out any left over or freeze it after 10 days.

Refrigeration, by the way, doesn't mean bringing the preparation to room temperature for an hour or so and then returning it to the refrigerator. It means taking what you need from the chilled mixture and not returning leftovers to the jar.

Botulism is no joke. It can result in months of hospitalization—or worse.

If a recipe instructs you to brown onions and garlic together, don't. Onions take infinitely more time to brown, and garlic that's actually browned becomes unappetizingly bitter. Always add garlic at the last minute to a browning pan or any situation where it might color. Very often it's enough to lightly sauté garlic in the olive oil or butter and then remove the cloves entirely—the Italians often do this, and it proves the subtlety of their cuisine.

Garlic is brilliant in sauces: Genoese pesto (with sweet basil, pine nuts, Parmesan, and olive oil), persillade (in your own proportions with finely chopped parsley), Greek skordalia (with olive oil, lemon juice, ground walnuts, and soaked bread or mashed potatoes), and Provençal aïoli (with olive oil and egg yolk). These are fist-on-the-table sauces of raw garlic.

CREAMY GARLIC TOASTS: In this recipe, blanching renders the lily bulb as mild as May and sweet. The toasts are enormously popular, so you needn't worry about friends worrying about eating straight garlic. They're especially suited to Mediterranean food, either as an hors d'oeuvre or as an accompaniment. Since you'll have a generous amount, experiment with the cream in small swirls over all sorts of seafood, as well as potatoes, eggplant, and zucchini. The play of hot cream and cold tomato is especially tasty. This makes about 1 cup, enough for about 24 toasts to serve 12 to 24. You can keep the cream refrigerated for 10 days.

Separate 4 large plump heads of garlic into cloves. Drop them into a saucepan with 2 quarts of water and 2 teaspoons salt. Bring to a boil over high heat, boil rapidly for 15 minutes, then drain. Skin by pinching a clove flatly in the center—it will pop out. Trim any brown spots.

Smoothly puree the cloves in a food processor or blender or through the fine blade of a food mill. Blend in 3 tablespoons of mild olive oil, about 3 large sweet basil leaves (very finely chopped if you won't be using a machine to blend the sauce), a few drops of fresh lemon juice, and salt and freshly ground white pepper to taste.

To serve, spread the cream on one side of lightly toasted triangles of thinly sliced French bread. Broil or bake in a 350°F oven until the cream has browned lightly—just a few minutes. Top with a thin slice of cold tomato, arrange on a flat basket or rustic tray, and serve.

PURE GARLIC TOAST: The way I like to eat garlic best is simple bruschetta. There's a complex version with fennel under that vegetable, but this is what's wanted at breakfast, lunch, or with drinks before dinner. Allow 1 to 2 slices per serving.

Thickly slice your favorite bread (homemade wheat or French bread is ideal). While the bread toasts, smash and split 1 garlic clove for each piece. While hot from the toaster, rub the toast with garlic—most of the clove will be absorbed. Drizzle with olive oil and serve hot.

Green Garlic

You'll know how to harvest and prepare green garlic if you think of it as baby leeks or scallions exquisitely flavored with garlic. Anytime a recipe calls for scallions, consider whether green garlic would be more interesting. The bulb and tender leaves are equally useful.

A puree of the white part of green garlic stalks softened in a little butter and then thinned with cream makes a heavenly sauce for grilled seafood, poultry, and vegetables. Naturally, garlic green is subtler than garlic grown to the height of its powers.

Tomato, Potato, and Green Garlic Soup

MAKES 4 TO 5 MAIN-DISH SERVINGS

This pale coral soup is an exceptionally delicate balance of flavors. It's made with spring-planted cloves, when new potatoes are just ready and tomatoes are in their glory. If your garden lacks green garlic, you can make this soup by substituting a scant 2 ounces of the white parts of young leeks and 1 or 2 big cloves of cured garlic.

The soup can be prepared a day before serving, then reheated. It's also marvelous cold.

- 12 green garlic stalks as thick as your little finger, trimmed
- 3 tablespoons mild olive oil
- 3 medium-large (a scant pound) tomatoes, coarsely chopped
- 5 medium-size (about 1¼ pounds) thin-skinned new potatoes, preferably yellow-fleshed, cut into eighths
- 2 cups vegetable stock or chicken broth
- 2 cups cool water
- salt to taste
- ½ cup half-and-half or whole milk
- freshly ground white pepper to taste
- a small handful of flat-leaf parsley leaves, chopped

Slice the white parts of the garlic in half lengthwise and crosswise. Reserve the tender leaves.

Warm the oil in a large heavy saucepan over medium heat. Before it's hot, add the garlic and sauté, frequently shaking the pot, until the garlic softens, about 5 minutes—do not brown. Add the tomatoes and potatoes and sauté for a couple of minutes so the pieces can be gilded a little, stirring once or twice. Add the stock, water, and salt to taste and bring to a simmer over medium-high heat. Turn the heat to very low, set the lid on askew, and simmer until the potatoes are tender, 20 to 25 minutes.

Puree the soup in a food processor or through the medium blade of a food mill. Return to the pot with the half-and-half. Add pepper, taste for seasoning, and heat, stirring a couple of times. Slice the garlic leaves into thin rings and garnish each bowl, adding a sprinkling of parsley for texture.

Serve with good bread and cheese, a glass of cold cider or white wine, and blackberries and cookies for dessert.

Elephant Garlic

It can take 2 years for 1 clove to increase to many little elephants, so pick your recipes with care. Harvest the same as true garlic. You can cook these enormous cloves—which aren't true garlic but a sort of leek—as a vegetable and eat them with cream sauce; that's how very mild they are. But use them soon after harvest, because they don't keep as well as true garlic. You can also slice raw elephant garlic into matchsticks and toss them into salad.

Elephant garlic can do anything garlic can do.

ROASTED ELEPHANT GARLIC BUTTER: Here's an especially delicious use of this allium—for seasoning vegetables, especially potatoes, and pasta. You can also do this with true garlic. This keeps well if covered in the refrigerator for a week.

Heat the oven to 325°F. Set separated but unpeeled elephant garlic cloves in a baking dish, sprinkle with mild oil, cover with a lid or foil, and bake 1 to 1½ hours until the cloves are thoroughly soft when tested with a thin skewer. Cool, then press the soft insides out of their skins into a small dish. Mash and blend with butter to taste—ours is 3 parts of softened unsalted butter and a bit of fresh lemon juice to 1 of garlic. Taste for salt and freshly ground white pepper. Smooth into a small bowl. Serve soft.

Rocambole Garlic

Use the underground cloves of rocambole as you would any garlic. The pretty purply topset bulbils are far hotter. Use them—the size of a kernel of corn—sparingly in salads.

One thing to do with whole unskinned garlic cloves is add them to the dish when you roast chicken. The cloves get creamy-velvety in texture and have a mild flavor. You have to remove the tough skins delicately before eating, but that's no big deal.

SPANISH GARLIC OF THE HAND: This complex and subtle Spanish vegetable dish is called *el ajo de la mano.* Serve it with grilled fish. This makes 2 servings and is easily made in advance and reheated.

Simmer 4 handsome whole unpeeled large red potatoes uncovered with 1 to 2 dried red chilies crumbled into water to cover. When tender (about 20 minutes), drain and slice the potatoes into a mixing bowl. Mince 3 garlic cloves (underground cloves when rocambole) and mix in a small bowl with a few drops of red wine vinegar and a drizzle of olive oil. Add to the potatoes and mix with your hands. Add salt and freshly ground white pepper, taste for seasoning, then either refrigerate or heat gently and serve garnished with marigold petals.

Herbs, Flowers, and Flavorings from the Kitchen Garden

You needn't grow a vast sweep of plants to have herbs to enjoy in your kitchen. One plant of a perennial and a pinch of seeds of most annuals will give you sampler leaves in a small space—then you can grow buckets of those you like. Intriguing leaves, flowers, seeds, and roots of these plants we call herbs add immeasurably to the pleasure of a dish.

TO KEEP FRESH HERBS FRESH: Gather them in the morning after the dew has dried but before the sun has touched them. Moisture will make the leaves sodden, so without washing, smash the tips of their stems and tuck them into a vessel of water, cover with a plastic bag secured with a rubber band, and refrigerate. Change the water every 4 to 5 days. To keep them for the longest possible time, when you change the water, snip off the smashed stems and smash again.

TO FREEZE HERBS: Best for the soft leaves of basil, borage, burnet, chervil, Chinese chives, chives, caraway, coriander (cilantro), dill, hyssop, lovage, parsley, perilla, and tarragon. Because flavor is retained best in leaves when they're blanched briefly before being frozen, drop them into boiling water for 5 to 10 seconds, lift out, dry thoroughly, and place in a plastic freezer bag. Submerge the bag in cool water up to the opening to force out air and seal. To use, chop off what you need. They'll keep for 2 to 4 months.

TO DRY HERBS AND PETALS: Good for the firm redolent leaves of anise hyssop, lavender, lemon verbena, mint, rosemary, sage, thyme, marjoram, oregano, and petals of marigold. If there's more dust on them than you can blow off, use a hair dryer at lowest setting or, as a final resort, rinse them lightly and pat thoroughly dry.

For leaves only, spread them on a cheesecloth-covered cake-drying rack and bake with the door open on your oven's lowest heat. Stir frequently until they're thoroughly dried—don't go away, because it doesn't take long. Store in super-clean tightly covered jars in a cool, dark, dry place and throw out after 1 year at the most.

For picturesque bunches of stalks, tuck bunches inside a thick brown paper bag and secure with paper clips. Hang the bunches, now upside down, in a warm, dry, airy place—an old-fashioned attic is ideal—until thoroughly dry. Keep all moisture away. They will retain their flavor for just a few months.

TO USE DRIED HERBS: We tend to forget that dried leaves are no different from dried mushrooms or dried tomatoes—a good soak in warm liquid makes them worlds more palatable. Heat a little of the liquid or oil or butter from a recipe, stir in the herbs, cover, and steep for 5 minutes or longer before adding them to a dish.

If that isn't possible, at least crumble dried herbs with your fingers as you add them to the dish to help release their oils.

As you know, drying intensifies flavor. Generally the dried herb is considered to have three times the flavor of the fresh. So when you have fresh herbs on hand and the recipe calls for dried, start with that many more.

TO SALT HERBS FOR KEEPING: You can use even less salt than usual when it has been stored with an herb. Tightly covered, the mixture keeps indefinitely in a cool, dark place and has remarkable depth of flavor. Sweet basil makes sensational salt; so do rosemary, oregano, chives, marjoram, thyme, tarragon, summer savory, lovage, parsley, and garden sage. Experiment with others you like.

FRESH HERB SALT: Alternately layer even measures of unblemished fresh herb leaves and bits of leaves and blossoms with sea salt in a jar with a tight-fitting lid. Start and end with a salt layer about ¼ inch thick, then make the remaining layers even (but evenness isn't crucial). Cover tightly and ignore until the leaves have dried—usually a few weeks, but it depends on their texture. Then stir the jar, mixing up the tags of leaves with the salt. They will have darkened, but they're quite delicious. Use sparingly, marrying the herb with the food, because the flavor is remarkably intense.

TO MAKE AN HERB BRUSH FOR BASTING: Tie a bunch of fresh herbs together—either all of one kind or a mix—and use them for dipping into oil or sauce when you're grilling or roasting.

TO SUBSTITUTE AN HERB IN ITS FAMILY: When you're out of an herb or feel adventurous about seasoning a dish, one notion is to turn to a member of an herb's family. Mint family: anise hyssop, basil, hyssop, lavender, marjoram, mint, perilla, rosemary, sage, savory, thyme. Parsley family: caraway, chervil, coriander, dill, parsley. Lily family: Chinese chives, chives. The rest are on their own in these pages.

Anise Hyssop

Alternative: For the flavor, combine mint with chervil or tarragon. For the leaf, mint alone will do.

Pick sprig by sprig. Anise hyssop is best added just before serving—cooking blunts its flavor.

This is a graceful member of the mint family, with thin shafts of purple flowers and longish pointed leaves. Their minty anise taste is mesmerizing. Blossoms are particularly delicious—sprinkle them in fruit cups.

Fresh Tagliatelle with Zucchini, Herbs, Shallots, Pine Nuts, Sun-Dried Tomatoes, and Lemon

MAKES 6 MAIN-COURSE SERVINGS

One of summer's glories is this extraordinary pasta dish. The warm flavors and colors—greens, golds, flashes of red and blue—are magical. The composition changes under my hand each time I make it, but the conception and the spirit are quintessential Deborah Madison (*The Greens Cook Book*).

If you haven't all the herbs called for, use those you do have—basil, chervil, tarragon, marjoram, and hyssop are good equivalents. As crucial to the success of the dish as the herbs and shapes of vegetables is thin homemade egg pasta. Made with anything else, the magic fades.

The ingredients can be prepared a few hours in advance, wrapped separately, and refrigerated.

24 large flat-leaf parsley sprigs
18 6-inch lemon thyme or garden thyme sprigs, including flowers
9 large anise hyssop leaves
3 5-inch oregano sprigs
6 large sorrel leaves, cut into thin ribbons
¾ cup matchsticks of sun-dried tomatoes, softened in hot water
zest of 1 large lemon removed with a vegetable peeler, then cut into slivers
4½ medium-size (1½ pounds) zucchini, sliced 1/16 inch thick on the diagonal
salt to taste
3 or more tablespoons olive oil
1 scant cup pine nuts
7 walnut-size shallots, thinly sliced, then roughly chopped

3 garlic cloves, finely chopped
3 recipes fresh tagliatelle (see Fresh Egg Pasta in The Cook's Notebook)
freshly ground black pepper to taste
a handful of borage blossoms or any blue or purple edible petals
about $\frac{1}{4}$ pound freshly shredded Parmesan cheese

Strip the leaves and blossoms from the herbs and chop medium-fine. The herbs with the sorrel should come to $\frac{3}{4}$ cup. Turn into your serving bowl with the tomatoes and lemon zest. Stack the zucchini slices and cut into $\frac{1}{16}$-inch strips.

To serve, bring a big pot of salted water to a boil. Film a medium-size skillet with some of the olive oil, heat it, then sauté the pine nuts over medium heat, stirring, until they begin to brown, about 1 minute. Add the shallots and garlic and sauté, stirring, until the shallots are soft and the nuts browned, $\frac{1}{2}$ to 1 minute more. Turn into the bowl.

When the water boils, add the zucchini and stir until just warmed through, no more than 1 minute. Skim out with sieve or colander and turn into the bowl.

Add the pasta and stir and boil until tender, adding $\frac{1}{4}$ cup of the pasta water to the bowl. Drain the pasta and turn it into the bowl. Drizzle on the remaining spoonful of olive oil to give gloss—or add more, if you like, to loosen the mix—add pepper and taste for seasoning, then toss everything lightly but thoroughly. Sprinkle on the flower petals and rush to the table. Serve on hot soup plates, passing Parmesan on the side. Drink a berryish Zinfandel, serve a crisp escarole salad and goat cheese to follow, then melon with port (see recipe under Melon)—soak the melon in a dessert wine instead of port.

Basil

Pick sprig by sprig, preferably before flowering.
Basils take well to cooking.

Here are the heavy breathers of the herb family—*so* sensuous! All basils have an affinity for the nightshade vegetables—tomatoes, eggplants, peppers, potatoes. The basils are indispensable in Mediterranean, Thai, and Indian cuisines—great with pastas, dried beans, garlicky dishes, eggs, and in salads. I especially enjoy whole basil leaves in my green salad.

Spicy sweet basil, the best known, is the soul of pesto, the incomparable Ligurian puree of leaves, olive oil, garlic, pine nuts and Parmesan or Romano cheese that graces everything from vegetables to pastas to fish to meat (you can adapt the recipe for Cilantro Pesto under Coriander to sweet basil).

When you'll use them decoratively as well as for flavor, look into the colorful sweet basils, particularly bronzy-purple Rubin and Purple Ruffles, with its deeply cut all-purple leaves. African Blue basil has a pungent, musky, sweet basil flavor—it's a perennial, so you can have basil all year.

Thai basil is also attractive, with red stems and small blue-green leaves that have an anise/sweet basil flavor with a hint of coriander woven through.

Lemon basil is divine in any dish in which you'd use both lemon and basil, such as spinach dishes.

Basil's pink or white flowers are flavorful, too.

A tisane of dried basil is a mild sedative and aids digestion. Basils are full of antioxidants, a plus.

To preserve the flavor of fresh leaves, stir chopped basil with mild olive oil to moisten, then pack in small quantities and freeze. Very long-keeping, up to a year. Or make basil salt (see Fresh Herb Salt in the introduction to this chapter). Whole basil leaves can be frozen—they will darken, but their flavor in cooked dishes is nearly as fresh as just-picked.

ROSY FRUIT COMPOTE WITH BASIL: Makes 4 to 6 servings. I stumbled onto an exquisite use of sweet basil—flavoring poached quinces. The basil delectably perfumes the fruit and rose-colored syrup. Make this in early autumn when a few quinces are ripe and frost hasn't taken all the basil. Use frozen leaves if need be. Out of season, apples and pears are also wonderful this way—in which case, use a purple- or blue-leaved basil to turn the syrup rosy. This lasts a long week in the refrigerator without losing quality. Quinces are ripe when they're so scented you can hardly bear it.

You'll need 8 medium-size ripe quinces, apples, or pears. Peel with a vegetable peeler, then quarter, core, and slice ¼ inch thick with a small sharp knife. Heat ⅔ cup sugar and 1 cup water in a skillet until the sugar dissolves, stirring once or twice. Add the fruit, the zest of a small lemon cut with the peeler in a strip, and 12 basil leaves. Simmer uncovered just until the fruit tests tender with a toothpick—don't overcook. Lift the quinces into a bowl and boil the syrup over high heat until syrupy. Remove the lemon and basil, pour over the fruit, and refrigerate. Serve cold with not-sweet cookies.

Borage

Alternative: Salad burnet, for its cucumber flavor. For the flowers, the only rival in blue is hyssop.

For the most part, use borage raw. Leaves can get squishy when cooked.

Plush cucumber-tasting leaves and ice-blue flowers on a plant that volunteers freely make borage a kitchen garden must. For salad, harvest young leaves, because the older they get, the fuzzier and tougher they are.

If you're out of cucumber but have borage in the garden, whatever is compatible with cukes is compatible with borage. Instead of chives, add finely chopped borage leaves to sour cream, yogurt, cream cheese, cottage cheese, creamy salad dressings, and such. The Niçois, like the Italians close by, add a chopping of borage leaves to the filling for ravioli and dip whole leaves in batter and fry them as fritters for dessert.

Young tender leaves and bright blue flowers lend their cucumber flavor to lemonade, white wine, and other summer drinks—one of borage's common names is *cool tankard.*

Remember the blossoms' cool blueness against warm reds and yellows for garnishing vegetable dishes. Drop the flowers into fruit cups, and they're gorgeous on cakes.

CRYSTALLIZED BLOSSOMS: Brush the flowers with slightly beaten egg white, dip in super fine granulated sugar—for a veil, not a coating—then dry. Store in a box in a cool, dry place and use as soon as possible. That's it.

BORAGE BLOSSOM TEA: The fresh blossoms make a mild, slightly spicy tea. To savor the blossoms' beauty in winter, I dry as many as I can, then brew a cup of tea. It's a watery blue-green with a fascinating flavor reminiscent of Japanese green tea. This is a model for all herb teas.

Drop as many dried blossoms as you can balance on a teaspoon into a deep teacup. Pour boiling water over them, cover with a saucer, and infuse for 10 minutes. Strain into another cup and perhaps stir in a flick of sugar.

Burnet/Salad Burnet

Alternative: For their cucumberiness, very young borage leaves.

Use salad burnet uncooked—cooking makes the leaf bitter. After flowering, use only the tips and the lightest youngest leaves, because the rest will be bitter.

Burnet's small, round lacy blue-green leaves grow in tall, airy rosettes. They are cucumbery, and the plants volunteer prolifically so you'll have lots. In spring, there are round buttons of flowers covered with ruby chips, a charming garnish.

Salad burnet is of course delightful in a green salad. As with borage, anything compatible with cucumber is good with it. Salad burnet flavors white wine vinegar beautifully—the leaves hold up for a long time. The herb is particularly good with beets, celery, and carrots.

Chilled Tofu Salad with Salad Burnet

MAKES 4 SIDE-DISH OR FIRST-COURSE SERVINGS

Cucumbers do so well with creamy things, here's a light, handsome, and refreshing salad inspired by a notion of Mitsuko Shrem's, of the Clos Pegase vineyard in the Napa Valley. To make this a main-dish salad, double the ingredients, setting four cubes of tofu on the plate.

Everything can be prepared in advance for composing quickly at serving time.

2 cucumbers, peeled only if the skin is bitter

2 large firm ripe red or orange tomatoes

1 pound well-chilled silken (soft) tofu

1/3 cup fresh lemon juice

2 overflowing tablespoons extra-virgin olive oil

salt and freshly ground white pepper to taste

1/4 cup young salad burnet leaves

Slice the cucumbers lengthwise into quarters, remove the seedy pulp, then cut into 1/2-inch dice. Cut the tomatoes into slightly larger dice—if the pieces are juicy, blot them in a towel. Cukes and tomatoes should be chilled at serving time, so start with cold ones or wrap separately and refrigerate them now.

About an hour before serving, drain the tofu, rinse, and pat dry. Cut into 8 equal squares and set in a rimmed dish. Blend the lemon juice, olive oil, and salt and pepper. Pour the marinade over the tofu, cover with plastic wrap, and marinate in the refrigerator for 30 to 60 minutes.

To serve, on each of 4 chilled rimmed plates, center 2 cubes of tofu corner to corner—a blocky figure 8. Strew the cucumbers and tomatoes around them, then pour on the marinade. Top each serving of tofu with 1 tablespoon salad burnet leaves. Serve with sesame crackers and a dry Sauvignon Blanc.

Caraway

Caraway seeds are best added during the last 10 to 15 minutes in a cooked dish. To plump dried seeds in the microwave, add 2 tablespoons water to 1 tablespoon dried seeds, cover, and cook for 1 minute.

Like small white lace doilies, flowers on a caraway plant bloom in the spring of the second season and taste like a blend of honey, caraway, and celery. The ferny leaves look like carrot's and taste like parsley. Pick both by the tender sprig or spray. I sprinkle flowers and leaves into fruit cups and over cream cheese on muffins. They're also lovely in dishes of delicate vegetables—the likes of carrots, celery, lettuce, and peas. The root, when large enough, can be cooked like carrot.

Smoky, bitey, silvery-tasting dried caraway seeds are traditionally scattered over cheese, cabbage, roasted apples, cookies, and, in Scotland, buttered bread. In England, at the end of the wheat-sowing season, husbandmen were rewarded with a caraway seed cake—a small handful of seeds added to a spiced coffee cake makes it marvelous.

Ah, but from your garden you can taste caraway seeds that you can't buy. Pick the seeds while they're plump and green on the flower spray, before they start to dry. They're intensely spicy and almost nutty. When you have a handful, make the following noodles.

Green Caraway Seed Noodles

MAKES 2 SERVINGS

When green caraway seeds aren't available, use a scant tablespoon plumped dried seeds.

Boil about 6 ounces broad egg noodles according to package directions, then drain. Brown ½ pound sliced mushrooms in a hot dry skillet, stirring frequently. Sprinkle with a few drops of fresh lemon juice. In a bowl, combine the noodles, mushrooms, ½ cup crumbled feta cheese (2 ounces), green caraway seeds from about 6 stalks (1 heaped tablespoon), and 2 tablespoons olive oil or melted butter. Toss to blend, add salt and freshly ground black pepper to taste, dust with paprika, and serve with chicken.

TOASTING SEEDS: Toasting seeds enhances their flavor the way it does a slice of bread. Toast them in a dry heavy skillet over low heat, shaking the skillet continually so nothing burns. Stop when you can smell the seeds or when they start to pop.

CHERVIL

Alternative: Flat-leaf parsley mixed with tarragon.

Chervil is good both raw and cooked, but add it in cooking only during the last few minutes or the flavor will disappear.

Lacy-leaved (they look like tiny fern fronds) chervil's flavor is that of delicate parsley dipped in licorice. The dainty flowers are creamy white. It's a darling—once in the garden, it will self-sow evermore. There is curly-leaved chervil as well, but I find the flat more appealing. The French prefer chervil to parsley for its subtlety, and we should use it more. In combination with parsley, tarragon, and chives, chervil composes the classic French *fines herbes*.

Chervil is marvelous in salads, especially with slightly bitter leaves like endive. Pick tender sprigs and young flowers and chop just before serving, since chervil's delicate flavor quickly pales. It makes a delicious vinegar and is beautiful in the bottle. Chervil adds an extraordinary element to soup, especially a puree of sorrel and potato. And it's superb with fish. Chervil is beautiful with eggs any style, its most celebrated use being a fines herbes omelet. Chervil also has an affinity for sweet vegetables such as carrots and garden peas.

Salad with Corn and Chervil

MAKES 4 SERVINGS

Chervil is best with foods that are themselves delicately flavored, such as chicken, lettuce, cucumbers, snap beans, and asparagus. It's very interesting with corn—the sweetness of the leaves warms the sweetness of the kernels. Combined, they make a terrific salad that's portable for a picnic or potluck, attractive—all those green ferny bits in the bright yellow and/or cream—and versatile; it goes with everything.

You can make this several hours in advance.

Roast 6 large ears of sweet corn in their husks in the microwave according to directions under Corn (in 2 batches). Cut off the kernels into a bowl—you'll have about 5 cups. Blend in ½ cup chervil leaves and flowers torn from the stems, ¼ cup rice vinegar or other mild vinegar, and 2 tablespoons olive oil. Toss to blend, then add salt and pepper to taste. Chill.

Chinese Chives

Alternative: A little garlic, a little chives.

Like garden chives, Chinese chives can be cooked briefly without losing quality.

For cooking, cut leaves an inch above the soil. For garnish, cut deeper to include the lovely pale pink or cream sheath. This is a part of the plant the Chinese particularly favor.

These are narrow, thin, flat dark green leaves that grow in a clump. Their flavor blends a ping of garlic with the mildness of sweet onion. When a recipe calls for scallion stalks *or* chives *or* garlic, you can use Chinese chives instead. Because the leaf is so flavorful and flat, it's a valuable addition to briefly cooked dishes such as steams and stir-fries—the leaf doesn't dissolve or collapse. When thinking how to use them, think garlic rather than chives.

Flowers of Chinese chives are a ball of individual creamy florets. They're delectable from the time they're soft poufs until the seeds have developed to succulence. Once the seeds are firming up, it's best to separate the florets and sprinkle them over a dish.

If you blanch a plant, toss the daffodil-yellow leaves with pale egg noodles.

PAN-ROASTED SALMON WITH CHINESE CHIVES: Makes 4 servings. Chinese chives are particularly good with fish. This is my favorite way to cook a fatty fish such as salmon or sea bass. This takes 10 minutes altogether.

Heat a large heavy nonstick skillet over high heat. When hot, lay in 4 salmon fillets or steaks of even thickness, preferably at room temperature and patted dry.

Sprinkle with salt and pepper and ½ cup chopped Chinese chives. Cook until browned on the bottom, 4 to 5 minutes. Turn (letting the chives fall where they may) and cook until the center of a small piece is opaque when you cut into it, another few minutes. Serve garnished with lemon quarters. Baked potatoes and a tossed green salad are good accompaniments. In season, spoon chopped fresh tomatoes over the fish before adding the chives—lovely flavors and colors.

Chives

To harvest, snip whole leaves of chives from the base, leaving ½ inch or so—don't give the plant a zany haircut by taking a few inches off the top. When chives are in bloom, snip the tasty lavender almond-shaped buds and puffs of pink blossoms for salads.

Garden chives can be cooked briefly without losing their quality.

These bright green leaves—like stiff hollow grass—are most decorative in sprinkles of snips. Chives may just be at their best combined with white cheeses—cream cheese, cottage cheese, even white cheddar. Their spice gives a bracing edge to the rich likes of crab, lobster, and smoked salmon but still doesn't overwhelm the delicate taste of scrambled eggs. Chives have the same compatibility as scallions, but their slenderness and deep green color make them more decorative.

Fresh Herbs and Flowers Pressed Between Leaves of Pasta

MAKES 54 TO SERVE 9

Here is a recipe that is a work of art, a creation you can serve anybody in the world. Fresh herbs and flowers are pressed between leaves of pasta so thin they're transparent when cooked. The flavors are dazzling, and the colors shimmer from within. Shapes may be triangles, squares, whatever you please. The dish is exquisite made with homemade pasta, but purchased wonton wrappers can be almost as good. You can produce more and thinner squares with the homemade pasta than the wonton skins, but that doesn't mean you have to. The wrappers freeze well, so you can purchase them in advance.

I've given the recipe to chives because I find they have the most distinctive flavor. But the recipe could be under almost any herb or flower in this book. I urge you to use a mix of fillings rather than just chives. Here are the arrangements for fillings

I've used. You can change them, of course—set tarragon leaves next to the tuberous begonia petal instead of blue basil, use 4 or 8 cilantro leaves instead of 6, and so on. If you roll supermarket wrappers to 4-inch squares, increase these numbers or sizes by about a quarter:

Two crossed chive buds bordered with two or three chive leaves on either side . . . one chive blossom bordered with its leaves . . . three small sage leaves . . . one tuberous begonia petal (no stamens attached) flanked with one or two small blue basil leaves . . . ½ teaspoon chopped rosemary needles . . . ½ teaspoon lemon thyme leaves pulled from stems . . . purple florets of blue basil stalks . . . three Thai basil leaves . . . nine small Greek oregano leaves . . . one young sorrel leaf . . . one nasturtium flower (tail pinched off, flattened to fit) . . . two large sweet basil leaves . . . five golden marjoram leaves . . . one young borage leaf . . . two small "Alaska" (variegated) nasturtium leaves . . . one hollyhock blossom . . . eight or nine pineapple sage trumpets with snippets of leaves . . . six cilantro leaves . . . eight tarragon leaves . . .

Some have sensational flavor—tangy sorrel, sweet lemon thyme, smoky Greek oregano, clean spicy coriander, warm sweet basil, and musky golden sage. Some have more drama than flavor—hollyhock, nasturtium, golden marjoram. But overall the taste is fresh buttered noodles, which is lovely.

Every season has its offerings from the garden—perhaps with choice additions from a farmer's garden—but certainly when there are lots of edible flowers blooming is the best time to make this. I make the packets in triangles. The design must be minimalist. I can't tell you how satisfying this all is.

These can be prepared and refrigerated a day before cooking. The recipe can be decreased or increased as much as you like.

A pinked pastry cutting wheel nattily finishes the edges and is worth finding.

2 recipes egg pasta (see The Cook's Notebook) or 14 to 16 ounces wonton wrappers (check the expiration date and be sure it's a long way off; at an Asian market, choose medium-thick wrappers, about 75 to the pound)

all-purpose flour

2 teaspoons cornstarch

2 teaspoons cool water

herbs and edible flowers of your choice for 54 squares

salt to taste

about 4 ½ tablespoons unsalted butter

freshly ground white pepper to taste

heaped ½ cup finely shredded Parmesan cheese, optional

Roll homemade pasta dough on the narrowest setting on the pasta machine. On a floured cloth, cut the dough into 3½-inch squares. Keep all dough you're not working with in a plastic freezer bag.

Medium-thick wonton wrappers from an Asian market will be thin enough. Three-and-a-half-inch supermarket wrappers are thicker and likely ¼ inch short on one end of making a square. You can roll that side to make it square. Or you can take an extra few seconds and roll each to a generous 4-inch square, making the sheets more delicate. Whatever you do, you can set sheets side by side and roll 2 at a time.

Cut 54 squares. Blend cornstarch and water in a small bowl (this holds the leaves of dough together and may add to the sheen from within—plain water doesn't hold as well).

Working with one square at a time, stir the cornstarch mixture with a brush and film the surface with the paste. Arrange leaves and/or blossoms diagonally to one side of the half in pretty patterns, leaving a ¼-inch border. Fold the blank half over, fitting it neatly, and press firmly to seal, starting at one end—force out as much air as you can while sealing the pieces. Trim edges with a wheel if you can.

Dust triangles of homemade pasta with cornstarch so they won't stick in the bag—store-bought wrappers are already dusted. Refrigerate now if you like.

To serve, bring a big pot (preferably broad rather than deep) of salted water to a boil. Heat ½ tablespoon butter for each serving in a serving bowl in the microwave. Boil 12 triangles at a time until al dente—2 minutes for homemade pasta, a scant 3 minutes for wrappers. Quickly lift them out with a skimmer, shake off water, and turn into the melted butter. You can cover the bowl and keep it warm in a very low oven while finishing the cooking or serve each batch fresh from the pot. Salt and pepper lightly if at all.

Serve on hot plates—the triangles are so ravishing they need no garnish. Pass the cheese separately. Serve as a first course or as an accompaniment to roast or grilled chicken. If you have round zucchini in the garden, they make a dreamy side dish for this menu when prepared in the style of Parma, under Squash. Either a sprightly Gavi or a Gamay Beaujolais will suit.

Coriander

Pick by the sprig. Use the leaves fresh, barely warming them up if added to something cooking—they don't heat to advantage.

Aka cilantro, these leaves look like feather-edged flat-leaf parsley. They're more delicate in texture but more powerful in flavor. The seeds, round and beige, grind to a perfumed powder that lifts chutney toward the sublime. They come in autumn of the first year. Fresh coriander is prized in Chinese, Middle Eastern, Indian, and Latin cuisines. I can't imagine a stir-fry or salsa that isn't made more exciting by a handful of leaves.

Few people like cilantro on first taste—it's a bit of a punch in the mouth from a delicate fist. Just go slowly. You'll probably come to adore it, as I do. Cilantro is compatible with other rich flavors—tomatoes, chilies, onions, garlic, corn—almost anything in the Latin larder, and the pork and pungent greens in the Asian.

CILANTRO PESTO: Makes ½ cup. Toast ¼ cup pine nuts and 2 garlic cloves in a dry small heavy skillet over medium-high heat until lightly browned, stirring frequently, about 3 minutes. In a mortar or bowl with a pestle or back of a heavy spoon, mash into a smooth paste. Add 1 cup (firmly packed—about 1½ ounces) finely chopped coriander (cilantro) leaves by large pinches, working the mixture to a coarse paste. Drizzle in 3 tablespoons extra-virgin olive oil and stir until you have a smooth, fluffy paste. Blend in 2 tablespoons freshly grated Romano cheese, then taste for salt. Cover and refrigerate until needed.

Stir this into any soup or pasta dish where the fresh leaf and the other ingredients would be welcome.

DILL

Pick dill from tender young leaves through the flowering stage through seeds—it goes quickly.

Dill is another leaf that's best briefly cooked, although branches beneath grilling fish, poultry, or meat are wonderful, as is dill in poaching broth.

When the big blowsy flower heads develop, use them as flavoring at every stage—as petals, when the seeds are soft and plump, and when the seeds have dried. Add dill flowers to potato salad.

Few herbs are more delightful with potatoes, tomatoes, carrots, cucumbers, cabbage, onions, mushrooms, beets, green beans, dried beans, spinach, summer squashes, cauliflower, cream cheese, hard-cooked eggs, seafood, salads, hamburger and meat loaf—and dill is particularly good with lamb.

LAMB POACHED WITH FRESH DILL. Makes 8 or more servings. This is a remarkable recipe inspired by one of Claudia Roden's (*A Book of Middle Eastern*

Food). The lamb cooks to succulence in a surprisingly short time and is suffused with the warmth of dill. It's the only lamb I've tasted that's still juicy when cooked past pinkness. I've cooked half a leg this way, using the same amount of ingredients, and it cooked to an ideal 135°F in 45 minutes.

My friend Philip S. Brown contributed the red wine and the sauce's creamy finish.

This lamb will wait patiently in a cool place for several hours and is lovely at room temperature.

Lightly salt and pepper a 5-pound bone-in leg of lamb (have the bone cut so it will fit in your pot). Spread a big bunch (about 2 ounces) of fresh dill in a large stew pot. Thinly slice a large lemon and arrange half the slices on the dill. Set in the lamb, fleshy side up. Thrust a meat thermometer in the center of the fleshiest part. Over it pour ½ cup dry red wine, ½ cup vegetable stock, and ¼ cup olive oil. Lay the remaining lemon slices on the lamb. Cover the pot tightly, set over medium heat, and when you hear simmering, turn the heat to the lowest heat maintainable.

Baste about every 15 minutes. After 45 minutes, use tongs to turn the joint over, replacing the lemons on top. In 15 more minutes, test with a meat thermometer thrust into the fleshiest part: 120°F is rosy pink, 135°F medium pink, 145°F medium-rare, and 160°F well done. Depending on how you like it, test every 5 to 10 minutes, basting each time.

When ready, remove from the heat and pour the juices into a skillet. Lay some of the dill over the meat, set the lid on askew, and set the pot aside to let the juices settle. You can serve it after 10 minutes or 3 hours.

To serve hot with a sauce, bring the juices to a simmer. Thicken with a slosh of heavy cream or a spoonful of yogurt. Taste for seasoning, then spoon over thick slices of lamb. Rice, steamed carrots, and a Cabernet Sauvignon go wonderfully with this. Apple tart for dessert.

GINGER

You can harvest all or part of the rhizome from a plant anytime you like as long as the rest of the root is big enough to sustain the plant's life. Young leaves have gingery flavor, so thinly slice them and add them to stir-fries or chop them finely and use them to flavor vegetables. Ginger is great with all fish, poultry, and meats, and practically every vegetable.

Ginger Tempura Nibbles

MAKES 5 OR 6 SERVINGS

Spicy hot gingerroot and crispy batter make this one of the most delectable morsels you'll ever put in your mouth. Serve as a finger food hors d'oeuvre or as garnish for a colorful Asian dish.

The ginger and batter can be prepared a couple of hours in advance. The frying takes about 10 minutes. The puffs should be served straight from the pan, but they're actually still tasty an hour later.

fresh tender gingerroot the size of 3 largish eggs, about 6 ounces

BATTER

6 tablespoons all-purpose flour
1 tablespoon cornstarch
1 teaspoon baking powder
¼ teaspoon sugar
¼ teaspoon salt
½ cup ice water
about 5 cups pure vegetable shortening or mild oil
salt to taste, preferably coarse
ginger leaves or other edible green leaves for garnish

If the skin is tough, peel the ginger with a vegetable peeler. Slice crosswise ⅛ inch thick, then cut into matchsticks. You can wrap and refrigerate the ginger at this point if you like. Prepare the dry ingredients for the batter as in the recipe for tempura batter under Burdock. Add the ice water about 15 minutes before cooking.

To serve, slowly heat the shortening or oil in a wok or broad heavy pot to 340°F. When it's ready, add all the ginger to the batter and stir until each piece is coated.

With a tablespoon, scoop up batter-moistened matchsticks and drop into the fat. Some spoonfuls will break apart and scatter—that's all right. Don't crowd—fry 6 to 8 spoonfuls at a time. Adjust the heat to maintain the temperature. When they're golden brown underneath, turn and fry until golden on the other side. Lift out onto several thicknesses of paper toweling and blot with towels on top. Heap on a platter, sprinkle with salt, and tuck green leaves here and there for decoration. Serve at once.

Hyssop

Alternative: Rosemary can substitute.

This is not the hyssop in the Bible. Authorities tend to think that was a marjoram.

Pick by the sprig. Hyssop leaves are smallish, long and narrow, and pungent—almost medicinal. Their astringence is appealing with rich fatty foods such as duck and goose. Their flowers are a fabulous dark blue—they can also be blush pink and white, but grow the blue.

HYSSOPED PEACHES IN SWEET WINE: When your hyssop is in bloom, the peaches will be at their peak, so make this delightful dessert. It's a perfect finish for an elegant dinner.

Just before serving, for each person, drop one luscious ripe peach in boiling water, wait about 40 seconds, then lift out. Peel the peach and slice into a stemmed glass containing a scant 3 ounces of chilled Moscato di Canelli or Sauternes—any delicious dessert wine. Pull the leaves from a 6-inch stalk of hyssop and sprinkle them over the peach, then sprinkle with the flowers. Serve with crisp delicate cookies.

Lavender

Alternative: Substitute rosemary or a little hyssop.

Lavender smells wonderful, but it's very tricky to use as an herb. Lavenders come in different strengths—English the strongest; the French and Spanish are perfumed but less intense. Lavender is used as a flavoring in the south of France, where it grows rampant. Its piney smoky fragrance can be used to season poultry and meat. My friend Russ Parsons takes about 2 tablespoons of chopped French lavender and rubs it over a chicken, then puts the remainder in the cavity. When roasted, the chicken tastes faintly lavender, delicious.

Lavender flowers are varied according to the plant, but all make fragrant garnishes. Often, however, the leaves are more scented than the blooms. Pick by the sprig.

LAVENDER PETAL SORBET. Makes about $1\frac{1}{2}$ quarts to serve 8 to 12. This sherbet is an adventure—if ever there was a taste of the Sun King's court, this would be it. Best within a few hours of freezing.

In a nonreactive saucepan over high heat, stir $5\frac{1}{2}$ cups water and $\frac{3}{4}$ cup sugar until the sugar dissolves. When it comes to a full rolling boil, add 1 firmly packed tablespoon pungent lavender blossom petals (a little more if the lavender scent isn't strong). Push the petals down into the syrup, cover, and boil for 1 minute. Remove from the heat and steep all day or overnight, then add 1 tablespoon fresh lemon juice and strain. Freeze according to your ice cream maker's directions. Serve in stemmed glasses with a fresh blossom on top and crisp sweet cookies.

Lemon Verbena

Alternative: Lemon-scented geranium or lemon zest.

The long pointed rough-surfaced leaves of lemon verbena hold an entrancing fragrance and flavor. Few leaves give such a rush of pleasure every time you brush by them. You need lots of these delicate fresh leaves to get the flavor, but the little shrub is generous with its leaves. They're suited to anything that goes with lemon, which is almost everything. The flowers are tiny and lavender—insignificant, really. Everything goes into the scent. Pick by the sprig.

LEMON VERBENA CATS' TONGUES: Makes 50 to 75 small cookies.

No cookie is better with simple fruit and iced desserts than cats' tongues, the French *langues-de-chat*. Lightly buttery and not too sweet, they are long, lyrical, and wafer-thin. They're easy to make and especially enchanting speckled with lemon verbena. If you have no lemon verbena, or if the flavor would distract from what you're serving, flavor the cookies with $\frac{1}{2}$ teaspoon vanilla extract. These thin, crisp cookies will keep in an airtight tin, or you can freeze them.

Heat the oven to 400°F. Butter and flour 2 large baking sheets. In a food processor or with a mixer at medium speed, blend 6 tablespoons minced fresh or 2 tablespoons finely crumbled dried lemon verbena leaves with $\frac{2}{3}$ cup sugar for 30 seconds. Add $\frac{1}{2}$ cup ($\frac{1}{4}$ pound) softened unsalted butter and process or beat just until blended, 5 seconds. Add 3 fluid ounces egg whites (3 eggs) at room temperature and process just until blended, 5 seconds. Sprinkle on ⅔ cup all-purpose flour and process just until absorbed, 4 seconds. The batter will be very soft.

Turn into a pastry bag fitted with a number 3 plain tube or into a plastic food storage bag with a corner cut off the bottom to make a ⅜-inch opening. On the cookie sheets, push out batter in 3-inch ribbons set 2 inches apart. Bake one sheet at a time until the edges of the cats' tongues are rich brown and the centers are pale, 6 to 9 minutes—don't leave the kitchen, because they can burn in a trice.

Transfer at once to a cooling rack—they crisp quickly. If you need to soften them again to get them off the pan, return briefly to the oven. When they're cold, store in airtight tins. If your air is humid, bake in a 300°F oven a minute or two and they'll be crisp again.

Lovage

Alternative: Any sort of celery.

Lovage leaves are reminiscent of celery's in form and flavor. But tasted side by side—even against the intensely celeried leaves of the Chinese sort—lovage is spicier, more complex. It has a silvery aftertaste edged with juniper and anise. Lovage grows easily, and one established plant provides lots of leaves. Harvest as you do celery.

Lovage works wherever celery does. It's particularly delightful paired with fish, giving warmth and a gentle snap to delicate flesh. I've discovered when you bake the two together tightly wrapped in paper—the classic method called *en papillote*—moist heat brings out every element of lovage's flavor. Whole fish are elegant prepared this way, but it's essential the flesh not be thicker than ¼ inch so the herb's essence can permeate the flesh in the brief cooking time. Whole boned trout is ideal, but any small fish or fillets of fish suit the method.

TROUT WITH LOVAGE BAKED IN PAPER: Makes 4 generous servings. The recipe can easily be increased. Don't substitute foil for the paper—foil doesn't breathe and you'll steam the fish instead of bake it.

The package can be prepared for baking hours in advance and refrigerated, but bring it to room temperature before baking.

You'll need 4 whole boned trout with heads and tails on, weighing about 10 ounces each, 1 packed cup lovage leaves, 8 long leafy lovage ribs, and 2 juicy lemons. If your fishes aren't boned, butterfly them—run a thin sharp knife inside down the backbone so the fish opens like a book.

Heat the oven to 450°F. Drizzle a large new brown paper grocery bag with oil and rub it in so all the paper is oiled. Crease the bottom widthwise so the bag will lie flat. Have ready a 9- by 13-inch baking dish, preferably glass.

Open up the fishes and sprinkle the flesh of each with 1 tablespoonful fresh lemon juice, salt, and freshly ground white pepper. Lay 1/4 cup lovage leaves down one side of each fish, then close. Lay the fish crosswise inside the bag, head to tail. Slip a lovage stalk under and lay one over each fish. Fold the bag closed and fit the bag in the dish so the fish lie flat and the excess ends are tucked.

Bake in the center of the oven 15 minutes, then open the bag and slip a meat thermometer into the bottom part of one of the fishes. It should be just short of 130°F. Cut open the bag and use two pancake turners to lift the fish onto a heated serving platter, arranging the lovage nicely. Lay a lovage leaf over each eye, garnish with crescents of lemon, and serve at once. Serve with steamed potatoes and asparagus in spring, peas in summer, snap beans in autumn. Drink a crisp white wine. For dessert, serve the sweetest melon you can find.

Marjoram—Sweet

Another ephemeral herb whose leaves are best added raw and just before serving. Pick by the sprig.

Marjoram is oregano to a lighter degree, the soprano voice. It's not that you can use less oregano in a dish and it will taste like marjoram. Marjoram is altogether subtler. Sometimes you want fist-on-the-table oregano, sometimes the restraint of marjoram. There is a golden marjoram that is chartreuse and lovely.

Traditional uses for the small lightly spicy-minty-musky leaves of sweet marjoram are with eggs and bean dishes. While too strong for fish, marjoram adds warmth to just about every vegetable, meat, and dish with cream and cheese.

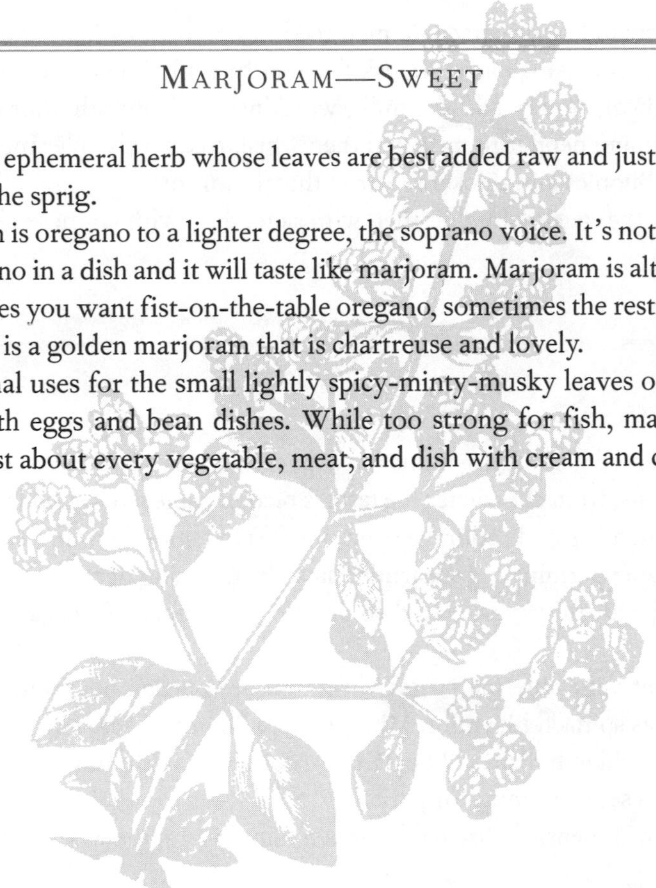

Marjoram Cream Sauce

MAKES ABOUT 2 CUPS

Marjoram can do wonders for a cream sauce. I use this often as an easy, distinctive sauce over vegetables for company.

If you wish to cover and refrigerate the sauce for a few hours, warm it up gently in a bain-marie (a pot set in a pot of water) or in a double boiler.

2 tablespoons unsalted butter
3 tablespoons all-purpose flour
2 cups cold milk (nonfat is fine)
2 to 4 tablespoons chopped fresh marjoram leaves
salt and freshly ground white pepper to taste

In a small heavy saucepan, melt the butter over low heat, then whisk in the flour to make a paste. Whisk frequently while it cooks for 2 minutes. Off the heat, slowly add the milk, whisking until smooth after each addition. Whisk in salt and pepper to taste and then whisk frequently over medium heat until the sauce bubbles and thickens. Stir in the marjoram.

Next try the sauce with dill, then with sage, then with Chinese chives.

MINT

Like scented geraniums, mints are copycats. There are dozens of sorts of mints in herb catalogs, from chocolate (the taste is recognizable) to Kentucky Colonel (ruffled and pungent), eau de cologne (hint of rose) to lemon bergamot (fruity lemon). For cooking, peppermint and spearmint have the true zing of mint, with pineapple or apple mint beautifully variegated in cream and green—fine garnishes. Pick as sprigs.

The great vegetable marriages with mint are garden peas and carrots. Leafy greens such as spinach like mint. Mint grows wild in Greece, and Greeks add mint to rice pilaf and lamb dishes. The Turks and Italians add mint to artichoke dishes. The rest of us seek out mint for jelly.

For a new dimension, use half as much mint in a recipe when it calls for basil.

Wappo Fresh Mint Chutney

MAKES 4 TO 5 SERVINGS

When a dish needs brightness, I often head for the mint. One of the brightest compositions I've tasted came with chick-pea-batter deep-fried sea bass under the grape arbor at the Wappo Bar and Bistro in Calistoga, California. Michelle Mutrux has generously given me her recipe. The flavor is wonderfully complex, its components elusive. This is in the tradition of Indian fresh chutneys served with fried and spicy dishes, but use it wherever you'd use mint or cooked chutney.

This can be refrigerated for up to 2 days.

Each mint naturally gives a different character to the blend. If you have other mints, try them by all means.

- 2 packed cups peppermint leaves
- ¼ cup shredded unsweetened dried coconut
- 4 dates, pitted
- 2 jalapeño peppers, seeded
- juice of 1 orange
- juice of 2 limes
- ¼ to ½ cup water
- salt to taste

Blend all but the water and salt in a blender. Add water to make it the consistency you like (traditionally it's like runny applesauce), then salt to taste.

Oregano—Greek

There are a number of oreganos, and their flavor varies from faint to powerful. Most fanciers regard Greek oregano as the oregano of choice since it's the richest in flavor. Pick by the sprig.

All the tastes that marry with sweet basil are happy with oregano—with a difference. I regard oregano as an earthy basil. Basil floods a flavor with its brightness. Oregano lifts a flavor from beneath.

Although it has a piquant flavor with some of oregano's characteristics, so-called Mexican oregano is a brash imposter—it's not even a member of the family.

OREGANO

Bakestone Herb Cakes

MAKES 18 2-INCH BISCUITS

You know how to strew oregano leaves over pizza, to combine their musky smoky warmth with tomatoes and eggplant and every other vegetable steeped in sunshine. To appreciate them in a new way, speckle the leaves through hot biscuits—they add wonderful depth and warmth. Based on an English recipe, these are quickly made and baked on the griddle—a boon in hot weather. They're splendid companions for any soup and salad in this book. They can be baked and reheated several hours later.

- 1/3 cup oregano leaves if using a food processor or 1/4 cup chopped leaves if made by hand
- 1 2/3 cups all-purpose flour
- 1 tablespoon baking powder
- 1/4 teaspoon salt
- 4 tablespoons cold unsalted butter
- 1/2 cup plus 2 tablespoons half-and-half or milk

Heat a cast-iron griddle or skillet (ideally 11 1/2 inches wide) over medium heat while you blend the herbs, flour, baking powder, and salt in a mixing bowl with a swish of your fingers or in a food processor, pulsing it 6 times. Add the butter in small dice, then rub it into the flour or pulse it 10 times in the processor, until the butter is the size of baby peas. At this point, turn the mixture into a bowl from the food processor. Stir in the half-and-half with a fork in as few strokes as possible. Knead briefly to pull the dough together into a ball.

Roll out 1/2 inch thick on a lightly floured cloth. Cut into 2-inch rounds, pat scraps together and reroll them lightly, then fit close together on the unbuttered griddle or skillet. Turn when the bottoms are browned, 5 to 6 minutes, exchanging biscuits on the center and sides. In another 4 to 5 minutes they'll be browned on the bottom. To be sure they're baked, split one open. Serve hot in a basket, to be split and buttered.

Parsley

Of the two sorts of parsley, curly and flat-leaf, curly is most popular here and in Britain and flat-leaf most prized in Europe and elsewhere. The flat-leaf type has come to be called *Italian parsley*—by and large it has the most flavor. Pick both parsleys by the sprig.

Try to regard parsley as an herb, not greenery to stick on the plate and then scrape into the compost jar after dinner. A chopped handful added at the last minute to almost anything—scrambled eggs, clam sauce for spaghetti, pot roast, coleslaw, chicken soup—brightens the dish. This is a worthy leaf, full of calcium.

Parsley Salad with Ravigote Sauce

MAKES 6 TO 10 SERVINGS

My grandmother adored a curly parsley salad—full of "vim and vinegar," she'd say—adding that parsley was good for the nerves. The salad's green astringence makes it a fine accompaniment to rich grills and roasts. If you find the dressing too sharp, use less vinegar. The dressing is superb on cold vegetables, fish, fowl, and meats. This can wait for a few hours in a cool place before being served.

10 cups leaves from about ½ pound curly parsley

RAVIGOTE SAUCE (MAKES ⅔ CUP)

⅓ cup mild oil such as peanut or safflower

3 tablespoons white wine vinegar or 1 tablespoon dry white wine and 2 tablespoons cider vinegar

1 tablespoon cold water

3 tablespoons finely chopped scallions, use white and green parts

1 tablespoon minced fresh tarragon or chervil

1 tablespoon finely chopped drained capers

salt and freshly ground white pepper to taste

Rinse the leaves well and spin dry. Blend the dressing, then pour it over the parsley in a big bowl. Toss with your hands, rubbing the dressing through the leaves. Add salt and pepper then taste for seasoning. Serve at once or cover and chill.

Any left over is good for breakfast the next morning, although it won't be as perky.

Perilla

Alternative: Mint mixed with coriander.

These leaves are gracefully oval and can be as large as the palm of your hand. Their edges are pinked, and the surface is lightly crinkled. They come in green and purple. Pick them leaf by leaf. The purple leaves are more colorful but less flavorful. Perilla's flavor is amazing—akin to coriander's take-no-prisoners pungence. It is minty, lemony, beefy, and grassy all at once, unlike anything you've tasted. Startling at first, it grows on you.

In Japan perilla is called *shiso* and also *beefsteak plant.* The green leaf is used the way Greeks use grape leaves—as a grace note under every conceivable presentation. Perilla makes a pleasing garnish, and the leaves are used in tempura. They're also often wrapped in sushi rolls, and the purple variety are brined and then used in umeboshi, classic pickled plums (really unsweet apricots).

KYOTEA: Makes 1 serving. In Kyoto there is a concoction called (for English-speaking tourists) *kyotea,* a blend of perilla leaves and broth that's delicious and restoring. In winter, make it with dried leaves.

Snip 2 teaspoons thin ribbons of fresh green perilla leaves into your teacup or crumble in a heaped ½ teaspoon dried leaves. Bring ⅓ cup chicken broth and ⅓ cup water to a simmer and stir into the cup. Cover the cup with its saucer and steep for 2 minutes.

A variation is the same delicate broth served in a soup cup with 3 or 4 overlapping thin slices (the size and shape of dominos) of tofu resting on a whole small perilla leaf.

Rosemary

Pick rosemary by the sprig—flowers included, when there are some. Rosemary smells like young pines on a sun-baked Greek island. Few herbs lend such warmth. Rosemary was made to flavor lamb—and to roast or sauté with chicken and rabbit, to roast with potatoes, to add to homemade fettuccine, to toss into summer squash at the last minute. The difference between fresh and dried leaves is amazing.

ROSEMARY SCRAMBLED EGGS: Makes 2 servings. This is one of my husband's exemplary ways with rosemary.

Melt 1 to 2 tablespoons unsalted butter in a large skillet over medium heat. Beat together 1/4 cup finely chopped rosemary leaves, 1/4 cup milk or half-and-half, 4 large eggs, a little salt, and lots of freshly ground black pepper. Pour into the pan and keep the eggs moving with a fork until cooked. Serve instantly with hot toast rubbed with garlic and drizzled with extra-virgin olive oil.

Sage, Garden

Rub these beautiful blue-gray or golden leaves between your fingers and you'll smell desert smoke. Yet sip a cup of tea of these leaves and you'll be surprised by their mintiness. Garden sages are at once strong and subtle. They have been relegated to turkey stuffing for too long. Discover their great affinity for the onion clan, cheeses, dried beans, ham and pork, veal, turkey, eggplant, and tomatoes. Pick them by the sprig.

Fritters of sage leaves sprinkled with grated Parmesan are sublime.

RESTORATIVE SAGE SOUP FROM PROVENCE: Makes 3 servings. An ideal place for toast is at the bottom of a soup plate of *aígo boulído*—literally "boiled water," a garlic-enhanced sage broth from Provence. Nineteenth-century herbalists prescribed the soup when the world was too much with one. *Aígo boulído* works.

In a large heavy saucepan, use a pestle or the back of a wooden spoon to crush 8 pungent fresh sage leaves, 3 garlic cloves, and 1 large fresh or 1 small dried bay leaf. Add 1 quart cool water, set the lid on askew, and boil for 15 minutes. Toast 3 thin slices of French bread, set a piece in each soup plate, and drizzle with olive oil. Remove the sage, garlic, and bay from the soup and stir in salt and freshly ground white pepper to taste. Whisk an egg in a hot mixing bowl, then slowly stir in the soup. Ladle the soup over the toasts and sprinkle with shredded mild cheese. Serve at once.

Savory, Summer

Summer savory is another undersung herb that deserves to be in your garden. It is much favored in Provence, particularly with the roasted white meats of veal and pork. The French have decided summer savory is the herb of choice for dried beans.

You might wonder how a winter dish is graced by a summer herb. But dried pulses are delicious sprinkled through tossed salad, and savory is as sweet with shelly beans as dried ones. This is an herb that dries with a true flavor. Pick it sprig by sprig.

Summer savory is one of the constants in herbes de Provence, that rich blend of dried herbs the French use over pizzas, roasted and grilled meats and fishes, and in rabbit stew, sauces for vegetables, salads, and fresh cheeses.

Every cook with an herb garden in Provence (that's every cook) knows the *best* blend of herbes de Provence. But in addition to summer savory, only thyme is common to all blends. As well as summer savory and thyme, one popular blend is speckled thickly with lavender buds, fennel seeds, and basil—equal parts of all.

A wonderful French custom is to preserve cheeses in herbs. They keep beautifully, increasing in their herbal flavor with each day. A semihard cheese is recommended. If you can buy such a goat cheese, that is ideal. Otherwise, use jack, Muenster, or Edam.

SAVORY PRESERVED CHEESE: Remove any rind or covering. Coat the cheese all over in coarsely ground white or black pepper and press it in. Cover the bottom of a small crock or jar with summer savory leaves, moisten with cognac or good brandy, lay in the cheese, and sprinkle with more leaves and cognac. If you have more cheeses to preserve, layer them in this way. Cover with olive oil, then cover the vessel and refrigerate, setting it in the least cold spot. Keeps 10 days.

Slice off pieces from the cheese as you wish to serve them—don't remove the whole cheese unless you plan to eat all or most of it. Bring to room temperature an hour before serving. If any cheese remains, wrap it and refrigerate, but not in the oil.

Rosemary and thyme are also delectable with cheese, and the leaves hold well in the process.

Tarragon, French

The long, thin luminous green leaves of tarragon taste like licorice drenched in sunshine. Tarragon is a classic companion to chicken, fish, lobster, and eggs, as well as artichokes, beets, green beans, carrots, and tomatoes. Again, pick it by the tender sprig.

Chicken with Tarragon Cream

MAKES 4 SERVINGS

One of the most sublime combinations in the world is this classic dish from Normandy—utter simplicity, pure ingredients in harmony. I've taken liberties—chicken parts instead of a whole bird—but guests have a better choice, and it's easier to manage. This is a celebration dish.

For finest quality, the chicken must go from browning to table.

3 pounds frying chicken parts, fat removed, patted dry, at room temperature

6 branched and leafy 6-inch tarragon stalks or the equivalent

salt and freshly ground white pepper to taste

1 tablespoon mild oil

1 tablespoon unsalted butter

⅔ cup chicken broth

⅓ cup dry white wine

¼ cup brandy

1 cup heavy cream

If you're using them and if they're joined, cut thigh and leg apart. Tuck 2- to 3-leaf sprigs of tarragon under the skin of each piece of chicken, spacing them evenly an inch or so apart. Chop some of the remaining tarragon leaves to make 2 tablespoons, cover, and reserve. The chicken pieces can be wrapped and refrigerated for a few hours. Bring to room temperature before proceeding. Dust with salt and pepper.

In a large heavy skillet, heat the oil and butter over medium-high heat. Add the chicken pieces and sauté, turning once with tongs, until golden all over, about 5 minutes on each side. Lift out onto a dish. Pour off the fat (good for sautéing potatoes another day) and wipe the skillet clean.

Add the broth and wine to the skillet and bring to a boil over high heat. Lay in the chicken, thickest sides down—include juices in the dish. Break the remaining tarragon stalks in half and set around the pan. Cover, then turn the heat to low. Cook until, when you make a small slash with a knife against the bone in the thickest part of a dark piece (if you're using both light and dark), there's no more pink—20 to 25 minutes.

If there's an exhaust fan, turn it off. Turn off the burner, then pour on the brandy. Carefully set it aflame and shake the skillet to move the brandy around until the flames die. Lift the chicken and tarragon onto a heated serving platter and set in a low oven. Turn the heat under the skillet to high and boil down the pan juices until syrupy, about 3 minutes. Stir in the cream and boil until a sauce consistency, about 1½ minutes. Remove from the heat, taste for seasoning, then pour over the chicken. Sprinkle with the reserved chopped tarragon and serve at once.

Rice, baby peas, and sautéed mushrooms are superb with this. Drink a Sauvignon Blanc or a Tavel rosé, have a salad of crisp Batavian lettuce or escarole, then a fine Brie to follow. For dessert, raspberries or other berries of the season over strawberry ice.

THYME

These tiny leaves are among the most valuable in the realm of herbs—their flavors are neither too pale nor too pungent. They seem to have captured the sweet outdoors in their leaves. The rosy flowers are tasty, although not as much as the leaves. Pick leaves and flowers by the sprig.

There are myriad thymes, some with flavors borrowed from other plants—caraway, orange, lemon. Lemon thyme is magic. If anyone you know hates cooked carrots, for example, you'll change his or her mind if you cook carrots quickly and sprinkle them with leaves of lemon thyme. Together with lemon verbena, these are the clearest lemon imaginable next to the fruit itself.

Europeans prefer wild thyme, which is actually milder than our domesticated garden thyme. Although it isn't incompatible with any food I can think of, garden thyme (sometimes named *French* or *English*) is perhaps most delicious with fresh beans, carrots, eggplant, mushrooms, onions, potatoes, tomatoes, cheese, and chowders.

THYME BETWEEN MELTED CHEESE AND TOAST: Allow at least 2 per serving. I was hurrying to try a new hors d'oeuvre of melted cheese and thyme one day, and I put the thyme beneath the cheese instead of on top of it. When it came out of the broiler, under the translucent gold were specters of green. Their deep flavor came as a delectable surprise. These can be prepared in advance and broiled just before serving.

Lightly brush one side of thinnish slices of French bread with olive, walnut, or hazelnut oil. Brown the oiled tops under a broiler or toaster oven. (That means the bottom isn't toasted, which gives the finished toast a certain sensual softness on the underside.) Sprinkle evenly with fresh leaves of thyme (for a baguette slice, leaves from one good sprig are about right). Cover the bread with thinnish slices of a delicate or spicy melting cheese such as jack, Swiss, or Muenster. Sprinkle with a light olive oil and a few turns of the black pepper mill. At this point the toasts can be tightly covered and kept in a cool place a few hours. Broil until bubbly and serve at once.

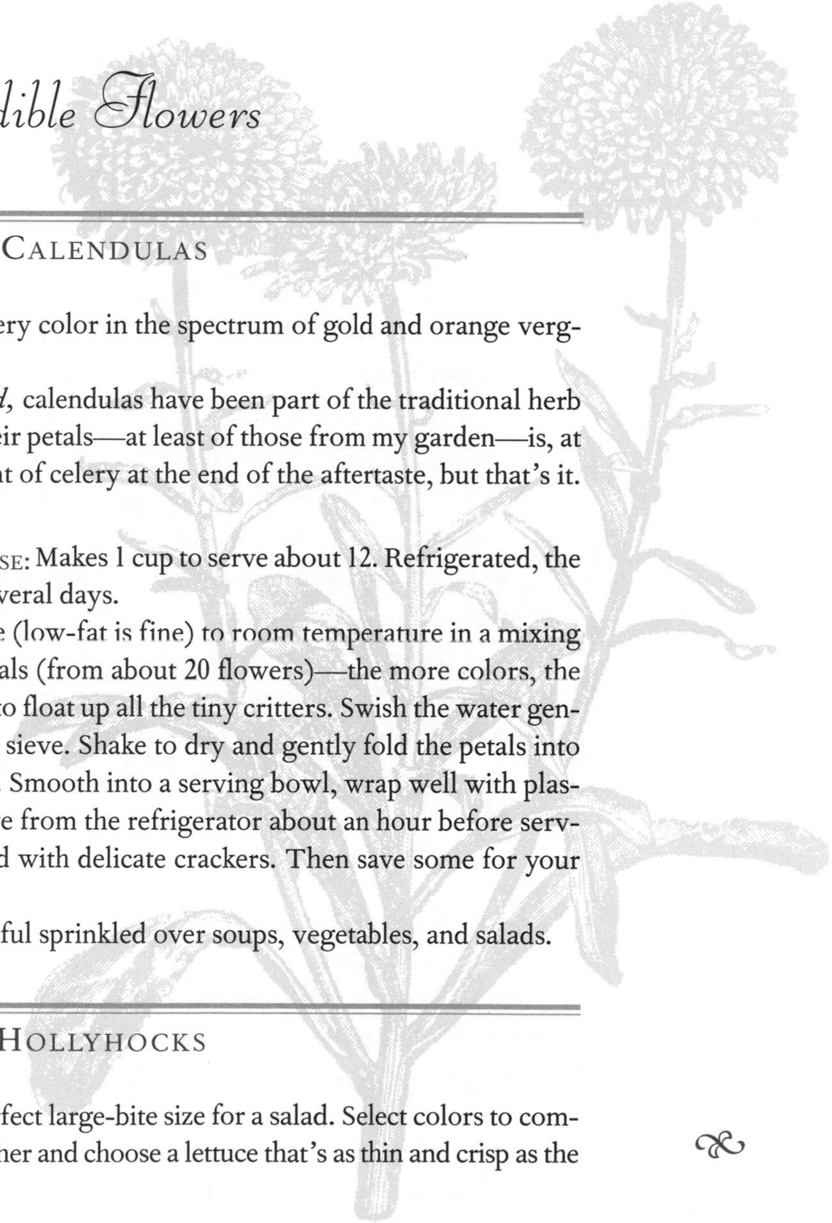

Edible Flowers

Calendulas

Bright daisylike flowers with every color in the spectrum of gold and orange verging on red.

Under the name *pot marigold*, calendulas have been part of the traditional herb garden forever. The flavor of their petals—at least of those from my garden—is, at best, elusive. There may be a hint of celery at the end of the aftertaste, but that's it. But their color holds up in food.

CALENDULA CREAM CHEESE: Makes 1 cup to serve about 12. Refrigerated, the petals hold their freshness for several days.

Bring ½ pound cream cheese (low-fat is fine) to room temperature in a mixing bowl. Drop ½ cup calendula petals (from about 20 flowers)—the more colors, the better—into a tub of cool water to float up all the tiny critters. Swish the water gently, then lift out the petals with a sieve. Shake to dry and gently fold the petals into the cheese with a wooden spoon. Smooth into a serving bowl, wrap well with plastic wrap, and refrigerate. Remove from the refrigerator about an hour before serving to soften. Serve accompanied with delicate crackers. Then save some for your morning bagel.

Calendula petals are wonderful sprinkled over soups, vegetables, and salads.

Hollyhocks

Hollyhock petals are the perfect large-bite size for a salad. Select colors to complement or contrast with one another and choose a lettuce that's as thin and crisp as the

Blossom Chocolates

Makes 32 candies. Tiny fresh flowers caught in small fluted rounds of white chocolate.

These can be refrigerated up to 4 hours.

Gather anchusa, English daisies, Johnny-jump-ups, violas, tiny marigolds, borage, lavender, radish flowers, dame's rocket—whatever's blooming—in the early morning, before the sun is on them, and keep stems in water in the refrigerator.

In about 32 double-thickness paper bonbon cups, arrange 1 to 4 tiny flowers facedown in each. The petals must lie as flat as possible: trim the sharp black point on the borage blossoms, and after the marigolds are tucked in, snip off their protruding hips. Have an assortment of sizes as well as colors and shapes of flowers—let an English daisy completely fill the cup, while 2 or 3 anchusa blossoms have lots of room to spare.

Chop 6 ounces white chocolate and melt it in a double boiler over hot, not boiling, water—the chocolate must never be more than tepid, although at some point you'll probably have to heat the water a bit. Stir until completely smooth.

Use a ½-teaspoon measure to gently plop chocolate over the flower(s). Fill the cups half full, just covering the arrangement, then use a chopstick to smooth the top. Be careful not to smear any chocolate on the paper above—that makes unmolding awkward. Cover and chill up to 4 hours. Just before serving, pull off the papers and arrange the candies on a beautiful plate.

hollyhock petals—nothing soft and languid. Often just one color of petals is most effective with lettuces. I like to use a peachy pink with green lettuce leaves tinged burgundy.

TOSSED HOLLYHOCK SALAD: Makes 4 servings. Hollyhock petals have a lettucey taste, so a light vinaigrette is appropriate. Served on pretty plates, this is elegant and simple. Petals, lettuces, and dressing can be prepared a few hours in advance.

Pull off the green calyxes at the base of 4 large hollyhock flowers, then gently pull each petal from its base, dropping petals into cool water. Rinse 24 small lettuce leaves—preferably decorative ones, such as Rosalita or some other pinkish red leaf—and spin or pat dry. Tear lettuce leaves into pieces the size of the petals. Wrap in a damp towel and refrigerate until needed.

In a small bowl, blend 2 tablespoons mild olive oil with 2 teaspoons rice vinegar, then add salt and freshly ground white pepper. Taste for seasoning.

Just before serving, blend the dressing and drizzle over the petals and lettuces in a mixing bowl. Toss with your hands until blended, then arrange the salad on chilled salad plates, giving the petals a prominent place. Serve at once.

Marigolds

The flavor of bright yellow, orange, russet, copper, white, and reddish marigolds hints of bitterness that's intriguing. Two small cultivars, Tangerine Gem and Lemon Gem, have a nuance of citrus that's more intriguing still.

Marigold Gem Fruit Cup

MAKES 8 TO 10 SERVINGS

Although any fruits you like can go into a fruit cup, a rainbow of colors and a variety of textures make it most appealing.

For company, this can be put together several hours in advance. Although it won't look as pretty, the fruit cup will be delicious for several days if kept tightly covered and refrigerated.

- 4 cups cubed watermelon
- 3 cups cubed orange-fleshed melon
- 2 cups blue, purple, or black berries
- 2 cups seedless green grapes
- 2 cups seedless red grapes
- heaped 1/4 cup Tangerine or Lemon Gem marigold petals with a few chopped leaves
- 1 Asian pear, when in season, or other type, cored and diced
- 1 crisp red apple, cored and diced
- 3 tablespoons fresh lemon or lime juice
- 2 tablespoons sugar, optional

Combine all ingredients in a pretty bowl, sprinkling the juice over the pear and apple as you prepare it to keep the flesh from darkening. Blend with your hands. Serve chilled.

Nasturtiums

Nasturtiums are among the gayest, most intensely colorful of flowers. Every part of them is edible and tasty. You can't have too many nasturtiums in your garden or too many colors, because you'll find you use them constantly for decoration on the plate. You can pickle the seedpods for delightful mock capers.

Try not to wash them—inspect for residents and shake or brush them off. Nasturtiums make the most beautiful vinegar of all. The tangle of primrose, canary, coral, tangerine, scarlet, gold, rose, and bronze buds, blossoms, and green coins of leaves couldn't be more art nouveau. Make the vinegar with rosé, and it will be luminous gold.

WINE VINEGAR WITH NASTURTIUMS: My house formula for wine vinegar can be prepared with red wine too, for peeled garlic cloves, shallots, and feisty herbs—but you won't see what's in it.

In the cool of the morning, take a clear-glass wine or champagne bottle with you into the garden. Choose perfect flowers, buds, and small leaves—a range of colors if you have them—picking the stems so the flowers will fit below the narrowing of the bottle's neck. Pick one lone heavy decorative stalk that will go in last to weigh the arrangement down; otherwise everything will float. Gently, using a chopstick or skewer, tuck flowers, buds, and leaves into the bottle one or two at a time.

In a measuring pitcher, blend 1½ cups rosé or white wine, 1 cup cider vinegar, and ½ cup distilled white vinegar. Pour into the bottle, leaving about ½ inch below the cork line. Cork. Keep in a cool, dark, dry place.

Pansies, Violas, Johnny-Jump-Ups, Sweet Violets

These darling children are invaluable in decoration: the large sweet and colorful faces of pansies, the smaller solid-color violas, the whimsical monkey faces of Johnny-jump-ups, and the Victorians' passion, sweet violets. Of them all, only violets have scent and flavor. But toss the rest into salads and fruit mixes.

A Flowery Salad

In a broad bowl, preferably glass to show off the colors, make a bed of tender leaves of varying textures and hues—soft green nasturtium, red and pale lettuce, dark coins of cress, and light crunchy bits of purslane as well as wisps of chervil and frizzles of endive are ideal. Tear the large leaves into largish pieces—too small, and the composition looks chopped.

Over the leaves scatter petals—copper and red nasturtiums, orange and neon calendulas, mahogany marigolds, any color of chrysanthemums or daylilies—and whole blossoms: hollyhocks, primroses, yellow-and-violet Johnny-jump-ups, blue borage, purple or blue pansies or violas, small pink English daisies, and buds of any of these.

Dress with just enough vinaigrette (made mostly with olive oil and very little lemon juice) to make each leaf and petal glisten. Toss gently with your hands and serve at once.

Sweet violets are candied in France, and you can buy them in elegant boxes at great expense. Crystallize your own as you do borage blossoms. Add their heart-shaped leaves to salads—they are as delicately flavored as lettuce. Fresh violets in fruit cups taste as perfumed as they smell.

A SPRING CLOUD: Makes 2 servings. For perhaps the most romantic dessert you'll ever serve, offer your significant other this.

Whip ¾ cup chilled heavy cream until stiff. Fold in 1 cup of the most scented violets you can find. Taste for sugar—you may want to fold in a spoonful or two. Pile into glasses, ideally stemmed and cut crystal. Cover and chill for up to 3 hours. Top with fresh violets and leaves. Serve with champagne and cats' tongues made with vanilla and without the lemon verbena (see recipe under Lemon Verbena).

Scented Geraniums

The blossoms of this brilliant group can be enchanting—pink, white, yellow, red, apricot, and lilac that look a bit like Johnny-jump-ups. But it's their leaves that are scented. Like those of mints, scented geranium leaves mimic other plants. There are scented geraniums flavored with rose, lemon, apple, lime, chocolate, peppermint, nutmeg, and filbert, all with the admixture of a sort of woody geranium taste. Rose is probably the best loved, but lemon and nutmeg geraniums are delectable. I love to flavor an old-fashioned bread pudding with them.

Scented Geranium Bread Pudding

MAKES 6 SERVINGS

Originally, bread pudding was a way to use up stale bread. In this house we let the bread stale so we can turn it into bread pudding.

The pudding can be prepared for baking an hour or two in advance.

1 heaped tablespoon very finely chopped leaves of fresh scented geranium, lemon verbena, or another sweet, not overpowering herb

3 cups milk (nonfat is fine)

about 2 tablespoons unsalted butter, softened

4 large ½-inch-thick slices of home-style white bread, 4 to 5 days old, trimmed of crusts

about ⅛ teaspoon ground cinnamon

3 extra-large eggs

¼ cup sugar

½ cup dried currants, plumped in warm water if necessary, or use small dark raisins

a sprinkling of ground mace or freshly grated nutmeg

a little red currant, strawberry, or other tart jelly as garnish, optional

Bring the herbs and milk to a simmer in a small saucepan, turn off the heat, cover, and let steep for an hour or more.

To make the pudding, heat the broiler. Butter a 5-cup baking dish. On both sides, lightly butter the bread and sprinkle very lightly with cinnamon. Set on a baking sheet and briefly slip beneath a hot broiler until toasted on both sides.

Heat the oven to 350°F. Cut the slices into 1-inch squares and turn into the dish. Blend the eggs and sugar into the milk and pour over the bread. Stir to distribute the herbs. Sprinkle the currants over the dish and stir them in just a little—they'll drift down of their own accord. Dust the top with mace.

Set the dish in a larger baking pan, fill with hot water two thirds of the way up the sides of the dish, and slide into the center of the oven. Bake until only a half-dollar-size circle in the center remains soft, about 55 minutes. If the top isn't crisp and brown, slip the dish beneath the broiler until it is. The custard will settle as it cools. Serve warm or cold with tart red jelly for dotting on top.

At high altitude, bake at 375°F for about 1 hour.

Sunflowers

Buds of sunflowers taste a bit like artichokes—toss them into salads. Use the colorful petals in salads. According to the cultivar, they taste from nothing to bitter.

SUNFLOWER NOUGAT: Makes about 11 ounces. Seeds are the bonus of sunflowers. When you feel the birds have taken their share of your seeds, and when a good store has been put away for your cereal, make this Old World candy for friends. The candy is a wonderful mixture of elevated and down-home tastes. Keeps in a cool place until eaten.

Smear a square foot of your work surface with softened unsalted butter. Butter your rolling pin. In a large heavy skillet over medium-high heat, blend 1 cup sugar and 1 tablespoon water, stirring with a wooden spoon after the first sign of melting. Stir in a few drops of pure vanilla extract and cook just until there are no lumps and all is tawny brown—it will quickly turn bitter past this point. Remove from the heat, add 1 cup toasted unsalted hulled sunflower seeds, and quickly stir until blended. Turn out onto the buttered surface and roll out until about ¼ inch thick or thinner. When cool, break into pieces. Keep in a tightly closed tin. Now see what you can do with peanuts and nougat, under Peanuts.

Herb Bouquets and Butters

You may see the term *bouquet garni* in a recipe. It is a bunch of fresh herbs tied together and buried in the center of a dish, then lifted out before serving. Loose dried herbs are tied with cotton string in a bundle of cheesecloth, then removed.

Swirled into vegetables just before serving or spread on hot breads (heat brings out their flavor), an herb-flavored butter is a luxurious touch. Any fresh or dried herb can flavor butter—a mixture can be used to savory effect. There are no rules about proportions. To softened butter (preferably unsalted for its pure flavor), blend in chopped fresh or steeped or crumbled dried herbs to please your palate. A few drops of lemon juice may be compatible and will heighten flavor. Let the butter rest in the refrigerator for an hour or more to absorb the herbal taste. Keep leftovers in the freezer.

Jerusalem Artichokes

Harvest about 3½ months after planting by digging gently at the base of the plant. Take only as many as you need, because they don't store well.

To prepare Jerusalem artichokes—crisp and fleshy, bland but not boring—scrub them gently and pat them dry. Don't peel, since many of their nutrients lie just below the skin—and the skin adds texture and flavor. Jerusalem artichokes are high in fiber, have a good supply of iron, and offer fair amounts of thiamine and phosphorus. Add raw slices or chunks to salad.

These days the tubers are smoother than the knobby knees they once were. The skin of Red Fuseau tubers is, of course, red, and the slender roots are rarely more than ½ inch thick. When the tuber is first harvested, its starch is in the form of insulin, absorbable by diabetics. When stored, the insulin slowly converts to the sort of starch found in potatoes.

Raw Jerusalem artichokes lend an aqueous crispness to a dish much like water chestnuts. Italians slice and simmer the tubers and sauce them with chopped anchovies and garlic or sauté them in butter and olive oil and finish them with lemon and parsley. Unpeeled Jerusalem artichokes are excellent roasted whole with poultry and meats. Look to recipes for cooking small whole new potatoes for inspiration with Jerusalem artichokes.

Steamed, fried, creamed, pureed, and pickled—lots of pickled Jerusalem artichokes in the South—are other delicious ways with these tubers.

Jerusalem Artichokes Merlot

MAKES 6 SERVINGS

This attractive and unusual side dish, ready in about 6 minutes, is my favorite. You can slice the roots a little in advance. Cover the pieces with water and a splash of vinegar to keep them from discoloring, then drain thoroughly and pat dry to cook.

about 50 small (1 pound) slender Jerusalem artichokes, scrubbed
2 teaspoons olive or nut oil
6 medium-size garlic cloves, finely chopped
½ cup dry but earthy red wine such as Merlot
salt and freshly ground black pepper to taste
a little fresh thyme

Slice the tubers crosswise into rounds ¼ inch thick. Pieces should be no wider than a dime—if necessary, cut them accordingly. In a wok or large heavy nonreactive skillet, heat the oil over high heat. Add the Jerusalem artichokes and garlic, stir to blend, then cover and cook for 2 minutes, shaking the skillet a couple of times. Pour in the wine, stir, cover, and cook for another 2 minutes, stirring once or twice. Remove from the heat when the wine has been completely absorbed and the slices are tender but still crunchy, russet, and starting to caramelize. Add salt and pepper then taste for seasoning and serve at once in small bowls sprinkled with fresh thyme. I like to eat mine with a spoon.

Kale

Kale is an ancient, primitive plant—thought to be the closest descendant of wild cabbage. Every other gorgeous member of the brassicas, from cabbage to broccoli to brussels sprouts, evolved after kale.

Kale can be harvested even though its leaves are heavy with ice crystals. Cutting with a knife, harvest leaves halfway from the center top to where mature leaves—past eating—begin.

If it isn't already, this can become one of your favorite vegetables—it just takes care in cooking. Rinse tender young leaves well in tepid water, watching for bugs. If the stalks aren't tender, fold each leaf over and pull the greens from the stalk. Chop the stalks and cook as you would celery. Although you can cook kale any way you can cook spinach—that's every way except roasting, and probably somebody will tell you it's divine roasted—I like to simmer it. Measuring kales is maddening—some are thick and heavy and some are feather light. Better to err on the generous side—use more leaves rather than less in a recipe. Bring a big pot of stock or salted water to a boil. Drop in the kale. If you're cooking lots of leaves, wait until the first big handful collapses, then add more by the handful. Simmer uncovered over medium heat, stirring occasionally. Generally, thin ornamental leaves will be tender in 7 to 8 minutes, peacock and Red Russian leaves will take 12 to 15 minutes, and thick curly kales will be tender in 25 to 35 minutes. Drain well in a sieve, pressing out most of the broth (this nourishing broth is fine added to soup if used half and half with water or another broth). Chop with a knife on a board (not in a machine—it would soon be mush) as you would spinach, then heat in a saucepan with a jot of olive oil and lemon juice or vinegar, butter and chopped shallots, garlic, or hot pepper sauce.

Consider deep-frying ribbons of kale—they cook in moments.

Kale is wildly nourishing as well as satisfying to eat: a thumping good source of vitamins A and C and beta-carotene, a moderately good source of fiber and vitamin E, a fairly good source of iron, calcium, vitamin B_6, and folic acid, and a fair source of magnesium, potassium, manganese, and copper. Pick young and don't overcook.

Kale is so easy to grow, so easy to cook, so delicious, and so nourishing that it ought to be frequently on our tables. Look to cabbage recipes for kale ideas. Like cabbage, it has an affinity for potatoes—from kale and potato soup to chopped cooked kale stirred into mashed potatoes to a skillet supper of simmered potatoes, kale, and frankfurters to ribbons of kale in potato salad. Add tender leaves to salad.

The leaves of most greens cook down amazingly—1 pound can be reduced to as little as 1/2 cup. Sorrel practically dissolves, but kale is one exception to this rule—it holds up quite well.

Creole Kale Soup

MAKES 4 TO 5 MAIN-DISH SERVINGS

Like its pal collards, kale loves being cooked in a savory broth.

The flavoring vegetables shouldn't simmer much more than 40 minutes. Know the different cooking times for the various sorts of kale so you'll know when to add your leaves to the pot. This soup is also wonderful the next day.

1 leftover ham bone or fresh ham hock

4 quarts cold water

4 unpeeled carrots

1 onion

1 small unpeeled turnip

1 leafy celery rib

2 garlic cloves, chopped

HERB BOUQUET

8 parsley stalks

8 fresh thyme sprigs

2 whole fresh bay leaves or 1 dried

1 small dried hot red chili, seeds removed (optional)

8 cups small pieces of kale leaves—including chopped tender stems—stripped from about 1 pound

½ cup lentils

salt to taste

freshly ground black pepper to taste

In a deep saucepan, simmer the ham bone in the water, covered, for 2 hours.

Meanwhile, slice the carrots, onion, turnip, celery, and garlic ¼ inch thick. Cut the turnip and onion slices in quarters. Tie the herb bouquet together with cotton string. Chop the kale into largish pieces.

When its time is up, remove the bone and add the vegetables, lentils, salt, and herb bouquet to the pot. Simmer uncovered 30 minutes, stirring occasionally. Add the kale. Cook until the kale is tender, then remove the bouquet, add pepper, and taste for seasoning. Serve with corn bread for dunking in the broth.

Bubble and Squeak with Kale

MAKES 4 SERVINGS

Kale's robust flavor combines well with meat. The English have been doing a tasty bit with beef and greens since Dr. William Kitchiner presented a piquant recipe called *bubble and squeak* in *The Cook's Oracle* in 1817.

The title comes either from the sound of the ingredients cooking or from the noises of happy eaters. Kitchiner's was made with cabbage, but we love the darker leaves and deeper flavor of kale. I add boiled red potatoes in their jackets for color and to complete the meal. Why this trio is so appealing a winter supper I cannot say, but people devour it. Just don't stint on the butter. Its nutted sweetness makes the dish.

All but the warming up is done in advance. Increasing the recipe depends on how many large skillets and how many burners you have. For these amounts, use two large heavy skillets for the meat and a large heavy skillet or saucepan for the kale. You can sauté the meat and the kale at the same time or do the meat first and then the kale. The important thing is to sauté the meat just until browned—slices must stay moist at the center.

6 tablespoons unsalted butter
4 thin slices (3/4 pound) cold lean boiled beef or pot roast
16 cups kale leaves, stripped from about 2 pounds, cooked, and chopped
freshly ground black pepper to taste
salt to taste
8 to 12 smallish red new potatoes, steamed or boiled and cut into eighths, piping hot
2/3 cup chopped curly parsley
12 or more pickled gherkins or cornichons

Over medium heat, melt 2 tablespoons butter in each of 3 large skillets. When hot, fit the beef slices in a single layer in 2 skillets and spread the kale in its pan (or have it wait its turn). Grind pepper over everything. Stir the kale to heat it up and to absorb the butter. After 1 long minute, turn the browned beef slices with tongs and brown the other side for another 60 to 90 seconds. Stir the kale. After 2½ minutes' total cooking, the beef should be browned on both sides and the kale hot and buttery. Taste the kale for seasoning.

Arrange the slices of beef, overlapping, near the edge of a large heated platter, leaving room for the potatoes. Blend any butter from the beef skillets into the kale and heap the kale in the center of the dish.

If you've waited to sauté the kale, cover the meat with foil, set it in the oven, and cook as directed.

Arrange the potatoes around the edges of the dish. Sprinkle the whole with parsley, and garnish with gherkins.

If you have them, serve with a pot of English brown mustard and pickled walnuts. Offer chilled hard cider or dark beer or a full-bodied red wine at room temperature. A peppery bit of Stilton cheese to follow, then an apple crisp for dessert.

Ornamental Cabbages and Kales

Alternative: Red Russian kale.

Harvest tender leaves from the base, trying as long as you can to preserve the shape of the whole plant.

These full-blown-roselike ornamental cabbages are at their best uncooked, as decoration—either whole or individually using their ruffled subtly colored leaves. That's not to say you can't cook them—method and time are under Kale.

When you have a lovely leaf shape, the last thing you want to do is chop it into oblivion. Other kales can be cut up, but not peacock kales with their art nouveau curls.

When the thick stems of the plant from which the peacock feathers sprout are very young, you can peel the stems, slice them into matchsticks, and treat them as celery. If the stalks are tender, you can chop them up and use them in a stir-fry. Alas, as the plant ages, the leafy green part of the leaves can be cooked to tenderness, but the stalks will be too tough. I've found that about half the weight of the leaf is green and half is stalk.

Bruschetta with Peacock Kale

MAKES 2 SERVINGS

Here's a composition with its roots in the French and Italian countryside—with a Vermont accent. Because the leaves are whole and sometimes a bit long, it can be messy to eat, but wonderful. Heaped on a crust perfumed with garlic, the rich green leaves and specks of orange cheese beneath translucent red or yellow tomatoes make this beautiful as well as tasty. Perfect for a picnic or lunch in the garden.

This recipe is for spring-planted kale, when tomatoes are still available in late summer. For overwintering kale, use a handful of sun-dried tomatoes reconstituted in boiling stock or water, then sliced into strips.

You can prepare all the elements several hours in advance, then put together the sandwich just before serving.

salt to taste
10 lightly packed cups peacock kale greens, no stalks or stems
2 large slices of sourdough or French bread
2 garlic cloves, sliced in half
½ cup shredded sharp cheddar or other tasty cheese, 1 ounce
1 tablespoon fruity olive oil
freshly ground white pepper to taste
2 ripe red or yellow tomatoes, thinly sliced, or strips of 2 reconstituted sun-dried tomatoes

Put a big pot of salted water on to boil. Swish leaves in a sinkful of cold water, then soak for 30 minutes to float any aphids. Examine them carefully for caches of bugs.

Drop the leaves into the water and boil uncovered over medium heat until tender but still bright, about 15 minutes. Lift out and press out moisture on a folded towel. Save the stock.

While the greens cook, toast the bread until browned and crisp, then rub both sides of each slice with garlic.

In a bowl, use your hands to blend the leaves, cheese, and oil. Add pepper and taste for seasoning. Heap the greens on the toasts and cover with overlapping slices of fresh tomatoes or strips of softened dried tomatoes.

Serve with a chilled fruity white wine or crisp beer. An icy apple is all you'll need for dessert.

KOHLRABI

Pull when you're ready to use them because these science-fiction-looking roots—with their appendages shooting out all over the place—don't keep. Harvest when the size of a plum. Young kohlrabis can be eaten like apples—they're crisp and have a nutted sweetness.

Never peel kohlrabi—much of the flavor lies just beneath the skin. Rinse, slice off the stalks, and save the leaves for preparing on their own. Steam rather than boil the roots to preserve their delicacy and cook them whole—start testing after about 10 minutes. Then slice or dice or quarter or mash. Kohlrabi is high in fiber and a fine source of vitamin C and potassium. Remember to add tender leaves and raw root to salads.

Young kohlrabi leaves—their flavor similar to but sweeter and earthier than cabbage—can be prepared in any recipe for cabbage or even spinach. The stems have the crisp nip of radish. You can also steam or stir-fry tender early shoots. Most recipes for turnips, daikon, celery root, and chayote are suitable for kohlrabi, but kohlrabi's flavor is subtler than these, so keep it simple. Cook as you like and finish with a little melted butter and lemon juice or browned butter or hot cream or sour cream or cream sauce, with chopped parsley, chives, chervil, tarragon, caraway seeds, or dill.

DELICATE KOHLRABI AND TOMATO SALAD: Makes 6 or 7 servings. Trim 4 medium-size kohlrabi. Cut into long shreds about 1/8 inch thick on the slicing blade of a food processor or Moulin Legume or a mandoline. Toss with about 2 tablespoons olive oil and 1 tablespoon fresh lime or lemon juice. Chop 2 large ripe tomatoes medium-fine and blend in with a handful of chopped summer savory. Add coarse salt and lots of pepper and taste for seasoning. At the end, pour the juice at the bottom of the bowl over a piece of toast and feed it to the cook.

MELONS

One of the greatest pleasures of the kitchen garden is growing melons you can't buy. Some of the sweetest—Crenshaws, for example—are so fragile that they cost a fortune at the market. Others—perfumed European true cantaloupes and Galia types, yellow watermelons—either are not available or are among the costliest wares of the produce stand. You certainly can't buy citron melons, the kind whose rind you turn into pale jewels. However, unless you live in Melonland, melons can be an iffy crop, sometimes less flavorful than you'd hoped. So among the recipes for the glories of the patch are a couple that turn disappointment into delight.

Making small balls of melon with a melon baller is fun and looks festive, but I don't do it with my homegrown melons—too much waste!

Speaking of waste, be sure to save the nourishing seeds and roast them—they have a melony flavor (although not all are 100 percent edible, they're tasty to chew on). In China some watermelons are raised for their seeds alone.

ROASTED MELON SEEDS: Makes about 1 tablespoon seeds per pound of melon. Turn the seeds and pulp into a vessel full of water and let stand awhile. The seeds will float, sink to the bottom, or cling to pulp. Scoop up the floating ones, pull off those clinging to pulp, then strain the water to get the rest. Spread on the baking tray of a toaster oven (bits of pulp won't hurt) and roast at 325°F until toasted, about 25 minutes for dessert melon seeds, longer for watermelon seeds. Salt or not, as you like.

Dessert Melons

Once a melon has been cut open, all ripening stops. If your melon is wonderfully scented and flavored, serve it barely cold rather than chilled so you can appreciate its bouquet. Chilling makes a melon refreshing but blunts its aroma and taste.

Time was when you were supposed to eat dessert melon with a silver spoon, since other metals react to the acid. It's still a pleasing idea.

The ancient Romans regarded these melons as vegetables, which they are, being cousins to cucumbers and West Indian gherkins.

ANCIENT ROMAN MELON SALAD: Makes 4 servings. If a melon proves to be handsome but has less flavor than you'd hoped, this dressing inspired by one from Apicius for *Pepones et melones* will liven it up. In fact, it's *delicious.* The salad can be prepared a few hours in advance.

Quarter and seed a ripe melon (about 3 pounds). Cut off the rind and slice each quarter into 8 crescents. Arrange them on 4 pretty salad plates.

In a 2-cup glass measure, cook ½ cup mild honey in the microwave a few seconds just until the honey thins out. Blend in 1 tablespoon plus 1 teaspoon cider vinegar, a scant 3 tablespoons minced fresh mint leaves, and salt and freshly ground black pepper to taste (I use about ⅛ teaspoon each). Pour over the melons. Serve cold but not icy.

For a truer Roman taste, add a drop of Thai fish sauce and a dot of chopped sweet marjoram leaves.

Netted Melons: Muskmelons, Cantaloupe, Nutmeg, Persian

We don't need to know a melon's botanical type to enjoy eating it. But indications of ripeness, whether it will ripen off the vine, and characteristics of flavor vary according to type, so that's why it's good to know which is which. A ripe dessert melon is usually a little soft on the blossom end (opposite where it is/was attached to the stalk).

The rind of these melons is clearly netted. The flesh is usually orange and musky. You'll know it's perfectly ripe when you take hold of the melon and it slips off the vine—this is called *slipping*. To choose from picked melons, the rind beneath the netting should be golden or bronzed, the netting prominent, and there may be tiny cracks at the stem end. Often a ripe melon has no scent. These melons don't ripen very much off the vine.

Persian Melon Rings

MAKES 6 SERVINGS

A perfumed ripe muskmelon is perfection in itself, especially if you've grown it. I don't gild this lily—I just try to make it as delectable to look at as it is to eat. This presentation makes an exciting first course or dessert—you can use any sweet large melon and any kind of blackberry.

To enhance dessert melons with flowers, choose smallish blossoms in yellow, orange, red, purple, and blue. I use nasturtiums and Johnny-jump-ups. Where summers are hotter, you can use Tangerine Gem, Lemon Gem, and African marigolds for the sunny hues and borage and annual clary sage for the deeper tones. If African marigolds are too big, heap just their petals in the center.

Everything can be prepared in advance for assembling just before serving, although most flowers will hold for half an hour in a cool place.

Directions seem complicated, but the arrangements go quickly, especially with another pair of hands.

3 medium-large perfectly ripe Persian melons of the same size
about 24 medium-size yellow to red edible flowers
about 24 small blue to purple edible flowers
36 small mint or other sweet edible leaves
36 ripe blackberries

To cut 6 melon rings, all as close in diameter as possible, slice 1-inch-thick rounds to either side of the center line (between stem and blossom ends) of each melon. Lay the rings on your work surface. Making the cuts so the melon ring is symmetrical and smooth, run the tip of a small sharp knife around the outside edge, cutting away the rind, then run the knife around the inside edge, cutting away the seeds. Now make 6 evenly spaced V-shaped notches—about 3/4 inch wide at the rim—around the edge. Wrap and chill the rings if you wish. (Of course, use the rest of the melon in a fruit cup.)

To serve, set the rings on 6 pretty plates. Set 4 of the yellow-to-red flowers in the center, then tuck in 4 blue-to-purple flowers. Slip a mint leaf, tip side out, under each notch and lay a blackberry on the leaf, tucking it into the notch—be sure you can see the leaf tip. Serve.

Resist the temptation to sprinkle a superbly flavored melon with spirits—it will muddy the delicate flavor. However, a glass of port is a classic companion for dessert. On the other hand, if you have muskmelons that are good but not great, port will make them festive.

CANTALOUPE WITH PORT: Makes 6 servings. Cut a triangular plug in the stem end of 2 ripe cantaloupes or other muskmelons—make it large enough for a small spoon to slip through. Scrape out the seeds, then stand the melon in a bowl and fill the cavity with port—about 1/2 cup. Fit in the plugs, butter the seams, and chill for 4 to 6 hours.

To serve, wipe off the butter, unplug, and drain the port through a fine sieve into a pitcher. Peel and slice the flesh into bite-size cubes. Heap into stemmed glasses and moisten with the port. Garnish with a flower and offer crisp cookies on the side.

For a more delicate steeping, use a dessert wine such as rosé, Muscat, or Tokay or experiment with other fortified wines such as Marsala, Madeira, and sherry.

Smooth Melons: Honeydew, Crenshaw, Casaba, Canary, Christmas, and Cavaillon

These melons are slow to mature, yielding large mildly scented fruit with white, green, or yellow-green flesh, with rind that's smooth or somewhat wrinkled. These melons don't slip. You'll have to get close to the vine and breathe in deeply at the blossom end—when the melon smells melony, cut it off with a knife. Smooth melons continue to ripen somewhat after picking. To ripen fully, tuck individually in a paper bag and close loosely. Set in a cool place, not the refrigerator, until fragrant. Casabas are good keepers.

PICKLED MELON: At season's end, remembering melons are related to cucumbers, you might pickle unripe melons, either sourly as in the recipe for gherkins or sweetly as for West Indian gherkins. Just cut the peeled flesh into small cubes and proceed.

HONEYDEW MELON WITH GINGER: Allow about 1/3 pound per person. In summer, this is one of my favorite first courses. It's easy, pure, versatile—goes with everything from down-home barbecue to a pull-out-the-stops curry—and it shows off a good honeydew to advantage.

The melon can be prepared well in advance—cut it into wedges, scrape off the seeds, then fit it back together to keep it best. Remember to serve the sweetest melons at room temperature.

To serve, chop 2 to 3 nice pieces of crystallized ginger medium-fine. Set each slice on a plate and sprinkle with the ginger. Garnish with borage or calendula blossoms.

COLD CRENSHAW MELON SOUP: Makes 12 servings. Spicy Crenshaws are my favorite of this group. They make a delightful cold soup. Muscat wine blends beautifully with melon. When you serve the soup depends on how sweet the melon is. If it's richly perfumed and sweet, serve the soup for dessert in the Scandinavian fashion, with glasses of the chilled wine and a crisp not-sweet almond-flavored cookie. I've also made this soup when the melon wasn't especially sweet, and it was more appropriate as a first course with cream cheese and crackers. A friend suggests that the not-so-sweet soup would be ideal as a palate refresher between rich courses instead of a sweet sorbet. Of course you can change the wine to suit the occasion.

A large cantaloupe makes half this recipe.

You can prepare this the day before serving. The wine slowly withdraws, so adjust the amount before serving. Serve barely cold so you can taste all the flavors.

Use a sharp knife to peel a large (about 5½ pounds) Crenshaw melon—leave no green. Seed and roughly cut it up, then puree it until smooth in a blender or through a food mill or sieve (a food processor won't get it smooth enough). If you've used the blender, let the frothy puree settle down awhile before measuring.

In a bowl, blend 6 cups puree, 2 cups Muscat or other wine, 1 cup fresh orange juice, and a pinch of salt. Cover and refrigerate until cold but not chilled, about 6 hours (½ recipe takes 4 hours).

To serve, stir well to blend froth and juice, then ladle into chilled soup bowls. Garnish with mint sprigs.

True Cantaloupes: Charentais, Ogen, Sweetheart

These are usually small and considered the most fragrant and tastiest of all melons. They have a hard unnetted rind with green, orange, or pink flesh. Not slipping melons, they're ripe when they smell fragrant and when the first leaf above the fruit turns pale—sometimes there will be a small crack on the melon close to the stem. Cut off with a knife. They won't ripen further off the vine and don't keep long once ripe.

These are the melons you don't fool with. Some people like to grind spicy black pepper over them—very nice. Others like a squirt of lime juice or a sprinkling of ground ginger. A small melon-half bowl for raspberries steeped in maraschino liqueur is heavenly. Italians have been wrapping crescents of melon in paper-thin slices of prosciutto forever, and it is one of those glorious connections in the mouth that makes you close your eyes. True cantaloupes are perfection in this way.

One of these small melons makes one serving, and it's flattering to receive the halves with pinked edges. Cut around the middle with a small sharp knife in Vs, alternating upside down and right side up. Make the last connection, lift, scoop out the seeds, then heap the center with flowers before serving.

Or fill the center with a small scoop of pure lemon or lime ice or the finest vanilla bean ice cream and top with a drift of golden petals.

LAOTIAN MELON IN COCONUT MILK: Alan Davidson (*Fruit*) describes a delectable Laotian way with sweet dessert melon. Heap large-matchstick-size pieces of melon in small bowls. Blend unsweetened coconut milk with sugar to taste, then mix with the melon and serve garnished with rose petals.

I sprinkle a dash of cinnamon over the top. Davidson's version involves thick and thin freshly steeped coconut milk. But you can use unsweetened canned coconut milk.

Mediterranean/Tropical

Somewhat confusing in terms of their heritage, these melons are intensely flavored with aspects of banana, strawberry, pineapple, pear, mango, and citrus. Most are ripe when the rind begins to change from green to yellow. After-harvest ripening varies with the cultivar.

These fruity melons lend themselves to mixing with other sensuous fruits.

Melon and Mango Ice Cream

MAKES ABOUT 1 QUART TO SERVE 6

The remarkable thing about this light ice is that, as beautifully as the flavors blend, you can clearly taste the melon, the mango, and the mint. Only make it with a deeply flavored Mediterranean melon, however.

As with all ice creams, this is best freshly made. Serve within a few hours of freezing or take out of the freezer 15 to 20 minutes ahead to soften slightly before spooning up.

- 2 cups puree of ripe Mediterranean melon (start with 2 pounds melon)
- 1 cup puree of slightly underripe mango (start with 1 large mango), or 2 firm ripe peeled peaches
- 1 cup half-and-half
- 2 tablespoons sugar
- 1 tablespoon fresh lime juice or to taste
- ½ tablespoon finely chopped fresh mint leaves
- 8 sprigs of lemon verbena or scented geranium, optional

Whisk all the ingredients together in a jar until the sugar has dissolved. Cover tightly and refrigerate for 12 to 24 hours. Freeze according to your ice cream maker's directions. Garnish with a sprig of lemon verbena or scented geranium.

Golden Crispy Hybrid Melons

Harvest when the rind is canary yellow and the melon is fragrant.

These white-fleshed Asian melons are remarkable—once you've set the seeds aside for roasting, the whole fruit is edible, the skin being almost as tender and crisp as the flesh. Slice as you would any melon, then relish the texture and flavor. A few drops of something equally exotic over the slices, such as orange flower water, is a lovely idea.

Watermelons

Although in the cucumber family, these are not cousins of cucumbers or dessert melons.

Gauging when a watermelon is ripe is difficult. Among all the signs, probably the most accurate is when the melon's underbelly turns from pale to yellow and the surface turns from powder or sheen to dull.

The highest and best use of watermelon, it seems to me, is to slice and eat it out of hand sitting in the garden or on a picnic—somewhere where the air is as sweet as the melon. I like my pieces in crosswise slices—rounds or rounds cut into wedges—and I like the rind off, which seems luxurious somehow. Even though it may blunt the flavor of a really great watermelon, there is no question that watermelon must be eaten cold.

WATERMELON WATER ICE: Makes 8 servings. A festive way to serve cold watermelon is as a European water ice, which the Italians call *granita* and the French *granité*. It's a cinch to make, has clear pure flavor, and glides down the throat. The idea of adding vodka to underscore its flavor is Wolfgang Puck's, and it wafts the ice up there with ambrosia. For freshest flavor, serve the same day.

Wrap roughly chopped watermelon in a damp cloth and squeeze out the juice to get 1 quart. Place a scant ¼ cup sugar in a glass measuring cup and add water to make ½ cup. Stir until the sugar dissolves, then blend into the juice with 1 tablespoon each of fresh orange juice and fresh lemon juice. Stir in about ¼ cup vodka if you like.

Turn into a shallow metal pan and set in the freezer. In about an hour, when ice has formed, use a spoon to chop and stir the ice back into the liquid parts. Do this every hour until, after 2½ to 3 hours altogether, the mixture is still slushy but frozen. Cover with foil. If the ice gets too hard, you can turn it to slush in the food processor, but the texture won't be the same. Serve garnished with a hollyhock or other edible blossom on each scoop.

Watermelon Party Basket

MAKES 14 TO 16 SERVINGS

Diced watermelon's grand in a fruit cup, lending color and that heavenly icy crunch—and it holds up. If you have a summer party coming up and a super watermelon ripening, plan to turn the melon into this gorgeous fruit basket. For the Fourth of July, I stick in paper flags on toothpicks. My thanks to Lynnda Hart for contributing her artist's eye to this recipe.

The basket and all elements can be prepared several hours in advance, but put it together just before serving.

This is one place where a melon baller is desirable—it makes getting the melon out easiest. But a teaspoon works, too. Turn the rest of the melon into granité (preceding recipe).

Any number of ripe fruits in any proportions would be splendid. There isn't any fruit that watermelon won't complement. Here are the easiest to prepare, all colorful and delicious together.

1 handsome oval (about 14 pounds) ripe red-fleshed watermelon
2 cups fresh orange juice
4 large (¾ pound) red plums, halved and pitted
1½ large (¾ pound) peaches, halved and pitted
1 pint (¾ pound) blueberries
2 cups (¾ pound) seedless green grapes
1 pint (¾ pound) small ripe strawberries with their leaves on
1 pint (¾ pound) blackberries
flowers to border the basket
16 mint sprigs
2 fifths champagne, chilled, optional

For a decorative edging, plan to scallop or pink it with a knife. When you slice the melon to make the basket, make the cut an inch above halfway.

Slice the watermelon in half—or higher—lengthwise through the middle. There's no handle on this basket. Leaving a margin of red, remove the watermelon's flesh in balls with a large melon baller or in ovals with a teaspoon (cut the ovals in half). You'll need 4 cups, so take the melon balls from the seedless heart, turning the pieces into a bowl. When one level is done, scrape the surface and scoop again. Refrigerate the melon balls.

Place the orange juice in a large bowl. Cut the pitted fruits into pieces the size of the watermelon pieces and toss them in orange juice so they won't darken. Heap the blueberries and grapes on top, cover, and chill.

Remove the rest of the melon and scrape the inside smooth. If necessary, cut off a small layer underneath to make the basket stable. Set it upside down in a cool place to drain.

At serving time, use your hands to mix all the chilled fruits together, then heap them into the basket, leaving the juices behind. Strew green-capped strawberries and the blackberries over the top. Tuck flowers and mint sprigs around the top here and there.

To serve, scoop up the fruit into a coupe glass or dessert bowl. You can pour on a splash of champagne if desired and serve the coupe or bowl on a plate. You can also spoon the fruit over a small scoop of raspberry or lime sherbet and then add champagne—you'll have 20 servings this way.

Citron Melon

Alternative: Watermelon with thick—repeat, thick—crisp rind.

These are small roundish blue-green melons grown just for their rind, which makes incomparable watermelon pickles for your—and your friends'—holiday table. Pick the melons underripe, just as their tendrils are beginning to turn brown (the last week of September for me). Choose fruit that's heavy for its size.

Crystal Watermelon Pickles

MAKES AT LEAST 7 PINTS

This is a nuisance to make—it takes almost 2 weeks, with a little fussing every day—and the cubes won't taste very promising when you're finished. But put the jars away on a cool, dark shelf until early December, then open one. Pick up a pickle with a fork and hold it to the light—you'll see the tines through the rind. Taste: the cubes will be crisp and absolutely delicious. Alas, there are no shortcuts. I've made the 2-day pickles, and they can't hold a candle to these.

This slow absorption of sugar is the process used to turn peaches, pears, apricots, and pineapple into glacéed fruits—the French call it *façon,* which means "making." This is a very old recipe.

It's hard to gauge yield from the starting weight of the melon. Weigh the prepared rind—you can expect at least 1 pint of pickles from every pound.

Canning details are in The Cook's Notebook.

about 18 pounds or 3 citron melons or small thick-rind watermelons, 5¾ to 6 inches

1½ tablespoons salt, preferably pickling salt

2 cups cider vinegar, 5 percent acidity

1 pint distilled white vinegar, 5 percent acidity

25½ cups sugar, about 11 pounds

a piece of fresh ginger the size of an egg, peeled and finely shredded

the zest of 1 large lemon, in a spiral

30 whole cloves

With a heavy knife, cut the melons into eighths from stem to blossom end. Discard the seeds and carefully slice off all pink flesh—it won't get crisp. Pare off the outer green skin and the paper-thin layer beneath it. Cut the rind into 1-inch squares and triangles or any shapes you please.

Bring a big pot of water to a boil and stir in the salt. Drop in the rind, return to boil, lower the heat, and simmer uncovered until a piece is tender with a trace of crispness at the center when tested with a thin skewer, no more than 10 minutes—longer and the pickle will be mushy. Meanwhile, prepare a big bowl of ice water.

Scoop up the cooked rind and drop into the ice water to stop the cooking, stirring. When cool, drain the pieces in a colander, then shake the cubes free of water. Turn into a 2-gallon crock or other nonreactive vessel.

In a nonreactive saucepan, bring the vinegars, 6 cups of the sugar, the ginger, lemon zest, and cloves to a boil over medium-high heat, stirring until the sugar dissolves. Pour the liquid over the rind, stir, cover, and set in a cool place until the next day.

Then, and in the days following, drain the syrup into the pot, add the sugar specified in the following schedule, stir over medium-high heat until dissolved, and bring *just* to a boil. Pour the syrup over the melon and cover. Here's the schedule: day 1, 3 cups; day 2, $2\frac{3}{4}$ cups; day 3, $2\frac{1}{2}$ cups; day 4, $2\frac{1}{4}$ cups; day 5, 2 cups; day 6, $1\frac{3}{4}$ cups; day 7, $1\frac{1}{2}$ cups; day 8, $1\frac{1}{4}$ cups; day 9, 1 cup; day 10, $\frac{3}{4}$ cup; day 11, $\frac{1}{2}$ cup; day 12, $\frac{1}{4}$ cup.

Should you miss a day, just pick up where you left off. On day 12, after adding the sugar, discard the zest. You'll have buckets more syrup than you need for the jars.

You can strain off the ginger and cloves if you want a delicate pickle or leave them in the syrup.

Fill hot pint jars two-thirds to three-quarters full of pickles, then pour boiling syrup over them, leaving $\frac{1}{4}$ inch of headspace. Remove air bubbles with a nonmetal implement. Seal, process for 10 minutes in a boiling water bath, cool, label, and store.

These are not just for holiday tables—they're wonderful as a condiment with roasts and curries.

Mustard Greens

Alternative: Any one of these greens can be used for any of the others. In addition, any Asian green or other leaf with character can be used in a mustard greens recipe—it just won't have the verve.

Here you'll find the hot mustard greens. Remember that once a plant starts to make flowers, all of its concentration is poured into the seed-making business. The leaves are thus neglected and consequently turn bitter and tough. This is not to say the leaves will be inedible, just less than their former tender selves. So the basic rule for the tenderest, sweetest mustards is to pick them before flowering. In fact it's a good idea to pick mustard greens when they're less than 12 inches long. Harvest from seedling stage to leafy to flowering. Choose the youngest leaves for a cut-and-come-again harvest, or take the whole plant.

Always rinse well, because all sorts of undesirables can gather in their folds. Submerge the leaves in a tub of tepid water, ruffling them around to release dirt and critters. Lift out, shake, and wrap in a large towel—you can refrigerate them, but not for more than a few hours. Pull tender greens from tough stalks, chopping the stalks into much smaller pieces so they'll cook at the same time as the tender leafy parts.

Simmer assertive mustard leaves torn into large pieces uncovered in lots of salted water in a broad pot. Some mustards are tender in 10 minutes, some can take 2 hours. Don't worry about how long it takes, just simmer merrily until tender. Add the traditional chunk of smoked or fresh pork to the pot if you like or a coarsely cut-up onion, even some pungent flavorings such as rosemary and garlic. To underscore mustard's spicy pungence, add a little lemon juice or vinegar. Then a hot-peppery sauce is optional but divine. Add tender leaves to salad.

Flowers of all the mustards are edible—and beautiful.

The wild bitterness of some greens makes you sit up and take notice. I relish a challenging flavor—you have to think about it and work at it to appreciate it.

These greens are high in vitamin C, with a moderate amount of beta-carotene and a little iron.

Broad-Leaf Mustards

This is a group of large coarse looseleaf cabbages as well as some that resemble a head that might be lettuce but is all stalk. Some are strong and pungent, some pungent and sweet. These leaves are best when not completely on their own. I find them at their best as part of long-and-slow-simmered soups. Rinse well in tepid water.

When you're looking for recipes in books, once you've looked under Mustards, remember to check for Cabbage, too.

ASIAN MUSTARD SOUP WITH BARBECUED DUCK: One gardening friend makes a spectacular soup with her thick-stalked broad-leaf Swatow Large-Headed mustard. At the Asian market she buys a portion of barbecued duck. She removes the meat and flavors mild chicken broth by simmering it with the duck bones, a few star anise, and a little fresh ginger. She strains that, then simmers chunks of her mustard in the broth until very tender—a couple of hours or so. At the end she adds the duck meat sliced into strips. A garnish of chopped scallions and cilantro, and it's served.

Spicy Mustard Leaf Soup, Somewhat Indonesian

MAKES 6 SERVINGS

With my broad-leaf mustards (I've also made it with collards and rapini), I make an interesting soup inspired by one from Indonesia. Floating in a golden broth are a green tracery of leaves, yellow kernels of corn, nubbins of black beans, and glints of red tomato. The flavors are light but complex. Good for supper on an Indian summer evening.

Rather than use frozen kernels of corn and canned tomatoes, save this soup for a seasonal treat.

- 10 cups chicken broth or 5 cups broth and 5 cups vegetable stock
- 1 large onion, thinly sliced and the slices quartered
- 4 garlic cloves, chopped
- 2 to 3 fresh Thai or other small hot green chilies to taste, seeds removed, finely chopped
- ½ tablespoon turmeric
- 6 cups packed (about 1 pound) young broad-leaf mustard leaves, leafy parts roughly chopped, stems thinly sliced
- kernels from 2 ears of yellow sweet corn, about 1½ cups
- 2½ cups drained cooked black beans (from about 1¼ cups dried, a generous ½ pound)
- 1 firm ripe tomato, cut into ¼-inch dice
- 1 teaspoon ground coriander
- 3 to 4 tablespoons fresh lime or lemon juice or to taste
- salt to taste

In your soup pot, blend the broth, onion, garlic, chili, and turmeric. Bring to a simmer and drop in the leaves and stems. Adjust the heat so the broth just simmers, and simmer uncovered until the leaves are tender, 20 minutes or more, depending on the leaves.

About 8 minutes before you plan to serve, stir in the corn and beans. When the corn is tender but still crunchy, 3 to 5 minutes, stir in the tomato, coriander, and lime juice. Add salt then taste for seasoning. Serve in soup plates.

A bowl of rice on the side would be an Indonesian touch and would add nourishment to the supper. To make this a substantial main dish, add a handful of cooked shrimp or cubes of tofu to each serving. Cold beer seems to go best with spicy food, I think.

Broccoli Raab

Broccoli raab has turnip greens' nippy taste—so cook it the same way. The broccoli moniker is attached because the buds resemble sprouting broccoli's and as the stalks thicken they're a bit like broccoli's. Peel them. Any recipe for turnip greens or collards or other mustard can be used for broccoli raab. These leaves are high in vitamins A, C, and K, have a moderate amount of potassium, and offer a fair supply of folic acid. Add tender leaves to salad.

THREE-FLAVORS VINEGAR OVER BROCCOLI RAAB: Makes 2 cups; allow 2 tablespoons per serving. A dressing of olive oil and lemon juice makes these full-flavored greens delicious. But for a fast no-fat extra-tasty vegetable, cook tender broccoli raab and sprinkle on this invaluable Japanese vinegar—you'll need no oil. There isn't a vegetable it won't complement.

This will keep indefinitely in a tightly covered bottle in the refrigerator, but warm it to room temperature before serving.

Combine in a nonreactive saucepan 1 cup cool water, 3/4 cup rice vinegar, and 2 tablespoons sugar. Stir over medium heat until the sugar has dissolved and the mixture comes to a simmer. Remove from the heat and blend in 3 tablespoons low-sodium soy sauce.

Common or Leaf Mustards

Here we have large leaves, a foot or so long, coarse, with saw-toothed edges. They are mild leaves as mustards go. Everything else about them is the same as for mustards generally.

Mustard Greens with Pork Chops, Italian Style

MAKES 4 SERVINGS

This savory sauce is especially suited not only to sweet pork but also to the assertive flavors of the mustards, turnip greens, and broccoli raab and of course the more delicate kale, chard, collards, beet leaves, and dandelions. I often mix greens together, depending on what's in the garden. The tougher the leaves, however, the more meticulous you must be in pulling off stems thicker than ⅛ inch, and the more finely the leaves must be chopped.

Start the greens first—they can be half-cooked several hours in advance. The chops must be last-minute, but they go quickly.

- 12 cups packed (2 pounds) tender common or any mustard greens, rinsed and separated into leaves and stems
- about ¼ cup olive oil
- 2 garlic cloves, finely chopped
- 4 loin or rib pork chops at room temperature, patted dry
- leaves from 2 4-inch fresh rosemary sprigs or 1 tablespoon dried
- 1 cup coarsely pureed fresh or cooked tomatoes
- ½ cup dry white wine
- 1 tablespoon fresh lemon juice
- salt and freshly ground black pepper to taste
- 1 heaped tablespoon drained capers

Chop not-so-bitter leaves into pieces as large as 2 to 3 inches; as they increase in bitterness, chop them more finely. Chop stalks the same way. Turn into a deep heavy pot with the water that clings to their leaves from rinsing, and cook uncovered over medium heat, stirring occasionally.

When the greens have reduced in volume considerably, add a generous 2 tablespoons of the olive oil and stir to mix. Continue cooking until the greens are glossy, about 10 minutes altogether. Stir in the garlic and a bit more oil if the greens are browning in the pot. Cook for 10 minutes more. At this point they can be covered and refrigerated.

In a heavy nonreactive skillet in which the chops just fit, heat 1 tablespoon olive oil over medium-high heat, adding the rosemary. Brown the chops for 1 minute on each side, turning with tongs. Add the tomato puree and wine, cover the skillet, and turn the heat to medium-low. Cook to 137°F on an instant-read meat thermometer or test with the tip of a sharp knife to see if the flesh is lightly pink. If you want the pork pure white, cook to 160°F, but no higher. It will take less than 3 minutes on each side for thin chops so double the time for thicker ones. Baste with the sauce frequently as they cook.

Lift the chops onto a heated serving platter, leaving the sauce in the skillet. Cover them with foil and keep warm in a very low oven.

Stir the greens into the skillet, cover, and simmer over low heat for 10 minutes, stirring occasionally. Blend in the lemon juice, then add salt and pepper and taste for seasoning. Arrange the greens around the pork chops on the platter, sprinkle capers over the chops, and serve. Potatoes are an essential complement.

If you'd like to enjoy these Italian greens on their own, add the tomatoes and wine when you add the garlic and seasonings. Cook for 20 minutes more, then finish with the lemon juice.

Curled Mustards

These very frilly crisp leaves are reminiscent of the curly kales. They're hot and spicy mustards, good in salads and razzle-dazzle when cooked. Everything else about them is basically the same as for mustards. Add the ruffly tender leaves to salad.

You can cook these greens in either of the preceding two recipes—or any mustard greens recipe for that matter—but mixing them with a milder leaf is more calming.

TWO GREENS MAKE ONE FINE DISH: Makes 4 servings. Rinse 6 packed cups of curled or any mustard greens and 6 to 8 packed cups of fresh spinach (about 1 pound each). Separate the tender leafy parts from the tougher stalks. Cook the mustard leaves in a large pot of boiling salted water until nearly tender, then throw in the spinach leaves and cook about 2 minutes, until nearly tender. Lift out and cook the stalks the same way—the time depends on their thickness and age. Start testing after 3 minutes. Turn all into a colander and press out excess liquid. Roughly chop everything together.

While the greens cook, chop and brown 2 smallish onions in a little butter in a large skillet. Add the greens, crumble in a suspicion of dried red chili pepper (seeds removed), and season with the juice of a lemon. Heat, enriching with a lump more butter, and serve accompanied by grits or corn bread.

You can make this supper by arranging a nest of the greens, laying in a poached egg, and sprinkling the egg with grated cheese.

Flowers of Mustards

When they are bright and the stems tender enough to eat, toss sprigs into salads, use them as edible garnish, set them in bouquets—they are invaluable hot yellows on the table as well as the plate.

Green-in-the-Snow Mustard

Large, vigorous, indented, hardy leaves that are mild when young, but as they mature, watch out. Basic mustard techniques and notes apply.

This is a worthy leaf. Usually I add ribbons to soup. Once in a while, after I've brushed the snow off a bunch, I cook it a Thai way. A bottle of Thai fish sauce keeps forever in a cool place and is appealingly piquant after the initial surprise.

THAI GREEN-IN-THE-SNOW MUSTARD: Makes 2 to 3 servings. If you've used up your last drop of Thai fish sauce, mince anchovy fillets and sprinkle them over the finished dish.

Using 6 cups young leaves, separate the greens from their stalks, rinse, and leave the rinsing water clinging to them. (The stalks may be too strong to eat. If not, chop finely and add to a soup.)

Heat a wok or large heavy skillet over high heat until smoking hot. Drizzle in a little mild oil, then add 3 to 4 chopped garlic cloves. Stir-fry for a few seconds, then drop in the leaves and stir-fry furiously to mix the garlic and greens. Sprinkle on 1 tablespoon Thai fish sauce, spread evenly in the pan, cover, and cook for 1 minute. Stir well, cover, and cook for another minute. Repeat until the leaves are tender but as crisp as possible.

Sprinkle on roasted unsalted sunflower seeds, grind on lots of black pepper, and serve at once with jasmine rice to accompany grilled fish or chicken. Beer goes splendidly with this.

Rapini

These are a form of turnip greens—prepare them accordingly. Nutritional information is about the same.

Sicilian Rapini

MAKES 5 TO 6 SERVINGS

Of course you can make this colorful Sicilian dish with chard or spinach or any other tasty leafy green.

- ½ cup pine nuts
- 1 tablespoon fruity olive oil
- 12 cups (2 pounds) leaves and tender stems of rapini or any mustard
- 3 garlic cloves, finely chopped
- ½ cup golden raisins
- 1 scant tablespoon red wine vinegar
- salt and freshly ground black pepper to taste
- 1 red sweet pepper, cut into small dice, for garnish

Toast the pine nuts in a large dry nonstick skillet over medium-high heat until browned, about 3 minutes. Remove them and drizzle in the oil. Slice the leaves into thin ribbons and finely chop the stems. Add the leaves and stems, still wet from rinsing, then sprinkle in the garlic, raisins, vinegar, and salt. Stir, turn the heat to medium, and cook uncovered, stirring frequently, until tender—the time depends on their age, but start tasting after about 8 minutes. Blend in the nuts, add pepper, and taste for seasoning. Serve topped with the sweet pepper. Delicious with chicken and fish.

NEW ZEALAND SPINACH

Alternatives: Spinach, Malabar spinach, or any large firm mild green leaf.

These fleshy not-quite-spinach-tasting leaves are appealing in form, with their triangular shapes and pointy tips. They're a hot weather substitute for spinach, because the heat doesn't faze the plant. Harvest in a cut-and-come-again way, as for spinach.

Wash branches of New Zealand spinach in a sinkful of tepid water, changing the water until clear. To serve raw, dry in a salad spinner or pat dry. Or leave the water on the leaves and steam them. To cook, drop whole stems into ample boiling salted water over high heat and boil uncovered until the color darkens and a leaf tests tender, about 5 minutes—older, tougher leaves may take longer. Drain quickly and proceed with the recipe.

A few leaves in salads add deep green and light crunch.

NEW ZEALAND SPINACH VINAIGRETTE: An easy and tasty way with New Zealand spinach—with all greens—is to cook branches, then sprinkle them while hot with a light vinaigrette, flavored with dry or Dijon mustard.

If you have some mustard vinaigrette left over from the hors d'oeuvre recipe under Celeriac, that would be ideal. For company, garnish each serving with a handful of sautéed mushrooms, themselves first tossed in vinaigrette.

ANOTHER COOKED NEW ZEALAND SPINACH SALAD: Add garlic cloves to the cooking water, chop them into the cooked leaves, and heap on slices of crisphead lettuce. Dress with a yogurt dressing—nice colors.

Okra

If you feel iffy about okra, know that it's not only sweet and roundly flavored but also very good for you. It's high in fiber, a good source of folic acid and vitamin C, and a fair source of magnesium, vitamin A, thiamine, potassium, and vitamin B_6. Harvest mature okra every day—like peas—so the pods won't get fibrous. Cut off with a knife when pods are 2 to 3 inches long, leaving the stems on the pod. Rinse and rub with a towel if they're fuzzy. The trick in cooking okra pods is to keep them whole, barely trimming the stem end and not touching the tip. This way the mucilaginous interior will stay on the interior until you eat it. Also, the cooking vessel mustn't be aluminum or iron—as with eggplant, the metal will darken the color.

Steaming uncut okra pods over a little water for about 3 to 4 minutes renders them tender without losing all their crispness. This is the way to make them most appealing—cooking them forever in a gumbo or stew is unfair to the pods. The beautiful flowers of okra are edible. Okra flowers resemble hibiscus—a relative. Rather than cook them, I use them for garnish. But don't forget that each flower you pick is one less pod of okra.

African Chicken and Okra Stew with Peanut Sauce

MAKES 5 SERVINGS

Since okra came to us from Africa, it is good to know how to make an African okra dish. This stew is East African in spirit. It's easy, with delectable flavors. Everything can be prepared in advance for cooking—which, to be its best, must be just before serving.

Cooking the okra pods whole and separately insures they won't be mucilaginous or overdone.

1 3¾-pound frying chicken, whole, at room temperature
3 cups chicken broth
4 garlic cloves, chopped
4 small red chilies, finely chopped, or 2 dried hot red chilies, crumbled, or to taste
2 medium-size onions, sliced ¼ inch thick
2 large ripe tomatoes, cut in ¼ inch thick slices, the slices quartered
about 5 cups (1¼ pounds) young okra pods
⅓ cup unsweetened unadulterated peanut butter
about 1 cup (5 ounces) chopped roasted peanuts

Set the chicken breast-down in a deep narrow saucepan. Add the chicken broth, then strew the garlic and chilies over the chicken. Cover the chicken with the onions and tomatoes. Cover and bring the broth to a simmer over high heat, then turn the heat to low. Simmer gently until an instant-read thermometer thrust in the thigh registers just short of 180°F, about 30 minutes.

Meanwhile, steam the okra until tender.

When the chicken is ready, add the okra to the pot, then drain the stock into a quart measure. Turn the peanut butter into a small heavy skillet and slowly whisk in 1½ cups of the stock. Bring this sauce to a simmer over medium heat, whisking until it's smooth—it will have the consistency of light cream. Turn into a bowl (save the spicy broth for another use).

Lift the chicken onto a large heated platter. Mix the okra with the other vegetables, then spoon them around the chicken. Sprinkle the chicken with some of the peanuts and turn the rest into a bowl. Serve over rice, thus: rice, vegetables, chicken, sauce, and peanuts. Offer cold beer and chutney, then a salad of sliced cucumbers, then icy watermelon for dessert.

CARIBBEAN OKRA IN CORNMEAL MUSH: Makes 4 servings. I'm especially partial to this recipe, since it can be made a day in advance, is unusual, and so good—the mush is silky, the okra at once crisp and soft. The cheese is my addition—perhaps not authentic, but a natural.

Steam 4 cups whole small okra pods (about 1 pound) over an inch of water until tender. In a medium-size heavy saucepan, whisk 3/4 cup white or yellow cornmeal with 3/4 cup cold water salted to taste. Whisk in 2 1/2 cups boiling water, then simmer the mush uncovered over medium heat, stirring frequently.

While the mush cooks, drain the okra (save the stock for another use) and slice the pods into 1/2-inch pieces. Stir them into the mush. Cover and cook the mush another 10 minutes for the two to blend, about 25 minutes in all. Before serving, stir in 1 cup shredded jack or other mild cheese, 2 tablespoons unsalted butter (optional), and 2 crumbled dried small hot red chilies, seeds removed. Taste for seasoning and serve as a vegetarian main dish heaped with sliced tomatoes or a side dish with seafood or heaped with crayfish or shrimp. Have sliced tomatoes on the side.

The Onion Clan

I'm keeping most of the clan together in this section because it's good to be reminded that when you find you haven't an onion for a recipe there are heaps of other alliums that will fill in—may even be more interesting. So have no qualms about moving your alliums around in your recipes—one of the joys of the kitchen garden.

Cooking and Slicing Onions, Including Potato and Multiplier Onions

You can use mature onions at the juicy just-pulled stage, but you must cure them for storage. After the tops have turned brown, pull the onions, then arrange them in a single layer in an airy place out of direct sunlight. Leave them for 1 to 3 weeks, turning them occasionally—the drier they'll be, the better they'll keep. Brush off the earth, then store the onions in an airy bag or container in a cool dark dry place. Most onions get hotter the longer they keep.

To Keep From Crying . . .

The best way to peel any of the onion clan is to pour boiling water over the bulb, wait a few minutes for the skin to loosen, then peel it under cold running water—or with the onion submerged in ice water.

Water rinses away some of the inherent sulfur, and cold suppresses it. To chop or slice without crying, have the onion well chilled. You may decide not to use the boiling water to loosen the skin if you have lots of onions to do.

Let the food processor chop, you say? Fine for the most part. But sometimes you'll want the uniform pieces that only careful hand chopping or slicing can produce.

Onions are low in nutrients, with only a bit of vitamin C and folic acid. But they make up for it: Studies indicate that onions may contain properties that lower blood pressure, inhibit blood clots, and reduce the bad sort of cholesterol.

Don't forget to take the tip of a small sharp knife and twirl out the small yellowish core at the root end of onions. Too often this is neglected, a small but telling detail.

Cooking onions are the sharper sorts, generally the onions that have been in storage. Slicing onions are the short keepers, the sweet guys—sometimes called *salad* or *Spanish onions.*

I'm sure you know what to do with your onions, but here are a few house favorites.

Cooking Onions, Red

Red onions are usually pink or cream-colored inside. I like the cultivars that are red clear through. Check the catalogs carefully.

Keep a jar of sliced red onions in a marinade in the refrigerator—use the same recipe as for red cabbage. Toss into salads, chop raw into bean dishes, mince and sprinkle over any vegetable or fish dish.

As a rule, red onions don't keep very well, so use them at their prime in summer.

I've come to feel that red onions are perhaps the most beautiful vegetable of all. Rosy skinny Purplette scallions, for example. They are surprisingly sensuous sliced into thin scarlet ringlets.

SMOTHERED RED ONIONS AND SWEET GREEN PEPPERS: Makes 4 to 6 servings. Cooked red onions are even sweeter than raw ones and just as pleasing to the eye. Try this old favorite of my grandmother's in lavender and green. You can make this several hours in advance.

Slice 2 large red onions and 1 large green pepper 1/4 inch thick. Heat 1 tablespoon unsalted butter in a large cast-iron skillet over medium heat. Add the slices, sprinkle with 1/4 teaspoon sugar and salt to taste. Cook gently, covered, shaking the skillet occasionally until tender, about 6 to 7 minutes. Add freshly ground white pepper then taste for seasoning. Mix in 1/4 cup finely chopped parsley and serve hot or at room temperature. Great over hamburgers.

Summer's Garden Pizza

MAKES 8 TO 10 SERVINGS

Here is a pizza celebrating the colors of summer—red onions light it from beneath. Because the crust is a marvel of lightness, the pizza is satisfying without being filling, and it reheats nicely. You can prepare all the ingredients and keep them refrigerated while the pizza dough rises.

- about 32 small or 18 large (3/4 pound) ripe red cherry tomatoes, cut in half
- about 1/4 cup extra-virgin olive oil
- 3 plump (1 generous pound) red onions, thinly sliced
- 3 large garlic cloves, thinly sliced
- salt and freshly ground black pepper to taste
- 3 medium-size (1 pound) mixed zucchini and yellow crookneck squashes, cut into matchsticks
- 1 recipe Pizza Dough in The Cook's Notebook
- 1/4 cup finely chopped fresh basil or marjoram leaves or 1 heaped tablespoon dried
- 1 1/2 cups (1/4 pound) crumbled mild goat cheese, feta, Gorgonzola, or shredded medium-sharp cheddar
- 2 1/4 cups (6 ounces) coarsely shredded mozzarella cheese

Turn the cherry tomato halves into a bowl, drizzle on ½ tablespoon of the olive oil, and toss gently to coat each piece. Heat the oven to its hottest. Set the rack on its lowest position. If you have a baking stone, set it on the rack.

Heat 1 tablespoon of the oil in a heavy skillet over medium-high heat. Add the onions and sauté, stirring occasionally, until limp, about 5 minutes. Stir in the garlic and cook for another minute. Season with salt and pepper, then spread on a large plate to cool. In another tablespoon of oil, sauté the squash the same way, until translucent, a long 5 minutes. Season and cool on another plate.

Stretch the prepared dough 13 inches wide on an oiled pizza pan, a heavy square baking sheet, or a square of wide heavy foil shiny side down sprinkled with cornmeal. Sprinkle half the basil evenly over the dough, leaving a ½-inch margin. Next make a bed of the onions; on them, strew the squash pieces; over them, strew the cherry tomatoes. Evenly distribute crumbles or knobs of the goat cheese, strew with mozzarella, then sprinkle with the remaining basil. Drizzle a thread of oil all over to moisten, about 1½ tablespoons altogether. Bake until the edges are brown and crisp and the filling is melting hot, 8 to 12 minutes. Serve at once.

This pizza can be a meal in itself, followed by a peppery/bitter salad of nasturtiums and arugula, and finishing with something mild such as chilled juicy pears. Cold Italian white wine is the thing to drink.

At high altitude, bake for 15 minutes.

Cooking Onions, White

Vidalias and Walla Walla onions are super-sweet white onions. They depend largely on the soil for their sweetness. Sweet white onions are best eaten raw—a recipe for them follows later in this section. White cooking onions can be pungent. The following recipe sweetens them.

Creamy Onion Pie

MAKES 8 SERVINGS

Here are creamy crispy common white onions with cheese, parsley, and caraway in melting pastry—as scrumptious as but less naughty than a traditional quiche.

Remember this easy treatment when you want onion slices that are extra-sweet and perkily crisp at the center without tasting raw.

The pie shell can be prepared a day or two in advance and the onions and other ingredients ready to go together hours in advance. But serve the pie warm, within a couple hours of baking.

1 recipe Flaky Pastry (in The Cook's Notebook)

1 tablespoon caraway seeds

4 large white onions, sliced ⅛ inch thick, then roughly chopped

2 tablespoons salt

1½ cups (about ¼ pound) medium-fine shreds of Swiss or medium-sharp cheddar cheese

3 tablespoons all-purpose flour

1 heaped cup chopped parsley, preferably flat-leaf

1 cup nonfat yogurt at room temperature

1 cup heavy cream at room temperature

freshly ground black pepper to taste

paprika for garnish

Make the pie dough as directed, but don't slice it in half. Pat into a ½-inch-thick round and chill for at least 15 minutes. Roll it out a whisper thicker than ⅛ inch and fit it into a 9½-inch pie dish (you'll have ample margins for error). Trim the edges ½ inch beyond the rim of the dish. Fold the extra under itself and flute this border against the lip of the dish if there is one or standing above the rim if there isn't a lip. Press the caraway seeds into the bottom and partially bake the shell. Cool.

To sweeten the onions put them into a big bowl along with the salt and mix well. Set aside for 15 minutes. Put a large pot of water on to boil. When the timer rings, fill the onion bowl with cold water and swish to free the salt. Drain the onions in a colander and turn them into the boiling water over high heat. Time 1 minute, stirring (it won't be boiling), then drain into the colander. Use a folded towel to press as much liquid as you can from the onions. Spread them on the towel to cool.

Heat the oven to 450°F and set a rack on the lowest shelf. Get out a large heavy baking sheet (fit 2 together if yours are light).

In the big bowl, use a fork to blend the cheese, flour, and parsley. Add the onions and mix with your hands. Blend the yogurt and cream in a bowl, then add and mix well. Add pepper. Smooth the filling into the pie shell, then sprinkle the top with paprika.

Set on the baking sheet and bake on the lowest rack until the whole pie bubbles and the top is nicely browned, about 45 minutes. If the pastry is in danger of burning, lay a sheet of foil, shiny side down, lightly on top. Or if you have an electric element right beneath your bottom shelf, move the rack up after 15 minutes.

Cool to warm and serve as a main dish for a luncheon or picnic. Serve with radishes, cherry tomatoes, and black olives. A dry Riesling would be perfect to drink.

Cooking Onions, Yellow

Golden onions are called *Spanish* in some parts of the country. They are full flavored, not so sweet as the sweetest whites. They make terrific fried onions—cook them slowly in a small amount of lard for the finest flavor.

Roasted Onion Soup

MAKES 6 SERVINGS

When the first snow flies (or when it gets as cold as it's going to get), make this haunting soup from your sweetest golden onions and invite people you love to share it. As mythical as onion soup may be, it's simple fare. This is our house soup, our version of one a French friend makes—inspired by the soup served in Paris's vegetable market, Les Halles. It goes together easily, roasting while you're getting ready and filling the air with an irresistible aroma.

The soup can be made a day or two in advance and reheated.

If you think of it in time, chill 4 medium-large sweet yellow onions, 1½ pounds, so you won't cry when you slice them. Heat the oven to 375°F while you slice the onions thinly. Turn them into a deep baking dish, preferably earthenware, and dot with 4 tablespoons unsalted butter. Roast the onions uncovered, stirring occasionally with a wooden spoon, until brown and very soft, about 1¾ hours in an earthenware casserole, about 1 hour in an enameled cast-iron pot.

Bring 1 overflowing quart beef broth and 1 overflowing quart vegetable stock to a simmer on top of the stove and stir into the onions. Turn the heat to 325°F and bake uncovered until the soup is bubbling and the onions are caramelized and melting tender, an hour or more. Stir in lots of freshly ground black pepper and 1¾ teaspoons balsamic vinegar, then taste. If you wish, add more balsamic vinegar by the 1/4 teaspoon until the flavor is very deep—but stop before you can taste the vinegar. Instead of balsamic vinegar, you can slowly add port wine to taste—or nothing. You can cover the soup, turn off the oven, and leave it there for an hour or two or remove and heat it later, covered, in a 325°F oven for about 30 minutes.

To serve, float a small thick slice of French bread for each person on top—you can toast the bread first to slow down the absorption of the soup. Heap the soup with shredded Gruyère or Swiss cheese (Gruyère adds a wonderful nuttiness)—2 cups or more. If you like, run the pot under the broiler to melt the cheese. Serve at once with more bread and cheese and a delicious Beaujolais or Pinot Noir.

Slicing Onions, White and Sweet

Onions like White Sweet Spanish, White Granex, and Crystal White Bermuda are ideal for salads, being marvelously sweet, crisp, fresh-tasting, and gleaming. They are best eaten raw, but look beyond salads to a broader use of their fine qualities. For example, this simple Indonesian sambal—a quickly made relish to serve with anything.

WHITE ONION SAMBAL: (makes 6 to 8 servings). Peel and thinly slice 2 sweet white onions, then cut the slices in half. Seed 2 fresh mild green chilies and slice them into thin matchsticks. Combine with the onions in a bowl and sprinkle with 1/8 to 1/4 teaspoon chili powder (or to taste) and the juice of 1 lime or 1/2 lemon. Add salt, taste for seasoning, and serve chilled.

For Thai food, add a sprinkling of shredded coconut. My friend Jeannine Perriseau adds chopped cilantro and toasted cumin seeds to this sambal and serves it with Indian dishes.

Slicing Onions, Yellow

Now that I've asked you to look away from salads for sweet raw onions, let's come back!

Japanese Onion Salad

MAKES 4 SERVINGS

Here is a quick Japanese way with yellow slicing onions—only fleetingly cooked. With thanks to Betty King for the fine touches.

This is easily prepared in advance. Do not use storage onions for this, but those in early winter that have been dried for only a short time.

1 teaspoon salt
4 sweet yellow onions, sliced into super-thin rings
¼ cup low-sodium soy sauce
2 tablespoons fresh lemon juice
¼ to ½ teaspoon sugar to taste
2 teaspoons toasted poppy or sesame seeds
freshly ground black pepper to taste
2 paper-thin slices of lemon, each cut into 6 triangles

Bring a large saucepan of salted water to a boil. Drop in the onions and stir. Count 1 minute, then drain and pat the slices dry.

In a mixing bowl, combine the soy sauce, lemon juice, and sugar. Add the onions, sprinkle with the seeds, then stir to blend all thoroughly. Add pepper to taste. Serve warm or cool in small bowls with the lemon pieces scattered over the top.

A Spanish Salad

MAKES 4 SERVINGS

This can be prepared well in advance. It is the Spanish custom to peel, seed, and chop all the vegetables. I don't.

Char the skins of 4 sweet red peppers on the burner or under the broiler. Turn into a paper bag, close tightly, and peel when cool. Slice the peppers into 1-inch chunks. Slice 4 ripe tomatoes the same size as the peppers. Cut 2 small sweet yellow onions into small dice. Combine all in a glass salad bowl with 1 cup pitted (or not) black olives, a handful of fresh tarragon leaves, and chopped flat-leaf parsley. Moisten with about ½ cup vinaigrette dressing and toss with your hands. Serve lightly chilled.

Green Onions, Including Bunching Onions and Scallions

For the most part these are the young things of the bulbing onions you cook and slice. Being young, they're delicate. Pull them as slender or plump as you please.

Trim off the roots, but use all the green stems—they're splendid if you have no chives handy. To serve these onions on their own, slice off leaves where they begin to grow thick and coarse—or limp and watery—slicing decoratively on the diagonal.

On a *crudité* tray add your smallest onions and serve them with what the Tuscans call *pinzimonio*—extra virgin olive oil, salt, and freshly ground black pepper.

Scallions are too little used for seasoning. There is a lightness, a sweet zing in young onions just pulled from the earth that makes them one of the most valuable of flavorings. See what happens when you finely chop up some scallion bulbs and stems when the recipe calls for parsley—more interesting. Scallions, aka green onions, shine with anything creamy—yogurt, sour cream, crème fraîche, the fresh cheeses. For example, the following version of a rich soup from the forties.

Cream of Scallion and Mushroom Soup

MAKES 4 SERVINGS

This is best freshly made because the mushrooms have barely cooked.

In a saucepan, simmer 1 medium-size potato, peeled and cut into small chunks, in 2 cups chicken broth and 2 cups vegetable stock or water. When tender—15 to 20 minutes—add 2 cups (about 30) chopped scallions, including tender leaves. Simmer uncovered just until soft, another 5 minutes.

Reserve 2 mushrooms from ½ pound. Puree the rest raw with the soup in a food processor or blender until smooth. Turn into the pot and blend in 1 cup half-and-half or yogurt. Add salt and freshly ground white pepper, then taste for seasoning. Heat gently just until hot, then serve garnished with thin slices of the reserved mushrooms and thinly sliced rings of scallion leaves.

Buttons, Boilers, and Pearls

Pull these little ones from pea to walnut size. Be sure not to waste their leaves.

Cipolline are button-shaped onions an inch or so wide and flattish on top and bottom. Although they're interchangeable with boilers—teardrops or rounds—*cipolline* have uncommon charm. The onions we love creamed for Thanksgiving are called *boiling onions* or boilers. They're the size of walnuts.

To cook small onions, pour boiling water over them. When they're cool enough to handle, peel them, then cut a shallow cross in the bottom. Soak the onions in ice water for half an hour to crisp and sweeten (an optional step). Simmer uncovered in a skillet in water to cover until tender when pierced with a thin skewer, about 15 minutes.

Italian Sweet-Sour Baby Onions

MAKES 4 SERVINGS

You can make this favorite with any small onions, and they can accompany any kind of meat, fowl, or fish in any season that you've got them. They are sleek and beautiful and fill your mouth with flavor.

These can be prepared a day in advance and warmed up.

Simmer 2 dozen (about 1 pound) 3/4- to 1-inch onions until tender. Meanwhile, in a large heavy skillet over medium heat, slowly melt 1/4 cup (2 ounces) finely chopped ham fat or bacon fat or lard. Add 1 tablespoon sugar and stir until dissolved, then blend in 1/4 cup white wine vinegar (or half white wine and half rice vinegar). Turn off the heat.

Drain the onions and pat thoroughly dry. Add them to the skillet, turn the heat to low, cover, and cook until tender, shaking the skillet frequently, about 30 minutes. Serve hot or at room temperature sprinkled with chopped capers. Broken toasted walnuts are a festive addition as well.

Leeks and Nebuka Onions

You can harvest a leek at any time. To harvest a leek, very carefully use a trowel to dig down until you can feel the roots of the leek. Worry and wiggle them until the whole leek comes up. Try to tug it out of the ground and you'll lose much of it.

Because they've been submerged in the soil, leeks and nebuka (Japanese bunching) onions are usually gritty in their layers. That's why it's wise either to slice the stalk lengthwise and flush out the sand or, if you slice it crosswise, carefully, gently, run a spray of cool water through the slices in a colander or sieve, then pat dry.

Leeks and nebukas can be used any way you'd use onions. Use their tender green leaves as part of the flavoring. If you've pulled gigantic hardy leeks in winter and the outside layers are tattered, just peel them away and use the sweet inner stem. Should you be surprised by a woody core in a leek, you've got one that's preparing to flower. Try to pull the piece out or slice around it and discard.

Leeks are infinitely useful in seasoning—soups and stews and sauces particularly—as well as being a delectable dish on their own. Simmer them in a skillet in broth for 10 minutes or more. Leeks cook to tenderness and then past it to mushiness in the blink of an eye, so be watchful.

Leeks have moderate amounts of folic acid, some vitamin C and iron, and a little vitamin B_6 and magnesium. Add tender bits to salad.

Baby leeks are sweet of themselves. If you're nervous about dirt, then slit and rinse them. If your experience has been that young ones don't gather much grit in their layers as they grow, you can roast them whole in a shallow dish with a sprinkling of sugar until golden.

Greek Leek and Rice Salad

MAKES 6 SERVINGS

This can be made a few hours in advance, but not so far ahead that the bits of tomato grow weary.

- 3 cups cooked long-grain white rice (preferably jasmine or basmati), with ½ teaspoon crumbled saffron tendrils or ½ teaspoon turmeric added to the water
- 2½ tablespoons fruity olive oil
- 4 cups ¼-inch slices of leeks, including tender leaves, about 2 medium-large leeks
- 1 large garlic clove, minced
- ¼ cup chopped fresh dill leaves, tender stems, and flower sprays (if in season)
- 1 tablespoon finely chopped mint leaves
- 1 tomato, cut in ¼-inch dice
- a handful of dried currants plumped in warm water and drained
- a handful of toasted pine nuts
- 2 tablespoons fresh lemon juice
- 1 tablespoon red wine vinegar
- salt and freshly ground black pepper to taste

While you're cooking the rice, heat ½ tablespoon of the oil in a large nonstick skillet over medium-high heat. Sauté the leeks until barely tender, stirring frequently, about 5 minutes. Stir in the garlic after 3 minutes.

In a salad bowl, use a fork to mix the warm leeks with the dill, mint, tomato, currants, and pine nuts, in that order. Add the rice and mix the same way, then blend in the remaining 2 tablespoons of olive oil and the remaining ingredients. Taste for seasoning.

Serve at room temperature in pretty bowls or heaped on leaves. Grilled fish or chicken go perfectly with this.

Shallots

Shallots are harvested like onions—when the tops die down. The bulbs are ready for storing at that point—no need to cure. They only last a couple of months, then they sprout—but they're still good to eat. Use shallots when you want a refined onion flavor—these are the aristocrats of the alliums. Shallots come in a wrapper, and sometimes there is an almost-separated young thing clinging to its mother. The easiest way to unwrap the bulbs is to cover them with boiling water and steep for a few minutes, then peel. Chop them finely and use raw in salads, egg dishes, pastas, and such. They are used mostly as seasoning, perhaps because they're so expensive in the market. But shallots are so easily grown and so sweet and mild that we should eat more on their own. Roast them in their jackets—350°F for 30 to 40 minutes—then drizzle with olive or a nut oil. Shallots are low in fiber, with a smallish amount of vitamin C and folic acid.

Shallots are one of those rare vegetables that seem to be always the bridesmaid and never the bride. Chopped shallots enhance classic French chicken simmered in white wine, fillets of sole simmered in white wine and finished with cream, the elegant duxelles—minced mushrooms and shallots sautéed together and finished with crème fraîche. But where are the shallots on their own?

Shallots can be cooked like boiling onions. Try braising them. Try candying them as you do carrots. Try slicing them into a salad with fennel. They make a terrific risotto.

SHALLOT VINEGAR: Shallot vinegar is one of the most useful of the flavored vinegars. It is classically used to season shellfish. It keeps in a dark, cool place for at least six months.

For every pint of white wine vinegar, blend in 1 cup minced peeled shallot bulbs, white part only. Pour into a clean dark green wine bottle and cork.

Shallot Greens

These greens, something between the size of small scallion and large chive leaves, are considerably more delicate than either. Use them as you would the stronger leaves, and keep a shallot greens pot going all year. If a recipe calls for shallots but you have just their leaves, you can substitute leaves for the bulb—if cooked, cook them much less since they're made of little more than pungent green and air. To chop these leaves finely, don't use a machine, because you'll lose essential oils. Stack them in a bunch, slice as thinly as you can with a sharp knife or snip with scissors, then chop until they're fine.

Sauce of Shallot Greens

MAKES 3/4 CUP TO SERVE ABOUT 8

Here is my adaptation of a classic French sauce, good with cold poultry and meats. A terrific way with leftover potatoes is to heat them in a skillet in this sauce. In a tightly covered jar, this keeps for at least 1 week in the refrigerator.

heaped 1/3 cup finely chopped shallot leaves
3 tablespoons hazelnut, peanut, walnut, or mild olive oil
6 tablespoons white wine vinegar or half white wine and half cider vinegar
salt and freshly ground black pepper to taste

In a serving pitcher, use a fork to blend the leaves, oil, and wine vinegar. Season to taste.

PARSNIPS

Wait until after a couple of nips of autumn frost before you harvest parsnips. As with all root vegetables, leave parsnips' skin on if you possibly can—a heap of goodness lies in their fine wrapping. Scrub the skin and cook them any way you please. Roast parsnips whole in the pan juices around a roast chicken, turkey, or any joint of meat. As with carrots and beets, roasting emphasizes the nutted flavor of sweet roots. While roasted parsnips are splendid, steaming is probably the most saving of flavor and nutrients—they take 15 to 20 minutes, but do not overcook. Parsnips are sweet, aromatic, and satisfying; they're also high in fiber. They are a moderate source of folic acid and vitamin C and a fair source of vitamin E, potassium, and magnesium. You can grate raw parsnips into salads.

PARSNIP SOUP: Sauté some onions and celery in a little butter or mild oil in a saucepan, add chopped parsnips and vegetable stock to cover, and simmer, uncovered until tender, about 15 minutes. Puree, thin to the consistency you like with milk, and heighten the flavor with lemon juice. Try adding grated apple to the soup another time. Frizzles of sautéed sliced scallions are good on top, too.

Parsnip Plops

MAKES 10 PLOPS TO SERVE 5 OR MORE

We're craziest about parsnips pureed, buttered, and fluffed with a little milk. When we have mashed parsnips left over, I make the following, inspired by Alfred Lunt and Lynn Fontanne's way with leftover mashed potatoes—they're crispy on the outside and creamy on the inside.

The plops can be prepared for baking several hours in advance.

4 tablespoons unsalted butter, plus more for the baking sheet
6 medium-large (about 1 pound) unpeeled parsnips, trimmed
1 large egg
¼ cup milk (nonfat is fine)
½ cup finely chopped parsley
a good pinch of freshly grated nutmeg
a good pinch of ground ginger
salt and freshly ground black pepper to taste

Brush a large baking sheet with butter. Cut the parsnips in half where they begin to taper and steam the pieces over an inch of water until tender, about 15 minutes (save the stock for another use). Send through a ricer or the medium blade of a food mill into a mixing bowl. Beat in 2 tablespoons of the butter, then the egg, milk, 1/4 cup of the parsley, the nutmeg, ginger, and salt and pepper to taste. Plop the puree onto the baking sheet by the scant 1/4 cup, spreading each to a scant 3 inches in diameter and swirling the tops. Cover and keep in a cool place if desired.

To serve, heat the oven to 375°F. Bake until lightly browned on top, about 25 minutes (a little longer if they've been chilled). Meanwhile, melt a generous tablespoon of butter. Serve the plops drizzled with the butter and sprinkled with the reserved parsley.

Mixing Roots Together

If you have a cache of lovely roots on the premises, and you find yourself needing to feed lots of hungry people (or needing to feed a few hungry people several times), I recommend this hearty delicious raspberry-colored soup contributed by Hildy Manley.

The finish of chopped raw onion—crisp against soft, bite against bland—was my husband's idea.

Root Soup

MAKES 10 TO 12 MAIN-DISH SERVINGS

You can make this a day ahead and keep it in the refrigerator, but don't boil the soup when you heat it up.

4 to 5 medium-size (1 pound) carrots
2 to 3 medium-size (1 pound) potatoes
1 medium-large (1 pound) rutabaga
6 medium-large (1 pound) parsnips
2 medium-size (½ pound) tender turnips
1 medium-large (¼ pound) beet, including greens
8 slender leeks, white part and tender greens
3 quarts water, vegetable stock, or water and stock
salt to taste
3 tablespoons fresh lemon juice
¼ teaspoon ground allspice
milk
½ cup chopped parsley, preferably flat-leaf
1 tablespoon chopped fresh winter or summer savory or 1 teaspoon dried
1 tablespoon chopped fresh dill leaves or 1 teaspoon dried
freshly ground black pepper to taste
2 cups plain yogurt
2 large onions, finely chopped, for topping, optional

Scrub and trim the carrots, potatoes, rutabaga, parsnips, turnips, and beet, then cut them into small chunks. Reserve the beet greens. Slice the leeks in half lengthwise, rinse out any sand, then slice into small chunks.

Turn the vegetables into your soup pot, add the water, and salt to taste. Cover and bring to a boil over medium-high heat. Turn the heat to very low, set the lid on askew, and simmer until everything tests tender, about 40 minutes, stirring occasionally. The last few minutes, slice the beet greens into thin ribbons and mix them in.

Coarsely puree the soup in a food processor or through a food mill, then return to the pot. Blend in the lemon juice and allspice, then add milk until the soup is the consistency you like. Gently bring to a simmer. Just before serving, whisk in the parsley, savory, and dill. Add pepper, taste for seasoning, and serve. Pass the yogurt and onions separately.

Good bread and cheese, a glass of red wine, and a fragrant pear tart complete the meal.

PEANUTS

What fun to grow your own peanuts! To harvest, loosen the soil around the plants with a digging fork, then carefully pry up the plant—pods won't be more than 6 inches below the surface. Shake off the soil and lay plants upside down so the pods will air-dry. Pods should cure for a couple of weeks on the plant, then for another week outdoors off the plant.

Shell peanuts just before using—the shell is a perfect storage container. Don't rinse and, unless directed to, no need to remove the skin, which adds flavor. It's lovely that our much-loved peanuts are so nutritious—these legumes are high in fiber, protein (more than nuts), niacin, folic acid, good sources of magnesium and phosphorus, and fair sources of thiamine, iron, zinc, vitamins B_6 and E.

Watch for Mold on Peanuts

Not that your peanuts will go uneaten long enough to get moldy, but be aware that a mold called *aflatoxin* can form on peanuts. You'd also have to eat a large amount of them to cause harm, but aflatoxin has been associated with liver cancer. Salt inhibits the growth of the mold, so if you're concerned, shell, roast, and salt your peanuts.

Otherwise, do not even taste peanuts that show a speck of mold or that look discolored or shriveled. And if you get one that tastes unpleasant, spit it out.

AUNT NELLIE'S MASHED POTATOES: My mother speaks, her blue eyes misty, of Aunt Nellie's mashed potatoes from her childhood. Where my California grandmother's sister learned to mix peanuts and potatoes is a mystery, but they are heavenly. Was it her father's Dutch heritage, I wonder—ultimately Indonesian? The potatoes are wonderful with poached fish, green beans, sliced yellow tomatoes, and chutney. For 4 servings, prepare 6 cups mashed potatoes with lots of milk and butter. Stir in 1 cup roasted whole Spanish peanuts. Add salt and freshly ground white pepper to taste and serve.

PEANUT NOUGAT CLUSTERS: Makes 4 cups. When you've harvested your own peanuts, you want to turn them into something terrific that's still pure peanuts. After stirring melted chocolate into part of our crop and dropping the nuggets onto waxed paper to cool, I make this simple sweet. Nougat is a very old candy, used in confectionery all over the world. It offers great possibilities. You can mix in sesame seeds or use honey as part of the sweetening or add a flavoring extract like vanilla or cherry. Chopped coarsely, the nougat is a great topping for ice cream. The clusters will keep in an airtight tin in the refrigerator until eaten.

Spread 2 cups raw Spanish peanuts in a thin layer in the microwave. Stirring every 2 minutes, roast until you can smell the nuts and test nuts are crunchy when cooled, about 6 minutes. Brush a large flat plate or pan with peanut or canola oil.

Turn the nuts into a large nonstick skillet and add a heaped ⅓ cup granulated sugar (or half granulated, half light brown). Stir constantly over high heat with a wooden spoon until most of the sugar has melted, about 3 minutes. Turn the heat to medium-low and keep stirring until every nut is coated in caramelized sugar, about 5 minutes more. Sprinkle with a little salt and spread the nuts on the plate. When cold, break into clusters.

PEAS

Seeds are full of nutrients because they provide the sustenance new plants must have to sprout into this perilous world. For my part, I couldn't care less whether sweet garden peas are good for me. Although not as nutritious as they would be if fully matured—i.e., dried peas—garden peas are almost as good for us as they are good to eat: a good bit of vitamin C and moderate amounts of fiber, folic acid, modest amounts of protein, thiamine, iron, and smallish amounts of phosphorus, vitamins A and B_6, niacin, and magnesium. That's a bundle when you consider these good things will be added to nutrients in other foods. Rinse before shelling, then save a few pods to sweeten the cooking water.

You've got to keep picking your peas, or the pea-factories will shut down. Pick when the pods are bright and gleaming and the peas inside are plump. Pick petits pois when the peas are just rounding up inside. As with old-fashioned sweet corn, the instant the fruit leaves the plant, peas' sugar begins converting to starch. That's why there are jokes about having the water boiling before you go into the garden.

To me the most felicitous way to eat my own peas, pure and simple, is to arrange the pods (their strings pulled off if necessary), only a few deep in a large skillet. (Remember, in cooking vegetables, that the more evenly spread out they are over the source of heat, the more evenly they cook—that's why skillets and woks are preferred to saucepans.) I add ½ inch of water, set the peas over high heat, cover, and bring to a boil—if I'm not indecently eager, I go back into the garden and pick a few sage or mint leaves and throw them in, too. After 3 minutes' boiling, I bite into a pod, then test every minute or two until the peas and pods are tender. I drain the pan, turn the pods into a bowl, add a lump of unsalted butter, salt and pepper, and serve everybody his or her fair share. To eat, we pull the pods through our teeth so the peas pop into the mouth along with a plush of pod meat (my grandmother would have a hissy fit at such vulgarity).

Garden Peas

When you simply cook a handful of shreds of lettuces with fresh peas, you'll have perhaps *the* classic pea dish.

Fresh Pea Pie

MAKES 8 SERVINGS

My mother's pea pie has been one of her favorite dishes for 40 years, inspired by a recipe from the gifted June Platt, author of graceful cookbooks in the 50s. Serve it as the accompaniment to simple roast poultry or meat or as the main dish for luncheon with crisp radishes and pickled beets.

Best straight from the oven, although everything can be prepared in advance.

½ recipe Flaky Pastry in The Cook's Notebook
6 cups peas, 4½ to 6 pounds unshelled
1 heaped lightly packed cup thin ribbons of corn salad or lettuce heart
2 fresh mint sprigs, finely chopped
½ cup (¼ pound) unsalted butter
½ teaspoon sugar
a little salt and freshly ground white pepper

Roll the pastry into a 12½-inch round. Cut a silver-dollar-size hole in the center. (You can cadge a little dough from the border and fashion decorative leaves to arrange over the lid if you like, attaching with a dab of cold water.) Lay the round on a plate, cover, and set in a cool place. If the peas are at all old, drop them into a big pot of boiling salted water over high heat. When the water returns to a boil, count a scant 2 minutes, then drain at once. Peas and the greens mixed with mint can be covered and refrigerated separately for a few hours. Bring to room temperature before continuing.

To make the pie, heat the oven to 450°F. In a smallish skillet, heat 3 tablespoons of the butter and sauté the greens and mint over medium-high heat just until wilted, stirring constantly. Add them to the peas and sprinkle on the sugar, salt, and pepper. Taste for seasoning. Mix well, then turn into a 10-inch pie dish preferably with a rim. Set a tablespoon of the butter in the center, then cut the remaining butter into flakes over the rest of the top.

Lay on the pastry lid, tucking the excess underneath itself at the edge of the rim. Pinch the border decoratively, pressing the pastry to the rim. (If your dish has no rim, make a border by doubling the dough at the edge and pinching it.) Bake 15 minutes, then turn the heat to 375°F. Bake until the peas are hot in the center (test with a fingertip) and the pastry has taken on color, about 15 minutes more.

Petits Pois

PETITS POIS: Makes 2 servings. Is there a smaller sweeter morsel in the vegetable kingdom than a petit pois? They're not baby peas but peas bred to be full-flavored when no bigger than a lentil. It's a labor of love to shell these peas for even two servings. But you must grow them—once at least—for this pleasure.

You'll need at least 1½ cups freshly shelled peas—from a generous 1½ pounds of pods. Finely shred a few leaves from the heart of a young butter lettuce. Put the peas in a heavy medium-size skillet, barely cover with water, then scoop out the peas. Add a pinch of sugar to the water and salt to taste, and bring it to a boil. Return the peas with the lettuce, and simmer uncovered over medium-high heat until the peas are almost tender. Taste after 5 minutes, although it will take longer. Drain the vegetables well, saving the stock for another day.

Melt 2 to 4 tablespoons unsalted butter—or heat that much heavy cream—in the skillet and return the peas and lettuce. Stir gently with a wooden spoon until the peas are tender and hot. Grind over a few grains of white pepper and turn the vegetables into small heated bowls. Rush to the table and eat with large spoons.

Soup Peas/Dried

Pick the pods and shell the peas when the pods are parchment dry. Store the peas in a jar in a cool, dry place. Do not overcook when reconstituting.

Bronze Age civilizations in the Indus Valley cooked dried peas in sesame oil and seasoned them with mustard, turmeric, or ginger. Swiss lake dwellers of the same period cooked dried peas and served them with fish caught in nets they'd woven of flax. In the classical age, Greeks bought hot split pea soup from vendors in the streets. Ancient Romans boiled dried peas, then added leeks, coriander, cumin, pepper, lovage, caraway, dill, basil, wine, and liquamen (essence of salted fish, the Worcestershire sauce of the day).

SPLIT PEA SOUP: I myself have always thought that split pea soup is its most delicious with only four ingredients: split peas, water, pepper, and salt. Well, maybe a little summer savory. Try it with 1 cup dried peas to 1 quart salted water. A handful of shredded lettuce and/or cooked fresh peas at serving time is lovely.

Snow Pea Shoots

These are the leafy ends of pea vines grown just for their leaves and tendrils. Pick the tender 3 to 5 inches at the tips of these vines and the plant will send forth new shoots a couple of times before being exhausted. The shoots droop the moment they're picked, so for maximum quality, this is from garden to plate or wok. However, they will revive in a jug of water in the refrigerator. Pea shoots should be rinsed lightly if at all.

In China, *dau miu,* tender pea plants that will never bear peas, are grown, a delectable idea. Rarely can you buy these even in the finest Chinese market—ah, the perks of having a garden! Because they are such an extravagance (in Hong Kong, they cost a fortune), if you're going to cook them, for simplicity's sake stir-fry the shoots with slivers of fresh ginger and a dash of sherry.

Pea Shoot Salad

MAKES 4 SERVINGS

Here is a salad that's as lovely as salad gets. It's crunchy and faintly pea-flavored.

Pick the top 3 to 4 inches of young pea shoots to glean a generous 3/4 pound. Turn them into a pretty bowl—preferably glass. Mix an overflowing 1/4 cup fresh orange juice with an overflowing 2 tablespoons fresh lemon juice and use your hands to mix with the shoots. Add salt to taste and serve at once.

I like these with thin egg noodles (Chinese or otherwise) and gingered chicken.

Pea Sprouts

You can sprout any sort of pea seeds for crispy pea wisps—delightful in salads and stir-fries. Harvest them about 2 inches long, when leaves are dark green but just emerging. (I've seen them only once at the Chinese market, but keep an eye out so you can taste them and be inspired to sprout them.)

Poached Egg in a Nest of Pea Sprouts

MAKES 2 SERVINGS

I love poached eggs on a bed of greens. The lacework of brilliant green around creamy white and gold is appealing, and a lemony veil complements both sprouts and egg. Last-minute but ready in less than 10 minutes. Blotting the eggs is an optional luxe touch.

½ tablespoon cornstarch
½ cup vegetable stock or chicken broth
½ tablespoon fresh lemon juice
½ tablespoon unsalted butter
2 large fresh eggs
heaped 6 cups (6 ounces) leafy pea sprouts
salt and freshly ground black pepper to taste

Set a clean folded kitchen towel beside the stove and heat 2 plates. Fill a 6- to 7-inch-deep saucepan with a couple of inches of cold water and bring to a boil. Whisk the cornstarch, stock, and lemon juice together in a bowl until blended.

Melt the butter in a medium-large skillet (preferably nonstick) over medium-high heat, whisk in the cornstarch mixture, and whisk until thickened, about 2 minutes. Pull off the burner while you carefully break the eggs into the water as close to the water as you can. Turn down the heat so the water just trembles and set the timer for 3 minutes.

Return the skillet to high heat. Add the pea sprouts and stir with a small pancake turner or spatula until the sauce is mingled evenly with the sprouts and the

Sprouting Seeds for Eating

Try cabbages (green and red), Chinese cabbages, leeks, cresses, green lentils, adzuki and mung beans, soybeans, all mustards, all radishes, sunflowers, and peas, of course.

Soak the seeds in cool water overnight. Drain, then keep the beans moist but not wet—you can sprinkle them in an earthenware or glass jar and cover them with a cloth. Rinse with fresh tepid water morning and evening, then drain through the cloth. Keep in a dark, airy place between 55°F and 70°F. Most will take from 3 to 8 days. The last day, set in indirect sunlight to green up.

There are all sorts of more efficient sprouters at health food stores.

sprouts are warmed through, about 1 minute. Arrange the saucy sprouts as nests on the plates. Use a slotted pancake turner to lift the eggs from the water, slip onto the towel to dry, lift, and place in the center of each nest. Add salt and pepper and serve at once with toasted sourdough or cracked wheat bread.

Snap Peas

These crunchy eat-them-all pea pods are best picked between the times the pods are three-fourths filled with peas (less starchy) and when the pods are full (sweeter). Rush to the table. Everything about snow peas applies to snap peas—even, in most cases, having to string them. With some, it's easiest to start at the bottom and pull the string up one side, nip off the flowery end, and zip the string down the other side. With others, start at the flowery end and pull down on the straight side.

These plump crunchy darlings are best eaten raw—wonderful in crudité baskets—or minimally cooked in stir-fries.

Garlic Stir-Fried Snap Peas

MAKES 3 TO 4 SERVINGS

If necessary, string 3 cups (1 pound) plump tender sugar snap peas.

Heat a wok or large cast-iron skillet over high heat until it starts to smoke, then drizzle in 1 tablespoon mild oil. Immediately add 2 large minced garlic cloves, stir for a few seconds to coat the bits with oil, then dump in the snap peas. Stir until they all glisten, about 20 seconds, then spread them evenly in the pan and cook for a long 30 seconds without stirring.

Repeat the stirring and quiet cooking until some of the skins have specks of brown and the pods are hot through and through, 2 to 4 minutes, depending on size. Remove from the heat and sprinkle with 1 tablespoon fresh lemon juice. Taste for seasoning—a little freshly ground white pepper? Stir to blend, then serve at once, leaving most of the garlic in the pan. A hint of minced perilla leaves at the end is marvelous. Rice is always welcome with such dishes.

Snow Peas

Snow and snap peas are not quite as nourishing as plump little shelled peas because the seeds aren't as mature and haven't had the time to develop all that sustenance. While snow peas offer more vitamin C, calcium, and iron, they have less protein and B vitamins. Do you care?

Rinse and string as for snap peas, if necessary. You can cook snow peas in boiling water as for green beans, but I never do it.

Not as rounded and succulent as snap peas, but flat and translucent, snow peas—edible podded peas—have been with us for generations. In fact, they are in part the forebears of snap peas. Harvest when the peas inside are barely there. It's curious that these exquisite gems are so identified with Asian cuisines, inevitably stir-fried. Instead, think of snow peas as a thin and delicate snap bean. All sorts of possibilities pop up.

ITALIAN SNOW PEAS: Makes 4 servings. Top and string 3 cups (1 pound) young snow peas. Heat a tablespoon of extra-virgin olive oil in a large heavy skillet over high heat. Add the peas and sauté, stirring frequently, for 2 minutes. Stir in 2 minced garlic cloves and 1 small tomato cut in small dice. Sauté another 2 minutes, then start tasting for doneness. When they're tender-crisp—another minute or so—stir in a small handful of chopped lemon basil. Serve.

Peeling Peppers

The thick-fleshed sorts of peppers are easier to peel than thin-fleshed ones, so bear that in mind when you're planning a peeled-pepper dish. Lay the peppers directly on a gas flame or an inch below a hot broiler and turn frequently with tongs until they're thoroughly charred. Wrap in a thick towel or turn into a paper bag, close the bag, and wait a couple of minutes—steam loosens the skin. If you're peeling chilies, wear gloves or be careful not to touch your face with your hands until you've scrubbed them with soapy water. With a knife blade, scrape off the skin (for most recipes you don't have to worry about a few charred bits—they're colorful and tasty). Trim out the stem, slice the pepper in half, and scrape out the seeds if you wish. *Please note: The seeds are the hottest part of a chili.* If you enjoy a chili's heat, include them. By contrast, the seeds of sweet peppers are mild as May, with a delicate pepper flavor. There's no reason not to include them in a dish unless their stippling would be unappealing.

Peppers

Harvest sweet peppers at any stage, any color, cutting off the stem with a knife. Leave a little of the stem attached. Whenever possible, let your peppers ripen on the bush to their finished color—they'll have more vitamins and be considerably more flavorful. Hot red peppers have more nutrients than sweet red peppers. While sweet red peppers are full of vitamins, hot red peppers have double the beta-carotene, almost double the vitamin A, and one-third more vitamin C—not that you can eat red hots in any quantity. The fruits are also fair sources of minerals.

Chili Peppers, Green—Unripe

Green peppers, whether chili or sweet, are like green tomatoes, immature. Their flavor will always be sharper, and they'll always taste as though they're short of the mark—which, of course, they are.

When a recipe calls for sweet green peppers, consider using a fresh green chili for a change. Such small exchanges can have big results.

As for the heat in chilies, Rosemary Brissenden (*South East Asian Food*) points out that hot peppers "have not so much a taste as a chemical effect—once the initial shock has passed you will find that chilies in food tend to stimulate the appetite, cool the body temperature, and bring about a general feeling of peace and benignity." Since the element that makes a pepper hot, capsaicin, lies largely in its seeds and the thin tissue surrounding them, when you remove these, the heat of the pepper is tempered.

GREEN CHILI LAMB STEW: Roasting a green chili partially cooks it, adds the flavor of the char, and sweetens it. A friend in New Mexico makes a fantastic green chili lamb stew by simmering browned chunks of lamb with chopped onion, garlic, tomatoes, and roasted green chilies—1 cup of chilies to every pound of lamb. He finishes by adding baby carrots and baby potatoes and baking the stew in the oven for an hour or so until everything is meltingly tender. Serve with hot corn tortillas.

Fast Fresh Green Chili Salsa

MAKES 1 CUP

My fast fresh green chili salsa has the warmth—not heat, but warmth—of the chilies, the nutty undertaste of garlic, and a lick of smoke from the roasting. It's a table sauce, like ketchup and the salsa verde under Tomatillos—a simple number that enhances everything from scrambled eggs to grilled halibut to roast beef to baked potatoes to anything in a tortilla. Tastes best fresh, but it's still good the next day.

2 Anaheim or other mild to medium-hot green chilies, roasted and peeled

2 garlic cloves

¾ cup chicken broth or vegetable stock

salt to taste

a little chopped cilantro

Scrape out the chilies' ribs and seeds only if you find the flesh sufficiently hot. Puree the chilies in a blender or food processor with the garlic and broth, then taste for seasoning. Serve in a bowl topped with cilantro.

Chili Peppers—Every Color but Green (Ripe)

Your mouth's on fire from chilies? Eat a banana.

I regard incendiary peppers not as a vegetable but as a spice. A judicious pinch or two of crumbled dried tiny Thai peppers in a dish of pasta—say with fresh tomatoes, mint, and orange peel—lifts it from "Lovely!" to "Oh, my *gosh*!"

Indonesian Red Chili and Garlic Paste

MAKES A GENEROUS 1/2 CUP

This sauce is thick, seedy, and a blazing red-orange of ripe chilies. Hot and toasty and deliciously garlicked, it was inspired by a concoction made in Hong Kong. You can track its course down your gullet. I smear it in tiny dabs over a slice of cheese, thin it with a nut oil as sauce for noodles, baste steaming fish with it, spread it in a veil over spears of cold cucumber or carrot or celery.

Tightly covered and refrigerated, this keeps until eaten and improves on keeping.

about 5 small ripe red chilies, hot to very hot
1/3 cup minced garlic, about 6 large cloves
1/2 tablespoon cornstarch
2 teaspoons sugar
1 tablespoon rice or distilled white vinegar
about 9 tablespoons cool water
salt to taste

Wearing rubber gloves and remembering not to touch them to your face, roughly slice the chilies, then finely grind them with their seeds in a food processor or blender (be careful when you lift the lid of the machine; the air is potent). You should have about 3/4 cup.

Combine the puree in a small heavy saucepan with the garlic, cornstarch, and sugar, then stir in the vinegar and 6 tablespoons of the water. Cook over very low heat, stirring frequently, for 1 hour, gradually adding 3 tablespoons more water as the paste thickens. The finished consistency should be that of thick jam. Add salt. Store in a jar in the refrigerator.

Paprika

Following the traditional Hungarian method, you and I can make our own paprika. String your paprika peppers in a loose garland, and hang them to dry in an airy place as chilies are strung in the Southwest. When the pods are crackling dry, finish drying them in a slow oven. For hot paprika, leave in the seeds and veins; for a sweet one, take them out. Warm the pods gently in the oven and grind to a fine powder with a mortar and pestle or in a coffee mill. The important thing is that the powder be bone-dry so it won't mold and be kept in tightly closed jars in a cool, dark, dry place.

Sweet Peppers, Green (Unripe)

Some of the richest, purest, most lustrous fruits in nature's giving are the family of peppers. Even in their unripe state they have a sensual warmth. Usually I prefer the rounded sweetness of ripe peppers, but I find the grand old favorite, stuffed bell peppers, is more flavorful made with the slightly bitter green fruits. However, for guests—yes, the following is a company dish—the presentation is more exciting if you bring in a platter of green, yellow, red, and orange or purple peppers. The filling, flavored with the chopped lids, is then colorfully speckled.

Greek Stuffed Green Peppers After Moussaka

MAKES 4 SERVINGS

The filling and custard topping here were inspired by moussaka, the delectable rich Greek dish of eggplant and ground meat. This version is wonderfully lean.

For dry bread crumbs, get in the habit of drying the odd scrap of bread in a low oven, then whirl a bunch in the food processor until fine and keep the crumbs in a jar. Sprinkled over baked dishes, they brown handsomely—giving the same effect as cheese with far fewer calories.

The peppers can be stuffed and the custard prepared a few hours in advance.

4 green sweet peppers of the same size, a generous 3 inches high
1 pound extra-lean beef chuck or lamb shoulder
1 onion, roughly chopped
½ cup dry bread crumbs
1 cup small diced drained plum tomatoes, about 4
3 tablespoons dried black currants, plumped in a little warm water if not soft
3 tablespoons chopped fresh sweet basil leaves or 1 tablespoon crumbled dried
1 tablespoon fresh lemon juice
dash of ground cinnamon
salt and freshly ground black pepper to taste

CUSTARD TOPPING

1 tablespoon butter
1½ tablespoons flour
⅔ cup cold milk (nonfat is fine)
1 large egg yolk
1 heaped tablespoon grated Parmesan cheese
pinch of nutmeg
dry bread crumbs for the top

Use a small sharp knife to cut around the outside edge of the peppers, then remove the lids. Cut the usable flesh from around the stem and chop the flesh into ¼-inch pieces; cover and reserve. Steadying each pepper on its side on the counter, scrape out the ribs with the side of a teaspoon—stems, seeds, and ribs to the compost. Set the peppers upside down on a rack in a pot and steam them for 10 minutes. Put the peppers on a plate.

Either grind the meat and onion together once through the largest blade of a food grinder, or process 1-inch pieces of meat with the onion in a food processor to a medium grind.

Heat a dry large nonstick skillet and sauté the meat, onion, and chopped peppers over medium-high heat until the meat is no longer pink, about 5 minutes, stirring frequently. Turn into a mixing bowl, add the bread crumbs, and blend thoroughly. Add the tomatoes, currants, basil, lemon juice, and cinnamon and use your hands to blend thoroughly. Add salt and pepper.

Holding a pepper case in your hand, spoon in the filling. You can cover the cases with plastic wrap and refrigerate now if necessary.

For the custard topping, make a thick cream sauce by melting the butter in a small heavy saucepan over medium heat. Whisk in the flour and cook for 2 minutes, stirring frequently—do not let it color. Whisk in the milk and whisk until thickened. Turn the heat to low and simmer for 2 minutes, stirring occasionally—it will be very thick. Whisk in the egg yolk, Parmesan, and nutmeg. Remove from the heat. To keep for a few hours, lay plastic wrap directly on the top and refrigerate.

To bake, heat the oven to 375°F. Divide the topping among the peppers, smoothing it to the edge and mounding as needed. Set the peppers in a pie dish, sprinkle the tops with bread crumbs, and bake in the middle of the oven until richly browned, about 30 minutes—add 10 minutes if the peppers have been chilled.

Serve with rice, a side dish of grilled mushrooms, a relish dish of Kalamata olives and unpeeled cucumber spears, beer or retsina to drink, and watermelon or a selection of melon slices for dessert.

Sweet Peppers—Every Color but Green (Ripe)

Relish of Peppers, Onions, Tomatoes, Garlic, and Sweet Basil

MAKES ABOUT 2 1/2 CUPS TO SERVE 4 OR 5

This peperonata is cooked more rapidly than the traditional version and is dry-skillet-roasted rather than sautéed in oil. The mix has uncommon dimension—velvety yet coarse, subtle yet tangy, muted yet glowing. And you can as easily heap it over slices of rough bread on a picnic as over polenta or pasta for a luncheon or over grilled fish, chicken, or lamb for a dinner party.

A large cast-iron or heavy nonstick skillet is invaluable here; it makes the unique pure browned sweetness of this composition possible. If none is available, film your largest, heaviest pan with olive oil before adding the vegetables and keep an eye on them, adding a drizzle more oil if needed to keep things from caramelizing.

This can be prepared a couple of days in advance.

olive oil, optional

2 large (1 pound) sweet peppers—green, red, yellow, purple, or mixed—stem scars removed

1 medium-size red onion

1 medium-large firm ripe tomato, cut into ½-inch dice

2 large garlic cloves, thinly sliced

a handful of chopped fresh sweet basil

salt and freshly ground black pepper to taste

lemon juice to taste

Cut the peppers and onion lengthwise into slices ¼ inch thick—use the slicing blade on the food processor if you have one; it won't do a uniform job, and part of the appeal of this dish is the way the mix of pieces looks.

Set a large heavy skillet over high heat. When hot, add the peppers and onion. Stir frequently until the vegetables have browned and softened but the peppers are still a bit crisp, 8 to 10 minutes. Blend in the tomato and garlic and stir occasionally until the tomato bits have softened, 2 minutes. Remove from the heat and stir in the basil and seasoning. Balance the sweetness with a little lemon juice. Serve hot from the skillet, at room temperature in an hour or so, or cold a day or two later.

Sweet Red Pepper and Pumpkin Seed Soup

MAKES 4 SERVINGS

When sweet peppers ripen red, I find their carmine exteriors more tempting than a new French lipstick. It's interesting that, when red peppers are cooked and pureed, carmine turns knock-'em-dead orange. A friend who's a brilliant cook created a soup of these peppers, and I couldn't get over its vivid color and subtle, unusual flavor. She thickened the puree with pumpkin seeds she'd just toasted. There are five elements in Maureen Wagstaff's soup, and the principal two come through clean and clear.

You will need a blender to refine the seeds and skins to creamy smoothness. Neither a food processor nor a food mill can do this. The soup can be served as soon as it's finished or in a day or two.

- 6 large (2 pounds) sweet red peppers, stem scars removed
- ½ large white onion, halved and thinly sliced
- ½ cup pumpkin seeds, toasted in a dry skillet or the microwave
- about 2 cups mild vegetable stock or chicken broth
- about 1 cup water
- 2 tablespoons fresh orange juice
- salt to taste
- a few cilantro or flat-leaf parsley stalks

Heat the oven to 475°F. Quarter the peppers and arrange them skin side up in a single layer on a large baking sheet. Roast for 15 minutes, then turn the peppers with tongs. Distribute the onion pieces over the sheet and roast until everything tests tender, about 15 minutes more.

Puree the peppers, onions, and pumpkin seeds in a blender, adding ingredients to the jar a few pieces at a time with the motor running and pouring in enough stock and water to make the puree flow easily. Turn the soup into a saucepan if you'll be serving it directly or into a bowl for the refrigerator. Blend in the orange juice, then taste for salt—pepper would be a distraction. If the soup is a bit too thick when it's heated, thin by slowly stirring in more stock and water (2 parts to 1, respectively).

Serve hot in soup plates, garnished with a few spangles of cilantro leaves—do not let this strong herb dominate the elegant flavors.

Sweet Red Pepper and Tomato Pissaladière Topping on a Crisp Neapolitan Pizza Crust

MAKES 5 TO 6 MAIN-COURSE SERVINGS

With the dough prepared, it takes just half an hour to get this pizza ready for the oven—the time it takes to heat the baking stone. It's not only fast but great. When you want a blaze of red with vibrant flavor to match on a thin crisp crust, serve this unfussy pizza. Simply cut out the stem of the peppers and the blossom scar of the tomatoes. The seeds and skin add their texture and flavor.

You can prepare the dough a couple of days in advance and the topping a couple of hours ahead, but put the pizza together just before baking.

You'll note I sauté the vegetables in a dry skillet and *then* moisten them with oil. I'm convinced this gives richer flavor and uses less fat, but if my backward technique drives you crazy, add the oil at the start.

½ recipe Pizza Dough (see recipe in The Cook's Notebook)

TOPPING (MAKES ABOUT 3¼ CUPS)

3 large (1 pound) sweet red peppers, sliced in rings ¼ inch thick
7 or 8 (1 pound) plum tomatoes, sliced ¼ inch thick
6 garlic cloves, thinly sliced
2 tablespoons fruity olive oil
¼ cup chopped basil leaves
whole fresh oregano leaves added to the basil to make a packed ⅓ cup
salt and freshly ground black pepper to taste

Prepare the dough as directed to the point where it is ready to be shaped. You can heat the oven while you make the topping or heat it later. When you're ready to serve, follow the dough recipe directions for shaping the dough.

To make the topping, heat a large heavy (ideally cast-iron) skillet over high heat. Chop the pepper rings into pieces 1½ to 2 inches long. Add to the skillet with the tomatoes and stir occasionally while you prepare the garlic. Add the garlic and herbs 7 to 8 minutes after the peppers. Turn the heat to medium-high. In a few minutes, when all the vegetables have softened but are still bright, remove the skillet from the heat and add the oil, then the salt and pepper. Cool—the topping shouldn't be set bubbling on the dough, but it can be warm to the touch.

To bake, about 15 minutes before serving, smooth the topping over the dough to the rim—not being a sauce but vegetables, it takes patting and poking to get them spread evenly. Slide out the bottom rack, have someone help you lay the foil with pizza on it onto the stone, pan, or baking sheet. Slide in the rack, and bake until the rim and bottom crust are lightly browned—check in 8 minutes, but because the topping is dense it can take 10 to 12 minutes. Serve at once. This is such a feast, you don't need more than a leafy salad to make it supper.

MARINATED SWEET RED PEPPERS FOR KEEPING: Makes 2 quarts. Because their vibrance is incomparable, both in color and in flavor, I'm grateful sweet red peppers can be preserved so easily and keep so well. A jar of marinated peppers—with a float of oil to keep the air out—lasts almost indefinitely in the refrigerator. You can buy big jars put up in Hungary, but your own will taste sweeter, I assure you.

Rinse, core, seed, and trim out the membrane of 6 large thoroughly ripe red thick-fleshed peppers (2 pounds). Cut into 2-inch squares. Four cups at a time, drop into a pot of boiling water and count 2 minutes, then lift out and drop into a bowl of ice water. When cold, drain, pat dry, and pack into clean hot pint or quart jars with a bay leaf, if you like, leaving 1/4 inch of headspace.

Bring 2 1/2 cups cider or rice vinegar, 1 1/4 cups water, 1/3 cup sugar, and 1/2 tablespoon salt to a boil. Blend in 1 1/2 cups mild olive oil and return to the boil, then pour boiling over the peppers, maintaining the headspace. Process for 10 minutes in a boiling water bath. Once opened, refrigerate and be sure there's a 1/4-inch layer of oil on top. Or don't bother processing and keep the jars refrigerated from the start.

POTATOES

Any time after the flowers appear, you can reach down into the soil and pull up walnut-size potatoes. However, not all potatoes produce flowers. If, by the end of August, there are none on a plant, work your hand down into the earth to feel what's going on below-ground.

When the vines droop and the leaves turn brown, the potatoes have matured. If you can, leave the tubers in the ground 2 to 6 weeks longer, and do not water. The skins will toughen and the tubers will last longer in storage. To keep them over winter, lay the potatoes in a single layer in a dark place at around 70°F for a week to heal any tears in the skin, then store in a cool, dark place with good circulation of air.

You know to leave the skin on your potatoes whenever possible and to cook them in their jackets, whole, when you can to preserve nutrients. Potatoes are a moderately good source of fiber and potassium, a moderate source of vitamin C, and a fair source of vitamin B_6, niacin, iron, and magnesium. *Note: Potato vine leaves are not edible.*

Even though we're told that waxy potatoes are best for salad and floury potatoes are best for baking, the first time a friend asked if I'd ever baked a new red potato, I was stunned. I did and was entranced. I'll give you the potatoes that have worked for me in the recipes that follow, but you decide which potato to use which way and for what. You grew them, after all.

Baking Potatoes

ONION-STUFFED ROAST POTATOES: This potato dish, at once curiously sensuous and plain, is my husband's invention. A thick slice of onion is sandwiched between halves of a garlicky buttered baking potato and roasted over coals. The onion melts and imparts its aroma to the potato. Serve with other grilled foods, whether vegetables, fish, poultry, or meats.

For each person, cut a baking potato in half lengthwise. Make slashes in the potato on the flat sides and force in chips of cold unsalted butter, a generous tablespoon altogether, and the slivers from 1 clove of garlic. Cover the surface of one of the halves with ½-inch-thick slices of onion, top with the other potato half, and wrap the two together tightly in heavy foil, shiny side in. At this point the potatoes can wait in a cool place for several hours.

Grill 6 inches above hot ash-covered coals or a medium-hot wood fire, turning the packages two or three times with tongs. Roast until the potatoes test tender when a thin skewer is thrust through the foil—about an hour. No harm will come to them if they cook a bit longer than they need to. Serve in their foil wrapping, to be unwrapped at table.

These potatoes can also be roasted in a 400°F oven until tender, an hour or so.

LEAN BAKED POTATO TOPPINGS: Baked is one of the most nourishing ways to eat a potato, and now that the days of butter and sour cream slathered on top are over, what good things can take their place?

I slosh my baked potato with the salsa of the moment, be it green chili or red. Chopped marinated peppers are splendid over a baked potato. When I've eaten all the inside of the potato, I fill the shell with my salad—folding the skin over and making a crispy potato/succulent green salad sandwich.

Consider also:

- golden zucchini caviar
- quartered mushrooms browned in a veil of olive oil in a heavy skillet
- green garlic
- roasted peanuts
- red chili and garlic paste
- shallot greens sauce
- caponata

Blue Potatoes

A PATRIOTIC SALAD WITH A TWIST: For the Fourth of July, if you got your crops in early enough, dress rings of red sweet peppers, sliced white tomatoes, and rounds of steamed blue potatoes with vinaigrette.

Puree of Blue Potatoes

MAKES 6 SERVINGS

Great-Aunt Nellie's heart would have stopped at the sight of a puree of blue potatoes. But this puree is gorgeous—made with the likes of All Blue, the color is like candied violets. Still the flavor is as familiar and comforting as your granny's arms.

This method and the resulting puree are a little more refined than the usual home-style mash, simply because the potatoes are uncommon and we want to prepare them to perfection. A great potato cook I know insists that mashing them roughly or using a circular motion in pureeing potatoes adversely affects their texture and taste.

For absolute freshness of flavor, serve these as soon as they're made. If they must wait an hour or so, beat in only a few tablespoons of milk and keep them warm over hot water, then beat in the rest of the flavorings and heat just before serving.

Peel 6 medium-size (2½ pounds) blue-fleshed baking potatoes and cut them into 1-inch-thick slices. Steam until thoroughly tender, about 10 minutes (save the stock for bread or soup). Dry out the potatoes for a few minutes either on a baking sheet in a 350°F oven or in a large nonstick skillet over medium heat.

While hot, gently but firmly press the potatoes through a ricer into the top of a double boiler or heatproof bowl. Set over simmering water and, with a wooden spoon, blend in a stick of soft unsalted butter (or to taste), then 2 to 3 tablespoons of hot whole milk or half-and-half. You want a creamy puree without its being too soft. Add a pinch of nutmeg and salt and freshly ground white pepper to taste.

If you'd rather, reverse the amounts, using ½ cup whole milk and 2 to 3 tablespoons butter. The puree will still be sublime.

New Red Potatoes

Tiny new red potatoes make an enchanting salad. It needn't be esoteric—let the potatoes be what's special. Just add plenty of chopped parsley, maybe bits of raw red onion, some chopped lovage or celery leaves, and dress with a light oil and delicate vinegar.

Don't forget how good these potatoes are roasted.

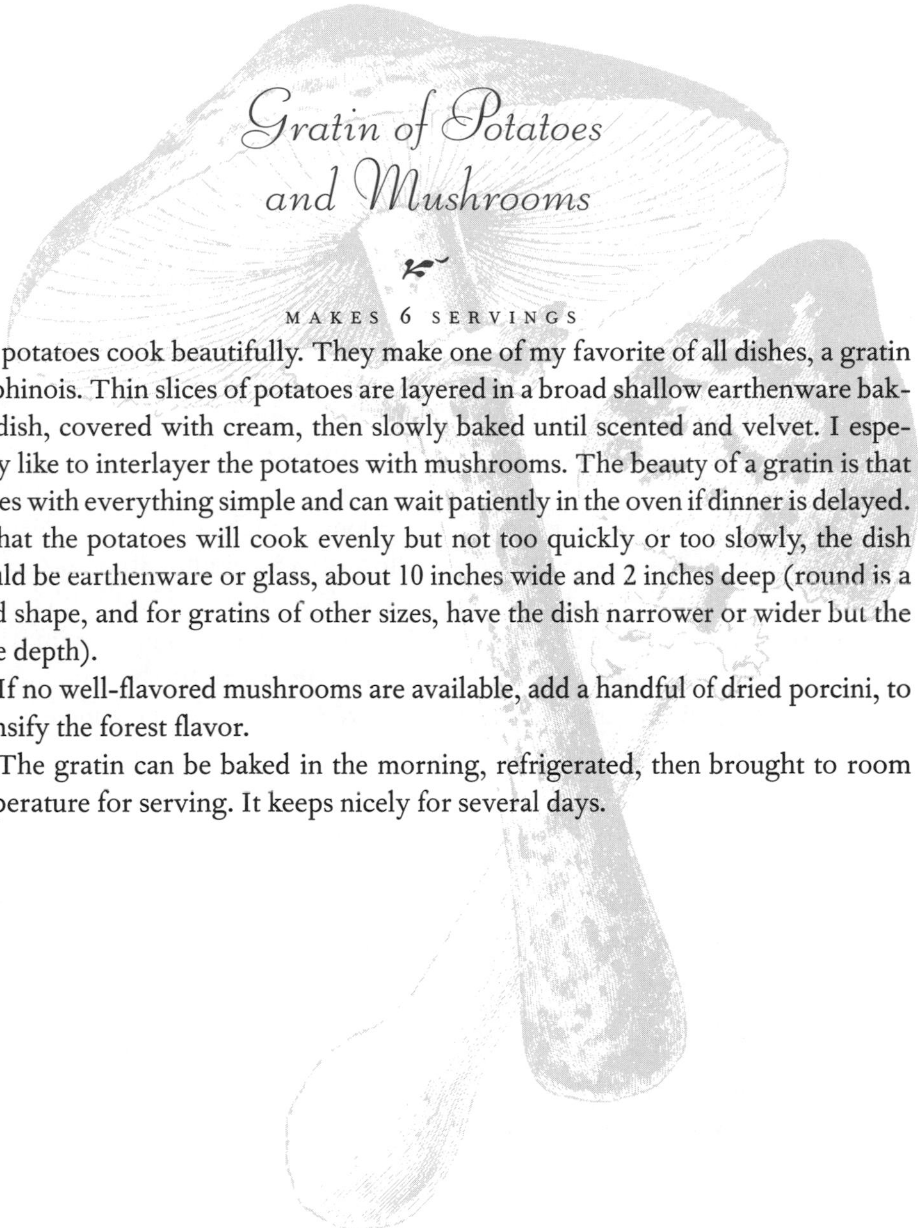

Gratin of Potatoes and Mushrooms

MAKES 6 SERVINGS

Red potatoes cook beautifully. They make one of my favorite of all dishes, a gratin dauphinois. Thin slices of potatoes are layered in a broad shallow earthenware baking dish, covered with cream, then slowly baked until scented and velvet. I especially like to interlayer the potatoes with mushrooms. The beauty of a gratin is that it goes with everything simple and can wait patiently in the oven if dinner is delayed. So that the potatoes will cook evenly but not too quickly or too slowly, the dish should be earthenware or glass, about 10 inches wide and 2 inches deep (round is a good shape, and for gratins of other sizes, have the dish narrower or wider but the same depth).

If no well-flavored mushrooms are available, add a handful of dried porcini, to intensify the forest flavor.

The gratin can be baked in the morning, refrigerated, then brought to room temperature for serving. It keeps nicely for several days.

a handful of small dried mushrooms, optional
½ cup hot water if you're using dried mushrooms
1 garlic clove, split
2 tablespoons unsalted butter, plus more for the dish
6 or 7 medium-size red boiling potatoes, 2½ pounds
salt to taste

CREAM SAUCE (MAKES A GENEROUS 2 CUPS)
2 tablespoons unsalted butter
2 tablespoons flour
2 cups cold milk
½ teaspoon fresh lemon juice
a good pinch of nutmeg
salt and freshly ground white pepper to taste

4 shallots the size of jumbo olives, finely chopped
2 tablespoons chopped parsley
1 tablespoon chopped fresh dill leaves and flower buds or 1 teaspoon dried
½ pound wild or cultivated mushrooms, thinly sliced

In a small bowl, cover the dried mushrooms with the hot water and let them soak until they swell handsomely; allow 20 to 30 minutes. Rub a broad shallow earthenware or glass baking dish with garlic, then brush with butter.

On the wide blade of a grater, Mouli-Julienne, mandoline, or with a food processor, slice the potatoes the thickness of a dime. Turn the slices into about 2 quarts of boiling salted water and, when the pot returns to a boil, boil uncovered for 2 minutes, stirring once or twice. Drain and cover.

To make the sauce, melt the butter in a small heavy saucepan over medium heat, then whisk in the flour. Turn the heat to low and cook for a couple of minutes, stirring once or twice. Don't let the roux color. Slowly whisk in the milk and, when smooth, the lemon juice, and nutmeg. Turn the heat to medium and whisk until the sauce comes to a good simmer. It will be lightly thick. Add salt and pepper, remove from the heat, and cover.

Heat the oven to 325°F. Blend the shallots, parsley, and dill (pretty colors, especially if you've used some yellow buds of dill). Arrange half the potatoes over the bottom of the dish. Use a big serving spoon to evenly smooth on a third of the sauce, then sprinkle with a third of the shallot mixture. Layer in the sliced mushrooms.

Drain the soaked dried mushrooms (save the water for soup) and strew them over. Spoon over half the remaining sauce and sprinkle with half the remaining shallots. Arrange the rest of the potatoes on top (in a tidy pattern or randomly), then cover with the rest of the sauce and shallots. Dot with flakes of butter and add a flourish of pepper.

Bake uncovered until the potatoes are tender when a thin skewer is thrust in the center and the top is a pale bisque, about 1¼ hours. If dinner looks to be delayed, just keep turning down the heat. Let cool a few minutes before serving or serve at room temperature.

This can be a vegetable main dish or an accompaniment for a roast or grill. All that's needed to complete dinner is a light (not creamy) soup to start, a crisp wild salad to follow with a plate of cheeses, and a brightly colored fruit with chopped candied ginger on top.

New White Potatoes

New whites are superb just simmered covered in their jackets until tender (10 to 20 minutes), drained, and rolled in melted butter and chopped young chives or garlic chives or finely chopped green garlic.

Creamers

MAKES 6 SERVINGS

In some parts of the country, these are called *creamers.* This extravagant but simple dish is one of the great American traditions to indulge in at the start of the harvest.

Simmer 2 dozen small new white boiling potatoes (2 pounds) in their jackets until almost tender, 10 to 15 minutes. Drain. (They can wait a few hours now, covered.)

To serve, slice the potatoes thickly into a large skillet. Barely cover with cream or half-and-half, about 1½ cups. Simmer, shaking the skillet frequently, until the potatoes are thoroughly tender and most of the cream has been absorbed. Season with salt and freshly ground white pepper—maybe a few grains of nutmeg—and serve hot in small bowls sprinkled with finely chopped chervil, lovage, or parsley as a course of their own.

Root Chips

All root vegetables can be sliced and fried into crispy chips. I like golden sweet potatoes best—toothsome and the color of a harvest moon. Carrots are carroty, intensely orange, and crisp. Jerusalem artichokes are amazingly crunchy and have a fresh clean taste. I love the garnet curls of beets, but the chips aren't uniformly crisp. Parsnips are crisp and a tad strong. Sadly, translucent slices of turnip and rutabaga fry up tough and bitter. Baking potatoes make the shapeliest, crispiest, subtlest chip of all—nothing commercially prepared can touch them.

When choosing the vegetables, bear in mind that slices of potatoes and Jerusalem artichokes fry up close to original size, while carrots, parsnips, sweets, and beets emerge half their size. Don't peel; just slice the roots $\frac{1}{16}$ inch thick on a mandoline or grater—carrots and parsnips on the diagonal for the largest surface. Drop slices into a bowl of ice water, separating them so every piece will chill. Leave for at least 1 hour, adding ice as it melts. Beets want a bowl of their own.

Lacking a fryer with basket, I use a cast-iron skillet or anything in which the fat can be $1\frac{1}{2}$ inches deep. Using part canola oil, part vegetable shortening, my 12-inch skillet requires 10 cups melted fat (2 cups

oil/melted shortening equal 1 pound solid shortening). Over medium-high heat, bring it to 390°F—a cube of bread should brown in about 50 seconds. When the vegetables are chilled and the fat is almost ready, arrange some slices in a single layer between two towels and blot them thoroughly dry. Keep in a covered bowl in the refrigerator as you blot the rest.

To fry, drop slices into the fat until you have an uncrowded layer—don't be too quick to stop, because some will curl and some shrink, making room for more. After a long minute, turn each chip with tongs. When lightly browned, another minute or so, lift out with a slotted spoon onto an absorbent towel and immediately blot fat with paper towels. Sprinkle with salt and serve or keep warm on a baking sheet in a very low oven.

For minimal absorption of fat, keep the fat at 390°F. Before each batch, drop in a test slice: it should sink, then zoom to the surface. When the party's over, strain the fat through a paper towel–lined funnel back into its vessel. Keep it refrigerated, and you can use it again.

Baked Crisp-Soft Potato Chunks

MAKES 8 SERVINGS

This dish is one of the tastiest and most versatile potato dishes imaginable. Potatoes are cooked in their jackets, then cut up and roasted in a quick oven until crispy on the outside and creamy on the inside, tasting of the earth. New white potatoes are especially good this way. Great for company—and for the family, a special way to use up leftover boiled potatoes. I can't imagine why this recipe, named *pommes de terre à la boulangère,* after the village baker's wife, isn't better known.

If you pale at the thought of cooking with lard, you should know that it has less cholesterol than butter and an even lighter, sweeter flavor.

If the potatoes are refrigerated in an airtight container, they can be prepared a day in advance. But be careful that the potatoes don't take on a stale refrigerator taste. Add about 10 minutes to the baking time if the potatoes are cold.

salt to taste

10 to 12 medium-large whole new white or red potatoes

1 large garlic clove, crushed

¼ cup fruity olive oil, rich nut oil, or melted lard

freshly ground black pepper to taste

Steam or boil the potatoes in salted water until tender. When cool, pat dry and cut into chunks about 1½ inches square. Wrap airtight and refrigerate until needed.

When you're ready to bake, heat the oven to 400°F. Rub a shallow earthenware baking dish—ideally just large enough to hold the potatoes in one layer (they will shrink)—with the garlic. Smear the oil or lard over the bottom. Add the potatoes and toss with your hands so all sides of the cubes glisten. Bake until crispy—they'll be ready in 45 minutes to an hour but can wait until you need them, roasting browner and smaller with time. Turn down the heat if they start to get too small. Stir gently every 20 to 30 minutes. Season and serve as you would french fries.

Waxy Yellow Salad Potatoes

Waxy yellow potatoes make splendid salads—the French slice hot steamed potatoes into white wine to cover, let them cool, then drain and dress them with vinaigrette (see Sauces in The Cook's Notebook). To accompany cold chicken or fish for luncheon guests, serve equal parts of this potato salad and watercress leaves garnished with sieved hard-cooked eggs. Small diced waxy potatoes combine well with young whole snap beans, garden peas, and florets of cauliflower, also dressed with vinaigrette. Cuts of beets and potatoes make a terrific salad dressed with half sour cream and half yogurt—you can add celery and/or apples and/or toasted walnuts to that one.

Brasserie Potato Salad

MAKES 4 SERVINGS

This lusty Alsatian salad is lighter than the traditional German potato salad. Most of the ingredients can be prepared for the final fast mixing a few hours in advance.

DRESSING (MAKES A GENEROUS ⅔ CUP)

3 tablespoons extra-virgin olive oil

2 tablespoons red wine vinegar

1 tablespoon fresh lemon juice

heaped ½ teaspoon Dijon mustard

2 small garlic cloves, minced

salt and freshly ground black pepper to taste

SALAD

8 cups torn leafy greens: a mix of mild chicory, arugula, mild mustard, and lettuces—about a quarter should be bitter

½ large red onion, fairly thinly sliced

1 pound, 8 to 10 small unpeeled waxy yellow potatoes, cooked and cut into 1-inch pieces, at room temperature

1 cup matchsticks of Gruyère or Swiss cheese

1 cup ½-inch croutons (cubes of home-style bread baked slowly until toasty dry)

½ unpeeled crisp red apple, cut into ½-inch dice

To make the dressing, in a small nonreactive saucepan, blend the oil, vinegar, lemon juice, mustard, and garlic. Add salt and pepper and taste for seasoning.

Combine the greens and onion in a large mixing bowl. Wrap in a damp towel and refrigerate for a few hours if you like. Keep the potatoes, cheese, croutons, and dressing covered and in a cool place. Don't dice the apple until the last minute.

To serve, bring the dressing to a simmer over medium heat. Meanwhile, add the potatoes, cheese, croutons, and apple to the greens mixture in a large salad bowl. Whisk the hot dressing until blended, then pour it over the salad. Toss until well mixed and serve at once with warm chewy French bread.

Potherbs

Alternatives: Each of these can fill in for the other—and any spinach for all of them.

What is a potherb? Just an herb that's boiled in a pot and eaten. And what's an herb? Botanically, it's a plant grown from seed without permanent woody stems. That does make lettuce an herb. And lettuce simmered and buttered a potherb. But not in this country, it's not.

As reckoned by gardeners and cooks, what makes a green a potherb is a we-know-quite-well-what-we-mean subtlety not yet in *Webster's*. Potherbs are greens with the breath of the wild still in them. They grow easily to the point of rankness. Their flavors are, on the whole, indistinguishable one from another—they just taste green. Few have named cultivars—neither nature nor plant breeders have taken these Cinderellas and turned them into princesses as they have lettuce and spinach and chard. In our gardens potherbs are for quickly filling the greens gaps and admiring the resourcefulness of nature.

Harvest the young shoots, tender leaves and stalks, and, later, the flowers of potherbs as you do other leafy greens. One thing they have in common: most are tastiest and tenderest in spring.

As for alternatives, these are all interchangeable, and, ultimately, good old spinach will fill in for any—just as a good way to get the feel for a potherb is to try it in simple recipes for spinach.

Amaranth/Tampala

All amaranths are colorful—some wildly. Most of their leaves have the texture of a delicate chard but some are crinkly, some fleshy. Amaranth has the pleasing bite of spinach. Rinse the leaves in cool water, then pat or spin dry. Separate leafy parts from stalks if the stalks are fibrous or tough and cook separately as you would chard. Stir-fry, steam, or cook the leaves uncovered in salted water until tender, very briefly. Green leaves supply some beta-carotene and likely vitamin C and calcium.

If you grow the cultivar Giganteus, the succulent stalks are as thick as a man's wrist, reminiscent of hearts of palm—slice them into salads. Young leaves are super in salads. Combine them with parsley and mint. Cook briefly in stir-fries.

Red Amaranth/Chinese Spinach Soup

MAKES 3 TO 4 SERVINGS

I'm especially fond of amaranth ribbons in soup. When the leaves are red, the broth turns watermelon pink.

Remove the leafy greens from about 4 amaranth stalks averaging 4 inches long. Stack the leaves, roll them up, and slice into thin ribbons—about 1 lightly packed cup of greens. Thinly slice the stalks as you would scallions. Peel and finely chop 1 garlic clove.

In an uncovered pot over medium-high heat, bring the amaranth leaves, stalks, garlic, and 3 cups chicken, pork, or vegetable stock to a boil. Reduce the heat and simmer until the leaves are limp but the stalk pieces are still crisp, about 5 minutes. Remove from the heat and stir in 1/4 teaspoon Asian sesame oil. Season with salt and freshly ground black pepper and serve in soup plates. Sesame seed crackers are a nice accompaniment.

Good-King-Henry

Gather only young shoots and later tender flowers when they come. The dark green arrow-shaped leaves cook down like spinach. Rinse well and, if stalks are coarse, send them to the compost. Turn the green leaves into a heavy skillet with just the water that clings to them. Cook uncovered over medium heat, stirring occasionally so leaves don't burn. They should be tender in about 10 minutes. Cool, press excess moisture from the greens, and chop. This can be done a few hours in advance of finishing.

In the 17th century the English naturalist Nicholas Culpeper said Good-King-Henry "is preferred to spinach, and is much superior in firmness and flavour."

I toss the leaves raw into a cool-weather salad with arugula and sorrel, a shuddery delight. Raw Good-King-Henry is good any way raw spinach is.

Indian Lentils with Good-King-Henry

MAKES 4 SERVINGS

To taste it cooked, give Good-King-Henry a lively Indian treatment that's good for all mild greens. This is based on a recipe called *dal aur bhagy.*

This dish can be reheated without harm. If you don't have all the spices, use 2 teaspoons curry powder.

1 cup lentils, rinsed and picked over
3 large handfuls of Good-King-Henry or other green leaves, roughly chopped
6 scallions, chopped
1 or 2 pickled hot chilies, seeds removed, finely chopped
2 cups vegetable stock or cold water
salt to taste
3 tablespoons unsalted butter or mild oil (if you have ghee, use it instead)
1 onion, finely chopped
1 garlic clove, minced
1 teaspoon turmeric
½ teaspoon ground cumin
¼ teaspoon ground cardamom
¼ teaspoon ground cinnamon
⅛ teaspoon ground cloves
½ teaspoon grated lemon zest
a handful of chopped cilantro or parsley

In a heavy saucepan, combine the lentils, Good-King-Henry, scallions, chilies, stock, and a little salt. Bring to a simmer, stir, cover, and simmer until the lentils are soft, 15 to 20 minutes, stirring occasionally.

Meanwhile, heat the butter in a large heavy skillet over medium-high heat. Add the onion, garlic, turmeric, cumin, cardamom, cinnamon, and cloves and stir for 2 to 3 minutes, until the onion softens. Add the lentil mixture and simmer gently over low heat for 10 minutes, stirring frequently. Stir in the lemon zest and taste for seasoning.

Serve over rice sprinkled with chopped cilantro or parsley. Accompany with hot flatbread and finish with slices of fresh pineapple sprinkled with coconut.

Nettles, Stinging

Nettles' pale green young spring shoots have a pleasing spring green flavor at a time when greens are scarce. But only spring's first new nettles—and the top leaves at that—are palatable, with a texture resembling cooked spinach. When the shoots are no longer than your longest finger, gather them, wearing leather gloves and cutting with scissors. Rinse well, still wearing thick gloves. Never fear. Once cooked, the barbs of the leaves' stinging hairs are softened to nothing. You really can use nettles in any spinach dish. Simmer uncovered in a little boiling salted water as for other tender leaves—5 to 10 minutes will do it.

Champ or Stelk

MAKES 4 SERVINGS

This ravishing country dish is called *champ* in Ireland and *stelk* in Scotland. It is infinitely flexible—you can also use parsley and/or kohlrabi tops or peas or chives or any green you like.

- 4 to 5 medium-size potatoes, any kind
- about 1 cup fairly finely chopped whole scallions or young leeks
- 1½ to 2 cups fairly finely chopped young nettles or other greens
- about ⅔ cup milk
- salt and freshly ground pepper to taste
- 4 or more tablespoons unsalted butter, melted

Steam the potatoes in their jackets. When they're about half done, start simmering the scallions and nettles uncovered in the milk. They'll be tender in 5 to 10 minutes.

When the potatoes are ready, peel and put them through a potato ricer or food mill. Beat in the hot greens and as much hot milk as needed to make a creamy mash. Season with salt and pepper, then spoon into deep warmed plates.

Make a well in the center of each and pour in melted butter. Some make a ritual of eating from the outside in, sweeping a forkful of potatoes into the butter until they reach the golden pool. I shudder with pleasure just thinking about it.

Orach

Orach is a small leaf, prepared in the same ways as others of its type—rinse, send the tougher stalks to the compost, and steam or simmer uncovered for just a few minutes, then finish as you might spinach. Orach adds yet another texture and shape to the soup pot or salad bowl.

A traditional French use of green orach is to mix equal parts with sorrel when cooking—orach's green helps neutralize sorrel's unfortunate tendency toward khaki.

ORACH ON ENGLISH MUFFINS: Like beets, red orach leaves turn everything cooked with them red. If you have enough, you can make this satisfying dish quite colorful. It's also good with green or yellow orach or any leafy green.

For each serving, cook, drain, and chop about 4 cups of any color of young orach leaves as directed. Melt 1 tablespoon unsalted butter in a small skillet and stir in the leaves. When hot, stir in a small splash of cream or half-and-half. Toast 1 split English muffin. Season the orach with salt, pepper, and a few grains of mace and spoon it over the muffins. Sprinkle with a heaped tablespoon of shredded melting cheese such as Swiss, jack, or Parmesan. Serve hot with sliced tomatoes on the plate. A grated carrot salad and thin slices of ham or chicken would make this supper.

Sorrel, Garden

These bright green spade-shape leaves are very good for you. Rinse them well. Use the stalks when you can, chopping them finely. Supposedly, the paler the leaves, the more delicate the flavor. In fact our leaves are pretty much all a verdant dark green. When they get large and tough, they'll be sourest, but there's nothing sorrel can be that I don't adore. You don't exactly have to cook sorrel—you just touch its leaves to heat and the leaves wilt, changing color dramatically. Since you could never eat a whole bowlful of sorrel, count on a couple of ounces per serving. Add tender leaves to salad.

Sorrel's shivery tartness is delectable in soups, especially *potage santé*—a puree of sorrel and potatoes with a little chervil and cream. Jewish cuisine loves its schav, a similar puree thickened with beaten egg instead of potato. And pureed sorrel saucing fish is classic.

You can use sorrel like spinach, except it will have a fraction of the volume after cooking. However, my friend Philip Brown taught me to wrap fish for baking or steaming in a sorrel leaf or two. The leaves help keep the flesh moist and add their flavor with each mouthful.

I'm sure the reason sorrel isn't popular is because the bright leaves, once cooked, turn army drab. I've found a way with sorrel that gives you the brilliant taste *and* color. It's a delectable March-April-May-from-the-garden dish, when your green things are perkiest.

Ribbons of Pasta with Ribbons of Sorrel and Herbs

MAKES 4 SERVINGS

This was inspired by an Italian recipe for *nastri,* pasta hand-cut into ribbons. To make it an even greener and more filling main dish, cook a pound of skinny asparagus cut on the diagonal with the pasta.

Herbs should be firmly packed in their measuring cups. You can mix the parsley, celery, chives, mint, and chili together and wrap and chill them a couple of hours in advance. Wrap and chill the sorrel separately. The dish goes together in about 5 minutes.

You can use dried pasta, but the dish will be markedly less exciting.

1 recipe Fresh Egg Pasta in The Cook's Notebook or 7 ounces store-bought fresh fettuccine

salt to taste

6 tablespoons extra-virgin olive oil

1 scant tablespoon finely chopped garlic

½ cup roughly chopped flat-leaf parsley

heaped ½ cup roughly chopped lovage or celery

heaped ¼ cup roughly chopped chives

1 heaped tablespoon chopped fresh mint

1 dried hot red chili, seeds removed, crumbled

¼ cup pine nuts, toasted quickly in a dry skillet

6½ cups narrow ribbons of young sorrel leaves, about 6 ounces; finely chop tender stalks

freshly ground white pepper to taste

lots of grated Parmesan cheese

Roll out homemade pasta as thinly as possible. By hand, cut into ribbons 4 inches long by ½ inch wide—the *nastri*. Cover with a kitchen towel until needed.

When you're ready to serve, bring a big pot of salted water to a boil. Cook the pasta as directed for just a few minutes, stirring frequently. Store-bought fresh pasta will take longer—time it according to the package instructions.

Meanwhile, in a large skillet over medium-high heat, heat ¼ cup of the olive oil. Add the garlic and stir frequently just until the garlic begins to color, 1 long minute. Remove from the heat.

Turn the noodles into a colander in the sink, letting the pasta water fall into the serving bowl, thereby warming it. Reserve ½ cup of the water and pour out the rest. At once turn the noodles into the bowl and moisten them with the reserved pasta water and the remaining olive oil. Cover and keep hot.

Stir the parsley, lovage, chives, mint, chili, and pine nuts into the olive oil. Pour this sauce over the pasta and at once add the sorrel. Toss to blend thoroughly so the sorrel is warmed. Add pepper, taste for seasoning, then serve at once, passing the cheese on the side.

Spinach Beets

First cousin to chard, these are generous plants. Any recipe for chard suits spinach beets fine. Also cook as you would beet greens or even spinach. Or, as the Roman Pliny recommended, add crisp leaves of spinach beets to salads with lentils and beans.

Hungarian Summer Herb Soup

MAKES 8 SERVINGS

This is a gorgeous soup for summer. Spinach beet leaves give it color and substance without overpowering it, as true spinach would. Another mild potherb such as red-leaved amaranth can be substituted, or try a mix of potherbs and other leaves, like lettuce.

This soup can be prepared almost completely in advance and gently reheated. It's also good cold. For best flavor and texture, chop the herbs by hand.

Beaten eggs make soup silky but take care: if it boils, the soup will curdle, but it will still taste good. Inspired by Füvesleves in George Lang's *The Cuisine of Hungary*.

2 quarts water
salt to taste
4 tablespoons unsalted butter
¼ cup roughly chopped chives
2 tablespoons chopped fresh mint
2 tablespoons chopped fresh marjoram leaves
2 tablespoons fresh thyme leaves
2 tablespoons flour
5 cups 2-inch ribbons of spinach beet leaves and finely chopped tender stems, ½ pound
2 whole large eggs
½ cup sour cream or plain yogurt
4 French rolls, sliced in half
freshly ground white pepper to taste
finely shredded zest of 1 large lemon

Bring the water and salt to a boil in your soup pot.

In a small heavy skillet, melt the butter and add the herbs. Cook over medium heat for 2 minutes, stirring frequently. Sprinkle in the flour, turn the heat to low, and cook for another 2 minutes, stirring frequently—don't let the flour color. Reserve.

Stir the spinach beet leaves and stems into the boiling salted water and cook over high heat, uncovered, for 5 minutes. Meanwhile, in a small mixing bowl, whisk the eggs and sour cream together.

Toast the rolls.

Whisk a ladleful of the cooking broth into the egg mixture. Turn the heat under the soup pot to low and whisk the egg mixture slowly into the soup. Whisk in the herbs and cook until the flour thickens. Add pepper and taste for seasoning.

Place half a toasted roll cut side up in each soup plate, ladle the soup over it, and sprinkle with the lemon zest.

Offer a fruity white wine with this fine first course for a summer night.

Radishes

Now radishes have come full circle—from being prized by pharaohs to being disprized for centuries and to being prized again along with the rest of the brassicas. They guard our health. Radishes are moderately good sources of vitamin C and fair sources of folic acid.

Spring radishes mature rapidly and don't hold their crispy sweetness for more than a few days. Keep an eye on them and pull them as soon as they're a size you like. Winter radishes are more patient. In both cases, let the seed packet guide you.

Spring Radishes

To know in a recipe how many of your radishes are needed to make a market bunch, figure about ½ pound—1½ dozen radishes with 1½ cups firmly packed leaves.

When you slice radishes into salad, leave a snippet of root and stem on. You'll soon get used to—and be fond of—the little tendrils of roots waving in the air and to biting down on the succulent bits of stalks.

When you have a bumper crop of radishes, cook them as though they were baby turnips—which you can cook as though they were carrots. Rinse the radishes until no earth remains in the bottom of the bowl. Cover with ice water and soak for 1 hour to crisp. When you poach little red guys, they turn delightfully rosy. It takes 6 to 7 minutes for sliced radishes to cook tender-crisp—don't overcook so they retain some crunch.

To me, the most sophisticated and the most innocent way to eat any sort of tender radish is to swipe one through my pat of soft sweet butter and pop it in my mouth.

SWEET AND SALTY SIMMERED RADISHES: Makes 4 to 5 servings. You'll be enchanted by this new cooked vegetable. Here's a Japanese example.

Trim off the leaves and rootlets of about 2 dozen radishes (about 1 pound). Rinse the leaves well and reserve them, then rinse and chill the radishes. Slice them into matchsticks, turn them into a skillet, and barely cover with vegetable stock. Simmer uncovered until tender-crisp, 6 to 7 minutes. Remove from the heat, drain (saving the stock for another use), and sprinkle lightly with sugar and low-sodium soy sauce. Stir, taste for seasoning, tuck the reserved leaves around the bowl, and serve as a side dish with rice.

MOROCCAN RADISH SALAD: Makes 4 servings. This delicate salad is beautiful as an accompaniment to white meats. The radishes and oranges are tastiest chilled. Combine them after they have spent a few hours in the refrigerator, but not long before serving. Save the leaves for another salad.

Thinly slice 3 dozen large but not pithy red radishes (the grating blade of the food processor is easiest). Peel and thinly slice 2 sweet oranges, then cut the slices in half, discarding seeds and draining off excess juice. When ready to serve, toss oranges and radishes in a glass bowl and dress with a little lemon juice and a spoonful or two of olive oil. Taste for salt and perhaps a dash of sugar. Serve on a bed of parsley and/or cilantro sprigs.

Radish Flowers

These are delicate but tasty, for salads and stir-fries. You can pick a lot of them, unless you relish the radish pods that would follow.

Radish Leaves

Do leave the leaves on the spring radishes when you put them out on the relish tray. Radishes without their leaves look denuded.

Think of radish leaves as baby cabbage leaves. Pick them before they get too fuzzy and add them to everything from salad to soup. Never again send a radish leaf to the compost. Many years ago, after wondering if I could eat the leaves I was throwing out, I began asking around, and an intrepid aunt came up with a recipe for soup.

Swedish Spring Soup

MAKES ABOUT 6 SERVINGS

This soup has wonderful texture and flavor, and the translucent radish rounds against the green are delightful.

2 to 3 tablespoons unsalted butter or nut oil

3 new carrots, scrubbed and coarsely grated

1 smallish leek, white and tender greens, trimmed, slit, rinsed, and thinly sliced

1 or 2 green garlic stalks or 2 dried garlic cloves, chopped

3 cups chopped radish greens

radishes that came with the greens, trimmed and very thinly sliced in a food processor or grated

½ cup freshly shelled peas (½ pound unshelled)

1 quart mild vegetable stock or half chicken broth and half water

salt and freshly ground white pepper to taste

1 tablespoon chopped fresh mint or parsley

plain yogurt or sour cream for topping, optional

In a broad heavy saucepan, warm the butter over medium-high heat. Add the carrots, leek, and garlic and sauté, stirring frequently, for 5 minutes. Add the radish greens and radishes, stir until they glisten, then add the peas and stock. Add salt to taste. Bring to a simmer and simmer uncovered until everything is tender, about 10 minutes.

In Sweden an egg yolk and a few tablespoons of thick cream are whisked in at the end to enrich the broth, but I prefer these delightful flavors unmasked. Add pepper, taste for seasoning, then serve in soup plates sprinkled with mint and dolloped with something creamy.

An assortment of mild cheeses, rye bread, and pale beer complete the meal.

Daikon—winter radish—leaves are delicious cooked in the manner of turnip greens, radish leaves, or any of the other sharply flavored leaves.

Radish Pods

Here are the seedpods of radishes—some are small and wispy, some are the size of big snap beans. All taste mustardy and crunchy. You might think there's no more to do with these than heap them in a basket and serve them with coarse salt at drink time and smile when people find out what they are. But in stir-fryland, these delicious seedpods are tossed into the wok. They need about 1 minute to be cooked tender-crisp.

In Britain the practice of pickling radish pods goes back at least to the 18th century, when E. Smith wrote about them in *The Compleat Housewife.* Follow the directions for white asparagus pickle.

Summer and Autumn/Winter Radishes

Alternative: Turnips.

Scrub and trim the radish, but peel only if the skin is tough.

There are so many shapes, sizes, colors, and flavors of radishes that are harvested in winter. To the Japanese the long stout snow-white daikon radish is more important than any other winter radish is to any other cuisine.

Japanese Steamed Fish with Daikon Shreds

MAKES 4 SERVINGS

This recipe was inspired by one in Shizuo Tsuji's *Japanese Cooking, A Simple Art.* The spirit and authenticity of the intriguing flavors are intact.

Everything can be ready ahead for this dish, which is last-minute but very fast. For added flavor, first marinate the fish in the sauce for a few hours in the refrigerator.

- ½ cup sake or pale dry sherry
- 1½ tablespoons low-sodium soy sauce
- ½ teaspoon sugar
- a piece of fresh ginger the size of a large egg, peeled and finely shredded
- 4 ½-inch-thick fillets or 1-inch steaks of succulent flavorful fish such as monkfish, rockfish, or shark
- 1½ cups thin daikon radish shreds
- ¼ cup chopped scallions, including some of the greens
- 7-spice powder (*shichimi*) or hot red pepper flakes to taste

Blend the sake, soy sauce, and sugar in a heatproof plate. Strew the ginger over it and set the plate in a steaming vessel (described in the accompanying box). Bring the water to a boil, then lay the fish on the plate. Cover

Steaming Arrangement for Fish and Poultry

This sounds fussy and difficult but it's simple and easy. Once you get it assembled you'll put it together in no time and be amazed at how often you steam food and wonder how you got along without this splendid technique.

The base can be a wok with a broad metal ring in it (the top and bottom cut out of an 8-ounce can of sliced water chestnuts is ideal—2 inches tall and more than 3 inches wide), a Chinese bamboo steamer set in a wok, or a broad metal steamer that fits in a deep pot or an 11-inch skillet.

The plate in which the food goes must be heat-proof and no more than 9½ inches wide, with a base that's 8 to 9 inches wide and at least ¼ to ½ inch deep. It should be narrow enough so you can get your fingers holding pot holders down between the plate and steamer to lift the plate up and out without burning your fingers. A pie dish works fine. Make sure the pan's lid fits on snugly.

Add hot water according to the depth of the steamer base (several inches for the Chinese steamer) to come up just below the plate's lip in a skillet. Bring the water to a simmer over medium-high heat. Lay the food to be steamed on the plate, cover the vessel, and steam until tender—it goes so quickly!—from 2 to 4 minutes for thin fillets of fish and chicken breast. You can turn with a pancake turner or tongs if the pieces are thick and firm enough, but a thin fillet won't need turning.

tightly, turn the heat to low, and steam for about 10 minutes per inch of thickness until when you open a flake of fish with the tip of a knife you can see the flesh is almost completely white with just a tinge of pink.

Quickly, evenly spread the radish over the fillets. Cover and steam for 2 more minutes.

Remove from the heat, carefully lift out the plate with pot holders, sprinkle the scallions over the top, and serve from the plate, spooning up sauce from the bottom. Serve with rice and pass a dish of *shichimi* or pepper flakes. A sweet bright green vegetable such as stir-fried snow peas or broccoli would be a fine complement. Offer tiny cups of hot sake to sip and a delicate fruit ice for dessert.

RHUBARB

Rhubarb was introduced in Europe in the 14th century or in the 17th, depending on your source. Whenever it was, the stalks of this fruit were cooked as vegetables and likened to the sourness of sorrel. Then in the 18th century, when sugar was more abundant and less costly, someone discovered that if you sweeten rhubarb you've got a velvety texture and an intriguing flavor.

To harvest after the second year, twist and snap off stalks when thick as your thumb. Don't take more than 1/4 of the stalks at once, and only half the stalks altogether.

Cut away all the green leaves, which are poisonous. When preparing rhubarb for a recipe, cut the leaf-end tips off where green turns to red.

RHUBARB SAUCE: For rhubarb pure and simple, cut the stalks into 1-inch pieces and cook them gently in a heavy saucepan with a squeeze of orange juice and a little sugar (you can add more later). The fruit will be tender in about 5 minutes. Nice warm with a plop of cold whipped cream and gingersnaps.

Rhubarb Crisp à la Mode with Strawberry Sauce

MAKES 6 SERVINGS

When they find they're getting rhubarb for dessert, inevitably one of our guests will whimper into his napkin, "But I *hate* rhubarb!" Then he'll bravely eat my crisp. Then ask for seconds.

The spices in the crumbles are the elements in 1 teaspoon of the country French spice blend called *quatre épices*—four spices. It's available in fancy food shops.

The sauce can be prepared and the crisp baked a few hours in advance.

SAUCE (MAKES 2 CUPS)

2 cups hulled ripe strawberries

about 3 tablespoons sugar or to taste

RHUBARB

½ cup sugar

1½ tablespoons cornstarch

finely shredded zest of 1 large orange

3 tablespoons fresh orange juice

10 to 12 (1½ pounds) bright red rhubarb stalks less than 1 inch thick (if larger, slice them in half lengthwise)

CRUMBLES AND FINISH

1 cup unbleached flour

½ cup firmly packed light brown sugar

heaped ½ teaspoon finely ground white pepper

scant ¼ teaspoon nutmeg

scant ¼ teaspoon ground ginger

a good pinch of cloves

½ cup (¼ pound) unsalted butter

3 cups vanilla ice cream

Make the sauce first so you can chill it. Puree the berries as smoothly as you please in a food processor or food mill. Add sugar to taste—not too sweet—cover, and chill.

For the rhubarb, blend the sugar, cornstarch, and orange zest in a large mixing bowl. Cut the rhubarb into 1-inch pieces (about 5½ cups), add them to the bowl, and mix with your hands until everything is blended.

To make the crumbles, in a food processor or a mixing bowl, blend the flour, brown sugar, and spices. Cut in the butter in thin chips, then pulse or work the mixture lightly with your fingertips until you have the texture of raw oats.

Heat the oven to 375°F. Arrange the rhubarb evenly in a 9½- by 2-inch glass pie dish, making sure all the sugar doesn't fall to the bottom—if it does, spoon it up and over again. Sprinkle with the orange juice, then spoon the crumbles evenly over the dish. Bake until bubbly and golden brown, 50 to 55 minutes. Serve warm. To reheat, bake at 350°F for about 20 minutes. Serve topped with a small scoop of ice cream and a splash of the bright red sauce.

RUTABAGAS

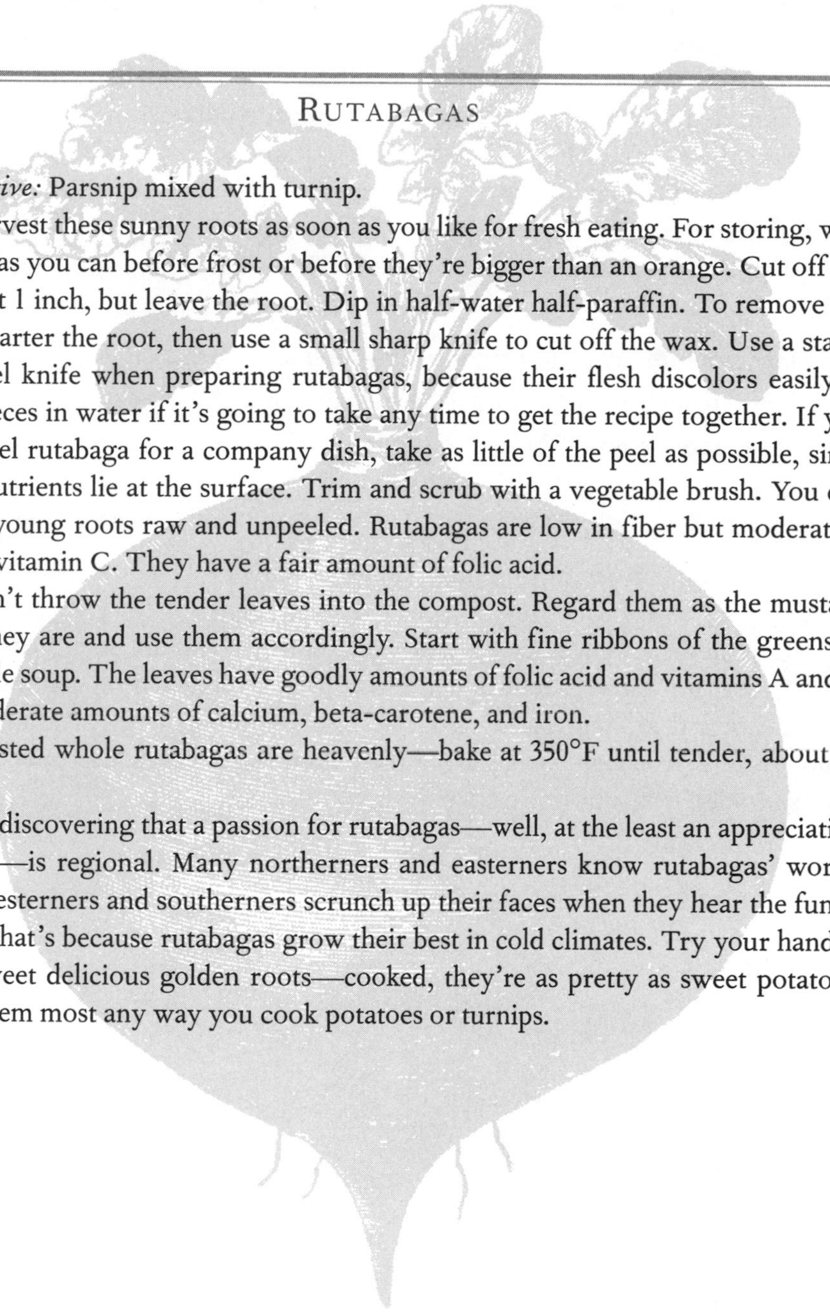

Alternative: Parsnip mixed with turnip.

Harvest these sunny roots as soon as you like for fresh eating. For storing, wait as long as you can before frost or before they're bigger than an orange. Cut off the leaves at 1 inch, but leave the root. Dip in half-water half-paraffin. To remove the wax, quarter the root, then use a small sharp knife to cut off the wax. Use a stainless-steel knife when preparing rutabagas, because their flesh discolors easily—keep pieces in water if it's going to take any time to get the recipe together. If you must peel rutabaga for a company dish, take as little of the peel as possible, since many nutrients lie at the surface. Trim and scrub with a vegetable brush. You can eat the young roots raw and unpeeled. Rutabagas are low in fiber but moderately high in vitamin C. They have a fair amount of folic acid.

Don't throw the tender leaves into the compost. Regard them as the mustard green they are and use them accordingly. Start with fine ribbons of the greens in vegetable soup. The leaves have goodly amounts of folic acid and vitamins A and C and moderate amounts of calcium, beta-carotene, and iron.

Roasted whole rutabagas are heavenly—bake at 350°F until tender, about an hour.

I'm discovering that a passion for rutabagas—well, at the least an appreciation of them—is regional. Many northerners and easterners know rutabagas' worth, while westerners and southerners scrunch up their faces when they hear the funny word. That's because rutabagas grow their best in cold climates. Try your hand at these sweet delicious golden roots—cooked, they're as pretty as sweet potatoes. Cook them most any way you cook potatoes or turnips.

Mashed Potatoes and Rutabagas

MAKES 4 SERVINGS

While they lend themselves to any form of cooking, I think most aficionados would agree that rutabagas are out of this world mashed. James Beard recommends mixing equal parts mashed rutabagas and potatoes. If you're expecting mashed potatoes, I find that's too much rutabaga—best two parts potatoes to one of rutabaga. But if you're expecting rutabagas, half potatoes is divine.

You can make this in advance and warm it up later, but this dish deserves to be savored at its moment suprême. This recipe is the half-and-half potatoes/rutabaga version, but you might start with a third rutabagas and see how you like it.

1 medium-size rutabaga, scrubbed and cut into ½-inch dice
1 large russet baking potato, peeled and cut into 2-inch dice
3 tablespoons unsalted butter, softened
6 tablespoons milk or half-and-half
salt and freshly ground white pepper to taste
the tiniest pinch of freshly grated nutmeg

Steam the rutabaga for a long 10 minutes, then add the potato. Steam until both are tender, about 20 minutes more. Turn into a bowl and mash while hot with a potato masher—not too finely, because there's pleasure in sweet lumps. With a wooden spoon, beat in the butter, milk, salt, and pepper. Serve at once sprinkled with nutmeg.

Salad Greens

Salads—even more than soups—are a pleasing uncomplicated way of eating a vibrant mix of vegetables. All of the following plants are interchangeable in the bowl.

Ambrosia

Alternative: Anise hyssop or perilla.

The small oak-leaflike leaves of ambrosia taste a bit as though ribbons of licorice and juniper had been pulled through spinach. Rinse them lightly, then pat dry.

Ambrosia and Purslane Salad

Here's an interesting combination for a light first course—dark green crisp spicy ambrosia leaves and green-gold crunchy tangy purslane. Everything can be prepared ahead, but toss it together just before serving. Allow $^3/_4$ cup per serving.

In a salad bowl, preferably glass, mix equal parts ambrosia and purslane leaves—if the purslane is the golden sort, all the handsomer. For sunny glints, add a few petals of calendula or marigold. Moisten with a dressing made of 2 parts fresh orange juice, 1 part extra-virgin olive oil, and sea salt and freshly ground white pepper to taste. Mix with your hands to coat each leaf.

Arugula

Alternative: Cress, chicory, dandelion, radish, or rapini leaves.

These lightly succulent, deep green, bright bitter leaves should be picked while young and piquant—older ones become sharp and chewy. They are beguiling in the seedling stage, and you can afford to harvest them tiny because if there's one thing arugula does, it's grow rapidly and easily. Rinse them lightly and pat dry. Ounce for ounce, the raw leaves of arugula hold $2^1/_2$ times the calcium of nonfat milk, twice the beta-carotene of cantaloupe, and a little less than twice the vitamin C of oranges.

Try tossing a few sprigs of arugula into a soup to perk it up. Add a snippet of arugula whenever spinach or chard is called for in a pâté or savory pie filling. It also makes a lively and pretty garnish, especially when in flower. The flowers are as peppery and edible as the leaves.

Mediterranean Arugula Salad Sandwich

MAKES 6 TO 8 SERVINGS

In this salad sandwich the arugula leaves add an incomparable snap. Proportions aren't crucial.

At its juicy best after an hour or so. To take it on a picnic, you'll also need six bamboo skewers.

FILLING

4 cups torn arugula leaves
about 24 (1 pound) cherry tomatoes, halved
1 medium-size cucumber, chopped
1 medium-large red onion, thinly sliced, then finely chopped
1 red or yellow sweet pepper, diced, including seeds, if desired
about 1 cup pitted black olives
about ½ pound feta or any cheese you like, crumbled
a handful of pine nuts, toasted in a dry skillet for a few minutes
½ cup chopped fresh oregano leaves
¼ cup chopped fresh basil leaves

DRESSING AND FINISH

¼ cup fruity olive oil
2 tablespoons fresh lemon juice
2 tablespoons red wine vinegar
1 to 3 minced garlic cloves
salt and freshly ground black pepper to taste
1 large Italian or Greek sesame seed bread ring
bright flowers for garnish

In a big bowl, combine the filling ingredients with your hands. In another bowl, whisk the dressing ingredients together. Drizzle the dressing over the salad, toss to blend thoroughly, then taste for seasoning.

Slice off the top third of the bread ring. Being careful not to pierce the sides and bottom crust, pull out the soft bread (feed it to the birds or dry it for bread crumbs), making a hollow case. Fill the case with the salad, set on the lid, press down, and wrap (butcher style) in foil. Chill if desired, but the sandwich is best at room temperature.

For traveling, cut the skewers in half and use them to hold the sandwich together. Fill the center with nasturtiums or other bright flowers.

When you get to the picnic, slice the sandwich into wedges big enough that they have to be held in two hands. Serve with cloth napkins and offer plates and forks to the decorous.

If no Italian or Greek baker is nearby, make individual sandwiches with hard French dinner rolls, following the same method. Or fill pita breads with the salad—pita bread won't hold the dressing well and should be eaten on the spot.

Capers and chopped fillets of anchovies, salami, artichoke hearts, and avocado are other possible ingredients.

Buck's-Horn Plantain

Alternative: Romaine lettuce cut in strips.

The thin dark green ribbons of leaves of these buck's horns taste like dark lettuce, and they're beguiling. Pick individually, rinse the leaves lightly and pat dry.

SALAD OF BUCK'S-HORN PLANTAIN AND CALENDULA PETALS: For each serving, pick about 20 leaves. Arrange them on a salad plate—blue, for preference—all going the same way. Sprinkle the petals of half an orange calendula over the greens, then those of half a yellow calendula. Drizzle very lightly with the oil of your choosing and a thread of red wine vinegar. Add salt and pepper and serve with soft Brie cheese and crisp crackers.

Chicory, Common

Alternative: Young cabbages.

Cut whole heads, leaving an inch or so to resprout, or pick leaf by leaf. Outer leaves of radicchio chicories—red Verona and Chioggia types—are more bitter than the leaves approaching the center, which have been naturally blanched to semi-sweetness.

Trim off any ragged or tough exterior leaves and rinse the chicory well, then pat dry if for a salad or leave wet if to be cooked. As with lettuce, that's the beginning and end of preparation. Chicories are a source of beta-carotene, vitamin C, iron, and a goodly amount of calcium—the outer darker leaves have the most nutrients.

Chicories are their deepest in hue and flavor just around autumn's first frost.

Some need a thump of frost to turn them the heady crimsons we love in radicchio and other *rossi*. Unless you're made of gold, you'll never be able to dine routinely on store-bought chicory salad—a mix of the purest and gayest slightly bitter, wonderfully vibrant greens and reds and frizzies and smooths. But all of these you can pluck every day in autumn and winter (if they're sheltered) from your garden.

Slice chicories for salad very thinly—the dressing best coats the leaves this way and seems to temper some of the bitterness. Drizzle with vinaigrette—a touch of dry mustard may be added. Translucent rings of shallots or tiny Purplette mini red onions are a fine addition.

The young leaves of Spadona chicory can be cooked as spinach and topped with chopped hard-cooked egg. Catalognas are tied with string, grilled, and garnished with onions and olive oil.

Chicories are marvelous braised. Follow the recipe for lettuce, using just the dark outer leaves. Save the lighter inner leaves for salad.

Gratin of Chicory

MAKES 4 SERVINGS

Here is a country French way of cooking chicory—you'll find it delicious beside roast poultry.

You'll need about 1½ pounds of leaves of any soft-leaf chicory you like, the equivalent of 2 large heads. With the rinsing water that clings to their leaves, lay them in a large nonstick skillet. Cook uncovered over very low heat, turning occasionally, until tender, 8 to 20 minutes. Drain if necessary and chop the leaves coarsely. Heat the oven to 375°F.

To make the sauce, in a bowl, stir 2 tablespoons softened unsalted butter and 1 tablespoon all-purpose flour until smooth. In a smallish heavy saucepan, bring ½ cup beef broth to a boil. Add the buttery paste and whisk furiously over medium heat until blended and smooth. Turn the heat to low and simmer, whisking occasionally, for 2 to 3 minutes.

Remove the sauce from the heat and add the chicory. Season with freshly ground white pepper (there will probably be enough salt from the broth). Smooth into a buttered shallow baking dish and sprinkle on about 1/2 cup dry bread crumbs. Drizzle with olive oil and bake until browned, about 20 minutes. Serve hot.

DARK-ROASTED CHICORY ROOTS: As an addition to or substitute for coffee, scrub the roots clean, cut into 1-inch pieces, and roast on a baking sheet in a 350°F oven until almost black—they will be very crisp and light. Cool, then grind finely in a coffee mill or blender. Blended equal parts with ground coffee makes the brew that's served in the coffeehouses of New Orleans.

Belgian Endive

Alternative: Young romaine lettuce hearts.

Cooked, classically the chicons of Belgian endive are braised in the manner of fennel and lettuce—and an interesting vegetable they are that way. But I find the blanched chicons want nothing more than to have their outer leaves removed, then for the center piece to be served.

One small whole chicon—"little head"—can be placed on a bed of watercress and dressed with a light vinaigrette. Or the wonderfully mild/bitter leaves can be cut into another composition, such as the salad that follows. Belgian endive, having been deprived of sunlight, has only a trace of beta-carotene, but it does offer a bit of calcium and iron.

Belgian Endive Salad

MAKES 4 TO 6 SERVINGS

Ever the artist, my mother serves her salad of pale green, vermilion, and black on brightly colored Chinese plates to accompany everything from roast Cornish game hens glazed with plum sauce to poached salmon with capers. Because of the bitter with the sweet and salty, this is an amazingly versatile salad.

Salad and dressing can be prepared hours in advance and refrigerated, but for best flavor, bring them to room temperature before mixing.

SALAD

4 chicons of Belgian endive, sliced crosswise 1/4 inch thick

1/2 cup chopped pitted oil-cured black olives

heaped 1/2 cup small strips of roasted peeled red sweet peppers (drained from a jar)

DRESSING (MAKES A GENEROUS 1/2 CUP)
1/4 cup fresh lemon juice
1/4 cup olive oil
scant 2 tablespoons water
scant 1 teaspoon dry mustard
salt and freshly ground black pepper to taste

In a mixing bowl, use your hands to gently mix the endives, olives, and peppers. In a measuring pitcher, blend the dressing ingredients. Drizzle over the salad, mix again until each piece is coated, and serve.

Corn Salad

Alternative: Leaves of mild cress.

Pick leaf by leaf from the pretty rosettes. The leaves are spoon-shaped and fragile, so rinse them lightly. The leaves are high in beta-carotene, a moderate source of vitamin C, and fair sources of calcium and iron.

This is one wild green tamed for salads that, as far as I know, isn't also cooked. There is, however, a hot corn salad composition from the vineyards of France that's charming.

VINEGROWER'S SALAD: For each serving, combine a handful of corn salad leaves and half a handful of torn dandelion leaves in a warm bowl. Sprinkle over a quarter handful of toasted walnut pieces. In a small nonreactive skillet over medium heat, warm a dressing of four parts walnut oil to one part red wine vinegar. When hot, drizzle it over the greens, toss, and serve. Matchsticks of cool cooked beets are often added to this salad, and sometimes crumbled bacon in place of walnuts.

Cresses

It's a delight to have a little patch of small dark-leaved cresses growing where you can bend down and pluck a hot mouthful. Pinch off the stems just above the soil by the bunch or one by one. In effect, cresses aren't much more than mustard seedlings. So if you pine for cresses and have only mustard seeds, sow some and pluck while the size of cress.

Rinse lightly and use tender stems. These brassicas are part of what we must eat heaps of every day with all their invaluable nutrients. They also contain moderate amounts of beta-carotene and vitamin C and a small amount of calcium.

Garden Cress

Alternative: Arugula seedlings or another cress.

A patch of garden cress is a delight in the border. It has the color and flavor of watercress, and its sharpness blends especially well with the tang of citrus.

A GARDEN CRESS SALAD: On one side of each chilled salad plate, arrange crescents of pink grapefruit, sweet orange, and strips of marinated sweet red peppers or roasted pimentos. Tuck a nosegay of garden cress with its stems on the other side. Drizzle with vinaigrette. Grind white pepper over the salad and serve at room temperature.

Upland Cress

Alternative: Arugula seedlings or another cress.

The little pinked shiny green leaves of upland cress really shouldn't be cooked. Just pick them at the last minute and toss into salads or heap in sandwiches instead of lettuce. Try it in a submarine between stacks of mortadella salami and provolone cheese—or simply tomatoes and fresh goat cheese—the sandwich moistened with vinaigrette.

Watercress

You can keep watercress happy in a big pot with ample water.

Pick by the sprig.

Savory Toasts with Watercress, Cheese, and Pear

ALLOW 2 SLICES PER SERVING

The British food writer Jane Grigson described an elegant use of cress—the recipe originated at Locket's Restaurant near the House of Commons. In Britain, savories are a course after dessert that ends the meal, but here I think this is best as a first course.

Heat the oven to 350°F. Trim the crusts from small slices of homestyle white bread and lightly toast the bread. Arrange two slices each in small buttered flat baking dishes or place all on a buttered baking sheet. Cover the toasts with cress, then cover the cress with thin slices of peeled sweet ripe pear. Cover the pear with thin slices of veined cheese (such as blue or Gorgonzola) and bake just until the cheese begins to melt and the scent of pear drifts out to the living room, 5 to 10 minutes—the cress must not wilt. Place the hot baking dishes on service plates or slide the toasts from the baking sheet onto a hot platter. Season with a few turns of the black pepper mill and serve garnished with fresh cress.

Dandelions

The toothed leaves of dandelions are delightfully bitter—but not too. Especially the young ones, especially in spring. Pick leaf by leaf. Rinse well, then use raw in salads or as garnish or cook them in the manner of a potherb—to flavor soups. Or slice the leaves and stems into thin ribbons the way you would a chicory. The surprising news is that these delicate leaves pack a nutritional wallop. Dandelion greens are high in calcium and beta-carotene and offer a moderate amount of vitamin C and a small amount of iron. When cooked, the value diminishes somewhat. Add the golden daisies of dandelions to salads.

The best way to eat dandelions is just to add them to salad. I never fail to get a little thrill of pleasure when I find one on my plate. Something about its wildness delights me.

COUNTRY FRENCH DANDELION SALAD: In other times, part of the dressing for this classic dandelion salad was melted bacon fat. Here olive oil takes its place. But it's surprising how a little crumbled crisp bacon can add that incomparable smokehouse touch.

Tear tender dandelion leaves into one or two pieces into a mixing bowl. Heat a vinaigrette of olive oil and red wine vinegar and pour it over the leaves, wilting them in the manner of wilted spinach salad. Garnish with a handful of crisp-cooked diced lean bacon, if you like, and serve at once, sprinkled with finely chopped hard-cooked egg.

Thin matchsticks of cooked beets are a nice addition, as are small diced cooked red potatoes.

Endive and Escarole

Alternatives: Mizuna for curly and butterhead for broad-leaved.

These leaves are either frizzy and disheveled or smooth and composed. All are bitter to a degree and so refreshing. Rinse them lightly. Pick leaf by leaf or cut the whole head. The leaves have modest amounts of beta-carotene, vitamin C, calcium, and iron.

Endives and escaroles add great interest to a tossed salad. Because they're so beautiful, they make a sit-up-and-take-notice first course, especially if you dress them with flowers—and little else.

If your climate is mild or if you've sheltered them in a cold frame, you can winter over early-summer-sown curly endives. Then when sweet violets come up, you can sprinkle them over the spidery leaves, where they'll catch and dangle in the branches.

SALAD OF CURLY ENDIVES AND VIOLETS: Tear a balance of dark green outer leaves and blanched inner leaves of curly endives into a glass bowl. Sprinkle on 6 to 8 violets per serving. At the table, drizzle on a little very light olive or nut oil, then a very little rice vinegar, then sprinkle with a little salt and freshly ground white pepper. Toss with your hands and urge everyone to eat with their fingers.

SALAD OF BROAD-LEAVED ESCAROLE AND ROSE PETALS: In early July, when spring-sown leaves are bright and tender and roses are ravishing, make this salad. Prepare the salad as for curly endives, using Batavian or other escarole leaves and clear pink or red rose petals from the garden.

Lettuce, Garden

Regarding beta-carotene, vitamins A and C, calcium, folic acid, and iron in lettuces, romaine is tops overall, then comes looseleaf, then butterhead, then Batavian, and at the bottom of the list is crisphead. Again and again we see that the deeper the green of the leaf, the more valuable.

Romaine lettuces, being stiffest and crispest, are the choice to stand up to heavy dressings and to last in long-held sandwiches.

For leaves tasting of earth and sunshine, we dine on butterhead and looseleaf lettuces. The textures of their leaves range from crunchy to crispy to melting. Their shapes may be a deer's tongue, an oak leaf, a frizzle, or a ruffle.

Crisphead and Batavian lettuces can be glorious: frilly green Webb's Wonderful, deeply notched Reine des Glaces, and wine-red Rouge Grenobloise.

Because raising lettuces is not quite as easy as falling off a log, for at least the first few tastes you'll want your lettuces pure and simple, letting their special qualities shine. A luminous oil—peanut, walnut, hazelnut, or a vibrant extra-virgin olive—and fresh lemon juice or a clear-eyed vinegar are all that's wanted, with sea salt and freshly ground pepper.

Before these good companions can grow fatiguing, often I combine nut and olive oils. Or I may omit the oil altogether and blend one part Dijon mustard and a splash of vinegar with two to three parts thin cream. Often I mix orange or tangerine or grapefruit or lime juice with the lemon juice or vinegar. Occasionally I'll crumble fresh goat or feta cheese or a fine chop of anchovy fillets into the dressing. Sometimes it's an enormous handful of minced fresh herbs.

Don't cut your lettuce with a knife unless you're serving it immediately—leaf edges will darken—and don't tear the leaves into itty-bitty bits. Larger pieces are more natural and easier to deal with. Slip the glistening leaves into your mouth with your fingers, not bruising the tender lettuces with the tines of a fork, the better to savor to the last such sensuousness.

We serve a leafy salad after the main course as a cool moment of repose. When there are guests, the green glass plates are whisked from the freezer. Even though the dressing is at room temperature, we enjoy chilled leaves—they're crispest. After everyone's finished their salad, we pass the cheese tray and cracker basket, for eating on the same plate—a hint of oil and lemon juice or vinegar anoints the cheese.

BRETON RED LEAF LETTUCE SALAD: We are so accustomed to oil and vinegar dressing that I was surprised to find this simple yet immensely refreshing idea for lettuce from Brittany. I especially like it with red lettuces, their color so rich on the plate. Sometimes I add thin circlets of baby red onions as well.

Slice rinsed and dried lettuces into ¼-inch ribbons. This can be done in advance and the lettuces chilled. To serve, heap the ribbons on salad plates. Using a bottle with a sprinkler top, for each portion sprinkle on about 1 teaspoon rice vinegar, then shake over ½ teaspoon sugar. Serve at once.

Lettuces are fully as delicious cooked. Soufflé of chopped wilted lettuce is light yet filling. Timbales (chopped wilted lettuce suspended in rich molded custards) are elegant accompaniments to meat. A ribbon of butter-poached lettuces makes a fine filling for omelets. And among the most useful ways with lettuce in the classic French repertoire are small braised heads combined with other vegetables as garnish. They're savory, but they still retain a delightful crunch.

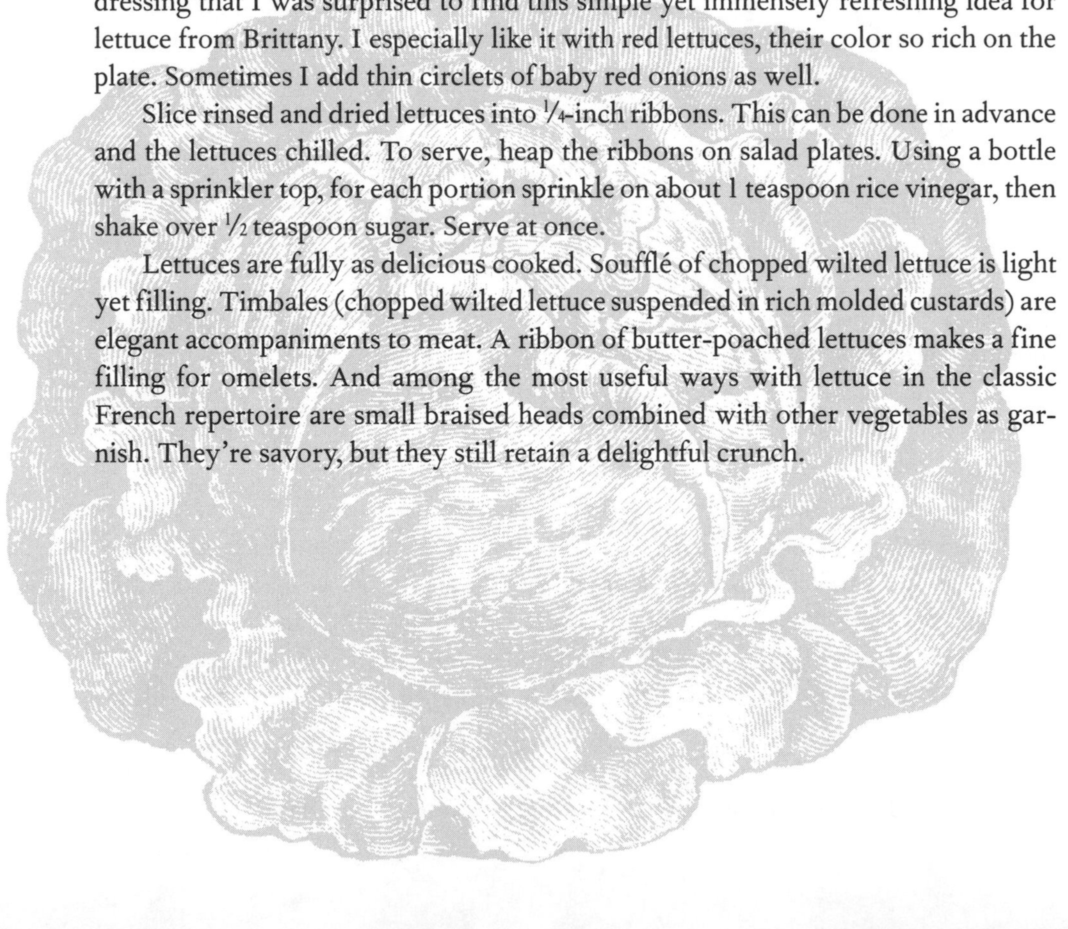

Braised Lettuce

MAKES 8 SERVINGS

The dish can be prepared for finishing a few hours in advance.

salt to taste
2 large heads crisp romaine or 3 to 4 large heads butterhead lettuces, trimmed
about ½ tablespoon olive oil
1 red onion, thinly sliced
1 unpeeled carrot, thinly sliced
a small handful of celery or lovage leaves, chopped
a small handful of flat-leaf parsley, chopped
1 large fresh sage leaf, chopped, or ½ teaspoon crumbled dried
½ tablespoon fresh thyme leaves or a heaped ½ teaspoon crumbled dried
1 cup chicken broth or vegetable stock
3 to 4 tablespoons unsalted butter to taste
freshly ground black pepper to taste

Have ready a big pot of boiling salted water. Drop in the lettuces and cook uncovered over high heat for 2 minutes. Lift out and drain, saving the broth in the pot. Heat the oven to 350°F if you plan to serve this immediately.

Film a large heavy skillet with oil and heat it over medium-high heat. Sauté the onion and carrot in it for 5 minutes, stirring frequently. Ladle in ½ cup of the lettuce stock and cook uncovered, stirring occasionally, for 5 minutes more.

Oil a shallow baking dish in which the lettuces just fit. Sprinkle the chopped celery leaves, parsley, sage, and thyme over the dish. Cut the lettuces into 8 pieces—lengthwise through the stem. Arrange in the dish, stems facing out. Add the chicken broth and onion and carrot mixture and shake the dish to settle everything. Cover with foil (dull side up). You can refrigerate it at this point, but bring it to room temperature before baking and heat the oven 20 minutes before serving.

Bake uncovered until hot, about 20 minutes. Drain the excess stock from the dish into the skillet, then keep the lettuces covered and warm in the turned-off oven while you reduce the stock to a syrup over highest heat, about 5 minutes. Add the butter and, when it has melted, season with salt and pepper, pour over the lettuces, and serve from the baking dish.

If you have Chinese artichokes in your garden, cook them and spoon them over your braised lettuces for an intriguing first course.

Lettuce in Flower

What to do when lettuce has grown or started to grow flowers to make seed and the leaves have turned bitter? If the lettuce has produced a thick stalk—I find it happens when the plant is sheltered and can bolt at a leisurely pace—regard the stalk as a primitive form of celtuce. It will be crisp and mildly bitter, but pare and slice it into a salad. The French call the stalks *moelles de laitue* and cook them as for asparagus. You can do that too if you have enough.

Then turn the leaves into soup. Their bitterness vanishes in the following refreshing summer puree.

Bolting Lettuce Soup

MAKES 6 SERVINGS

I like this rough with flecks of colors, but my husband prefers a silky cream. Use this recipe for proportions, depending on how much lettuce you've got to salvage. The soup is equally good hot or cold—a splendid pick-me-up after weeding in the sun. It keeps for several days in the refrigerator.

2 quarts cold water, vegetable stock, or water and stock
3 large unpeeled potatoes, coarsely chopped
3 medium-size unpeeled carrots, coarsely chopped
salt to taste
2 tablespoons olive oil
1 large onion, preferably red, chopped
2 large garlic cloves, chopped
1 large head of bolting lettuce, trimmed and cut into broad ribbons
½ cup dry white wine
2 tablespoons fresh lemon juice
½ teaspoon celery seeds
freshly ground white pepper to taste
plain yogurt for garnish

In your soup pot, combine the water, potatoes, carrots, and salt. Bring to a simmer, turn the heat to low, and simmer uncovered until tender, about 15 minutes. Meanwhile, in a skillet, warm the oil. Sauté the onion over medium-high heat until softened, stirring frequently, about 5 minutes. Add the garlic and sauté for another minute. Mix in the lettuce and cook, stirring, until the lettuce turns limp. Add a splash of stock from the pot if you need it. Stir these vegetables into the soup.

Puree in a food processor, blender, or food mill as coarsely or finely as you like, then return to the pot. Blend in the wine, lemon juice, and celery seeds, then taste for salt and pepper. Bring to a simmer over medium heat, stirring occasionally. Serve hot or cool, passing yogurt for each bowl.

Malabar Spinach

Alternative: Red orach or young beet leaves.

The red stems of these large shiny crispy green leaves are appealing raw in salads. The greens have a basic green taste. Pick individually and rinse lightly (since they're a vine and grow off the ground, leaves won't be sandy).

Although the decorative leaves are known for being a spinach substitute in hot weather, in fact the leaves are more palatable uncooked. Cooked, they can be strong and mucilaginous. Use them for garnish; the red and green are handsome. Especially pretty when paired with the gold and white of hard-cooked eggs.

MALABAR SPINACH, WALNUT, AND CHRYSANTHEMUM SALAD: Tear the leaves into large-bite-size pieces, dropping them into a salad bowl. Chop up the tender red stems for color and crunch. Drizzle on a dressing of two parts walnut oil and one part low-sodium soy sauce sweetened with a bit of sugar. Sprinkle the leaves with chopped roasted walnuts—a couple of tablespoonfuls per serving—and toss. If yellow chrysanthemums are in bloom, sprinkle their petals over the top or use yellow calendulas. Serve.

Mallows, Curled

Alternative: Common bean vine leaves hint of their flavor.

Looking very much like hollyhock leaves, when picked no larger than the palm of your hand these dark green leaves are delightfully flavored—close to spinach but closer to okra. They have a slightly succulent quality that is a pleasant change from just plain leaves. The hollyhocklike flowers are edible, too.

Rinse well. To cook, steam in a skillet over low heat in the water that clings to their leaves after rinsing until they droop, about 5 minutes. Although they have an unusual melts-in-the-mouth quality, the leaves don't utterly collapse as most greens do.

In our garden the mallow plants come back each spring and grow with abandon. The leaves are smallest and most delicate in early spring, but I can hunt down small ones for salad here and there on the plant until frost. I toss young leaves and mauvy white flowers into salads and soups.

The leaves are cooked as a potherb in a number of cultures, but my experiments with cooking mallow have been disappointing. So I take their pleasures in my salads and in making a bed of them on the platter when serving fish.

Mesclun/Misticanza

Many seedsmen offer collections of seeds that all but toss a mixed green salad for you in the bowl. The notion of growing a blend of leaves all in one place originated in the South of France—where mesclun is classically composed of lettuce, endive, arugula, and chervil—and in the Piedmont district of Italy—where misticanza is traditionally composed of five chicories and four lettuces.

You can grow these pretty mixes, or (what I prefer) sprinkle pinches of myriad salad makings through the garden and pick and choose leaves for each salad as the spirit moves you. Before you know it, you'll have your own house blend of greens.

Miner's Lettuce

Alternative: Very small leaves of spinach or New Zealand spinach.

More beta-carotene, vitamins A and C, calcium, and iron. Rinse well.

Some miner's lettuce leaves are as big as a minute, some are the size of a quarter. Pick one by one. I don't expect ever to have enough leaves to try cooking miner's lettuce, and I probably wouldn't anyway. The charm of these unusual cup-shaped leaves for me is straight from the garden onto a plate. Rather than lose them in a tossed salad, I make an arrangement where I can see them. They have a tiny star of a blossom in the center.

MINER'S LETTUCE AND FRUIT SALAD: Make a pretty border of miner's lettuce leaves around orange slices strewn with sliced fresh strawberries. Dress with raspberry vinegar and hazelnut oil at the last moment.

Purslane

Alternative: Miner's lettuce or pea shoots for their crispness.

A rollicking plant that, once it has found you, will always fill your salad bowl with flavor. Pick by the sprig and rinse the purslane lightly but thoroughly, since it is one to revel lustily in the dust. The oval leaves are green or green gold, succulent, and slightly tangy. You'll come to a time when your gleanings seem to drop millions of pepper specks all over the place. These seeds are why purslane will never be an endangered species.

Leaves and stalks are chockablock with astonishing amounts of nutrients: omega-3 fatty acids, beta-carotene, vitamin C, potassium, iron, calcium, phosphorous, and riboflavin!

Purslane's stalks and leaves have such a refreshingly tangy crunch I never tire of them. Drop the flowerlike clusters of small wild cultivars whole into salads. You're supposed to eat just young leaves because the older ones get tough. I guess we eat them so fast they haven't a chance to coarsen on us because I haven't yet found a purslane leaf I didn't like.

PURSLANE SALAD WITH RUBY GRAPEFRUIT AND LEMON GEM MARIGOLDS: Whether you have the small green or large gold leaves of purslane, it makes no difference. This salad with marigold petals is delectable; most marigolds have an acrid scent and flavor, but the small Gems—Tangerine and Lemon—have a faintly citrus taste.

In your bowl, have bite-size pieces of purslane of whatever cultivar, two handfuls per serving. Peel sweet ruby grapefruit—depending on its size, one for every two to three servings. Carefully remove the white membrane. To produce bite-size pieces, slice the grapefruit in half crosswise, then slice the other way. Pull segments apart. Add petals and chopped leaves of Lemon Gem marigolds, two or three per serving.

Make a dressing of equal parts extra-virgin olive oil and fresh orange juice, plus salt and freshly ground white pepper. Lightly dress the salad and toss with your hands to mix. Heap on salad plates on waiting leaves of red lettuce.

Purslane Salad in the Mexican Style

MAKES 6 SERVINGS

Here's a sensational salad inspired by flavors from farther south. The salad can wait a few hours in the refrigerator.

Put 8 cups bite-size sprigs of purslane into a salad bowl. Slice 2 medium-size sweet white onions very thin, then cut the slices in half. Add to the purslane, separating the pieces. Mix in ½ cup (packed) chopped cilantro leaves.

Peel and thinly slice 2 sweet oranges, removing any seeds. Cut the slices in quarters and add to the bowl. Slice 2 mildly hot red chilies in half, remove seeds, and cut the chilies in very thin strips—or cut thin strips from ½ sweet red pepper. Add 6 tablespoons fruity olive oil, 3 tablespoons red wine vinegar, and salt to taste. Mix with your hands, then taste for seasoning.

OTHER PURSLANE SALADS:

- purslane sprigs with equal parts finely chopped tomatoes, dressed with crème fraîche
- purslane sprigs with lots of chopped chervil, dressed with crème fraîche thinned with lemon juice
- purslane sprigs with half the volume of chopped mixed herbs—parsley, dill, and chives—dressed with garlic-flavored yogurt

COLD PURSLANE SOUP: A smooth puree of sprigs (in a food processor or blender) thinned with buttermilk, heightened with a little fresh orange juice and lemon juice, then served speckled with finely chopped watercress.

Purslane can also be pickled according to the recipe for samphire. The same amount will shrink to a fourth its size and be slippery. Still, it's a European favorite.

Samphire

Alternative: Purslane for its lively flavor and crunch.

Samphire is marvelous. It looks like a cross between caraway and a plant from the sea. Its flavor is a lightly tangy mix of dill, anise, and who-knows-what, and although its branches are thin, they're crunchy. Rinse lightly.

Mix pieces of samphire's thin fleshy stalks, leaves, parsleylike flowers, and aromatic seedheads in salads. Nothing resembles its graceful branches as garnish. I've never done it, but you can simmer samphire until tender (about 10 minutes) and serve it with melted butter. But in England, samphire gets pickled. It holds up amazingly, and has a bit of a spicy grassy taste—welcome in winter.

PICKLED SAMPHIRE: Makes 1 quart. Rinse 4 cups perfect sprigs with their plump seedpods and lay them in a bowl. Cover with brine: proportions are ¼ cup salt (preferably pickling salt) dissolved in 3½ cups cool water. Lay a saucer on top to keep the samphire beneath the brine. Cover for the night. The next day, drain and rinse several times with cold water, then pack the branches into jars to within an inch of the top. Cover and refrigerate for at least 3 weeks before serving with roast meats.

Shepherd's Purse

Alternative: Young arugula.

By the middle of May our garden is graced with rosettes of shepherd's purse all over the place. This little weed—yes, it is—is as welcome as the robins. Its leaves are long and indented, very like dandelion's, but they're not prickled. In springtime shepherd's purse is wonderfully mild and tender; even the stalks are sweet and crisp. The leaves begin with a mild bite—they contain mustard oil. As the weather warms up, so does their heat, and they also can become chewy. Pick stalks individually.

You can cook the leaves as a potherb, chopping them up and cooking in a nonstick skillet with just the water that clings to the leaves from rinsing. It's very delicious with a few drops of lemon juice and a thread of olive oil. These leaves are rich in minerals and vitamins—shepherd's purse is said to contain more vitamin C than oranges.

BLOOD ORANGES AND SHEPHERD'S PURSE: Shepherd's purse springs up when blood oranges are ripe, and they make a tasty pair in a salad. Arrange the shepherd's purse leaves in a star on a plate and set overlapping rounds of peeled sweet blood orange on them. Drizzle with hazelnut or peanut oil and then a hint of red wine vinegar. A speck of salt is needed, but really no pepper—the leaves are peppery enough.

Salsify and Scorzonera

Alternatives: Burdock, parsnip, pale carrots.

Both carrot-shaped roots, salsify has beige skin and scorzonera dark skin. Both have cream-colored flesh, the flavor in both is delicate and unique, and the two, for all practical purposes, are interchangeable. After a few nights of sweetening frost in autumn, pull the roots. Trim off the pretty leaves—reserve them for salad—and scrub the roots in cold water. Steam the roots unpeeled and whole until tender when pierced with a skewer—start testing after 10 minutes. Don't overcook, because these roots quickly pass from tender to mushy. Lift out pieces individually as they're cooked. Gently rub off the peel under running water and pat dry.

Taking the delicacy of their flavor into account, you can adapt simple carrot, parsnip, turnip, potato, and cauliflower recipes to these roots. Salsify offers slight amounts of vitamin C, potassium, and some B vitamins.

Norman Salad of Salsify or Scorzonera

MAKES 6 SERVINGS

To illustrate how well these roots adapt to recipes designed for other vegetables, this salad began as one for potatoes. It's from the Norman coast of the English Channel, where the cows produce exquisite milk and cream—Norman cooks make the most of this. The vaguely artichoke taste of the roots, the crunch of celery, the mild nip of vinegar, and the sweetness of cream play beautifully together.

If you'd rather, you can blend in yogurt instead of cream. And if you're out of salsify, make this salad with its original potatoes.

The salad can be prepared hours in advance up to the point of adding the cream.

Steam 10 medium-size (2 pounds) salsify or scorzonera roots (or a mix of both) until tender, then quickly peel. Slice into 2-inch pieces. Toss in a bowl while hot with 1/4 cup cider vinegar. Blend in 1 cup thinly sliced celery (some leaves included) and 1/2 cup finely chopped watercress or other cress leaves (flat-leaf parsley can be substituted). The salad can be prepared in advance to this point.

To serve, drizzle 1/3 cup heavy cream over the salad and use your hands to blend it in. Season with salt and freshly ground white pepper and blend again. Sometimes a dash more vinegar is wanted.

About 1 1/2 cups finely diced lean ham makes this salad supper.

SPINACH

This graceful dark green plant gives us some of the garden's best flavor. Harvest leaves individually or pull the whole young plant before it bolts. The leaves of Wolter spinach, small, smooth, and spade shaped, collect no dirt, so a quick swish in lukewarm water in the sink is all they need. Crinkly leaves may need several rinsings.

The ideal way to rinse spinach leaves of earth is to fill a large salad spinner with tepid-to-warm water and drop in the leaves. The warmish water relaxes the leaves just enough for the sand to slide off. Swish the leaves gently up and down a few times, then lift out the liner and pour out the water. Repeat until the water is clean. Then, if you're going to use it raw in salad, spin the leaves dry. Otherwise, leave the water on the leaves for cooking. Rinse just before using, or the leaves will quickly wilt.

Always use the stems of spinach in a dish when you can. Unless the plants got away from you, these are not tough cookies as are some of the mustards, but dainty things that are quite chewable—and they're packed with valuable nutrients. And see the next section, about the pink crowns of spinach bunches, a delectable conceit.

You can blanch spinach—cook it in an abundance of boiling water in the manner of kale and other tougher greens, but the only reason to do this is if you want to serve the brightest and most flavorful of your spinach to guests. Spinach cooks to tenderness in about 5 minutes, and it's never strongly flavored, so why waste a scrap of its nutrients in all that water? Simply arrange rinsed leaves evenly in a suitably sized heavy skillet or big pot—preferably nonstick—and cook uncovered over medium heat until tender, stirring the leaves occasionally. It's easier to chop the leaves after cooking—squeeze out excess moisture so the spinach will absorb its seasonings. Spinach is very high in vitamin A and beta-carotene, high in folic acid and potassium, moderately high in vitamin C and iron, and a fairly good source of magnesium, vitamin E, manganese, calcium, riboflavin, and vitamin B_6.

So many recipes call for chopped spinach that we forget what it's like to eat fresh whole branches of cooked spinach—I find them uncommonly aesthetic.

SPINACH IN BRANCHES: Lay whole rinsed plants with the pink rootlet attached side by side in a heavy skillet with the water that clings to their leaves. Cook over low heat until wilted. You may have to add a splash of water to keep them from sticking—or use a nonstick skillet. You can also cook spinach this way by drying the leaves and sautéing the branches in a bit of oil. Lift out and arrange on a platter and moisten with a little olive or nut oil and a jot of soy sauce—perhaps sprinkle with a pinch of toasted sesame seeds. Serve hot or cold.

In classical French cuisine, spinach has been compared with virgin beeswax in its ability to receive any impression—other vegetables impress their own character on a dish.

SPINACH WITH FRESH CREAM: This, says Elizabeth David, is ". . . one of the most delicious vegetable dishes in the whole of French cookery." Cook 3 large bunches (3 pounds) of spinach and squeeze it of excess liquid in the usual way, finely chop it and stir in 4 tablespoons of unsalted butter, then ½ cup boiling heavy cream. Serve as a first course. Follow with fresh fruit.

MANZI'S SPINACH: Here is the secret of making spinach utterly divine. After cooking your fresh spinach leaves, squeeze, then roughly chop them. Stir in lots and lots of softened unsalted butter. That's it. I wouldn't dream of telling you how much because you might discover the moment suprême for you is a little more than mine. But even a tiny bit of butter is a revelation with garden-fresh spinach. Season to taste with salt and freshly ground white pepper.

A Greek Spinach

MAKES 4 SERVINGS

I'm glad the Greeks have so many wonderful ways with spinach that don't involve butter. This can be prepared and reheated without harm.

Rinse 2 pounds (2 bunches the size you'd get at the market) of spinach, saving the crowns to be enjoyed on their own. Cook uncovered with the water that clings to them in a big pot, just until wilted, a few minutes. Press out excess moisture, then chop. Mix in a large nonstick skillet with a small handful of fresh oregano leaves and 2 minced garlic cloves. Sprinkle with fresh lemon juice to taste and moisten with a little olive oil. Taste for salt and freshly ground black pepper and either heat up, stirring, or refrigerate until needed. Top with chopped scallions.

This is especially good spread on a heated platter as a bed for grilled lamb or fish—the charred juices add their flavor.

Spinach, Lemon Basil, and Raspberry Salad

MAKES 4 SERVINGS

Spinach is a leaf that does beautifully with herbs—its flavor is strong enough, but not so strong that it slams down an herbal companion. This is a surprising and felicitous combination of flavors. All elements can be prepared in advance for tossing. Since this is special, we'll save the stalks for a family salad.

Rinse and dry about 2 pounds (2 market bunches) spinach. Tear the leafy parts into large bite-size pieces into a salad bowl. According to their strength, add a handful or two of lemon basil leaves—sweet basil or one of the purple basils can be used instead. Chill under a damp towel until cold and crisp.

To serve, toss the leaves with about ⅓ cup vinaigrette. Heap on chilled plates and strew each with about ⅓ cup fresh raspberries or strawberry halves.

Spinach Crowns

Gathering enough of these to serve them to anyone more than yourself depends on whether you cook for a commune. To tell the truth, I take every crown from the branches I clean, and I eat their sweet crunch all by myself.

SPINACH CROWNS IN SOLITUDE: Slice off the crowns—the pink rootlet at the base of the stems—of your branches. Toss in a small skillet with a little water over medium-high heat until tender—briefly. Turn into a bowl and add a few drops of Asian sesame oil or walnut oil. You might add a touch of lemon juice and salt and freshly ground white pepper.

Spinach in Flower

July's Bolting Spinach

MAKES 3 OR 4 SERVINGS

Older leaves are best pureed. Here is something nice with leaves and flowers of plants going to seed. Bring the plants in from the garden, cook, and serve at once. Proportions are a rule of thumb.

Melt 2 or 3 tablespoons unsalted butter in a large heavy nonreactive skillet. Add 10 to 12 spring-sown spinach plants, about to bloom, buds and all—you'll probably have to cut the plants in half to fit them into the skillet. Cover, turn the heat to low, and cook just until the spinach turns limp, a minute or two. Turn into a food processor and whirl until as much as is going to be chopped has been chopped. The odd thickish stalk won't chop finely, but no matter.

Turn the chop into small shallow dishes and sprinkle with lemon or lime juice and salt and freshly ground black pepper.

Some of the stalks may be chewy, but so what? The spinach will be fresh and—surprise—creamy and delicious.

SQUASHES AND PUMPKINS

Squashes

A summer squash has a soft shell and is ready to eat in summer. A winter squash's shell is too hard for your thumbnail to pierce—and isn't ready to eat until winter. All winter squashes pass through the summer squash stage, but few summer squashes get to see autumn, much less winter.

Squash Blossoms

The time to cook with squash blossoms is midsummer, when the plants are still cheerily sending up flowers but the winter squashes have set all the fruit you want them to and you'll welcome a break from the stream of summer squashes. If you're hungry for blossoms but still want their fruit, cut only male flowers—the ones on long slender stalks with no bulge at the base—leaving at least one or two male flowers to service the ladies. Gather blossoms that have just opened and at the last possible moment. Cut them off cleanly with a knife. Then, while you're still outdoors, gently open each one and peer inside. I've often found the ochre chamber of a squash blossom sanctuary to an exhausted bee. If you can't gently shake her out onto another flower (she'll tumble out, no harm to you), cut a small escape hatch in the stem of the flower where she's resting, and ease her out through it.

In an airtight plastic bag in the vegetable drawer of the refrigerator, the blossoms will stay crisp for a few hours. Since you haven't sprayed them, they don't have to be washed. A little dust never hurt anybody—just blow it off. Squash blossoms are a good source of beta-carotene, vitamin C, and potassium.

Add the squash's flowers and tender vine leaves and stalks to salads.

These stuffed squash blossoms are delectable creations from Suzanne's Cuisine, a superb restaurant in Ojai, California. Amazingly, the flowers are as perky as jaybirds yet filled with hot creamy cheese. Owner-chef Suzanne Roll was generous enough to give me the secret for you.

STUFFED SQUASH BLOSSOMS: Blend equal parts soft goat cheese and ricotta cheese. Season to taste with salt and freshly ground white pepper. Trim the stems from the squash blossoms. Gently squeeze the flower open and spoon in enough cheese to make a layer 1/4 inch thick at the base. Lay the flowers on a plate, cover with wax paper, and microwave at full power for 10 seconds or just until the cheese is hot; the flower should not be affected. Serve at once as an hors d'oeuvre, garnished with nasturtium blossoms and leaves.

Fettuccine with Squash Blossoms

MAKES 6 FIRST-COURSE SERVINGS

Usually, cooked slices of squash blossoms quickly dissolve into a vaguely flavored silky mouthful. But the blossoms are so sensuous and beautiful that if you can capture their color and fleeting crispness you'll have fantasy in your dish. Here it is. With the green of basil and oregano, the gold of blossoms, the red of tomatoes, and the purply black of olives on your plate, you could be dining with Picasso in Provence.

The dish is last-minute but very fast.

salt to taste
1 pound dried fettuccine, preferably Italian or fresh homemade
12 large crisp squash blossoms, firm green stalk trimmed off
about 1/2 cup mild olive or hazelnut oil
6 ripe flavorful plum tomatoes, chopped
1/2 cup roughly chopped basil leaves
2 tablespoons roughly chopped fresh oregano leaves
about 24 small unpitted black Italian, French, or Greek salt-cured olives
freshly ground white pepper to taste
freshly grated Parmesan cheese

Bring a big pot of salted water to a boil. Add the pasta and stir frequently so it won't stick together. Cook according to the package or recipe directions until al dente.

Meanwhile, loosely stack the blossoms and slice them into inch-wide rings.

When the pasta is ready, drain and turn into a serving bowl. Drizzle on about 1/4 cup of the oil, toss to moisten each strand, then cover to keep warm. Quickly heat about 1/4 cup oil in a large heavy skillet over high heat and sauté the tomatoes for 2 minutes, stirring and shaking the skillet. Add the basil, oregano, and olives and stir just until everything is blended and warmed through, 1 long minute. Add pepper, taste for seasoning, then pour over the pasta and strew with the blossom pieces. Rush the dish to the table. Toss again to mix in the blossoms so that the hot pasta warms them. Pass a bowl of Parmesan on the side.

We like a piquant Zinfandel with these colors and flavors, but before you toast the garden that has provided such delight, warn everybody about the olive pits. There might be pieces of roast or grilled chicken to follow with a bit of wild salad and blackberries after that.

Squash Seeds

Squash seeds are very nutritious, having all sorts of exotic trace vitamins and minerals—the ones that nourish the gleam of squash in the seed's eye while it's growing. Never waste them. Even those with thick shells are worth roasting.

The thinner the hull, of course, the better the eating.

Any spice you like will probably taste just great here.

CHILI-ROASTED SQUASH SEEDS: Spread the seeds without rinsing them on a lightly oiled baking sheet. Sprinkle with chili powder to taste and toss with a fork to distribute the seasoning. Toast in a 250°F oven, stirring occasionally, until crisp and richly browned, about an hour and a half. Remove from the oven, sprinkle lightly with salt, and stir again. When cool, store in a tightly covered jar.

Squash Vines

The Hmong—remarkably resourceful in the garden—harvest the tender vines of winter squashes—not summer's squashes, because those are needed to sustain bearing fruit. After the first blossoms have set, the tender tips of vines—7 to 8 inches—are taken down to a mature leaf. Harvest is done by twisting off the shoot—soon a new tip will grow, which will be harvested in its turn. The vine is peeled if necessary, then all of it—including tendrils and flower buds—is chopped and stir-fried until tender-crunchy.

Near the end of the season, when the immature winter squashes are picked so the vines will pour energy into the larger fruits, these babies (resembling summer squashes) are sliced and stir-fried with the vines.

Summer Squashes

Always harvest summer squash as small as possible. If it still has its blossom attached, that's ideal (though not always practical). As you amble through these recipes, regard the connections between a squash and a given recipe as a loose link. Any young squash can be prepared by any recipe for any other young squash. What matters is that you'll begin to discover the nuances of flavor among all these progeny. Sautéing preserves a tender squash's color and flavor the best. Rinse and quarter squashes of any shape lengthwise. Toss in a hint of olive or nut oil over

Cakes Using Overflow Squashes

The uncooked flesh of all summer and winter squashes, finely shredded and blended into cake batter, contributes moisture that makes the cake particularly long keeping—and golden winter squashes add their umbered flavor. These will keep in the freezer until the holidays.

To adapt a cake or sweet bread recipe to squash as an ingredient, find a recipe with 1 cup liquid—anything from water to coffee to buttermilk—and 2 cups flour. Reduce the liquid to ⅓ cup and add 1 pound finely shredded squash (peel only hard-shelled squashes). Have all other ingredients measured before grating the squash, then put the batter together without delay—the longer the squash sets, the more liquid it exudes. Why, you ask, would it matter *where* the liquid is—in the shred or out of it? Flour can absorb only so much liquid before it collapses to a gummy paste. If the moisture stays inside the bit of squash, the batter can wrap pleasingly around it, and most of the moisture isn't released until you bite into it.

Because squashes have native sweetness and because I don't like cloying cake, I use 1 to 1¼ cups sweetening, often less than what's called for. Nuts and raisins are a festive addition for grown-ups, but most small children hate bumpy bits in their cake.

You can bake the batter as cupcakes, layers, loaf cake, or Bundt cake, but moist batter takes longer to dry out than average batter, so baking time may need to be increased.

medium-high heat until just tender, 3 to 6 minutes. Heighten the flavor with a little lemon juice, salt, freshly ground white pepper, and sweet marjoram mixed with flat-leaf parsley. Serve hot or cool.

Gingery Summer Squash Cakes with Lemon Icing

MAKES UP TO 36 BARS

Some think these are even better than brownies. The flavor is best the day after baking.

CAKE

10 tablespoons unsalted butter plus extra, softened, for the pan
½ cup light brown sugar, firmly packed, with no lumps
½ cup light molasses
⅓ cup hot brewed coffee
2 large eggs at room temperature
2 cups all-purpose flour, lightly spooned into the cup
1½ tablespoons ground ginger
1 tablespoon unsweetened cocoa powder
1 teaspoon ground cinnamon
1 teaspoon baking soda
¼ teaspoon salt
2 well-packed cups raw, finely shredded summer squash, ¾ to 1 pound

LEMON ICING

about 3 cups confectioners' sugar, sifted if lumpy
6 to 8 tablespoons fresh lemon juice to taste

Heat the oven to 350°F. Brush the bottom of a 13- by 9-inch baking pan with the butter. Cover with wax paper, then butter the paper.

In a large saucepan, melt the butter without browning it. Turn off the heat and whisk in the brown sugar, molasses, and coffee, then the eggs. Sprinkle the flour, ginger, cocoa, cinnamon, baking soda, and salt over the batter. Whisk for a minute or two, until any lumps disappear. Blend in the squash with a wooden spoon. Smooth into the pan, pushing the batter slightly up against the sides.

Bake in the middle of the oven until a toothpick emerges clean from the center, about 35 minutes.

Unless you'll be freezing the cakes, combine 3 cups confectioners' sugar and 6 tablespoons lemon juice in a small bowl or a food processor and beat until smooth—don't overprocess, or the icing will thin out. If it's too thick to spread easily, add a little more juice. If too thin, add a little more sugar.

Cool the cake in the pan for about 10 minutes, run a knife around the edges, then turn out onto a cake rack (removing the paper, bottoms up). To serve fresh, spread the icing at once over the cake. When the icing has set, cut the cake into diamonds, rectangles, or bars and finish cooling.

To freeze, cool completely, and don't ice it. Wrap the uniced, uncut cake airtight in foil, then ice and cut after it thaws. Best eaten within 4 to 6 months of freezing.

At high altitude, bake at 370°F for 20 to 25 minutes.

Cocozelle Summer Squashes

These are like long, skinny zucchini—use them any way you like. Trim off the stems. Cocozelles have fundamentally the same nutrients as zucchini: a bit of beta-carotene, vitamin C, and folic acid. Add the squash's raw flowers and tender vine leaves and stalks to salads.

COCOZELLE WITH ITS VINES: Slice the squash in matchsticks, cut their leaves into thin ribbons, and chop tender tips of vines. In a large cast-iron or nonstick skillet, heat a film of fruity olive oil. Add the squash and sauté over medium-high heat, stirring frequently, until crunchy, about 2 minutes. Add the vine leaves and cook until they collapse and are tender-crisp, another 3 minutes.

Add coarsely chopped cocozelle flowers if you have them to spare (check for bugs first), minced garlic to taste, and a sprinkling of dried red chili flakes. Moisten with the juice of half a lemon and sauté, stirring, over medium-high heat until the flowers are warmed through, about 1 minute. Season with salt and pepper and serve.

Crookneck Summer Squashes

Anything you can do with zucchini you can do with beautiful golden crookneck squashes. Only these will have more flavor. They lend themselves better to sautéing than zucchini, not being so watery. Prepare according to the basic recipe. Add the flowers and tender vine leaves and stalks to salads.

Provençal Crookneck Squashes, Tomatoes, Onions, and Herbs

MAKES 7 TO 8 SERVINGS

This composition using the bounty of summer's squashes fits all my hopes for a party vegetable dish: beautiful flavor and looks—lilac, green, gold, red, and cream—easy to make, prepared in advance, and complementary to the simple grills we like to serve. In addition, potato chunks are slowly crisping on the rack below.

The only problem you might have making this dish—called a *tian*—is the dish itself. *Tian* is Provençal for gratin dish, and a gratin dish must be shallow (under 2½ inches) and earthenware. Any shape suits, and of course you can use a good old glass baking dish instead.

For an informal late Sunday breakfast, the last 5 to 6 minutes of baking I quickly make a depression in the vegetables with the bowl of a spoon, then drop in an egg for each person. I sprinkle each with a bit more herbs and bake just until the white has set.

Usually in such compositions there is cheese on top. I used to do that, but once I left it off and found the sunlit flavors of the vegetables and herbs even brighter.

The herb blend gives a complex, lively, and supportive dash to the vegetables. If some aren't available to you, compose your own blend, gauging the quantity by the strength of the herbs—use only enough to enhance, not dominate.

With a food processor, a mandoline or a good sharp knife, the cutting goes quickly.

A friend who made this with me recently said she would prefer the slices thinner. If that's your taste also, do that. The layers would settle down more firmly, and the quality, I suspect, would be less earthy.

1 large red onion, sliced a scant ¼ inch thick
¼ cup chopped Swiss chard or spinach leaves and tender stems
a handful of chopped parsley, preferably flat-leaf
a handful of chopped celery leaves
a handful of chopped fresh basil leaves
1 heaped tablespoon fresh thyme leaves—lemon thyme if you have it
1 heaped tablespoon chopped anise hyssop or delicate sage leaves
2 large garlic cloves, chopped
3 medium-large yellow crookneck squashes or any summer squash, sliced a scant ¼ inch thick
4 medium-large flavorful tomatoes, sliced a scant ¼ inch thick
scant ¼ cup extra-virgin olive oil
salt and freshly ground black pepper to taste

Heat the oven to 375°F. Heat a dry heavy skillet until hot, then cook the onion over high heat, stirring often, until lightly browned, about 5 minutes.

Meanwhile, blend the chard, parsley, celery leaves, basil, thyme, anise hyssop, and garlic. Roughly divide the onion, squash, and tomatoes into 2 parts and the herb mixture into 3 parts.

Film a large shallow baking dish, preferably earthenware (mine is oval, 10 by 14 inches), with a scant tablespoon of the oil. In it layer the vegetables as follows, seasoning each with a drizzle of oil and a sprinkling of salt and pepper: onion, squash, herbs, tomato. Repeat, then top with herbs, oil, salt, and pepper. Cover loosely with foil (shiny side down) and bake in the middle of the oven until the squash tests tender but still slightly crisp when pierced with a thin skewer, about 45 minutes.

Serve at any temperature.

There will be ample flavorful juices, so offer good bread for sopping them up. Some mild slicing cheese for the bread, a glass of Merlot or Gamay Beaujolais, and watermelon granité (see Watermelon) would complete a delightful hot-weather lunch or supper.

Pattypan Scallop Squashes

Lumpy old-fashioned pattypans have more vitamin C than the other summer squashes, and just maybe the richest flavor.

Pattypans in the Style of Parma

MAKES 4 SERVINGS

Many squash fanciers prefer their fine-flavored pattypans plain. For a party, though, here's a gorgeously easy and delectable way to cook these charming round nubbins. The Parmesan cheese is prepared in little bits so it melts bumpily, and once in a while you get a taste of it in a large lump unmelted, spicy and tangy. Of course you can just grate the cheese if it's easier. Small round zucchini can be substituted.

You can cook the squashes in the morning, then finish them in a few minutes before serving.

5 small (1 pound) pattypan squashes, sliced into quarters

2 tablespoons unsalted butter

¼ cup chopped Parmigiano-Reggiano or good domestic Parmesan cheese (whirl a chunk in a food processor until it's like clumpy cornmeal)

salt and freshly ground white pepper to taste

Sauté the squashes until barely tender-crisp according to the basic recipe. Remove from the heat, cover loosely, and set in a cool place until needed if you're doing this in advance.

To serve, heat the butter in a large nonstick skillet over medium-high heat. Pat the squashes dry if moist and sauté them, turning occasionally, until hot and lightly browned, about 5 minutes. Serve in a heated colorful bowl, sprinkled with the cheese and salt and pepper.

This is wonderful with roast chicken and pasta. Do try other vegetables Parma style—asparagus, fennel, cardoons, cauliflower, broccoli, and on and on.

Zucchini Squashes

Not wildly nourishing, but an amiable vegetable indeed.

All you have to do to trim zucchini is slice off the remnant of stem and blossom at either end. Add tender vine leaves and flowers to salad.

As you know, there are all sorts of marvelous ways to cook zucchini. Here are two of my pets.

TWO FRIENDS, TWO WAYS WITH ZUCCHINI: As a friend said recently, the best way to eat summer squashes is to cut them thin. Do this in coins or matchsticks, on

Sautéed Vegetable Shreds

This may just be the best way—next to baking—of tasting your vegetables. Sautéed shreds of unpeeled vegetables—crisp yet tender, with all the flavor still vibrant—are superb.

Anything firm will shred: all the roots and tubers, artichoke hearts, thick snap beans, broccoli stalks, celery, cucumbers, fennel, onions, squashes.

For four servings, shred a generous pound of the vegetable on a 3/16-inch blade using a grater, a food processor, or a mandoline. Ideally, the shreds should be about 1½ inches long so they'll hold their shape in cooking. Shred at the last minute before cooking to retain vitamins.

In a wok or large heavy skillet over high heat, warm 1 tablespoon flavorful oil until hot. Add 2 finely chopped garlic cloves (optional) and stir for a moment, then dump in the shreds. Spread them evenly in the pan without packing and sprinkle lightly with salt. Stir frequently until tender-crisp—or tender in the case of some. Sprinkle with a little fresh lemon juice, then taste for freshly ground pepper and serve at once because the shreds will continue cooking. You can add herbs, but I find it distracting.

a mandoline or grater, toss them over high heat in a little olive oil or butter until barely tender (a wok is ideal), salt and pepper them, and maybe flavor them with chives or garlic chives or chopped oregano or basil and a spritz of lemon juice.

When our children were small, another friend taught me (friends are the best teachers) to pile long, skinny shreds of zucchini in a shallow baking dish, drizzle them with olive oil, and bake the dish at 400°F just until the heap begins to collapse, about 20 minutes. Easy when kids are screaming at you, and delicious, and kids love the long strings.

Tortino of Young Squashes

MAKES 6 SERVINGS

When we've had our fill of perfectly pure young squash, I welcome this herbal composition. And when the summer squash patch goes crazy, I can mix deep and light greens, bright and pale yellows. This is a classic Italian way to use all of summer's squashes.

Both squashes and sauce can be prepared and refrigerated a few hours in advance, but put the dish together just before baking so the squash's juices won't thin the sauce.

1½ tablespoons olive oil

2 pounds mixed young summer squashes, cut into walnut-size pieces

1 cup freshly grated jack or other mild cheese

a good pinch of freshly grated nutmeg

salt and freshly ground white pepper to taste

1 recipe Marjoram Cream Sauce (under Marjoram in Herbs)

Warm the oil in a large heavy skillet over medium-high heat. Sauté the squash pieces, turning frequently, just until browned on their cut sides, 10 to 15 minutes. Turn into a 10-inch glass pie dish or earthenware gratin dish. Sprinkle with cheese and nutmeg and salt and pepper to taste.

Prepare the cream sauce. Cover squashes and sauce and keep cool.

About 35 minutes before serving, heat the oven to 400°F. Pour the sauce evenly over the dish. Bake until browned, 20 to 25 minutes—do not overbake, or the zucchini will turn limp. Cool for a few minutes, then serve.

Baby Zucchini Squashes

BABY ZUCCHINI ANTIPASTO: When the babies are tiny, still nestled beside their mama flowers, this recipe is most appealing. Although it's last-minute—once the flowers hit the heat, they'll wilt, so it must be served a presto!—you're not likely to have more baby zucchini with flowers than for a few lucky friends. For each person, pick three to five little-finger-size zucchini with their flowers on (if you can mix green and gold fingerlings, so much the better). From the tip, slice the squashes in half lengthwise just to the stem, leaving them connected.

Heat a large heavy nonstick skillet with a film of unsalted butter over medium-high heat until hot. Spread the squashes gently in the pan and sauté until lightly browned, turning once with a pancake turner, 5 to 6 minutes altogether. Serve hot on small plates garnished with a crescent of lemon.

This can be an hors d'oeuvre on its own or the hot centerpiece of a handsome arrangement—rolled paper-thin slices of salami, thin rings of red, orange, purple, or gold bell pepper, a chunk of Gorgonzola, and a few anchovy fillets curled around capers.

Golden Zucchini Squashes

Golden Zucchini Caviar

MAKES 4 CUPS TO SERVE ABOUT 20

I grew up with what my Russian-born grandmother called *peasant caviar*—eggplant baked slowly, then seasoned and spread on rye bread. After all these years, a Kremlinologist friend told me that in Russia there are also squash, bean, mushroom, and beet caviars. Another use for zucchini! *Chudesno!* (Our Kremlinologist friend says that's Russian for marvelous!)

The gold in zucchini doesn't taste enormously, but I've found Butterstick to be indeed buttery—or is it my imagination? It makes a beautiful spread.

It's fun to cook the zucchini partially in the hot sun, an Italian method.

All the better for being made a day or two in advance. This recipe can be multiplied or divided. It will keep for at least a week.

12 medium-size (4 pounds) golden zucchini, trimmed and sliced 1/4 inch thick
1 teaspoon coarse salt
2 tablespoons olive oil
4 garlic cloves, thinly sliced
1 tablespoon mild vinegar
1 yellow onion, fairly finely chopped
1 1/4 teaspoons crumbled seeded dried hot red chili or to taste
2 tablespoons fresh lemon juice
salt and freshly ground white pepper to taste

Arrange the zucchini in a single layer on baking sheets or trays lined with towels. Sprinkle the slices evenly with the salt and set out in the noonday sun for an hour or two (if there are insects, cover lightly). If there's no sun, set the trays in the warmest spot in the house for a few hours. You want the flesh only to exude some of its moisture, not cook. Gently rinse the slices in a colander under cool running water, then pat dry.

Heat the oven to 325°F. Arrange the zucchini in a large shallow baking dish (earthenware if you have it). Drizzle with oil, strew with garlic, then toss with your hands to mix. Bake uncovered until the squash is soft, about an hour, stirring occasionally.

In comfortably sized batches, process the squash in a food processor just enough to chop it into a rough puree, then turn it into a mixing bowl. When the baking dish is empty, loosen the bits with the vinegar and scrape them into the bowl. Mix in the onion, chili, and lemon juice. Taste for seasoning. Cover and chill for a day or two to ripen if there's time.

Serve lightly chilled with drinks accompanied by sesame seed crackers or rye bread.

Round Zucchini Squashes

Steam or simmer or roast as for the usual zucchini.

Seedsmen seem enchanted with round green zucchini. Me too. Ronde de Nice, the one we grow, has an aftertaste of nutmeg.

Panful of Small Round Zucchini and Small Red Potatoes

MAKES 3 TO 4 SERVINGS

Since you must pick round zucchini young and my one bush doesn't supply more than a handful at a time, this is what I do to make the most of them. The colors—rose, pale, and dark green—are delightful.

Cut 10 to 12 plum-size squashes in half. Quarter 10 to 12 red potatoes of the same size. Turn them into a large nonstick skillet and add cold water or vegetable stock ¼ inch deep. Drizzle with a thread of extra-virgin olive oil and strew on 2 minced garlic cloves. Cover, bring to a simmer over medium heat, then turn the heat to low.

Simmer until tender, about 20 minutes, shaking the skillet occasionally. Lift into a serving bowl—with or without the spoonful of broth at the bottom. Sprinkle with 1 tablespoon chopped rosemary—or lovage, marjoram, or any basil—a handful of parsley, and squeeze on the juice of half a lemon. Taste for salt and freshly ground pepper. Serve hot or cool.

Winter Squashes and Pumpkins

The same philosophy applies to winter squashes as to those of summer: play with them. Although mature (winter) squashes are more distinctively flavored than when young (summer), they are all pretty much interchangeable when you cook them in their season. Texture would be the only reason not to make every recipe here with every winter squash—some call for dry flesh, some for moist. But do get to know these squashes well. In their gorgeous variety they are among the most nourishing and satisfying crops you'll harvest from your garden. Harvest when the shell is hard—a thumbnail cannot easily pierce it. Leave a couple of inches of stalk on the fruit, at least, and store in a cool dark dry place.

Roughly speaking, 1 pound of untrimmed winter squash will come to about 13½ ounces of trimmed squash and yield about 1¾ cups of pureed cooked squash.

It's always easiest to remove the hard shell after cooking. Either steam or bake winter squash. To steam it, remove the seeds and strings and cut the rest into 2-inch pieces. Steam over a scant inch of boiling water until tender, 15 to 20 minutes (save the stock in the pot for another use). Peel the pieces, then use as desired. You should bake a small squash just as it came from the garden: Set it whole in a pie dish or on a baking sheet, pierce it with a knife in a couple of places, and bake at 350°F to 375°F. Start testing for tenderness after 45 minutes. The average time is an hour, although a whole butternut can take 1½ hours. Cut it open the long way (if there is one), scoop out the seeds and strings, and use the flesh as desired—maybe that's simply adding a lump of sweet butter, salt, freshly ground black pepper, and a pinch of mace or nutmeg. You can also cut the squash into large pieces, remove the seeds and strings, brush the flesh with oil, season with salt and pepper, and bake it on a baking sheet at 350°F—again, it will be 45 minutes to an hour. The flesh of winter squash doesn't suffer by being cooked ahead and reheated.

Winter squashes are good sources of nutrition: all have calcium and vitamin C, some have beta-carotene.

Always save the nutritious seeds for roasting.

How to Eat the Summer Squash Overflow

After you've made all these lovely dishes with all your squashes and you still have a mess of them chasing you through the garden, you can:

Bake them simply. Slice and layer the squashes in a shallow oiled baking dish, sprinkling them heavily with a mixture of chopped fresh basil, parsley, and oregano leaves, then a little salt and freshly ground white pepper as you go. Cover with grated mild cheese (mozzarella, jack, Swiss) and a drizzle of olive oil and bake at 350°F until tender, 20 to 30 minutes. Serve hot or at room temperature.

Make a salad. Toss matchsticks of raw young squashes and red sweet peppers in a salad bowl with thin ribbons of lemon basil. Dress with vinaigrette and serve within the hour at room temperature (if you wait, the squash will start to exude juices, and the salad will be soupy).

Make a frittata. Grate a mixture of green and gold squashes into a bowl of beaten eggs. Add finely chopped green garlic or scallions and chopped parsley. Turn the eggs into a hot buttered heavy skillet and cook covered over low heat for 5 minutes, then remove from the heat and let the eggs finish cooking, 10 to 15 minutes—they should be firm but moist. Use a spatula to slip the frittata out of the pan and serve hot or at room temperature, sprinkled with grated cheese. Great for a picnic.

Acorn Winter Squash

Dark green to black to ivory acorn-shaped squashes, their golden flesh is mildly sweet, smooth, and at its best baked.

ACORN SQUASH SUPPER: These make engaging bowls for a whole supper. While the squash is baking, sauté cubes of apple (1 small one per person) over medium heat in a little unsalted butter. Cover and keep warm. When the squash is tender, add a good handful of diced ham or cooked rice to the apple and toss to heat up. Season

Make soup. Soften a couple of chopped onions in a saucepan in a little olive oil, add a couple of pounds of diced summer squashes, and stir over medium-high heat for a minute or two. Add 3 to 4 cups vegetable stock or chicken broth and simmer, covered, until tender. Puree as roughly or smoothly as you like, then add a squeeze of lemon juice to heighten the flavor. If the soup is too thick, whisk in yogurt or buttermilk. Serve hot or cold.

Put up relish (canning details are in The Cook's Notebook). Grind coarsely or chop finely with onions, celery, and red sweet peppers—have the total volume of the other vegetables equal the zucchini's. Turn into a big bowl. For every 20 cups, stir in ⅓ cup salt, then cover with cold water. Let soak overnight. Drain and rinse through a colander four times. Turn into your preserving kettle or soup pot and blend in 2¾ cups cider vinegar, 6⅔ cups sugar, 1 heaped tablespoon turmeric, 1 heaped tablespoon celery seeds, and ½ tablespoon freshly ground white pepper. Cover, bring to a boil, and simmer until tender, about 30 minutes. Turn hot into hot jars, leaving ½ inch of headspace. Use a nonmetallic utensil to force out air. Process in a boiling water bath for 15 minutes.

Make pickles. You can exchange sliced unpeeled summer squashes in any recipe for cucumber pickles. They're especially good as icebox pickles.

with salt and freshly ground black pepper, heap into the squash cups, dollop with your favorite chutney, sprinkle with chopped parsley and roasted peanuts, and serve.

Banana Winter Squash

Shaped like a fat banana, here is lightly sweet and finely textured flesh that resembles pumpkin. Banana squash can be used in any recipe calling for winter squash or pumpkin. Because it's enormous, bake as you would a Hubbard. Allow about ½ pound (uncooked untrimmed weight) per serving. Bananas have a fair amount of beta-carotene and vitamin C. Add the squash's flowers and tender vine leaves and stalks to salads.

Potage of Winter Squash

MAKES ABOUT 4 SERVINGS

The French make a soup that is simple, pure, and profoundly—wildly—pleasing. Before I knew how absurdly easy it was to create a *potage,* I was in awe of them. A *potage* is just a thinned thick puree. It's easy not just in terms of effort but also because you can create one of whatever vegetables you enjoy and chances are it will be grand.

Here's a model recipe made with winter squash. A base of softened onions or onions and garlic—any allium, really—is a good idea. Some part of the mix should be a dense vegetable such as potatoes or winter squash to provide the thickening. Liquid can be water or stock. Sometimes cream or egg yolk is added at the end for silkiness and richness, but that's never essential—a *potage* can be as lean as you like.

Follow the recipe loosely, adding flavorings to your taste. Banana squash is a tussle to peel raw, but other squashes are easy to peel and cut up. It's easiest to add the main vegetable to the soup pot after the onions have been softened, then simmer the mix until tender. That's the way many if not most *potages* are put together.

In a veil of olive oil in your soup pot over low heat, lightly brown 1 chopped onion or 2 large whole leeks, stirring occasionally. Add 2 finely chopped garlic cloves and sauté, stirring occasionally, for another 2 to 3 minutes. Cover and reserve.

Steam a 2½-pound piece of banana squash. When the squash is tender, remove the seeds (save for roasting) and strings. Scoop the flesh into the soup pot, chopping up pieces with the side of a cooking spoon to make them more or less uniform. Add 4 cups chicken broth or vegetable stock, heat, and pass through the medium blade of a food mill or puree in a food processor—be careful not to overprocess, or it will thin out. Return to the pot.

Warm up over medium heat, stirring often. If necessary, thin it to the desired consistency with more broth or milk. Season with salt and pepper. Serve hot with lots of chopped cilantro or chives on top.

Buttercup Winter Squash

Most buttercups have a belly button. Their orange flesh is sweet with a smooth dry texture—you can use it in any recipe calling for any winter squash or pumpkin. Because their shells are hard to work with and because they're small enough, it's easiest either to bake them whole, or to whack them into pieces and bake as a Hubbard. Add the squash's flowers and tender vine leaves and stalks to salads.

BUTTERCUPS WITH STAR ANISE: The sweet flesh of a buttercup is enhanced with the sweet licorice taste of Chinese star anise. You can buy these fetching eight-pointed stars in cellophane bags at Asian markets. Grind a small handful to a powder in a coffee mill or blender just before using it. Sprinkle the spice sparingly over the hot squash as you would nutmeg, whether still in its shell or scooped out and mashed.

You may be able to find Chinese five-spice powder more easily—star anise is an ingredient in the mix.

Butternut Winter Squash

Resembling an elongated pear, the warm orange flesh of butternuts is sweet, smooth, and just moist enough for baking. They can be used in any recipe calling for any winter squash or pumpkin. Butternuts are very high in vitamin A, moderately high in vitamin C, and fair in folic acid, magnesium, and vitamin B_6. Add the squash's flowers and tender vine leaves and stalks to salads.

BUTTERNUT SQUASH WITH A BURMESE FINISH: Makes about 8 servings. Inspired by a recipe in *Sundays at Moosewood Restaurant,* this is an exhilarating way to season the sweet orange flesh. Bake the squash whole, about 1½ hours. Meanwhile, sauté 2 chopped onions in a little mild oil until golden. Finely chop 2 garlic cloves, an egg-size knob of peeled fresh ginger, and a seeded fresh green chili (as hot as you like) and mix in. Cook until the chili is tender. Cover and keep warm.

Discarding the strings and reserving the seeds for roasting, scoop out the squash flesh with a large spoon and turn it into the baking dish. Mash with a fork, then blend in unsalted butter and salt to taste. Smooth on the onion mixture, warm up in the oven if you like (it will wait patiently), or serve immediately. Serve sprinkled with chopped cilantro.

Cheese Winter Squashes

Large, fat, and ribbed cheeses give us at least 10 pounds of delicious moist orange-for-the-most-part flesh. To serve as winter squash, bake as for Hubbard. You can use a cheese in any recipe for any winter squash or pumpkin. Add the squash's flowers and tender vine leaves and stalks to salads.

Because of their size, it's grand to have a place to preserve some of the crop—

true of all the large squashes. Chutney is a place. One reason I'm partial to chutney for stashing the excess crop is that unlike preserves that might mold, sugar and vinegar and spices ensure refrigerated chutney will keep until eaten.

Cheese Winter Squash Chutney

MAKES ABOUT 7 PINTS

Here is a chutney from an English friend you'll find deliciously useful. Feel free to be creative with the ingredients, adding apples or pears, fresh ginger or fresh chilies, cayenne pepper, or mustard. Of course you can make this with any firm-fleshed winter squash.

Although delightful the moment it's made, chutney is invariably mellower after aging in a cool, dark place for a month or two.

Canning details are in The Cook's Notebook.

4½ pounds chopped peeled sweet firm-fleshed cheese squash, about 7 pounds whole

3½ pounds light brown sugar, almost 8 cups firmly packed

1 pound seedless dark raisins

4¼ cups cider vinegar

1 white onion, chopped

6 large garlic cloves, finely chopped

juice of 1 large juicy lemon

juice of 1 large juicy orange

2 tablespoons mustard seeds

1 tablespoon salt or to taste

½ tablespoon ground ginger

1 teaspoon turmeric

1 teaspoon ground white pepper

1 teaspoon ground coriander

Combine all ingredients in a large heavy nonreactive kettle and stir with your hands to mix. Cover and steep in a cool place for 3 to 4 hours. Bring to a boil over high heat, stirring frequently. Turn the heat to medium and boil gently, uncovered, until the squash is thoroughly tender and the mixture has thickened, about 2½ hours. Stir frequently at the beginning of the cooking and almost constantly at the end to prevent sticking and burning. You can stop at this point or cook it longer and more slowly until dark and mysterious.

Pack hot into hot pint canning jars to within ¼ inch of the top. Seal and process in a boiling water bath for 20 minutes. Refrigerate once opened.

Serve as a condiment with every sort of poultry and meat.

Cushaw Winter Squashes

The golden flesh of bulb-shaped cushaws is renowned for making superb pie. They're big squashes, so you can easily freeze cooked pureed flesh for turning into filling when it's convenient. To bake and eat cushaw cum winter squash, cook following the directions for Hubbard and season any way you please.

Add the squash's flowers and tender vine leaves and stalks to salads.

Winter Squash/Pumpkin Pie

MAKES 8 TO 9 SERVINGS

If you've never eaten pumpkin pie made with fresh—not canned—pumpkin, you're in for a surprise. The canning process caramelizes the puree, and it has a deeper flavor than winter squash that's simply cooked and pureed. Not to say better flavor, just deeper. Since most of our palates are accustomed to that, and since baking squash gives richer flavor, we bake the squash rather than steam it for pie. Besides, it's easier.

Partially baking the shell, having the custard filling warm before baking, and baking the pie on a hot metal sheet cooks the custard more evenly and rapidly with less chance of the filling overbaking and then weeping.

This is my mother's—the best pumpkin pie anyone who's eaten it ever ate.

Because the custard will make the pastry soggy, serve within 4 hours of baking.

1 partially baked and cooled 9-inch pie shell (see recipe under Pastry in The Cook's Notebook)

FILLING

2½ cups pureed baked cushaw or other winter squash, 3 pounds whole

1¼ cups half-and-half

¾ cup firmly packed light brown sugar

3 large eggs at room temperature

½ tablespoon ground cinnamon

1 teaspoon ground ginger

½ teaspoon ground mace or freshly grated nutmeg

½ teaspoon ground allspice or cloves

heaped ½ teaspoon salt

¼ cup bourbon

TOPPING

5 tablespoons unsalted butter

1 cup firmly packed light brown sugar

1 cup (about 5 ounces) broken pecan pieces

pinch of ground cinnamon

vanilla ice cream

For the pastry shell, follow the recipe in The Cook's Notebook for the dough, then shape and partially bake according to the technique in a standard cookbook.

Heat the oven to 450°F and set the rack in the top third of the oven. Slip a baking sheet onto the rack.

In a large heavy saucepan, combine the squash, half-and-half, and ¾ cup brown sugar. Whisk over low heat until the mixture feels lukewarm to the touch. Remove from the heat and whisk in the eggs, cinnamon, ginger, mace, allspice, and salt. When smooth, blend in the bourbon. Pour into the shell.

Set the pie on the baking sheet and bake for 10 minutes, then turn the heat to 300°F. Bake until a circle in the center the size of a silver dollar jiggles when you gently move the baking sheet—and when a thin knife inserted at the edge of this circle comes out with specks of the filling on it—not entirely clean—another 25 to 35 minutes. Be careful not to overbake, because the custard will go on baking after it's out of the oven. Remove to the counter. Heat the broiler.

Immediately make the topping: Melt the butter in a smallish heavy skillet over low heat. Add the brown sugar, the pecans, and cinnamon and stir until the sugar caramelizes. Spoon this hot mixture evenly over the pie. Broil about 5 inches from the heat until the sugar melts and darkens, about 3 minutes—watch that it doesn't burn. Set on a rack to cool.

Serve warm or at room temperature with vanilla ice cream and strong coffee.

Hubbard Winter Squashes

The flesh of the great big warty blue-green melon-shaped Hubbards I've eaten was thick, sweet, and dry although I understand they can be bland and watery. You can pierce and bake a whole Hubbard squash on a baking sheet in a 300°F oven for 2½ to 3 hours. To bake it faster, heat the oven to 350°F and divide the squash up: Make a short deepish stab into the squash with a strong sharp knife running lengthwise somewhere in the center. Fit a cleaver or heavy chef's knife in the cut to steady it, then use a rubber mallet or the side of a hammer to tap the blade through. Scoop out the seeds (save them for roasting) and scrape out the strings. Cut the squash into largish pieces, then set them close together on a rimmed baking sheet or pan and cover with foil. Bake until the squash tests tender with a thin skewer, 1 to 1¼ hours. You can simply butter the pieces and serve at this point. Add the squash's flowers and tender vine leaves and stalks to salads.

MAPLE HUBBARD MASH: If you find you have a watery squash, this is a good way to serve it. If the flavor is sweet, the maple will underscore it without being cloying. If the Hubbard's flavor is bland, the maple will brighten it.

Scrape the cooked flesh from the shell and puree through the medium blade of a food mill or mash with a potato masher or a fork. If the puree is soupy, turn it into a skillet and stir over medium heat until the excess moisture has evaporated. Drizzle in maple syrup (the real stuff if you can) to taste and stir in a little unsalted butter, then salt and pepper. Serve piping hot with a shake of cinnamon on top.

Japanese Winter Squashes

Here's teardrop-shaped Red Kuri, an example of this fascinating group of squashes. Mine was the size of a small icebox watermelon. After curing, I kept it on the cool stone floor of the entry hall because I loved to look at it. In the middle of February we baked it. I sliced it into four pointed ovals, scraped away the seeds (saved them for roasting) and most of the orange strings, then stuck the pieces on a baking dish and into a 425°F oven to roast alongside a chicken. In an hour there was a small orange pool in the center of each piece. Out of the oven, the broth settled back into the flesh. I added a little butter, a sprinkling of turbinado brown sugar crystals, salt, and pepper. At first there was a hint of coconut in the taste, but that disappeared. The brilliant orange meat was sweet and rich, and the skin was as thin as zucchini's.

Add the squash's flowers and tender vine leaves and stalks to salads.

Kabocha and Similar Winter Squashes

Kabochas are the winter squash non pareil. Round and flattish, their shells are usually a rich forest green, their flesh deep orange, fairly dry, sweet and *rich*.

Bake a whole squash until tender, about 1 hour. Remove from the oven and slice in half—halfway between the stalk and blossom ends. Discard the stalk and set these two squash vessels on a platter. Spoon out the seeds (save for roasting) and strings and pat down any pieces that might be dislodged. Butter, salt, and freshly ground white pepper are all you need. Cover with the foil and set the platter in the oven with the heat turned off until serving.

Use flowers and tender vine leaves and stalks in salads.

Scallops and Shrimp in Kabocha Bowls

MAKES 4 SERVINGS

This combination may sound unpromising, but trust me. Halves of a baked kabocha, prepared as just described, are set on a platter—they might be Japanese pottery for their vivid orange and squarish shape. The vessels are heaped with cream-colored scallops and coral-colored shrimp in a translucent lemony sauce speckled with scallions and parsley. The squash is scooped from its shell with the seafood. The dish goes together with little effort and no fat.

My kabochas are about 2½ pounds, perfect for four people. You can also bake a larger squash and increase the remaining proportions for more people.

The scallions and garlic can be prepared and the seafood thawed if frozen a few hours in advance and refrigerated. Cooking the squash takes no attention, and the rest of the preparation takes scant time at the last minute.

The squash should be evenly drum shaped so that when it's cut in half the bowls are identical. The flesh should be richly colored, dry, and sweet. A buttercup can be used lacking a kabocha.

If you have green garlic, you can use three stalks of it instead of the scallions and garlic cloves.

1 2½-pound kabocha squash
2 cups chicken broth
2 tablespoons fresh lemon juice
3 scallions, white parts and tender greens, sliced into thin rounds
3 garlic cloves, finely chopped
2 tablespoons cornstarch
⅔ pound small scallops, thawed if frozen, thawing juices saved
⅓ pound small shrimp, thawed if frozen, thawing juices saved, and cooked
½ cup chopped parsley, preferably flat-leaf
salt and freshly ground white pepper to taste

Bake and slice the squash and keep it hot in the oven. Omit the finish of butter.

In a large nonstick skillet, combine the broth, lemon juice, scallions, and garlic and bring to a simmer over medium-high heat. Meanwhile, sprinkle the cornstarch over the scallops and shrimp in a bowl and mix with your hands to distribute the cornstarch.

When the broth simmers, add the seafood mixture and stir frequently until the sauce has thickened and the scallops have cooked—taste one; it will only be 2 to 3 minutes after the sauce has thickened. Stir in the parsley, remove from the heat, and taste for salt and pepper.

At once spoon the seafood mixture into the squash bowls. Turn any extra sauce into a small bowl. To serve, spoon up the squash from its shell together with the seafood and sauce. Pass the extra sauce.

A Chardonnay is lovely with this. To complete the dinner, add a green salad—either on separate plates on the side or afterward—and a tart brightly colored ice such as raspberry for dessert.

Pumpkin Winter Squashes

Think of all those glowing orbs lolling about the pumpkin patch not just as amusing jack-o'-lanterns for Halloween and spicy Thanksgiving pie, but as a valuable (four times the vitamin A of sweet potato, just for starters) winter squash that even children love baked or pureed and buttered. Any winter squash recipe applies to pumpkins, which are botanically just a type of winter squash. Bake as for my Japanese winter squash. Add the squash's flowers and tender vine leaves and stalks to salads.

Pumpkin Polenta

MAKES 6 SERVINGS

This country dish inspired by the daily bread of the Piedmont part of Italy is—with a slice of cold chicken—one of my favorite suppers. It's meltingly delicious, nourishing, and easy. Baking cornmeal with pumpkin in milk results in a texture that's creamy and a flavor that's suave beyond telling. Toasted onions and rosemary with a little freshly grated cheese melting over the slice are heavenly.

If you have flint corn or dent corn or a combination corn such as Mandan Bride, you can coarsely grind your own corn for this meal. Otherwise, find a natural foods store that will freshly grind whole kernels for you, or buy its ground whole-kernel meal that's kept in the refrigerator. The oil in the germ spoils quickly. Refrigerate or freeze the meal once you get home. Whole-kernel cornmeal is an infinitely richer source of calcium and minerals and tastes infinitely sweeter than the "enriched" stuff you buy in a box.

Best warm from the oven, but you can bake this at your leisure and heat it up without harm.

1¾ pounds fresh pumpkin

½ tablespoon olive oil

1 onion, finely chopped

2 teaspoons chopped fresh rosemary leaves or 1 scant teaspoon crumbled dried

softened unsalted butter for the baking dish

1 cup whole-kernel coarsely ground cornmeal

1 teaspoon salt or to taste

2 cups milk (nonfat is fine)

freshly grated Parmesan cheese

Cut the pumpkin into 8 pieces, and steam them until tender, about 20 minutes. While the pumpkin cooks, film the bottom of a large heavy skillet with the olive oil and sauté the onion in it until pale gold, stirring frequently, about 5 minutes. Blend in the rosemary. When the pumpkin is tender, cool until you can handle the pieces, then zip off the skin with a vegetable peeler. Pass the flesh through the medium blade of a food mill or a ricer into a mixing bowl. You'll have about 2 cups puree.

Heat the oven to 300°F and butter a fairly deep 6-cup baking dish. Sprinkle the cornmeal and salt over the pumpkin while you beat it in, blending thoroughly. Add the milk little by little, stirring until smooth after each addition. Smooth into the baking dish, then sprinkle the onions evenly over the top. Bake for 2 hours. The onions will be deeply toasted and the sides deeply gold. Serve in thick slices with a little grated cheese. (I like to eat mine with an oversize spoon.)

To bake in advance, cover and refrigerate, then reheat, covered, at 325°F for about 30 minutes.

Spaghetti Squashes, Vegetable

Ovals, these, with amusing golden strands of squash in place of solid flesh.

Bake the whole squash until tender, about 1 hour. Cut in half the long way and scoop out the seeds. In this case it's a game of hide-and-seek with some of the seeds because they're buried in the "spaghetti"—but the seeds are large and white, and it's not an enormous nuisance. (Save the seeds for roasting.) Scoop all the flesh into a big bowl and separate the strands with a cooking fork. Add the squash's flowers and tender vine leaves and stalks to salads.

Chicken Breasts and Garlic in a Nest of Spaghetti Squash

MAKES 6 SERVINGS

This is about as effortless as dinner gets, and good. Last-minute, but it takes very little time.

1 spaghetti squash, baked until tender, seeds removed
12 garlic cloves, chopped
6 boneless, skinless chicken breast halves, frozen or not
about 3 tablespoons mild olive or walnut oil
salt and freshly ground black pepper to taste
a good handful of chopped fresh oregano or sage leaves (or fresh flat-leaf parsley mixed with some of these dried herbs to taste)
½ tablespoon hot red pepper flakes, optional

When the squash is ready, set 2 nonstick skillets over medium-high heat. When hot (about 3 minutes), sprinkle half the garlic in each skillet and lay 3 chicken breast halves on top. Cover and sauté until lightly browned, then turn with tongs and brown the other side—about 5 minutes on each side for frozen, about 2 minutes on each side for fresh. The garlic will be cooked either to nutty bits or until just tender. Continue to cook another minute or two, if necessary.

The chicken is done when you cut into the center of a piece with a thin sharp knife halfway down and see that the flesh is no longer pink.

Meanwhile, turn the squash into a heated mixing bowl and separate the strands with a cooking fork. Drizzle with oil, season with salt and pepper, and toss to blend. Make a nest of the squash on a heated platter.

Arrange the chicken pieces in the squash nest, discarding the browned garlic. Sprinkle with herbs and pepper flakes if desired and serve at once.

Sweet Dumpling and Delicata Winter Squashes

Sweet Dumplings are single-serving squashes of exceptionally sweet and fine orange flesh. Delicatas are similar but twice as large and elongated. Usually their flavor is Sweet Dumplings' to a lesser degree. Bake either for about 50 minutes. Cut in half, scoop out the seeds, and serve with a big spoon, a little butter, salt, freshly ground pepper, and chopped chives or Chinese chives.

Small Sweet Dumpling squashes, stored in the cellar until the end of January, turn from their native ivory and green stripes to a pale sunshine yellow and green. The deep orange flesh is suave and just sweet enough. A baked Sweet Dumpling, a glass of buttermilk, and a heap of peppery salad greens dressed with olive oil and orange juice make a soothing supper.

Add the squash's flowers and tender vine leaves and stalks to salads.

Gourds, Edible

There's a wealth of interesting cooking and eating in gourds—you'll find it in Asian cookbooks. For starters:

ANGLED LUFFA: Looking like a curved ridged cucumber, the young fruit is sweet, but older gourds get bitter. Pick 4 to 6 inches long. Flavor is that of most immature squashes, more texture than taste. Pare down the peaks, leaving the skin on the valleys so you'll have stripes (should you have picked the squashes too late and the skin is tough, peel it all off). Cook angled luffas as you would zucchini or cucumber, but the Chinese reserve their *sze gwa* for stir-fries. This sort of gourd has a little beta-carotene in the green skin, and a fair amount of folacin and Vitamin C.

BITTER MELON: Bitter melons look like warty cucumbers, and when cooked, they taste like thick, crunchy, quinine-flavored sweet peppers. Startling at first, the flavor grows on you—all over Asia, their tang is welcomed as cooling in hot weather. Pick young and close to cooking time. Prepare as you would cukes, but use these challenging vegetables with discretion. Bitter melon is low in calories. The quinine-bitter leaves resemble small grape leaves—they add a wonderfully surprising note to a dish.

CHINESE FUZZY GOURD: This is a favorite of Cantonese cooks, perhaps because it's a blank canvas. Its flavor is a barely there blend of cucumber with a hint of zucchini. Mixed with vegetables with more definition and seasoned with a flavorful sauce, fuzzy gourd contributes a luminous green crisp base. Any recipe for cooked cucumber can be adapted to fuzzy gourd, and vice versa. Pick small—the fuzz can be rubbed off or ignored. Nutrition would be about the same as for zucchini.

CUCUZZI/LAGENARIA: Pendulous and pale but not watery, one giant vine gives so many of these gourds that you've got to engage your wits to use them up. Bitter when small, pick these at least 8 inches long—they're even tasty larger. One of my most successful cucuzzi inventions was for a potluck for 24: I made a humongous salad with matchsticks of one large gourd, adding kidney beans, chickpeas, cherry tomatoes, oranges, black olives, snap beans, scallions, shredded carrots, diced celery, and cucumbers—everything else equalled the cucuzzi—finished with vinaigrette, Chinese chives, and toasted sunflower seeds. Everybody loved it, and still I had to bring some home.

Strawberries

Pick berries when it's cool and they're ripe but still firm—don't wash or hull them until just before preparing.

Fresh strawberry juice is a revelation.

For instant strawberry ice, set whole hulled strawberries on a baking sheet, freeze, drop the berries into freezer bags, expel the air, then return the berries to the freezer. When it's time for the ice, drop frozen berries into a food processor or blender, whirl, and you've got it. Of course you can add sugar or a little orange juice or minced leaves of lemon basil or lemon verbena. You can do the same with any freezable fruit.

FESTIVE STRAWBERRIES: Makes 4 servings. Good store-bought angel food or sponge cake makes a lighter, easier alternative to the rich biscuits in strawberry shortcake. When strawberries are at their peak, scented geraniums are blooming their heads off, too, so use them as garnish. All elements can be prepared several hours in advance.

Hull 3 pints of ripe sweet strawberries. Slice half the berries lengthwise in half and sweeten lightly. In another bowl, mash the remaining berries to a coarse puree and sweeten lightly—if desired, add a splash of cherry-, raspberry-, or orange-flavored brandy. Cover both bowls and chill.

To serve, heap a portion of sliced berries over a serving of cake on a dessert plate. Top with a scoop of vanilla ice cream or frozen yogurt. Make a diagonal ribbon of mashed strawberries over the cake. If available, sprinkle the ribbon with the pink petals of a rose or scented geranium.

Danish Strawberry Fromage

MAKES 6 SMALL SERVINGS

A Danish friend taught me about the light, smooth, creamy sort of puddings Danes call *fromage*—the French word for cheese. Classic fromages are flavored with orange, lemon, and chocolate. Here is my slimmed-down homage to strawberry fromage. Egg yolks and heavy cream are traditional, but I've omitted the yolks and used sour cream. This is a velvety pouf, perfect at the end of a rich meal. You might want to garnish the fromage with grated semisweet chocolate or a sifting of cocoa.

Make this at least 4 hours in advance—overnight or the next day is fine.

1 cup fresh strawberry puree, made from about 10 ounces, a generous pint, of ripe sweet berries

1 tablespoon unflavored gelatin

3 large egg whites at room temperature

pinch of salt

½ cup sugar

1 cup sour cream, chilled

6 gorgeous unhulled strawberries

In a small saucepan, whisk the puree and gelatin together. Let sit for 5 minutes, then stir over very low heat until the gelatin dissolves. Remove from the heat.

Meanwhile, beat the whites in a bowl until foamy, add a pinch of salt, then beat on high speed, slowly adding the sugar, until the whites are stiff but still moist. Use the unwashed beaters in another bowl to beat the sour cream until doubled in volume. Fold the puree into the sour cream, then fold in the whites. Divide among 6 pretty bowls, cover, and chill until set. Serve topped with a strawberry.

Creole Sweet Strawberry Vinegar

MAKES ABOUT 7 CUPS

Now for the brightest imaginable color and flavor, an elixir of strawberries. Use the syrup as a flavoring for summer drinks, to shake over salads—fruit, green, and otherwise—and for roasting chicken. Tightly closed, this keeps in a cool place until used.

You need one-third the amount of berries on each of three days, so don't pick the lot the first day.

about 2½ pounds (2⅓ to 3 pints) ripe strawberries

1 quart distilled white vinegar

about 1½ cups sugar

Hull a third of the berries, cut them in half, then thinly slice—there should be about 3 cups. Turn into a glazed ceramic bowl or enameled pot and pour the vinegar over them. Cover and set in a warmish place.

Twenty-four hours later, scoop out the berries with a strainer. Turn them into a damp cloth and squeeze out as much juice into the vinegar as you can until it starts becoming cloudy.

Hull and slice the next third of berries into the vinegar. Steep, drain, and squeeze as before. Repeat the steps one more time with the last berries—3 days in all.

Turn the vinegar into a large nonreactive saucepan. Stir in a little less sugar than you'd like—the turn-of-the-century recipe calls for an impossible heaped cupful for each cup of vinegar. Bring to a boil over medium heat, stirring until the sugar has dissolved. Turn the heat to low and simmer for 30 minutes. Strain through damp filter paper into squeaky-clean bottles. Cork or cap and keep in a cool dark dry place.

Alpine or Wild Strawberries

ALPINE STRAWBERRIES IN CHAMPAGNE: Makes 4 servings. Past heaping them in a beautiful bowl, powdering them with sifted confectioners' sugar, and dolloping them with crème fraîche, this is my favorite way of enjoying wild strawberries.

A long hour before serving, turn a heaped ½ cup of alpine strawberries into each of 4 stemmed glasses—the broader the bowls, the better. Add 1 tablespoon orange-flavored brandy, maraschino liqueur, or kirsch, swirl the glass to mix and level out the berries, then just cover with cool dry white wine (about ½ cup each). Set in a cool place, not the refrigerator, to steep.

To serve, bring the glasses to the table on dessert plates (with a spoon and 2 or 3 plain crisp cookies on the side). Open a bottle of chilled champagne and fill the glasses.

Sweet Potatoes

Did you know that the sweetness in sweet potatoes increases as it matures, then finally even more as it cooks? What a jolly vegetable. Simply dig sweets for fresh eating when they're large enough to suit you. To keep them, wait till the vines have died. Sweets are cured the same as are potatoes. Sweets are sensationally rich sources of vitamin A and beta-carotene. They offer moderate amounts of fiber and vitamin C and smallish amounts of vitamin B_6, manganese, and copper.

Scrub the tubers with a brush, but try not to peel your sweets. As always, the skin provides nutrients and fiber. Use stainless-steel tools to work with sweet potatoes—

carbon steel discolors the flesh. You can cook them any way you like, but moist-fleshed sweets take a bit longer to cook than dry-fleshed ones. Baking potatoes at around 400°F for an hour or so is probably the best way to conserve nutrients and gives the flesh a caramelized undertone.

Malabar Sweet Potato Curry

MAKES 6 SERVINGS

To me, sweet potatoes baked, split, and buttered, with salt, pepper, and nutmeg, are all the heaven I need. A friend likes hers with a squeeze of lime.

For company, here is a pungent Indian way that makes a superb vegetarian entrée—others will perhaps offer slices of chicken or turkey on the side. Include lots of condiments—bowls of raisins, chopped apples, sliced scallions, chopped cucumbers, sliced radishes, crisply browned bits of onion, the chutney recipe under Slicing Tomatoes, chopped peanuts, and lime pickle from India.

Most of the curry can be put together a few hours in advance. Drop the sweets into water to keep their color as you work. Dried coconut tastes fresher when covered with equal parts milk and water and steeped for an hour or two, then drained and patted dry.

9 medium-size (generous 2 pounds) sweet potatoes, preferably dry fleshed, peeled for the finicky, and cut into 1½-inch chunks

about 6 small fresh mildly hot green chilies or to taste, sliced in half and seeds removed

1 tablespoon unsalted butter or mild oil

1 tablespoon curry powder

1 small onion, chopped

a piece of fresh ginger the size of a walnut, peeled and shredded, or 2 teaspoons ground ginger

1 garlic clove, minced

1 large tomato, fairly finely chopped

2 cups plain yogurt

1 cup (about 3 ounces) unsweetened shredded fresh or dried coconut

Steam the potatoes until tender when pierced with a thin skewer, about 20 minutes. Meanwhile, roast the chilies in a dry heavy skillet over high heat, turning frequently with tongs, until tender. Slice into small, thin strips.

Warm the butter in a large heavy skillet (preferably nonstick) over medium heat, then add the curry powder, onion, and ginger. Sauté, stirring, until the onion has softened, a few minutes, then blend in the garlic and tomato. Sauté for another minute or two, until the tomato has absorbed the curry. Remove from the heat and gently blend in the sweets and chilies. Cover lightly if you're doing this in advance.

When you're ready to serve, gently stir the curry over medium-high heat until nearly hot. Blend in the yogurt and coconut and cook, stirring frequently, until the sauce barely comes to a boil. Turn into a heated serving bowl and serve over steamed white basmati or jasmine rice. Let guests help themselves to condiments.

For the rest of a dinner party menu, start with a light and tangy (not creamy) vegetable soup—for example, the chrysanthemum leaves in broth in Asian Greens (substituting any tasty leaves you like if necessary). Offer cold beer or hot Ceylon tea and, for dessert, pistachio ice cream sprinkled with toasted pistachios and rose petals.

Tomatillos

Alternative: Small firm green tomatoes.

Not related to tomatoes, these enchanting custom-wrapped fruits are usually picked unripe, when the flavor has an appley tang—ripe, it's like strawberries. For underripe, pick just when the husk turns buff. The husks of tomatillos are always removed just before cooking, and the fruit is rinsed, but there's no need to wash away their stickiness, and never peel them. These are very good simmered—their classic use is as an ingredient in sauce. Still, there's no reason they can't be used any way tomatoes are. Raw crescents add crispness to salads. Purple slices turn translucent in soup.

My recipe for salsa, which follows, evolved from one in *La Tradicional Cocina Mexicana* and from a friend who taught me that sweet tomatoes cool torrid sauces. There is no right way to compose a Mexican table sauce, except that you must use the freshest ingredients possible. Just as in this country, every cook in Mexico makes salsa in his or her own style. Some don't skin the chilies. Some throw the chilies in with the tomatillos to simmer a bit. Some grind the chilies straight off the bush. Some use a mountain of cilantro. Some think two cloves of garlic one too many. Some flick in chopped white onion. Start with the following proportions to get accustomed to the flavor, then see where it leads you.

Salsa Verde

MAKES ABOUT 3½ CUPS TO SERVE 14

Always best fresh, but if refrigerated in a tightly covered jar, leftovers will be acceptable for a day or two.

- 1½ pounds tomatillos, about 16 large or 32 medium-size
- cool water barely to cover
- 3 fresh serrano chilies or 1 small jalapeño, roasted, seeds removed, and peeled (see Peppers)
- 2 garlic cloves, peeled
- at least 2 cilantro sprigs
- 2 medium-small (about 6 ounces) ripe tomatoes
- salt to taste

In a nonreactive saucepan over medium-high heat, bring the tomatillos and water to a boil, turn the heat to low, and simmer just until the fruits feel soft with the side of a spoon (long before they break open), 5 to 10 minutes. Lift into a bowl.

In a food processor, blender, or, for the most authentic texture and flavor, with a mortar and pestle, grind the chilies, garlic, and cilantro together until finely chopped, then add the tomatillos and tomatoes. Puree, leaving small bits for texture, then season to taste. Serve in a bowl at room temperature.

Quick Garden Breads

Wouldn't you love a pale-orange-colored slice of bread with rosy bits of tomato, green-gold chunks of walnuts, and a sunny tomato taste? Or bread made from delicate summer or winter squash shreds threaded with orange zest? Or bread bright with carrots, the tomatoes' match for gaiety? And instead of mashed cooked sweet potatoes, how about moist nutted bread made with their creamy flesh uncooked? Finally, there's the intoxicating slice thick with onions just as they're pulled from the ground.

These breads from four seasons and one master recipe are intense with the pure flavor of their fresh vegetable, underscored with fresh orange juice and zest, crunchy with toasted broken walnuts or pecans, gilded with olive or walnut oil, and given depth with a soupçon of whole-wheat flour. The breads are great for breakfast drizzled with the oil that's in them or brushed with butter or for brown-bag lunches with slices of mild cheese. They are elegant with a luncheon salad or soup and cheering with afternoon cups of herb tea. Not only do these loaves give a home to a pound or more of the larder's overflow, but they do so with élan. And, of course, they're a gift that's loving and easily made anytime. Freeze some for the holidays.

Quick Fresh Vegetable Nut Bread

MAKES 1 LOAF

The bread will crumble unless you wait a day to slice it; still I can't resist buttering one crusty end piece warm from the oven.

The recipe can be doubled for two loaves, or you can bake a single recipe in two smaller pans for about 30 minutes.

unsalted butter for the pan

1⅔ cups all-purpose flour, lightly spooned into the measuring cup

⅓ cup whole-wheat flour or another ⅓ cup all-purpose flour, measured the same way

2 teaspoons baking powder

¾ teaspoon salt

½ teaspoon baking soda

finely shredded zest of 1 large or 2 small oranges (optional)

⅓ cup fresh orange juice, 1 large or 1½ small oranges, at room temperature

2 large eggs at room temperature

½ cup sugar

¼ cup olive or walnut oil at room temperature

1 cup (about 5 ounces) toasted broken walnut or pecan pieces

FLAVORING

2 cups lumpy puree or fine shreds (firmly packed into the measuring cup) or coarsely chopped or ground . . . *carrots:* about 3 very large, finely shred or grate; use walnut oil and walnuts or pecans; *onions, fresh or dried, or whole*

scallions, or shallots: 1 pound, peel and finely grate; use olive or walnut oil and walnuts; increase the orange juice to ½ cup; *summer squash* (zucchini, pattypan, crookneck): a generous pound, discard any tough seeds and finely shred or grate at the last moment; use olive or walnut oil and walnuts; *sweet potatoes:* the same as winter squash; *tomatoes, ripe but firm pear or plum or slicing tomatoes with fairly dry flesh*—or slice salad or cherry tomatoes in half and squeeze their excess juice into a jar, saving it for soup: Weigh them now—you'll probably use ⅓ to ½ pound more—1 pound, puree roughly; use olive or walnut oil and walnuts and omit the orange zest; *winter squash or pumpkin:* 1 pound peeled flesh, finely shred or grate; use olive or walnut oil or walnuts or pecans

Pulsing in a food processor will give the ideal rough puree for this recipe. You can try pureeing in the blender—work in small batches and be careful not to end with a mush. To produce the puree by hand, roughly chop the tomatoes (preferably on a surface with a lip to catch juices). For the remaining vegetables, the medium grating blade of a food processor will produce ideal shreds. Or use a hand grater, mandoline, or anything that gives ⅛-inch-wide shreds. Carrots grate successfully in a blender (the trick is to cover them with water, then drain it off when they're grated).

Have all ingredients at room temperature. Heat the oven to 350°F. Brush the bottom of an 8½- by 4½- by 2½-inch loaf pan (or one slightly larger or smaller) with unsalted butter. Line the bottom with wax paper and butter the paper. Blend the flours, baking powder, salt, and baking soda together. Remove and reserve the orange zest before juicing the orange(s). Have the warmed eggs, sugar, oil, and nuts ready before preparing the flavoring fruits or vegetables.

Combine the orange juice, eggs, sugar, oil, and puree, shreds, or bits in a large mixing bowl. Beat until blended. Add the dry ingredients and stir just until mixed, then thoroughly blend in the nuts and orange zest, if used. Smooth into the pan, slightly pushing the batter up against the corners.

Bake in the middle of the oven until a toothpick emerges clean from the center, 50 to 60 minutes. Cool in the pan on a rack for 15 minutes, then run a thin knife around the edges and turn out onto the rack, top side up, to cool completely. Wrap airtight and refrigerate, then slice fairly thickly the next day. The loaf will keep for several days.

Some loaves will rise higher than others, depending on the texture of the puree or shreds. Not to worry.

At high altitude, use ¼ teaspoon baking soda and bake at 375°F for about 50 minutes.

TOMATOES

Harvest your beautiful fruit when it smells like a tomato and its color—whatever aspect of the rainbow that may be—is uniform. Unsprayed deeply flavored sun-ripened nontraveling tomatoes—no matter what shape or size—are the most persuasive argument for cultivating a patch of earth.

Leave the tomato's skin on and keep the seeds in when you can, for added flavor and nutrients. Rinse your tomatoes lightly. For slices that best hold their shape and juice, cut from top to bottom, not through the center. Like peppers and the onion tribe, tomatoes are an invaluable seasoning vegetable as well as one that's eaten for its own self. They're low in fiber and offer a moderate amount of vitamin C and fair amounts of vitamins A and E.

Do not use these vine leaves in salad. They are toxic.

In late summer, my breakfast is a slice of good bread rubbed with garlic, drizzled with fruity olive oil, and covered with thinly sliced tomatoes—the rounds aren't overlapping but set shoulder to shoulder so I can admire their luminous color and almost oriental pattern. For the top I've been working my way through the herbs in the garden, strewing shreds of basil or sage or needles of rosemary or hyssop or lavender or leaves of marjoram or oregano or thyme. The way the character of each herb affects the tomato's flavor is stunning—try it.

How about cold sliced tomatoes around hot mashed potatoes or with green chili salsa?

Among the most memorable combinations with tomatoes I've ever made was spinach fettuccine (green) dressed with olive oil and lemon juice (glistening) tossed with shelled steamed mussels (apricot) and tomato quarters (red).

Salad Tomatoes

Salad tomatoes are a group that are larger than plum tomatoes but smaller than the usual tomato. It's a fine point, but a number of tomato cultivars have been bred to be sweet and firm and modestly sized, perfect for salads.

AVOCADO-STUFFED TOMATOES: Equal parts diced salad tomatoes and diced avocado brightened with lime juice and tarragon leaves are handsome heaped in shells of beefsteak tomatoes.

A GREEK TOMATO SALAD: Greeks blend crumbled feta into yogurt and use it as a dressing for sliced tomatoes and cucumbers speckled with chopped fresh mint.

A SIMPLE SHAKER TOMATO SALAD: The Shakers peel fine salad tomatoes, slice them, and dress them with fresh lemon juice, period. Remarkable, especially when the tomatoes are richly sweet.

Sicilian Tomato Salad

MAKES 4 TO 6 SERVINGS

Smallish salad tomatoes are beautifully suited to this treatment.

Slice 8 firm ripe salad tomatoes into a bowl. Slice and add ½ pound raw mushrooms, 1 cup cooked shelly beans or any cooked dried beans you like, 1 finely chopped small red onion, 2 dozen salt-cured olives, a scant 2 tablespoons drained capers, and a small handful of chopped fresh sage leaves. Pour over enough vinaigrette dressing to moisten (about ⅓ cup), toss with your hands to mix, taste for seasoning, and serve on leaves of escarole or endive. Warn everyone about the olive pits.

Slicing Tomatoes

Slicing tomatoes are the larger tomatoes, including beefsteaks. Of course they can be used in salad as well as cooked.

LIGURIAN BAKED BEEFSTEAK TOMATOES: Here are great tomatoes seasoned with a flavorful filling and baked. Makes 1 serving. Slice the lid off one large firm ripe tomato (1 pound). Express the seeds and juice into a bowl, using a finger to nip out the little globs from each chamber (save this to strain into stock). Turn upside down on a cloth to drain. Finely chop a handful of any sort of basil leaves, a large garlic clove, an inch strip of lemon zest, and a walnut-size knob (¾ ounce) of Parmesan or other grating cheese. Mix in a bowl. Holding the tomato over the bowl, drop the filling into the tomato's chambers. Don't pack. Sprinkle the top with dry bread or cracker crumbs and moisten them with olive oil. Bake on a shallow earthenware or glass dish in a 350°F oven. When the crumbs are golden and you can smell the tomato, remove—about 35 minutes. Serve at room temperature. Excellent to accompany almost any other vegetable, or fish, fowl, or meat.

Santa Fe Tortilla Soup

MAKES 4 TO 6 SERVINGS

Use your ripest, richest, reddest tomatoes to make this simple soup with spectacular flavor. Except for the broth that makes it a soup, there are just three ingredients, and you can taste each one clearly: tomatoes, white onions, and chipotle chilies. The chilies are what make an otherwise delicious soup extraordinary.

Chipotles are ripened jalapeño peppers that have been dried and smoked. You can find them in Mexican or ethnic markets dried or canned (usually in a tomato-based sauce, even though the label may say "pickled"). For this dish, choose the canned chipotle. Even in small quantities, chipotles add a profoundly sensual pungence to a dish. You need only one chili for this soup, so keep the rest in a jar and fold a small chop into mashed potatoes, a dish of beans, cream cheese for a spread, and so forth.

If you can't buy chipotles, substitute jalapeño, poblano, or any small hot chili. If dried, soak it in water until softened. If it's raw, roast it as described under Peppers, leaving the blackened skin on and the seeds in.

Freshly made, the smoky flavor of the chili is discernible. A day or so later there's less smoke, more pungence, and it's marvelous cold.

With a bow to the Canyon Cafe for an inspired Southwestern soup.

about 16 medium-large (5 pounds) ripe red tomatoes

3 large (1 pound) white onions

2 inches chipotle chili; use a little less for timid palates, a little more for aficionados

1 cup homemade chicken broth or half good-quality canned broth and half water

½ cup water

about 5 slightly stale 5½-inch corn tortillas

salt to taste

about 2¼ cups (6 ounces) shredded cheddar cheese

about ¾ cup sour cream

a handful of cilantro leaves

In batches, cut up the tomatoes and onions into a food processor or blender and process until smooth, adding the chili to the last batch. Turn into your soup pot, then blend in the broth and water. Bring to a simmer over medium-high heat, turn the heat to low, cover, and simmer until the onion has lost its raw taste, about 20 minutes. Stir frequently.

Meanwhile, stack the tortillas and slice them into 6 strips.

Taste for salt, then ladle the soup into hot soup plates. Arrange 5 or 6 tortilla strips over the top, sprinkle lightly with cheese, dollop with sour cream, and decorate with cilantro. Be careful not to heap on too much garnish—it will smother the delicate soup. Serve with cold beer.

To serve cold, strew crisp tortilla chips on top instead of soft tortilla strips, then add the same garnishes. Some people prefer the soup this way.

Scalloped Tomatoes and Corn

MAKES ABOUT 8 SERVINGS

a little mild olive oil
2 medium-large onions, chopped
½ green pepper, diced
½ cup chopped parsley
3 large ears of sweet corn, kernels freshly cut
salt and freshly ground white pepper to taste
a pinch of dried or fresh rosemary leaves, minced
2 cups fresh coarse whole wheat bread crumbs, about 4 slices (crusts on or off)
6 medium-size (2 pounds) tomatoes, sliced ¼ inch thick

Heat the oven to 350°F. Lightly brush a 9- to 10-inch square baking dish with olive oil. Sauté the onions and pepper in a hot dry nonstick skillet over medium-high heat until softened, stirring frequently, about 3 minutes. Remove from the heat and blend in the parsley, corn, salt, and pepper. Blend the rosemary into the bread crumbs.

Make layers in the dish in this order: crumbs, tomatoes (cut as needed to fill the space), salt and pepper, corn, in two layers. Add a final layer of crumbs, then the remaining tomatoes and salt and pepper. Drizzle the top with mild olive oil or dot with butter and bake until thoroughly hot, 35 to 40 minutes. Good hot or warm and versatile enough to take to a potluck supper.

Tomato Chutney

MAKES ABOUT 16 PINTS

Tomatoes make glorious chutney. Lida Schneider's tomato chutney is the richest and most luscious I've ever tasted. The recipe, her grandmother's, was a family secret for more than 100 years until Lida generously gave it to me for this book. As you stir, think of her namesake, Lida Bonfield Schneider, in a hot kitchen on a ranch in San Jose, California, on an autumn day in the 1880s, with Sing, her Chinese cook, peeling and chopping and stirring her world-class chutney.

Once open and refrigerated, this chutney keeps until eaten. I nursed along one pint for 4 years.

Tomatoes and apples are peeled before measuring (drop tomatoes into boiling water for about 1 minute, lift out, and slip off the skins).

8 quarts chopped ripe tomatoes, about 32 large
4 cups chopped onions, about 4 large
4 cups chopped green apples, tart and juicy, about 5 large
2 pounds raisins, half dark (preferably seeded muscats), half golden
3 pints cider vinegar
3 pounds brown sugar, half light, half dark, about 6¾ cups firmly packed
2 tablespoons ground cloves
1 tablespoon ground allspice
3 to 5 tablespoons salt to taste
1½ teaspoons cayenne pepper or to taste
¼ cup mustard seeds

Mix everything together in a big nonreactive kettle. Simmer over low heat, stirring frequently, until the mixture is very thick and very dark—at least 3 hours. Pack, seal, and store (canning notes are in The Cook's Notebook), letting the chutney ripen for at least 2 months before serving if you can bear it. Don't keep your glorious chutney hidden away in a corner of the refrigerator. Bring it out and serve it with simply cooked fowl, fish, or meat.

Orange Slicing Tomatoes

These may be the most luminous tomatoes of the lot. In Portugal many native tomatoes are orange-red and have splendid flavor.

Portuguese Orange Tomato Salad

MAKES 4 SERVINGS

Here's a way with them that takes little time and—in orange, yellow, red, green, and pink—makes a fetching summer dish. As you can see, there are lots of options for putting it together.

Good at room temperature, so all but the shrimp can be prepared an hour or two before serving.

a little olive oil
2 ripe firm orange or any yellow or gold tomatoes, chopped
1 large red onion, fairly finely chopped
1 small fresh hot red chili, seeds removed, chopped, or ¼ red sweet pepper
1 large garlic clove, finely chopped
a small handful of cilantro or oregano or basil leaves, chopped
2 sweet oranges, peeled and chopped
salt and freshly ground white pepper to taste
a good bunch of cress or other peppery leaves such as escarole or endive
4 medium-size firm orange or red tomatoes, sliced about ¼ inch thick
a little white wine vinegar
4 nasturtiums or other edible flowers of different colors with leaves
1 pound cooked small shrimp, optional

A Della Robbia Wreath of Vegetables

Midsummer, you can compose an arrangement of garden vegetables for your guests as ravishing as any enameled terra-cotta wreath from the Italian Renaissance.

The greens might be verdant shoestrings of filet beans, darker fingers of zucchini, pale pattypans; the golds could be plump curlicued crookneck squashes, sprays of dill flowers, sprigs of golden sage; the reds and scarlets balls of cherry tomatoes and beets; the purples whole snap beans and opal basil; the creams top-shaped turnips, florets of cauliflowers, and perhaps spirals of Chinese artichokes; for oranges, use tiny carrots, ruffled nasturtiums, and sleek daylilies.

Ahead of time, make a map of where you'll put everything on your largest platter or tray, balancing colors and shapes. I find it helps to use uncooked samples of the vegetables and flowers I'll be using when planning the arrangement. The vegetables can be cooked or prepared raw a few hours in advance. Cook by the method that preserves color and flavor best—simmered in a big pot of boiling salted water or in a skillet with ½ inch of water. Cook until barely tender or to your taste.

To serve hot, toss cooked vegetables individually in skillets in butter or oil until heated through. To serve at room temperature, moisten each element with delicious oil. Garnish the platter with fresh herbs and edible flowers.

This gala presentation is a first course on its own, a vegetarian main dish with an assortment of sauces, or can be accompanied by roast chicken or fish.

Film a large heavy skillet with oil and sauté the 2 orange tomatoes, onion, chili, and garlic over medium-high heat until softened, stirring frequently, about 5 minutes. Turn into a bowl, blend in the cilantro and oranges, add salt and pepper, and cool to room temperature.

To serve, make a bed of the cress on 4 plates. Arrange a ring of overlapping orange tomato slices on the leaves. Sprinkle lightly with vinegar, salt, and pepper. Heap the yellow tomato mixture in the middle, set a flower on top, and border with the shrimp, if using. Pass a small bottle of olive oil, dishes of black olives and toasted walnuts, and drink a dry white wine—then have sponge cake and grapes for dessert.

Yellow Slicing Tomatoes

YELLOW TOMATOES AND HERBS DRESSED WITH BRANDY: Here's a startling dressing for tomatoes and herbs—the flavors jump out at you. Although the salad is delicious with tomatoes of any color, yellow tomatoes seem to have the special richness and sweetness of their glowing color. Inspired by a recipe of Helen Evans Brown's (*Helen Brown's West Coast Cook Book*).

For each serving, sprinkle 1 tablespoon chopped fresh herbs—chives and tarragon or thyme, basil, and Italian parsley—over a thickly sliced large golden tomato in a bowl. Sprinkle with about ½ teaspoon brandy. I add no salt and pepper, but you may wish to. Serve while the brandy still sparkles.

This is excellent with fish or poultry.

Yellow Tomato Ice with Red Chilies

MAKES ABOUT 8 SERVINGS

With my zippy yellow Taxis or orangey Caro Riches, I make this ice. Served in wineglasses, it's an appetite-tingling first course on a hot night. The color is the gold of a desert sunrise, and the dash of heat after icy tomato is splendid. Made with red tomatoes, its color is sunset red.

Botanically tomatoes are berries, and if you leave out the chili, you'll be delighted at what a splendid dessert this makes with a plop of whipped cream.

Serve within hours of making. Ices rapidly lose their freshness and texture on standing in the freezer.

I like this ice made with 3 chilies, but most of my guests prefer 1 chili with the delicate tomato.

¾ cup plus 1 tablespoon cool water

⅓ cup plus 1 tablespoon sugar

3 cups finely strained tomato puree, from about 6 medium-size (2 pounds) flavorful yellow, orange, or red tomatoes

2½ tablespoons fresh lemon juice

1½ tablespoons fresh orange juice

salt to taste

1 to 3 small dried hot red chilies to taste, including seeds

In a mixing bowl, stir the water and sugar until the sugar is dissolved. Blend in the tomato puree, then heighten the flavor with the lemon and orange juices and a few grains of salt.

Grind the chili(es) finely in a mortar and pestle (or with a wooden spoon in a bowl), stir into the tomato, then immediately strain out through the tomato-straining sieve.

Freeze in an ice cream machine according to the manufacturer's instructions.

White Slicing Tomatoes

The only invention needed here is which herb to choose to dramatize the remarkable hue and to counterpoint the sweetness of these translucent tomatoes. Each time you arrange them on a colorful plate, try another herb. Whether you'll want a glistening of extra-virgin olive oil or walnut oil and a dash of rice vinegar is something to decide each time after a taste. Fine tomatoes do *not* need to be dressed.

Make these a course on their own.

SOME HERBS FOR WHITE (AND OTHER) TOMATOES:

- thin ribbons of any basil
- chopped young borage leaves, including a few sky-blue flowers
- tiny marbled leaves of lemon thyme
- pineapple sage
- apple mint

- Greek oregano
- salad burnet
- purple perilla
- tricolor or golden sage
- flat-leaf parsley
- Chinese chives
- green garlic
- lavender

A BEAUTIFUL MEATLESS MAIN-DISH SALAD: Mix chunks of white tomatoes, tender-crisp baby green beans (or larger beans sliced on the diagonal), matchsticks of red sweet peppers, a small dice of sharp cheddar cheese, pitted black olives, chopped hard-cooked egg whites, and their yolks put through a sieve. Toss in a bowl with a vinaigrette made with mustard and serve on spinach leaves.

Green Tomatoes (Unripe)

Pick these green or half-green or however they come to you.Green tomatoes ripen indoors, but if I have plenty of Garden Peaches for ripening, I use my harvest of green tomatoes green. I've tried green tomato pie, but I don't like it—there's something that doesn't work for me in green tomatoes when cooked as fruit; their flavor seems a little like oversweetened rhubarb.

On the other hand, have you ever eaten a green—that is, underripe—tomato out of hand? Another sensational fruit, akin to none I can think of. Perfection is when the green is blushed with gold or rouge and the texture is crisp with just a relenting bit of softness.

Nashville Fried Green Tomatoes

MAKES 4 SERVINGS

Our son-in-law Jim Whelan is a great cook, and has generously given me his recipe for fried green tomatoes. It's simple and perfect. The method also works with ripe yellow and red slicing and plum tomatoes as long as they're not juicy.

Heat ⅛ inch olive oil in a cast-iron skillet. Slice 8 green tomatoes ¼ inch thick. Dip in stone-ground cornmeal blended with freshly ground black pepper, cayenne pepper, and salt to taste (Jim likes them spicy). Fry over medium to medium-high heat about 5 minutes on each side until golden brown and crisp. Pat with a paper towel to remove excess oil and serve immediately.

Green Tomato Piccalilli

MAKES 14 TO 16 CUPS

At summer's end when there are too many to eat—and you'd get a stomachache—put up green tomato piccalilli that is as good as piccalilli gets. I usually find myself trebling the recipe. Canning details are in The Cook's Notebook.

16 medium-large (4 pounds) firm green tomatoes, stem scars removed
16 medium-large (4 pounds) onions
6 medium-size (2 pounds) firm sweet peppers, stems removed, seeds included
1 cup coarse sea salt or ½ cup pickling salt
3 cups white vinegar, 5 percent acidity
1 cup cider vinegar, 5 percent acidity
1 cup mild honey
1 tablespoon prepared mustard
2 teaspoons dry mustard
½ tablespoon paprika
1 teaspoon celery seeds
freshly ground black pepper to taste

Chop the tomatoes, onions, and peppers fairly coarsely (the mixture will cook down, and you don't want too fine a finished texture). Turn into a big bowl or nonreactive pot, add the salt, then use your hands to blend thoroughly. Cover and refrigerate overnight or for up to 24 hours.

Drain the vegetables in a colander, then with both hands squeeze out all the liquid you can. In a large nonreactive kettle, blend the vinegars, honey, mustards, paprika, celery seeds, and pepper. Cook over medium-high heat, stirring occasionally, until the honey has dissolved. Blend in the vegetables. Raise the heat to high and bring to a boil, then reduce the heat to keep the simmering at a good clip. Cook, stirring frequently, until all the peppers have changed color, about 10 minutes.

Divide the piccalilli among hot 1- or 2-cup jars, leaving 1/4 inch of headspace. Seal, process for 15 minutes in a boiling water bath, cool, label, and store. Store for at least 2 weeks for flavors to develop before serving.

Plum/Pear Tomatoes

Slow-Roasted Plum or Pear Tomatoes

You can slow-roast plum/pear tomatoes until they're almost jam. They are heavenly, and even if you never got to eat them, the scent of roasting tomatoes that fills the house is a feast for the senses. Serve the tomatoes hot or at room temperature, spooned over or beside anything you please, from bread to fish to pasta.

- about 24 (3 pounds) plum or pear tomatoes, stem scars removed, sliced in half lengthwise
- 2 large garlic cloves, pressed
- sea salt to taste
- a little olive oil

Line a jelly-roll pan with foil, shiny side up. Arrange the tomato pieces closely on it, cut sides up. Smear a speck of garlic on each tomato half, then sprinkle with salt and very lightly drizzle with oil. Roast in a 300°F oven until velvety soft, about 3 hours. Serve in an earthenware dish or mix with pasta or cooked dried beans or rice or potatoes.

EFFORTLESS PASTA WITH TOMATO-ORANGE SAUCE: One of the sunniest compositions I've ever tasted is this sauce for spaghettini: Chop plum tomatoes, then barely heat them through in a skillet with a drift of toasted pine nuts, crushed dried red chilies, and—the magical ingredient—wisps of orange zest. Add some French golden olive oil to moisten the pasta and you have one of those splendid dishes that use imagination in place of effort.

Cherry Tomatoes

CHERRY TOMATOES ON TOAST: From my friend Hildy Manley, one of those remarkable combinations that is greater than the sum of its parts: sautéed small tomatoes on toasted English muffins or French bread. Mix as many types of small tomatoes as you can because the reds and golds complement one another not only in color but also in taste. Great for breakfast, lunch, hors d'oeuvres, or supper.

For each muffin half (and three or four halves per hungry person is not too many), figure a mix of something like three or four larger cherry tomatoes and six or eight currant-size ones—double that of either size alone. Stem them.

Start toasting split English muffins or sourdough or French bread as you barely film a heavy nonreactive skillet with olive oil. Warm it over medium heat, then add the tomatoes, turn the heat to medium-low, and shake the skillet until the tomatoes are warmed through and their skins begin to wrinkle, 2 to 3 minutes. Turn the tomatoes into a bowl and the muffins onto a serving dish. Each person should balance tomatoes on a muffin, then mash them with a fork—carefully, because some spurt. A pinch of coarse salt, a turn of the black pepper mill, then nip in and enjoy. Since the tomatoes spurt so irreverently, I tuck my napkin under my chin.

Inspired by a notion of Diane Worthington's, sometimes we cook the tomatoes in a splash of heavy cream with a handful of thin ribbons of sweet or lemon basil.

Currant Tomatoes

Serve and eat these warm gold or sparkling red darlings as you do bunches of grapes. Remember them for a beguiling garnish.

Red, Yellow, and Green Currant Tomato Tartlets Provençal

MAKES EIGHT 3-INCH TARTLETS

A friend's mention of a green tomato tart her sister once ate in Provence inspired these tartlets, which are pretty, amusing, and delectable. The unusual shape is a flat square with pinched corners. Colors are dots of bright red, warm gold, pale orange, celadon, leaf green, cream, and purply black. Perfect for a special autumn first course. Grilled or roast chicken rubbed with lemon and garlic might follow, accompanied by shredded zucchini, orange slices as garnish, and a soft light red wine such as a Gamay. After a leafy salad and a selection of cheeses—the Provençal Banon is perfect—offer ripe figs.

Of course if you have just red or just yellow currant tomatoes, that would be fine, too. And you can do this with small cherry tomatoes, same or different colors. Green grapes are especially recommended.

As with all tarts based on ephemeral pastry, these must be served on the day of baking. That's not to say you won't enjoy one the next day.

1 recipe Crisp Short Lemon Pastry for Tarts (in The Cook's Notebook)
1½ tablespoons unsalted butter
egg white left from the pastry
½ cup (¼ pound) creamy feta cheese
about 3⅓ cups mixed unripe and ripe currant tomatoes, all sizes, leaves removed
3 tablespoons finely chopped fresh sweet or lemon basil
8 Kalamata olives, the flesh cut lengthwise so 4 equal pieces can be removed from the pit

On a well-floured cloth, roll the dough to an evenly thick rectangle 8 by 16 inches. Patch as needed to get straight edges (press together and roll lightly to blend). Cut into eight 4-inch squares. Butter a large baking sheet with a bit of butter, then melt the rest.

You'll form square boxes that will relax in baking, but the sides will keep the heap of tomatoes in place. Make a ½-inch diagonal cut at each corner of the first square—cut from the corner toward the center. Lift up one edge of the square at a right angle to make the side of a ½-inch-deep box. Lap over the corner tips of the side, using egg white as glue. Repeat with the remaining 3 sides. Pinch the corners to make little points—they will last and be very pretty. Set the shell on the baking sheet—placed as diamonds, all will fit on one sheet. Construct the rest of the shells the same way, then brush the bottoms with the melted butter.

For best texture, cover and set in the freezer for 15 to 30 minutes or refrigerate for another couple of hours or up to 3 days.

To bake, heat the oven to 425°F. With a teaspoon, gently spread 1 tablespoon of the feta evenly over the bottom of each shell. Turn about ⅓ cup tomatoes into the shells, pressing the tiny orbs lightly but firmly into the base. Sprinkle each with about 1 teaspoon basil and top with a star of black olive pieces.

Bake in the middle of the oven until the pastry is golden brown around the edges, 13 to 15 minutes. Wait a minute for the pastry to firm, then lift the tartlets onto racks and cool. You may want to rearrange the olive pieces. Serve within a few hours.

At high altitude, bake at 440°F.

TURNIPS

Pull baby turnips whenever you like—no bigger than a walnut. After that, just pull them before they get big and woody. For storing, sun-dry them a few hours before setting in a cool dark dry place—do not cut off the root.

Sweet, tender large-plum-size turnips just pulled from the earth, still dripping from their rinsing under the hose, have little relation to strong, tough, rubbery market turnips. Leave the greens on the roots until cooking, then cut the stems off flush with the top. Refrigerate the leaves if you're not using them right away. Nip off the rootlet. Scrub the roots, leaving the skin on if you can. If it's thick, use a vegetable peeler. The creamy flesh of turnips shares a reaction with potato, eggplant, sweet potato, and okra: aluminum, iron, and carbon steel discolor it. You can cook turnips any way, but they're especially flavorful baked or braised. Turnips are moderately good sources of vitamin C, but the reasons to grow and eat them are their deliciously crisp texture, their reviving taste, and the all-important variety they add to our diets. Add tender raw leaves to salad.

To find appealing ways to serve your turnips, treat them as though they were carrots. For example, turnips make a heavenly creamy pureed soup, and they make an equally delicious salad of raw shreds.

Here a celebrated French recipe for carrots lends its luster to garden-grown turnips. As you can imagine, there are as many nuances of the recipe as there are cooks. This is the simplest I've found. The water cooks down and, mingled with the butter and sugar, becomes a delicate glaze.

SWEET YOUNG TURNIPS: Makes 4 servings. For fastidious guests, lightly peel the turnips. Slice 4 medium-size (1 pound) turnips 1/4 inch thick—slice from top to bottom. Arrange in a large heavy noniron skillet and barely cover with cool water. Add 2 tablespoons unsalted butter in small pieces and sprinkle on 2 teaspoons sugar.

Bring to a simmer uncovered over high heat, then adjust the heat so the water simmers briskly. Cook until tender, watching carefully toward the end, about 10 minutes. Season with salt and freshly ground white pepper and turn into a heated serving bowl. Sprinkle with finely chopped parsley and serve hot.

Another time, omit the water and simmer to tenderness in dry Marsala.

Turnip Greens

These greens are snappy, so the younger they are, the milder—but then you want your turnips young and mild, too. Rinse the leaves well, and if the stems are tough, pull the leafy greens from them (double the leaf over and tear). You'll find simmering them in a big pot of water the best way. Turnip greens are a very rich source of beta-carotene and calcium and a good source of vitamin C and iron. Tear young leaves into salads.

Turnip Greens in Pot Liquor

MAKES 4 SERVINGS

Perhaps the best way to cook turnip greens is the traditional way of the South—where they know their greens. The main thing is to cook the leaves whole to preserve their flavor. The pot liquor—the broth—that's left from this is divine. See the black-eyed pea soup made with it under Dried Beans.

The greens can be cooked in advance and heated up.

- 1 gallon cold water
- ½ pound lean salt pork
- 1 dried hot red chili, seeds removed, finely crumbled
- 16 cups lightly packed (2 pounds) torn turnip greens, tender stems included
- salt to taste

Bring the water, salt pork, and chili to a boil in your soup pot, then adjust the heat so the water simmers. Cook covered for about an hour. Drop in the greens, stir, and simmer uncovered until tender, 20 to 30 minutes.

Drain the greens through a colander—saving the pot liquor—and press out excess moisture. Chop, then season with salt if it needs it. Serve with buttermilk and corn sticks or muffins.

The Cook's Notebook

Blanching

This is a process of boiling vegetables to the point where they're almost cooked but not quite, then draining them and plunging them into ice water to stop the cooking ASAP. This is a culinary step comparable to the gardening step of sowing seeds indoors rather than into the garden—you have control over the process rather than being reduced to hoping things go well. You lose some vitamins and minerals in the blanching water you dump out, but it does cut down on any acrid flavors in the vegetable. Blanching should really be used only when vegetables are being prepared for company. It's valuable because most of the cooking is done in advance (a big help in the last-minute schedule), and blanching best preserves color, texture, and flavor.

Canning

I've recently discovered that a number of friends who put up preserves are leery about canning them—i.e., processing them in a boiling water bath. My friends either cover their preserves with paraffin or refrigerate the jars. I used to do this, but then I learned the advantages of the vacuum seal you get from canning: there's no danger of spoilage, the contents can keep for years, and a guest can throw a jar of our asparagus pickles into a handbag or suitcase and carry it from here to Timbuktu with no worry about spilling. One friend said she was afraid the processing would ruin the quality of her preserves. It won't. Others said they were afraid of botulism. But the process itself has nothing to do with botulism. (For more on botulism, see the box under Garlic.)

Here's all you need to know about canning.

JARS: Wide-mouth jars are the easiest to fill, to fit into the kettle for processing, and to serve from. But the look of "regular" jars is sleeker. Use only jars manufactured for home canning, jars without nicks or cracks. Wash in hot soapy water and rinse well. If the food will be processed in the boiling water bath for less than 10 minutes, boil the jars for 10 minutes to kill any bacteria and fungi hanging around. Either way, keep the jars in very hot water until needed.

STERILIZING JARS: Traditionally we've been told by canning authorities that when filled jars are to be processed for less than 10 minutes the jars must be sterilized. But when you lift "sterilized" jars out of the water, unsterile food is put into them, an unsterile implement is used to force out air bubbles, and an unsterile cloth wipes the lip clean. It's impossible to achieve a sterile atmosphere in a home kitchen. So fill and cap soap-and-hot-water-clean jars and boil them the required length of time to get a good seal. That way you'll be certain the contents are sealed against contamination and will stay so until opened.

When the jars are to be filled with a foodstuff that would suffer from boiling—pickles, for example—the jars *must* be boiled first:

Place jars on a folded towel or rack in a deep kettle and cover with hot water by 1 inch. Cover the kettle and bring to a rolling boil over highest heat. Remove the lid and begin counting. Maintain a boil: count 10 minutes from sea level to 1,000 feet—adjustments for higher altitudes follow. Keep the jars in the water until needed, then lift using tongs on the outside of the jar. Also boil any implement that will be poked into the jar for releasing air bubbles.

The dishwasher and microwave oven don't sterilize jars.

Altitude	Increased boiling time
1,001–3,000 feet	5 minutes
3,001–6,000 feet	10 minutes
6,001–8,000 feet	15 minutes
8,001–10,000 feet	20 minutes

LIDS AND RINGS: Use only lids with sealing compound that has no indentation from previous canning. Use only rings that are neither rusty nor bent. Wash lids and rings in hot soapy water and rinse well. To soften the sealing compound, place lids in a pot of water and bring to a simmer, then remove from the heat. Keep in the water until needed.

PACKING: Lift jars from the hot water with a jar lifter or tongs, shake out water, and ladle in the preparation, leaving the required headspace. As a rule, leave 1 inch for canning low-acid foods (generally every vegetable except tomatoes); 1/2 inch for canning fruits, tomatoes, and sauerkraut; 1/4 inch for jellies, preserves, pickles, chutneys, and juices. Run a clean nonmetal implement down through the jar to force up air bubbles.

SEALING: Wipe rims with a clean damp cloth, lay on the lids, then screw on rings as tightly as you comfortably can with your hand. Process as directed in the recipe or the required amount of time needed to sterilize the jars.

Cooked foods are processed just enough to get a good seal—if not to sterilize the jar. As a rule of thumb, process jellies (in sterilized jars) for 5 minutes; fruit butters, jams, preserves, conserves, marmalades, and chutneys for 10 minutes.

COOLING: Lift jars onto a cloth or board away from a draft and give each jar a little elbow room for cooling. Do not disturb for 12 hours. Test for a seal: press down in the center of the lid. If it pops up with a plink, you must replace the lid and process again in the boiling water bath—or refrigerate the jar and use the contents as though you'd just opened it.

LABELING: Nothing like opening a jar of red pepper jam when you thought it was strawberry. Even when the contents of a batch are obvious, label the jars, including the date. Time flies when you're having fun.

STORING: In a cool, dark, dry place, properly canned goods will keep for at least 1 year.

Refrigerate jars once opened and keep an eye out for signs of spoilage, such as mold of any hue—if there's even a speck, toss it out. Once bits of mold on open jars of refrigerated preserves were simply scooped out and the rest was considered sound. But now we know that microscopic molds can also be present in the jar, and they, like the larger clumps, are considered potentially carcinogenic.

CHEESE—HOMEMADE CREAMY, WITH HERBS

Want to make creamy fresh cheese that takes one minute to prepare and is ready to serve in a few hours? Fresh cheese that can become your trademark with the herbs you add to it? Creamy cheese that's delectable whether nonfat, low-fat, or full fat? If you're not partial to tang in your cream cheese, make or buy the freshest yogurt available—it will be the least sour.

CREAMY FRESH CHEESE: Makes about 2 cups. Wring out a clean dish towel, line a colander or strainer with it (single thickness), and set over a bowl. Turn in a quart of unflavored yogurt, cover with film, and refrigerate. Check after about 3 hours to see if it's ready to serve. Don't let so much whey drip out that the cheese becomes crumbly. Too, the drier the cheese, the more intense its flavor. When it's the consistency you like, turn your cheese into a mixing bowl. Add a little salt, if you like, and freshly ground pepper, white or black. Smooth it into a bowl, or pat it into a round or log or block. You can dip it into a dish of herbs or spices for a coating.

HERB AND SEED CREAM CHEESE: Don't worry about measurements, don't worry about combinations, just take a handful of leaves whose flavor you like, chop them medium-fine—too fine and the flavor can disappear—and stir them into your cheese before seasoning. Then add salt to taste, some freshly ground white pepper, and maybe the thinnest shreds of lemon zest. Smooth into a bowl, press a few whole leaves into the top, cover with plastic wrap, and refrigerate at least a few hours for the flavors to marry. Spread on great bread or crackers, or a slice of apple or pear.

Crudités

Hors d'oeuvre of raw vegetables: A basket or bowl of raw vegetables whisked fresh from the garden is one of the most appealing beginnings to a meal imaginable. The more you can bring the garden indoors the better. A few examples: leaves and wisps of rootlets on radishes, baby carrots, kohlrabi, turnips, and beets, tops and tails on snap beans, unhusked baby corn, blossoms on small squashes, a bit of vine and tendrils attached to tomatoes.

For dipping, offer something just to moisten and not distract from the young vegetable—a shallow dish of extra-virgin olive oil (under Dressings) or a pot of softened unsalted butter is best, with a little dish of coarse salt mixed with coarsely ground white pepper on the side.

Dressings

Sesame Miso Dressing

MAKES ABOUT 1 CUP

Based on intensely-flavored soybean paste, this is a delicious, nourishing, and versatile dressing for everything from greens to fish. It keeps about 1 month in the refrigerator. Response to salt differs considerably in all our palates, so adjust proportions to please yours.

3/4 cup miso, white or red

2 tablespoons toasted sesame seeds

3 tablespoons mild vegetable stock or chicken broth, or to taste

1 teaspoon low-sodium soy sauce, or to taste

1 teaspoon sugar, or to taste

In a food processor, blend the miso and sesame seeds. With the motor running, add 3 tablespoons broth, 1 teaspoon each soy sauce and sugar, then taste. If desired, slowly blend in more broth, soy sauce, and/or sugar until a pleasing consistency and flavor.

Foolproof Mayonnaise

MAKES 3/4 CUP

This keeps in a tightly covered jar in the refrigerator for at least 2 weeks.
When served with very delicate foods, use peanut oil for a portion of the olive oil.

2 tablespoons lightly beaten egg set over hot water until warmed

2 teaspoons fresh lemon juice

pinch of salt

1/2 cup mild olive oil, warmed

Combine the egg, lemon juice, and salt in a food processor or blender. Process just until blended. Put the oil into a small pitcher. Steady your hand on the processor work bowl or blender jar and, with the motor running (medium speed on the blender), let the oil fall into the jar in a stream no thicker than a thread. It will take a few minutes, but the mayonnaise will be thick and shiny.

Vinaigrette: Basic French Salad Dressing

MAKES ABOUT 2/3 CUP TO SERVE 8

The dressing can be prepared several days in advance and refrigerated in a covered jar.

Suit the acid and the oil to the salad makings—stronger for hearty flavors, subtler for delicate flavors.

2 tablespoons vinegar or lemon juice or a combination of vinegars and citrus juices

salt to taste, preferably fairly coarse sea salt

1/2 to a scant 2/3 cup oil—extra-virgin olive oil or nut oil

freshly ground pepper to taste

pinch of dry mustard, optional

a handful of chopped fresh herbs or 1 heaped tablespoon crumbled dried, according to the salad, optional

In a small bowl, whisk the vinegar and a pinch of salt together. Set the bowl on a towel and slowly whisk in the oil until you get the balance of acid and oil you like. When blended, taste for seasoning. Add the mustard (if the salad would be improved by it) and herbs. Whisk or shake well before pouring it over the salad.

I like the proportions of 5 or sometimes 6 parts oil to one of vinegar or fresh lemon juice. With delicate foods, half lemon and half orange juice is even more pleasing than just lemon. Sometimes wine vinegar and sherry vinegar are mixed. Be sparing with freshly ground pepper and salt until you've tossed and tasted the salad. Vinaigrette also can include minced shallots, a hint of garlic—rubbed over the bowl—and lots of chopped fresh herbs such as flat-leaf parsley, tarragon, chervil, basil, or chives.

Figure a tablespoon to dress one serving of most leaves. The aim is not to have a speck of dressing left in the bowl once the salad is tossed.

Mix the salad at the table and use your hands. You'll mix it better—and it's good theater.

TUSCAN DUNK FOR RAW VEGETABLES: Into an earthenware plate, pour a golden pool of your finest olive oil. Sprinkle with coarse sea salt and grind on spicy black pepper. *Pinzimonio,* as this simple sauce is called in Italy, is wonderful with almost any fresh raw vegetables.

PASTA, HOMEMADE

If you can invest in the modest expense of a hand-operated pasta machine, you'll quickly find yourself breezing through these steps and making pasta at the drop of a hat to show off your glorious vegetables. The pasta is infinitely lighter, more delicate, and more exciting than any you can purchase.

Fresh Egg Pasta

MAKES 7 OUNCES TO SERVE 2 TO 4

Pasta keeps fresh for 4 days, dried for 1 month.

It is important to keep the dough on the dry side so the paste won't be gummy and the noodles flabby. But if the dough is too dry, it will crumble going through the rollers. The correct texture, instantly obvious, is a dough that is easily pressed into a ball and holds together when kneaded. Begin without water, but don't hesitate to add a little if needed.

1 cup unbleached flour, lightly spooned into the cup

pinch of salt

1 extra-large egg

2 teaspoons olive oil

1 teaspoon to 1 tablespoon cool water if needed

In a food processor, blend the flour and salt. Add the egg and olive oil and process until the mixture turns into tiny beads, about 10 seconds.

If you know from prior experience that your dough will need water, add it now and process for 15 seconds. Scrape the bowl and process for 15 seconds more. Otherwise, wait.

Turn the dough onto your work surface and squeeze it together to form a ball. Knead until the pieces cohere. If they won't hold together after a few strokes, sprinkle lightly with water and knead again—sprinkle and knead until they will hold together.

Wrap the dough airtight in plastic wrap and set it in a cool place (not the refrigerator) from a long half hour to overnight.

Flour the work surface around the pasta machine. If you've multiplied the recipe, work with one recipe portion at a time. Keep the rest of the dough covered so it won't dry out.

Set the rollers at their widest aperture (about 1/2 inch). Flatten the dough and pass it through the rollers, pulling it out from underneath with your free hand. Draw the bottom of the sheet through the flour, lightly dusting the dough, then fold the sheet into thirds, making a rectangle. Press out the air. Open end first, pass it again through the rollers. Repeat this folding and rolling 8 to 10 times, until the dough is ultra-silky.

Set the aperture at the next narrowest opening. Lightly dust both sides of the dough with flour and, without folding, pass it through the rollers once, resting the sheet over your free hand as you draw it out.

Repeat this rolling, each time setting the rollers on a narrower aperture, dusting the sheet with flour when sticky, until it is either 1/16 inch thick (the last or next-to-last setting) or perhaps 1/32 inch thick, whichever you prefer or whichever the noodle classically ought to be—or whichever your machine produces.

Cut the sheet into even pieces 12 to 15 inches long. You can dry the pieces for 10 to 15 minutes or proceed (if your air is dry, keep going).

Attach the cutting mechanism (unless you'll be cutting by hand). Although authorities don't always agree, usually tagliatelle is the thinnest you can make and 1/4 inch wide, fettuccine is not quite paper-thin and is about 1/8 inch wide, and the narrowest pasta the machine makes—about 1/16 inch wide—is ultra-thin tagliarini/tagliolini.

If the noodles are to be cooked within the hour (they may be cooked within minutes of cutting), lay them on a lightly floured board, uncovered. If to be cooked within 12 hours, lightly flour two kitchen towels and spread in a single layer between them. If to be cooked within 4 days, dry the pasta, uncovered, for about 2 hours, then turn it into a plastic bag, tie loosely, and store at room temperature. If to be stored, hang the noodles from a clothes drying rack or a stout cotton line strung across the kitchen (be careful the line isn't too thin, or it will cut the paste, and the noodles will fall) or lay the noodles out straight and let dry until brittle. Gingerly arrange them in a shallow vessel and store uncovered in a cool, dry place.

To cook, bring to a boil about 5 quarts water with a heaped tablespoon of salt per pound of pasta. Add the pasta, stir with a wooden spoon so nothing sticks, and cover. When the water returns to a boil, uncover and start timing. Just-made tagliarini cooks in 15 seconds, tagliatelle in 30. If made within 2 hours to 4 days, 1 minute is maximum for both widths. Taste frequently and don't overcook. Cook fresh egg pasta until just tender.

Drain in a large colander over the serving bowl (the water heats the bowl). Dump out the water, shake the bowl dry, and turn the pasta into it.

That's just the beginning. There's a world of richly tinted and amazingly flavored pastas you can make with vegetables, fruits, herbs, and spices.

Unless otherwise noted, the method and yield will be the same as for this master recipe. When vegetable purees are added, the paste will be softer than usual. This takes more flour in the rolling, so be careful not to overdo it.

The important thing, once you've created such pleasure, is to be able to taste it, so keep the finishing sauce very light.

FRESH HERB PASTA: Use flat-leaf parsley, lovage, celery leaves, cilantro, basil, or summer savory, for starters. These delicate leaves retain their flavor better when briefly blanched.

Pour boiling water over 1/2 cup very finely chopped herbs in a bowl. At once drain and press dry in a towel. Turn 3 tablespoons into a small bowl with the egg and oil. Beat until blended, then add the egg and oil as usual.

LEAFY GREEN PASTA: Although there will probably be more color than flavor to this pasta, it's very pretty.

Any fresh flavorful greens with body will make it. Traditional leaves are beet greens, chard, kale, and spinach. Many Asian greens are splendid here: garland chrysanthemum, komatsuna, mizuna, and rosette pak choi. Of the mustard greens, broccoli raab is the mildest. Of potherbs: amaranth, Good-King-Henry, orach, and spinach beets are good. Experiment with peppery salad plants: arugula, chicory, cress, and shepherd's purse.

Decrease the egg to 2 1/2 tablespoons and omit the olive oil. Thoroughly rinse 3 ounces of the leafy parts only of young greens (no stems, no spines). Cook in boiling salted water until tender (time will be in the entry on each vegetable). Drain and squeeze out all excess moisture, then finely chop. Beat in a small bowl with the egg, then add to the flour as usual.

Green pasta is especially suited to creamy sauces—flavor a white sauce with freshly grated Parmesan cheese or stir in a goat's milk cheese. Green pasta also makes great lasagne with fresh tomato sauce.

PAPRIKA PASTA: In a food processor, blend the flour and salt with 3/4 teaspoon best-quality paprika. Increase the egg to 1/4 cup plus 1 tablespoon and make as usual.

This is a gorgeous pasta, created for the elegant lasagne recipe under Chard.

ROSEMARY PASTA: This pasta is ethereal. The flavor quickly pales, so make this no more than a day before serving. It's almost as good made with thyme.

Add 1 tablespoon minced fresh rosemary leaves to the dough with the olive oil and make as usual. Serve in soup plates dressed with no more than a drizzle of extra-virgin olive oil and several turns of the black pepper mill.

SAGE PASTA: Tear garden sage leaves into tiny pieces to make 1 1/2 tablespoons and add to the dough with the olive oil.

This wants only a little olive oil and crumbled salty cheese.

SWEET RED PEPPER PASTA: Makes about 9 ounces. Although you can make this with green peppers, they are bitter, whereas the red is sweet and glorious.

Increase the flour to 1 cup plus 6 tablespoons and decrease the olive oil to 1 teaspoon. Stem and seed a large (5- to 6-ounce) pepper. Cut up roughly into the food processor, add a spoonful of water, and puree until perfectly smooth. Turn into a fine sieve and press out the juice until the puree is dry and thick. Add 3 tablespoons to the egg and beat until blended. Add the egg and continue as usual.

To appreciate the flavor of this pasta, simply toss noodles of it with extra-virgin olive oil, a few grated cloves of garlic, and flat-leaf parsley leaves—called *aglio e olio,* garlic and oil sauce.

TOMATO PASTA: Increase the flour to 1 cup plus 2 tablespoons and 2 teaspoons and omit the olive oil.

In a small bowl, thoroughly blend 1 tablespoon tomato paste and 1/2 teaspoon paprika with the egg, then add this to the flour as usual.

As with green pasta, there's more color than flavor here, but it's beautifully coral, and I like it with mixed finely chopped fresh herbs—hyssop, parsley, and a purple basil, for example—and half olive oil, half melted unsalted butter.

Pastry

Crisp Short Lemon Pastry for Tarts

MAKES ONE 10-INCH SHELL OR 8 TARTLETS

This pastry holds up better longer than pie pastry. The dough keeps fresh for 1 week, wrapped and refrigerated.

1 cup all-purpose flour, lightly spooned into the cup

1 tablespoon sugar

1/4 teaspoon salt

6 tablespoons very cold unsalted butter, cut into thin chips

1 heaped tablespoon fine shreds of lemon zest

1 tablespoon chilled egg yolk

3 tablespoons cold heavy cream

In a food processor or with a mixer, blend the flour, sugar, and salt with 6 pulses. Add the butter and lemon zest and process just until the butter is the size of baby peas, about 20 pulses or briefly with the mixer on low speed. Add the yolk and cream and process or beat just until the bits of the dough start to cohere, about 30 seconds.

Turn the crumbles onto your work surface. With the heel of your hand, starting at the top of the pile, push about an inch of the crumbles straight ahead, smearing them across the counter. Do this with the next inch of crumbles below that and so on until the whole batch has been smeared across the counter. Pull it together and—voilà!—it's a cohesive dough. Pat into a flattish round, wrap in foil, and chill for 2 hours or up to 3 days. Set at room temperature for about 30 minutes before rolling as directed.

Flaky Pastry

MAKES TWO 10-INCH CRUSTS

The dough can be wrapped and chilled a day or two ahead.

A great secret in flaky pie pastry is the less handling the better—especially if you have warm hands.

1½ cups all-purpose flour, lightly spooned into the cup, plus more for rolling

¾ cup cake flour, lightly spooned into the cup

slightly heaped ½ teaspoon salt

10 tablespoons cold vegetable shortening or lard

5 tablespoons cold unsalted butter

about 1 extra-large cold egg, beaten, ¼ cup

3 tablespoons ice water

2 teaspoons cider vinegar

Combine the flours and salt in a food processor and process for 10 seconds. Add shortening in 20 blobs and cut in the butter in 20 chips. Pulse just until the largest pieces of fat are pea size, about 12 times.

In a bowl, blend the egg, ice water, and vinegar and pour over the flour mixture. Pulse until the mixture masses to the point of being crumbles, 8 to 10 times.

Turn the crumbles onto the counter and pat into a ball (blobs of unincorporated fat are correct). Slice the ball in half and pat each half into a 5-inch round. Wrap in foil and chill for at least 30 minutes—2 hours is better—before rolling out ⅛ inch thick. When patching is needed, press pieces together without water.

PIZZA

This Neapolitan-style crust, is light, crisp, and tender. Fresh herbs add great flavor—use any leaf compatible with the filling and chop by hand or snip.

Using a food processor, the dough is on its way in 5 minutes. To use a mixer, double the processing times. You can also double the recipe.

Pizza Dough

MAKES 1 13-INCH CRUST (10 SERVINGS)

The dough may be prepared in advance, put in a freezer-weight bag, and refrigerated—punch down as needed—or frozen. Bring to room temperature before shaping.

¾ teaspoon active dry yeast

1 cup all-purpose flour, plus more for the board

½ cup very hot water

½ teaspoon salt, preferably sea salt

1 tablespoon fruity olive oil, plus more for the pan and baking

1 tablespoon finely snipped fresh herb leaves, optional

a little cornmeal

In a food processor, using the steel blade, pulse the yeast and 1/2 cup flour briefly to mix, then add the water and process 30 seconds. Scrape down the bowl, add the remaining flour, and process 1 minute. The dough will be sticky. Lightly oil a quart glass measure, add the dough, then turn the dough over, oiled side up. Cover with plastic wrap and let rise at around 70°F until its shoulders hit 2 1/2 cups, 30 to 45 minutes.

Punch the dough down and knead on a lightly floured surface a dozen times. Pat 1/4-inch thick and dimple all over with your fingertips. Sprinkle over the salt, olive oil, and herbs. Fold the dough in thirds one way, brushing off excess flour, then repeat, folding the other way. Knead 2 to 3 minutes until the herb is evenly distributed and the dough is silky. Oil the quart measure again, add the dough, oiling it, then let rise until its shoulders hit 3 cups, 1 to 1 1/4 hours. Punch down but do not knead.

About 40 minutes before serving, place a baking stone, if you have one, on the lowest rack of the oven. Set the oven at 500°F. If you don't have a baking stone, heat a 14-inch pizza pan or large square baking sheet. Sprinkle the shiny side of a square of heavy foil with cornmeal.

To shape, about 20 minutes before serving, on a floured surface, pat and roll and *very* gently pull the dough to make a round a scant 14 inches wide—this is rustic pizza, so don't worry if the round isn't even. Fold over the edge to make a rim no more than 1/4-inch thick. Lift onto the foil and coax again to make it about 13 inches wide. Lightly dimple. It's ready to receive the filling. The dough needn't rise before baking, but a little puffing won't hurt.

Salt

Although every vegetable contains natural salt, adding a few grains of pure sea salt makes flavors glow. But when should we add the salt and how much?

The French and Chinese (who consider one another their only culinary rivals) add salt to everything at or near the beginning of cooking. But for most of my life I've added salt just before serving, on the theory that salt not only draws out juices but can also make food tough.

Then I discovered the dramatic effect salt has on dried beans when added to the simmering water at the start. Beans cooked with salt are not only more flavorful (and not at all tough), but—as I learned from Russ Parsons of the *Los Angeles Times*—in trying to approximate the taste, I had to use *more* salt at the end than the amount added at the beginning—and still the beans didn't taste as good.

The same is true for all vegetables: roots, leaves, whatever. There's an astonishing gap between the depth and roundness of flavor salted early and salted late. Try it for yourself.

Although I don't use much, unlike the French and Chinese, I now always salt at the start. My rule of thumb:

- *added to mixtures or sprinkled over food that will be dry-cooked,* from a scant 1/8 to 1/4 teaspoon sea salt per serving
- *added to water or other unsalted cooking liquid,* a scant 1/2 tablespoon (about 1 1/4 teaspoons) salt per quart

The most natural salt I've tasted—particularly flavorful because it's produced in flakes—is Maldon sea salt, from England.

Sauces

Cream Sauce/Bechamel/White Sauce, Light and Basic

MAKES ABOUT 2 CUPS

To keep the sauce a few hours, cover and refrigerate it. When you're ready to serve it, warm it up gently in a bain-marie (a pot set in a pot of water) or in a double boiler.

- 2 tablespoons butter or light oil
- 3 tablespoons flour
- 2 cups cold milk (nonfat is fine)
- a few grains of grated nutmeg
- salt and freshly ground white pepper to taste

In a small heavy saucepan, melt the butter over low heat then whisk in the flour. Whisk frequently while the mixture cooks 2 minutes. Off the heat, slowly add the milk, whisking until smooth after each addition. Whisk in the nutmeg, salt, and pepper and then whisk frequently over medium heat until the sauce bubbles and thickens. Taste for seasoning.

SAVORY CREAM SAUCE: Prepare the recipe above, but first flavor the milk: add a small handful of chopped celery or lovage leaves, a chopped carrot, a little chopped onion, parsley, thyme, whatever flavorings will suit the dish your sauce is saucing. Start with a little more milk than you'll need for the sauce and simmer it gently for 5 to 10 minutes, then let it set another half-hour or so. Strain the milk and proceed with the recipe.

Crème Fraîche

This instant version makes 1 cup and keeps a week.

- $^2/_3$ cup sour cream
- $^1/_3$ cup heavy cream

Blend together and store in a jar in the refrigerator.

Sautéing in a Dry Skillet

Long ago in *The Art of Fine Cooking,* Paula Peck introduced the idea of browning vegetables in a heavy skillet with just a modicum of fat. This brilliant pupil of James Beard's pointed out how the heat of cast iron slightly caramelized the sugar in onions, for example, thus emphasizing their native sweetness. The onion's juices became the essential moistening ingredient, thus concentrating their flavor even more.

As *fat* became a four-letter word and nonstick skillets came into their own, I found myself sautéing almost everything this way without using any fat at all.

You can of course use a soupçon of fat in the pan to carry the flavor throughout the dish. Or try a splash of flavorless vodka or other high spirits in the skillet—another way of moistening an ingredient and capturing its essence. So when I ask you to sauté dry, do what makes you comfortable, using a little fat or a spoonful of spirits or both or nothing.

Soup

Here's an example of an ad lib height-of-the-season soup.

Summer Vegetable Soup

MAKES ABOUT 9 QUARTS TO SERVE 2 FOR A WEEK

Everything except onions and garlic is unpeeled, so there's as little waste as possible. The cooking is a casual matter, but because the soup will be reheated, I'm careful not to overcook the vegetables the first time. If you're in a hurry, after the beans are cooked, you can throw everything into the pot and let it simmer until tender.

The calf's foot, if you can find one (available in Latin markets), gives a silky texture.

about 1 cup dried black-eyed peas or other dried legumes

salt to taste

1 split calf's foot, optional

12 large carrots, cut into 1/2-inch rounds

6 medium-size tomatoes, coarsely chopped

5 medium-size potatoes, cut into eighths

5 medium-size beets, cut into 1/4-inch-thick matchsticks

2 medium-size green sweet peppers, cut into 1-inch dice, seeds included

2 medium-size onions, thinly sliced

1/4 head of red cabbage, thinly sliced and the slices halved

1 medium-size yellow summer squash, quartered lengthwise and thinly sliced

1 small Chinese cabbage, cut crosswise every inch and then into 1 1/2-inch pieces the other way

4 enormous garlic cloves, finely chopped

2 cups coarsely chopped green leaves

1 or 2 small fresh green chilies, seeds removed, minced (optional)

1/4 cup chopped fresh dill, or basil, summer savory, or parsley

a few squirts of fresh lemon juice

plenty of freshly ground black pepper

Cover and simmer the black-eyed peas in about 6 cups salted water until tender. When they're ready, stir them with their broth into the soup.

Meanwhile, in your soup pot, cover the calf's foot with about 4 quarts vegetable stock or salted water, bring to a simmer, and simmer gently, uncovered for an hour or two. Add the carrots, tomatoes, potatoes, beets, peppers, onions, and red cabbage, stir to blend, and return to a simmer. Turn the heat to very low and, if you can, set the pot over a Flame-Tamer so the soup barely bubbles. Cook until the root vegetables are nearly tender. Stir in the squash, Chinese cabbage, garlic, greens, and chilies and cook until everything is tender—add more stock, if necessary. Remove the calf's foot and add the herbs and lemon juice to heighten flavor. Add pepper and taste for seasoning. Keep refrigerated.

This is very good cold with yogurt on top.

Sun-Dried Tomatoes

Before you even sow your seeds, please know the proper way to store these gems.

Sun-dried tomatoes, no matter what their pH, can be kept safely and indefinitely dropped into a box or bag and kept in a cool dry place.

If they are standard old-fashioned tomatoes with ample acid—pH of 4.7 or lower—they can be dried and packed *all by themselves* in any oil and stored indefinitely at room temperature. Once garlic or herbs are added, the jar must be refrigerated and used within 10 days. Please see the box Garlic and Herbs in Olive Oil under Garlic.

Small tomatoes as well as white or yellow tomatoes tend to be highest in acid, whereas pear and other elongated tomatoes—the most popular for drying—tend to be lower.

To dry tomatoes, use those no more than 2 inches across. Rinse and slice in half lengthwise. Whole tomatoes usually will not dry properly—their top skin just puffs up like a bullfrog. Lay on something airy that will let air but not insects pass through—I use tulle from the dime store set on cake cooling racks. Lay cut sides up and sprinkle generously with coarse sea or kosher salt, cover with netting, and set in the sun. If mornings are dewy, bring in the racks every night. When the tops of the tomatoes are leathery, turn them over. Leave in the sun until crackling dry with no puffy spots. Some advise finishing the tomatoes in the shade, but I find it surer to keep the whole process in the sun.

If rain or humidity interferes with this project, finish drying the tomatoes in the oven on the lowest temperature setting with the oven door open.

To reconstitute sun-dried tomatoes, cover them amply with boiling liquid—water if you won't be using the resulting stock in the dish, otherwise use something that adds flavor. Dried tomatoes vary enormously in texture, from pliant to brittle, so soaking time varies.

Here's *la maestra* Diana Kennedy's handsome salad combining fresh and sun-dried tomatoes from the garden.

DK'S TOMATO SALAD: For each serving, soften 1 medium-size or 2 smallish sun-dried tomatoes until flexible in a little hot stock or water. Pat dry and slice them lengthwise into thinnish strips. Cover the bottom of a luncheon plate with thinly sliced ripe tomatoes. Over them, in a decorative pattern, arrange the strips of dried tomatoes, a few whole sweet basil leaves, and pieces of goat or smoked mozzarella cheese. Drizzle with good fruity olive oil and serve with country bread.

Stock

VEGETABLE STOCK: Whenever a vegetable is cooked in liquid—no matter how small the amount of liquid—vitamins and minerals are leached into that liquid. There can be more good left in the pot than in the vegetable. To glean the most from your kitchen garden, use the cooking stock. Pour the precious liquid into a jar, cover it tightly, and keep it refrigerated. Or freeze it. Instead of using water or canned broth to simmer the next vegetable, pull out your tasty stock.

It's fun to mix stocks for an adventurous anything-goes soup, but take care and remember that the stock will add an element of flavoring to the composition at least as much as any herb or condiment. A touch of celery adds brilliance to the taste of carrots, and the sweetness of carrot enhances the earthiness of turnips—but the flavors of celery and turnip have very little to offer one another. So it's wise to keep stocks separate and to use them as soon as you can for maximum flavor and nutrition.

Now if you're vegetarian, a fine vegetable stock is the backbone of your cooking. Here, from *La Cuisine Moderne* (1907), is a lovely freehanded stock.

"Take carrots, turnips, parsnips, onions, leeks, a stalk of celery, a head of lettuce, a small cabbage, some new peas, a little parsley; cut all in small pieces; toss them in butter for a few minutes without their coloring; sprinkle with a little confectioner's sugar, salt and pepper them, and cover generously with boiling water. Let the vegetables simmer gently for three or four hours. Strain the broth through a napkin and use for preparing lean soups."

VEGETABLES

COOKING YOUR VEGETABLES: Your beautiful vegetables are waiting to be cooked. What about cooking and flavor? Heat releases the aroma molecules in plants, so cooking enhances every vegetable's flavor.

Then how best to preserve a vegetable's color, shape, and nutrients?

Rule Number One: The less cooking, the fewer the nutrients lost. That's not to say that every vegetable is more nutritious in its raw state. A small amount of heat breaks down cell walls in carrots, for example, releasing imprisoned nutrients—so, surprisingly, lightly cooked carrots are more valuable than raw ones.

Rule Number Two: The more a vegetable is cut up, the more nutrients are lost. Although this rule applies particularly to vegetables cooked in water, it's true of all cooking methods. A whole baked sweet potato retains 89 percent of its vitamin C; cut in half, all but 31 percent is lost. So in that sense, cutting up vegetables to cook them faster is a devil's bargain.

Every plant contains acids and enzymes that are potential destroyers of their own color and nutrients. When a vegetable cooks, its tissues release these elements into the vessel. The trick is to dissipate the acid and enzymes as much as possible—and/or to cook the vegetable before it has a chance to release the terminators.

For maximum nutrition from your vegetables, pressure cooking them whole or microwaving is the most efficient method. Steaming is next, but significant amounts of folic acid, niacin, and thiamine are lost. Otherwise, cook them in a tightly covered skillet in as little liquid as possible and serve any leftover stock with the vegetables or reserve it for another use.

For best color, no matter what the vessel or technique, cook the vegetable uncovered. A cover not only traps the released acids so they're in the air, but they can condense on the underside of the lid, then drip back onto the vegetable, darkening it.

Steam can also collect acids, which can be released to darken colors.

For best color and true flavor in green vegetables, cook them in a great quantity of boiling water, leave the pot uncovered, and try to get the job done in less than 5 minutes, even if you have to cut them into small pieces. Unless you use the cooking water, this method is spendthrift of vitamins.

Green vegetables cooked in a copper pot or with something else alkaline such as baking soda vividly retain their color but at the cost of most of their nutrients. There are two other cautions about the alkaline method: Copper can destroy folic acid and vitamins C and E, and it can also be harmful in itself. Vegetables cooked in alkaline water tend to be mushy. If your water is on the alkaline side, you can neutralize it by adding a squeeze of lemon juice or a splash of vinegar to vegetable-cooking water.

A jot of the acid of lemon or vinegar also helps preserve the color in red vegetables. An acid fruit like apples adds flavor as well as preserves color. A touch of acid also helps preserve the white of onions, eggplant, and mushrooms in cooking.

For other than green vegetables, stir-frying best preserves color. The pan gets hotter than boiling water, and since pieces have been cut into the traditional small bits, they are cooked through in minutes.

The yellow and orange pigments in fruits and vegetables and the red in tomatoes, sweet peppers, and watermelon are called *carotenoids*, and they're comparatively stable, just as the pigment in beets is also little affected by cooking. When cooked in simmering water, the yellow in carrots and tomatoes is largely preserved, although temperatures in a pressure cooker darken their hues.

When roasted, vegetables retain and often develop their flavor but can't cook fast enough to avoid the destructive acids and enzymes.

To preserve color and a reasonable amount of nutrients, simmer colorful vegetables uncovered in a minimum of liquid—with leafy greens the water that clings to them from rinsing, with others ½ inch of water. The resulting stock contains leached nutrients, so use it as soon as possible in sauce or soup.

GRILLING VEGETABLES: Roasted over an open fire, vegetables (and fruits) succumb to the same primeval magic that overtakes poultry, meat, and seafood.

Grill over fruitwood or add soaked chips to a charcoal fire. Or throw branches of herbs on the fire during the last minutes of grilling for a wreath of herbal smoke.

For maximum juices and flavor, grill vegetables as they come from the garden—in their skins or husks or shells. Small vegetables grill most uniformly—slender Asian eggplants rather than fat European ones. Baste frequently with oil to keep surfaces moist and turn frequently for even cooking. Test frequently for tenderness with a thin skewer, then note how long your vegetables took since your vegetables and your fire are unique. You can turn pieces halfway through cooking on one side so the grill will make an appealing crosshatching on the flesh, but this doesn't affect flavor.

I like grilled vegetables best at room temperature, when I don't have to deal with heat but can devote my attention to sweetness. A chunk of lemon for verve, a drizzling of tasty oil, and perhaps a sprinkling of herbs is all you need.

For details, I recommend Deborah Madison's grilling chapter in *The Savory Way* (Bantam Books, 1990).

MICROWAVING: I should be but somehow I'm not yet in the habit of routinely cooking vegetables in the microwave. The method is remarkably saving of color, flavor, and nutrients. I do love corn on the cob as it came from the stalk and cauliflower in a moist paper bag cooked in the machine—and small new potatoes, snap beans, and garden peas. Tender vegetables are fast, easy, and superb. When I roast nuts in the machine—a habit I do have—I throw in some vegetables and have them cool for supper.

SERVINGS AND WEIGHTS: Unlike buying leaves by the bunch at the market, it can be absurdly difficult trying to stuff the unusual types of leaves and sprigs we harvest into a measuring cup. Very often I must call for a vegetable by weight. If a kitchen scale is still on your wish list, you can weigh the vegetable on your big scale on a sheet of wax paper—or weigh yourself with and without the vegetable, then subtract the difference. If your scale isn't 100 percent accurate, don't worry. I usually measure by the handful, and a handful this way or that can do no harm.

Allow 5 to 8 ounces of a vegetable per serving: 5 ounces if it has no waste, like carrots, ½ to ¾ pound if there's lots of trimming or it's a favorite like asparagus or snap beans you haven't topped and tailed.

Index

A

B

C

D

E

F

G

H

I

J

K

L

M

N

O

P

T

V

W

Z